Founders of Modern Political
and Social Thought

PLATO

FOUNDERS OF
MODERN POLITICAL AND
SOCIAL THOUGHT

SERIES EDITOR

Mark Philp

Oriel College, University of Oxford

The *Founders* series presents critical examinations of the work of major political philosophers and social theorists, assessing both their initial contribution and their continuing relevance to politics and society. Each volume provides a clear, accessible, historically informed account of a thinker's work, focusing on a reassessment of the central ideas and arguments. The series encourages scholars and students to link their study of classic texts to current debates in political philosophy and social theory.

Also available:

JOHN FINNIS: *Aquinas*
RICHARD KRAUT: *Aristotle*
GIANFRANCO POGGI: *Durkheim*
MAURIZIO VIROLI: *Machiavelli*
CHERYL WELCH: *De Tocqueville*

PLATO

Political Philosophy

Malcolm Schofield

OXFORD
UNIVERSITY PRESS

Great Clarendon Street, Oxford OX2 6DP

Oxford University Press is a department of the University of Oxford.
It furthers the University's objective of excellence in research, scholarship,
and education by publishing worldwide in

Oxford New York

Auckland Cape Town Dar es Salaam Hong Kong Karachi
Kuala Lumpur Madrid Melbourne Mexico City Nairobi
New Delhi Shanghai Taipei Toronto

With offices in

Argentina Austria Brazil Chile Czech Republic France Greece
Guatemala Hungary Italy Japan Poland Portugal Singapore
South Korea Switzerland Thailand Turkey Ukraine Vietnam

Oxford is a registered trademark of Oxford University Press
in the UK and in certain other countries

Published in the United States
by Oxford University Press Inc., New York

British Library Cataloguing in Publication Data

Data available

Library of Congress Cataloging in Publication Data

Schofield, Malcolm.
Plato : political philosophy / Malcolm Schofield.
p. cm. —(Founders of modern political and social thought)
Includes bibliographical references and index.
ISBN-13: 978–0–19–924946–6 (alk. paper)
ISBN-10: 0–19–924946–6 (alk. paper)
ISBN-13: 978–0–19–924961–9 (alk. paper)
ISBN-10: 0–19–924961–X (alk. paper)
1. Plato—Political and social views. I. Title. II. Series.
JC71.P62S36 2006
321'.07—dc22 2006016279

Typeset by Laserwords Private Limited, Chennai, India
Printed in Great Britain
on acid-free paper by
Biddles Ltd., King's Lynn, Norfolk

ISBN 978–0–19–924961–9
ISBN 978–0–19–924946–6 (Pbk.)

For Matthew

Preface

This book had its origin (I believe) in a suggestion from Myles Burnyeat to Mark Philp, general editor of the *Founders of Modern Political and Social Thought* series. Serious thinking began in response to an invitation to deliver Carlyle Seminars on the *Republic* in Oxford in Trinity Term 2000. The philosophers, historians and political theorists who participated gave my ideas a warm and argumentative reception. Through the good offices of Myles Burnyeat I was privileged to enjoy the hospitality of the Warden and Fellows of All Souls during my visits. Serious writing was made possible by a year's sabbatical in 2003–04. I thank my colleagues in the Faculty of Classics at Cambridge for shouldering burdens in my absence. Another leave in Lent Term 2005 and the honour and stimulus of the John and Penelope Biggs Residency at Washington University, St Louis, set me up for the final push. I am most grateful for the challenging week I enjoyed in St Louis as a guest of the university and its classics department. I was showered with generous hospitality: I hope it will not be too invidious if I thank Bob Lamberton and Eric Brown above all for their many kindnesses.

I have profited from the observations and criticisms of colleagues on numerous occasions, both when I have delivered versions of particular chapters as talks in various parts of the world and in innumerable private conversations. A whistle-stop lecture tour in March 2004, taking in Northwestern, Brown and Princeton Universities and the University of Toronto, was particularly helpful; and I returned with a draft of Chapter 5 from an unforgettable stay in May of that year at the Fondation Hardt—itself a sort of utopia. A number of friends gave me extensive written comments on the first draft of the whole book: Christopher Gill, Melissa Lane, Geoffrey Lloyd, David Sedley and Christopher Taylor. It is much the better for their varied input, both in detail and in its broader horizons. Two anonymous readers for the Press wrote encouragingly about the draft and the project as a whole, and were again very helpful in highlighting things to work on further. Finally, Mark Philp for the series and Peter Momtchiloff for the Press have been the most relaxed and kindly of editors. When Mark finally got a full draft, he sent me one of the most searching and beautifully nuanced set of responses I've ever had to anything I've written, at once supportive and delicately quizzical. My thanks also go to Jenni Craig, Helen Gray, and Andrew Hawkey in the editorial team for their friendly efficiency.

The book attempts both to ground an analytic account of Plato's political philosophy in its historical context, and to suggest some of the resonances it finds or might find in more contemporary concerns and more recent political thought. I don't suppose I could have conceived that ambition or worked out a strategy for carrying it through without the different sorts of examples set by three scholars in particular: Moses Finley, Quentin Skinner and Josh Ober—whose advantages over me include being proper historians. Learning to read Plato is a continuing adventure. I am particularly indebted to colleagues in Cambridge, who have frequently returned to Plato in our Thursday evening reading group, and above all to Myles Burnyeat, for all we have learned from him, especially during his time as Laurence Professor of Ancient Philosophy.

In the years through which this book was in the making I had as always the unassuming loving support of my wife Elizabeth. She died at the end of July 2005, trying to complete the massive, hugely demanding, and often lonely archaeological writing project on which she had been working for a decade and a half.

Contents

Introduction

Is Plato our contemporary? Well, yes and no. When he philosoph-
ized about politics, he was thinking of the long-vanished Greek
polis or 'city-state' of ancient Athens and Sparta. Democracy for
him meant the direct participation of all adult male citizens in
the decision-making processes of the popular assembly and the
courts of justice, not the representative systems of today. The
intensity of his obsession with political rhetoric as an inbred
democratic disease is intelligible only against the background of
an interpretation of fifth-century Athenian imperialism and its
downfall in the Peloponnesian War that he probably borrowed
(not without twists of his own) from the historian Thucydides.
One particular event dominated Plato's conception of politics:
the trial and execution of Socrates in 399 BC. So this book will
begin by immersing the reader in the historical contexts of Plato's
writing; and there will be recurrent re-immersions.

When Nietzsche spoke with enthusiasm of Plato's 'genuine,
resolute, "honest" lie' (he had in mind the Noble Lie of Book 3 of
the *Republic*), however, he was thinking about general questions
to do with morality, and more specifically of a contrast with the
'dishonest' lying—as he took it to be—of Christian morality.[1]
Similarly Hegel thought 'the Idea' of Plato's *Republic* contained
'as a universal principle a wrong against the person, inasmuch as
the person is forbidden to own private property'. Hegel, of course,
believed like Nietzsche that a philosophy such as Plato's could
appear only at a particular moment in the historical process.[2]
Nonetheless in these remarks about lying and property Plato
is treated *not* as a writer simply of a certain time and place,
but someone still to be disputed with or invoked in aid. The
assumption is obviously that at a certain level of generality there
are themes and questions in moral and political philosophy, as in
other areas of philosophy, which stay close enough to being the
same over the centuries for a conversation of some sort between
us and Plato to be possible and profitable.

That at any rate is an assumption I shall be making in this
book. My expectation is that most people interested in reading
about Plato's political philosophy come to it precisely because

this is their assumption, too. Accordingly the book takes up a sequence of major themes: alienation from politics, education, democracy, knowledge, utopia and the idea of community, the power of money, and ideological uses of religion. Between them these define what Plato takes to be the fundamental problems for politics. All remain live issues. On all of them Plato took radical and uncomfortable positions. On none of them does contemporary politics or political theory offer particularly convincing answers. Many see the legacy of the Enlightenment—above all its focus on individual subjective human preferences—as close to bankruptcy.[3] For that reason it is worth revisiting Plato's adoption of a transcendent critical (and self-critical) perspective that demands more holistic solutions. The Platonic terrain we shall be exploring—as with any foreign country—has aspects partly familiar, partly unfamiliar. The fascination lies in watching a powerful and subtle mind attacking problems we can recognize with conceptual weapons we can recognize. And it may be that we will get a sense from Plato, whether in critical or constructive mode, of the kinds of resources we need to tackle them.

Books on Plato often proceed dialogue by dialogue, usually following a standard scheme of chronological sequence, and attempting to trace developments in his ideas.[4] All such chronological schemes, however plausible, are conjectural: there is very little direct historical evidence on the order of composition of Plato's dialogues. In this book the standard division into an early, middle and late period will be assumed, but not much will turn on it, and on some items—notably *Euthydemus*—judgement will be suspended. Thus I suppose with virtually all scholars that the *Laws*, the *Statesman*, and *Timaeus-Critias*, which share with the *Sophist* and *Philebus* an array of highly distinctive stylistic features, are productions of Plato's latest period (from roughly 360 to his death in 347 BC). With most scholars, too, I take the *Republic* to be a work of Plato's mature middle years, probably belonging to the 370s. Most of the other writings to be discussed in the book I put earlier: *Apology* and *Crito* in the 390s, *Protagoras*, *Gorgias* and *Menexenus* in the 380s. They all evoke different moments in recent Athenian history, in ways which suggest to me dates of composition early in the fourth century. But the rationale for that dating derives also from an impression partly of a less involved prose style, and partly of a more single-minded engagement with demonstrably Socratic themes and ideas than in the *Republic*. In Chapter 4 I discuss political aspects of two other dialogues: *Charmides* and *Euthydemus*. These works are peculiarly difficult to place in any such sequence, for reasons briefly explained in Section 2 of the chapter.[5]

Developmental interpretations of Plato are currently under something of a cloud.[6] I do not myself doubt that Plato's thought evolved, in politics as in other fields. Few writers communicate so intense a sense of the life of the mind. And life means change and growth and eventual decay. So far as the *Republic*, the *Statesman* and the *Laws* are concerned, however, it seems to me that the chief differences between them are to be explained (as the book tries to do in a number of places) by difference in purpose and point of view adopted. The dialogue form enables Plato to speak with various principal voices, and to give expression to such differences in viewpoint that way. We listen not just to Socrates (as in the *Republic*), but (in the *Statesman*) to an anonymous visitor from Parmenides' city of Elea, and (in the *Laws*) to an Athenian Visitor to Crete meant to remind us of the great legislator Solon.

I have indicated that and why the approach I adopt is thematic, not chronological or developmental. The themes are all themes to be found in one dialogue in particular: the *Republic*—although, as we shall be seeing, all appear elsewhere too. What emerges from the *Republic* is the idea that a person's well-being will be secured only by living the life of justice. For that we need education—a rigorous and systematic moral and intellectual preparation for life that permeates all our development as human beings, from physical exercise through music and poetry to the demands of mathematics. Such an education is designed to achieve a highly specific goal: the rule of reason—as shaped in the end by philosophy itself—over heart and mind. The dialogue maps and indeed explicates these notions against a parallel conception of a well-ordered society.

Key to that conception is the idea that political rule must be based on knowledge (examined in Chapter 4), if the harmony of a just social and political system is to be created and sustained. Plato's vision of what constitutes true community, in a world dominated by appetites and the pursuit of the wealth needed to satisfy them, and so by war, is the subject of Chapter 5. Without the rule of knowledge the appetites, above all insatiable greed, will run riot, destroying the possibility of true community. Why these are the forces posing the prime threat to well-being in city and soul alike, and how they can be made to 'listen to reason', is the topic of Chapter 6. The two main instruments of rational political control Plato envisages are law and ideology. Law is discussed at various points in the book (notably Section 3.3 of Chapter 2, Section 5.1 of Chapter 3, and Section 7 of Chapter 4). Ideology—in the form of the *Republic*'s Noble Lie and the *Laws*' provisions for religion—is discussed in Chapter 7.

The book does not provide an exposition of the main argument of the *Republic* itself or as such. For that I refer the reader to my chapter 'Approaching the *Republic*' in *The Cambridge History of Greek and Roman Political Thought*, which also contains accessible accounts of the *Statesman* (by Christopher Rowe) and the *Laws* (by André Laks).[7] The *Laws* and the *Statesman* are probably less familiar than the *Republic*. So I include some material introducing these dialogues as dialogues at appropriate points (see Chapter 2, Section 3.1, for *Laws*, and Chapter 4, Section 5.1, for *Statesman*). In general, I assume a broad range of readers—with backgrounds in varied fields (politics, philosophy, classics, history)—who may have little prior knowledge of Plato. But the book is problem-oriented. The idea is to move from and through exposition to analysis and (where appropriate) controversy that will also provide those who know Plato well with food for thought.

The nexus of ideas I have been describing plays a central role in much of the *Republic*'s philosophizing. One of the book's ambitions is to offer an exploration of those ideas which enhances understanding of the dialogue by situating them in a wider context—both in a multidimensional historical setting, and in the light of Plato's engagement with similar issues in earlier or later works. The philosophy of the *Republic* is fed by a heady mixture of profound reflection on the teaching, life and death of Socrates, ambiguous admiration for ancient Sparta, and fierce but thoroughly engaged rejection of the democracy of Plato's and Socrates' native Athens. This is why the first three chapters of the book examine in some detail these dimensions of Plato's thought, as they present themselves to us in a number of dialogues. In other words, we approach Plato's political philosophy through a study of the matrix from which it emerged.

The author of a book like this needs to be five very different animals: a philosopher, a political theorist, a cultural and political historian of ancient Greece, a reader, and an intellectual looter. The first three of these explain themselves. The skills of a reader are demanded above all by Plato's use of the dialogue form to communicate his ideas. Not only has he recourse to a huge cast of characters and a wide range of imagined dramatic contexts, but he has many different tones of voice and styles of argument—all of them in some sense 'his'. Learning to read these takes time, experience, discipline and imaginative sympathy. No straightforward or uncontroversial guidance on how to do it has ever been formulated. The book reflects on the question from time to time, but mostly aims to instruct or persuade by example. The looter is a more brutal figure. Looting is simply extracting from Plato ideas or questions that from our point of view still strike a resonance. Where a historian says: 'This argument or preoccupation can only really be appreciated if we understand its relation to (say) Pericles' funeral oration in Thucydides', the looter asks: 'Whatever its original contexts, is the *Republic* still good to think with?'

If political theory is 'a dialogue across the centuries',[8] other voices than Plato's need to be heard. In the following pages Aristotle, Proclus, Rousseau, de Tocqueville, John Stuart Mill and Benjamin Jowett make more or less brief appearances, as do John Maynard Keynes, Karl Popper, Leo Strauss, Rawls, Dworkin, Habermas and Bernard Williams from more recent decades. Nobody could write a book on this subject without drawing inspiration and insight from the work of other contemporary scholars, and without disagreeing with them from time to time, too. References to the huge scholarly literature are mostly confined to the endnotes: the argument of the main text is designed to be intelligible and complete as it stands. They vary in frequency and quantity. Where what is at stake is historical background or intellectual controversy (as for example over the question of Plato's 'feminism'), there are more. Where it is more a matter of expounding or analysing argument, supply is much more sparing. I have largely confined references to books and articles I have found particularly helpful. I regret that little of what I cite is in any language other than English, which is only partly because I have borne in mind the importance of guiding English-speaking students to key items accessible to them. Work by French scholars, however, is often available in translation now, and I have tried to exploit this as fully as possible. I want to acknowledge the help I have received from the invaluable resources contained within the major Italian commentary on the *Republic* being published by Mario Vegetti and his team of collaborators. They have now—with volume 6 (2005)—got to the end of Book 9; we look forward to the completion of the whole project.[9] Finally, translations of Greek texts are sometimes my own, sometimes borrowed or adapted from other well-known versions. I am grateful to Cambridge University Press for permitting use of Tom Griffith's translation of the *Republic*, and to Penguin Books and Mrs Teresa Saunders for that of Trevor Saunders' translation of the *Laws*.[10]

Notes

1. See Geuss 1999: 179–80.
2. See Waldron 1995: 146.
3. Hence no doubt the huge impact made by a book such as Alasdair Macintyre's *After Virtue*: Macintyre 1981.
4. For brief recent discussions of the issues, see Cooper 1997b: vii–xviii; Kahn 2002: 93–127 (also Kahn 1996: ch. 4). H. Thesleff has argued that the versions of Plato's writings we possess are in many cases 'the products of a successive revision' (Thesleff 1982: 84): not an intrinsically improbable proposition, but one for which it is hard to find any unequivocal evidence.
5. For an overview which sets out my own account of the development of Plato's thought as evidenced in his writings, see Schofield 1998.
6. See e.g. Annas and Rowe 2002.
7. Rowe and Schofield 2000: chs 10–12.
8. Waldron 1995: 146.
9. Vegetti 1998–   .
10. Ferrari and Griffith 2000; Saunders 1970.

I

The *Republic*: Contexts and Projects

---

1. The Centrepiece

This book will inevitably be mostly, if by no means solely, about Plato's *Politeia* or *Republic* (its familiar English title): 'the first great work of Western political philosophy', in G. R. F. Ferrari's simple statement, introducing what was perhaps the first new translation into English of the new millennium.[1] There may be grumbles about that. Plato's capacity for literary production was formidable, and few of his writings lack political resonances. A good number besides the *Republic* address substantial political issues in political philosophy more or less head on: the *Crito*, for example, our earliest philosophical text on political obligation, or the *Gorgias*, probing the unhealthy relationship—as Plato's Socrates represents it—between rhetoric and democracy. Two of Plato's later dialogues have titles and topics that are explicitly political, the *Statesman* and the vast *Laws*, a work even longer than the *Republic* itself. It has recently been claimed that it is in fact the *Laws* (probably written mostly in the 350s BC), not the *Republic* (probably completed by the mid-370s), which 'can be considered the first work of genuine political philosophy in the Western tradition'—on the ground that it builds an elaborate legal and theologico-political superstructure on the foundations it discusses. By comparison, 'the *Republic* is at best a sketch, whereas the *Laws* breaks ground for future political thought'.[2]

The *Republic*'s prime claim on our attention is not, therefore, uncontested. Some might feel other kinds of disquiet about Ferrari's formulation. On one side, readers of Thucydides would concede that he is no philosopher, but yet reckon him a writer earlier than Plato by a generation, who remains unsurpassed in the profound and sustained reflections on politics that he puts in the mouths of his historical protagonists or articulates on his own account: on might and right; calculation and fear; the fragility of civilization; and the compulsive dynamic of imperialism. We might want to call him the first political *theorist*. But 'theory' was not a concept Thucydides or his contemporaries had available in their vocabulary. And he was crystal clear that what he was writing was the history of an eyewitness, proudly presented as an innovative mode of rational enquiry transcending all existing discourses about the past.[3] On the other hand, 'political philosophy' may seem to suggest the appropriateness of a taxonomy of genres of philosophical writing and thinking ill-suited to the fluidity and ambition of the project undertaken in the *Republic*, as it weaves ethics, politics, psychology, epistemology, mathematics, metaphysics and cultural criticism into something utterly unique. Most of these modern categories do have an ancient Greek origin. Aristotle uses many of them, systematizer that he is, although not always under those labels. Readers of the *Republic* quickly realize that mathematics at least (and its constituent sciences) was already achieving the status of a discrete structure of disciplines and sub-disciplines in Plato's day. But if the idea that philosophy itself might usefully be conceived as a discipline with a number of different branches ever occurred to Plato, his favoured modes of writing seem calculated to resist expression of any such idea.

'Philosophy', 'philosopher' and 'philosophize' were words which had only recently achieved any significant currency by Plato's time. The evidence suggests that intellectual practitioners with different agenda (Plato included) were appropriating them for their own distinctive purposes, not least in the attempt to define and legitimate their own activities against those of their competitors.[4] 'I deny', writes Plato's rival Isocrates, 'that the thing called "philosophy" by certain people is in fact philosophy.' So 'it is fitting that I define and make clear to you what it is that is justly called by this name' (*Antidosis* 270–1). A philosopher is literally a 'lover of wisdom'. Plato's Socrates gives both elements in the expression thorough exploration, above all in the *Symposium* and the *Republic*. The focus is on what it is to *love* wisdom, and on what constitutes the knowledge and understanding that wisdom requires. Philosophy as the *Republic* conceives it involves a passionate desire for unifying comprehension of everything there is. No doubt Plato could recognize points of view from which such knowledge might properly be parcelled out into different departments, but philosophy itself is basically undepartmental. Any reader who asked Plato: 'But what *sort* of philosophy—moral, political, metaphysical—are you doing in the *Republic*?' would be entirely missing the point.[5]

Still, a lot of the philosophy in the dialogue is preoccupied with political questions. And there are several compelling reasons for according the *Republic* pride of place in any treatment of Plato's political thought. First and foremost is that the dialogue contains most of Plato's most striking ideas in political philosophy. For example, this is the work in which his Socrates argues for philosopher rulers, female as well as male, and for the abolition of the nuclear family. It is here that he suggests that lies and myths are necessities in politics. And it is here that he makes the psychological motivations (and their pathologies) that are characteristic of particular forms of society the key to understanding their political discontents, and—by the same token—finds in the politics of the soul and of the forces operative within it the explanation of what in the individual makes for happiness or for dysfunctionality. In political philosophy—and a fortiori in the study of the history of political philosophy—perhaps we learn most by seeing what happens to all the other major values when a thinker takes one central ideal (knowledge, for instance, or fairness, or liberty) as fundamental to a proper politics.[6] From this point of view the *Republic*, which has a highly distinctive grand vision, is likely to be more rewarding than the *Laws*, which proportionately devotes much more space to working through detailed constitutional, educational and legal provisions within the overall framework it establishes.

Then Plato himself seems to give the *Republic* primacy among his writings on the principles of politics. He intimates in the later *Laws* that *its* main agenda is set by the *Republic*. The *Republic* had already indicated that we must be content if in practice we can achieve as good an approximation as possible to the ideal political order it proposes. The *Laws* briefly recapitulates that ideal, and then announces as its own project an enquiry into the political system that so far as *humanly* possible approximates to it—with the investigation keeping a grip on the ideal as the enquiry is conducted. Similarly, Socrates launches the never-completed late work *Timaeus-Critias-Hermogenes* with a reprise of the main features of the *Republic*'s political system. He then expresses a desire to see that system put into action, with the ideal city pitted in warfare against other cities. The idea is worked out in the narrative—quite imaginary—of the ancient conflict between Athens and Atlantis, sketched a little later in the *Timaeus* and designed to be the main subject of the unfinished *Critias*. Again, the autobiographical *Seventh Letter*—whether authentically Platonic or not—makes the *Republic*'s idea of philosopher rulers pivotal to *its* narrative.[7] As these later writings carry forward programmes inspired by the *Republic*, so for its part the *Republic* seems to attempt a definitive treatment of key themes from earlier writings: Socratic quietism (in the *Apology*), justice, the soul and the good life (in the *Crito* and the *Gorgias*). In short, the *Republic* is in the sphere of politics as in much else the centrepiece of the entire Platonic corpus.

Many subsequent contributions to political philosophy in antiquity also make the *Republic* their main point of reference. Aristotle in his *Politics* certainly engages with the *Statesman* and the *Laws* at crucial junctures in his argument. But when after the preliminaries of Book 1 he turns at the beginning of Book 2 to consider previous views on the main official topic of the work—'what form of political association is best for people so far as it is possible for them to live as they would wish'—the *Republic* is what he starts discussing right away, and in highly critical terms. It occupies him for the next four chapters. He thinks it sufficient to devote one only to the *Laws*, which he sees as virtually identical in the institutions it proposes except for the issue of communist arrangements regarding women and property.[8] A generation or so later Zeno of Citium, the founding father of the Stoic philosophy, entitled his own short radical treatise on political association *Politeia* or *Republic* (perhaps to be dated around 300 BC), evidently as a challenge and riposte to Plato's great work. The *Laws*, too, interested the Stoics, but it was left to Persaeus of Citium, Zeno's devoted but undistinguished lieutenant, to write *Against Plato's Laws*, in seven books.[9] The most substantial text in political theory to survive from the second century BC, Polybius's treatment of constitutions in the fragmentary Book 6 of his *Histories*, is heavily indebted to discussions of moral and political questions in Greek philosophy. The only thinker he names in the general theory elaborated in the opening chapters is Plato (at 6.5.1), in connection with the idea that changes from one form of constitution to another exemplify a determinate diachronic pattern. He clearly has Books 8 and 9 of the *Republic* in mind.[10] A century later (54–51 BC) Cicero composed two closely related dialogues addressing fundamental questions of political philosophy: his own *Republic* and *Laws*, both incompletely preserved, in emulation although not imitation of Plato (he conveys disapproval of the utopianism of Plato's sketch for an ideal city).[11] Like Plato, Cicero conceives of his *Laws* as rounding off the project undertaken in his *Republic*, although as with Plato's its literary presentation is quite independent of the earlier work. After the foundational first book, subsequent books developed a legal code appropriate to the Scipionic republic represented by the *Republic* as the best constitution for a commonwealth.[12]

From the Roman imperial period and later in antiquity, the volume of material surviving that is marked by the general influence of Plato's writings on political philosophy is much more substantial. This is the era when Platonism of one form or another becomes the dominant strain in much philosophical discourse. I shall be referring later in this chapter to one text that deals specifically with issues in the *Republic*: the collection of essays on political as well as other topics in the dialogue by the late and prolific Neoplatonist philosopher Proclus (fifth century AD). Here are two other voices which still speak vividly to us about the dialogue. The first belongs to Dio of Prusa, a versatile exponent of philosophy for the general educated public, who was writing at the end of the first century AD. He defends his own digressive method of writing (*Euboicus* 130–2):

So we should probably not criticize the writer who set out to discuss the just man and justice, and then, having mentioned a city for the sake of illustration, expatiated at much greater length on the topic of the social and political system (*politeia*)—and did not weary until he had gone through all the kinds of system and all the transformations they undergo, and had set out very clearly and magnificently the features characteristic of each. There are those who do take him to task for spinning out the discussion and for the time he spends on an *illustration*. But if the complaint is that his treatment of political questions has no bearing on the project of the dialogue, and that not the least light has been shed on the subject of its enquiry—these are grounds, if grounds there are, which make it not altogether unfair to call him to task. So if it became apparent that I too am going through material that is not pertinent or germane to my project, then it would be reasonable to charge me with prolixity. But otherwise it is not fair to commend or to criticize either length or brevity in a discourse on that ground alone.[13]

Photius—learned Byzantine patriarch, writing eight centuries later—was less measured in his dissatisfaction. He is inveighing against the fourth-century pagan emperor, Julian the Apostate (*Amphilochia* 625A):[14]

Yet ought not a writer who is close to worshipping Plato's ideal cities, filled though they are with innumerable forms of immorality and innumerable contradictions, utterly opposed to every political system (*politeia*) known to man, unrealized and non-existent throughout the course of history—if a writer calls these to mind and takes pride in doing so, ought he not to be ashamed of letting the very word *politeia* pass his lips?

By now it will be obvious that there has never been a time when the *Republic* did not succeed in irritating intelligent readers.

A book on Plato in a series concerned with founders of *modern* social and political thought can scarcely avoid an emphasis on the *Republic*. This is not the place for a potted history of modern engagement with its political ideas, of the 'Plato to NATO' variety. Suffice to mention here by way of example the intense and incompatible reactions of Karl Popper and Leo Strauss in the mid-twentieth century, which were central components in their authors' own political philosophies, and hugely important in sustaining the influence of their thinking.[15] The significance of Benjamin Jowett's success in establishing the *Republic* as a core text of the Oxford Greats curriculum from 1853 onwards has been much discussed, particularly the impact on the minds of a young elite that was made by the combination of moral idealism and acknowledgement of political responsibility found in the dialogue by the Master of Balliol and many who taught in the tradition he established.[16] But it would be a mistake to think that perception of the *Republic* as a classic document of social and political thought is entirely a consequence of the rise of Hellenism and the revival of Greek studies in the nineteenth century. After all, Sir Thomas More's *Utopia* took much of its inspiration from the *Republic*, as in the most different way imaginable did Rousseau's *Emile*.

2. *Some Dubious Platonic Autobiography*

Near the end of his argument in the *Republic* for the need for philosopher rulers, Socrates introduces one of the most radical elements of this radical proposal (6.501A):

They would take as their slate a city, and the character of human beings. They would begin by wiping it clean, which would be far from easy. All the same, you should be in no doubt that they would differ from other draftsmen in refusing, right from the start, to have anything to do with any individual or city, or draft any laws, until they were either given a clean slate or had cleaned it for themselves.

The grave condition of existing cities and of the human race itself was highlighted in Socrates' initial formulation of the thesis that either philosophers must exercise the powers of a king, or else kings and those in power engage genuinely and successfully in philosophy (5.473C–E); and it has formed at least the backcloth of much of the intervening discussion in Books 5 and 6. This new pronouncement confirms that he judges that condition irremediable. Starting again from scratch is the only option. And it is a philosopher ruler who must make the fresh start. What led the Plato who makes Socrates say these things to this conclusion? Is it right to assume that it *is* in some strong sense Plato's conclusion, not just 'Socrates''?

I am going to sketch two different sorts of answers to these questions. The first we might dub the appeal to Platonic quietism. It is a heavily biographical and indeed autobiographical account. The second might be called Platonic reflection on Socrates' quietist activism. Insofar as that reflection is rooted in Plato's response to the life and death of Socrates (not just his philosophical discourse), the second account too has a biographical dimension. But it is essentially philosophical in character. My preference for the second of the two approaches to the issue will quickly become apparent.

13

Ancient writers tell us a great deal about Plato's life. Much of it is highly and unreliably anecdotal, and sometimes evidently reflects partisan traditions sympathetic or hostile to him and his philosophy. Some basic information is nowadays generally accepted as sound. Plato was born probably in 427 BC of parents who both came from aristocratic Athenian families, and in the case of his father Ariston traced a lineage back to one of the legendary first kings of Athens. He had two elder brothers, Glaucon and Adeimantus, whom he makes Socrates' interlocutors in the *Republic*. His sister Potone was mother to his nephew Speusippus, who succeeded him in the leadership of the philosophical school he founded, the Academy, on his death in 347 BC. There were two great formative experiences in his early life: exposure to the charismatic figure of Socrates, and the dramatic sequence of political upheavals in Athens in the latter stages of the Peloponnesian War, culminating in the judicial execution of Socrates in 399 BC (Critias, a member of his own extended family, took a leading role in the ugly oligarchic junta—known as the 'thirty tyrants'—that seized power briefly in 404 BC). Plato was never politically active himself, except for two ill-judged visits to Syracuse in Sicily in 366 and 361, when he appears to have attempted to exert an influence on the young despot Dionysius II. He did so at the invitation of his friend Dion, Dionysius' uncle, and a powerful figure at court. He ended up caught as a more or less innocent and certainly ineffectual bystander in political machinations which were to culminate in Dion's death as he was engaging in an abortive coup. 'The important thing is...simply and solely the fact that he was somehow involved, that he thought he should participate. When the opportunity came, he decided—sensibly or foolishly—to get stuck into contemporary events.'[17]

There is one surviving document which purports to tell us a great deal more about some of these experiences. Among the extant writings attributed to Plato is a collection of thirteen letters. Its centrepiece—the *Seventh Letter*, much the longest and most interesting in the sequence—is devoted to an autobiographical account of his Sicilian adventures, in the guise of an explanation of their real character addressed to the political faction with which he had become associated. The production of fictive letters under the names of distinguished writers or public figures of the past became a significant literary industry in the Hellenistic and Roman periods, and it is generally agreed that most if not all of the items in this 'Platonic' collection are later fictions. The jury is still out, however, on the issue of the authenticity of the *Seventh Letter*, not least because on some tests its diction, sentence rhythms and other stylistic characteristics turn out to be indistinguishable from those of the latest group of Plato's dialogues (which includes the *Laws*).[18]

'Plato'—to describe him neutrally for the moment—prefaces his elaborate Sicilian narrative with an account of the political outlook he developed prior to his very first visit to Italy and Sicily at around the age of forty (i.e. about 387 BC). His line is that an initial appetite for public activity had been dulled and thwarted by observation of the unfolding development of Athenian politics in his early manhood. The rule of the junta led by his own relatives made people look back on the previous democratic regime as a golden age; and he was particularly distressed by the appalling treatment that his friend Socrates—'the most upright of men then living'—received at the hands of the thirty, and then by his trial and execution under the restored democracy. Reflection increasingly made 'Plato' realize two things. To achieve a proper management of affairs one would need, first, trustworthy friends and, second, a framework of sound laws and customs. Finding the friends would be an uphill struggle, and even the existing framework was rapidly deteriorating (*Ep.* 7.325D–326B):

Consequently, although at first I had been full of zeal for public life, when I looked at all this and saw how unstable everything was, I became in the end quite dizzy. I did not cease to consider how the situation and indeed the whole political system could be improved, but so far as action was concerned I was always in the position of waiting for opportunities. In the end I realized something about all contemporary cities: the whole lot of them are badly run—the state of their laws is pretty well irremediable without exceptional resources and luck as well. And I was compelled to say, in my praise of the right philosophy (because from that vantage point all forms of justice both political and relating to individuals are discernible), that the classes of mankind will therefore find no release from their troubles until either the class of those who engage properly and truly in philosophy take on political positions, or the class of those who wield power in the cities engage in real philosophy by some dispensation of divine providence.

'Plato' therefore adopts a pragmatic quietism as his own political posture, as the rational response to a political situation which he

---

claims could be transcended only by the advent of a philosopher ruler.

If the author of the *Seventh Letter* really was Plato, we have a quick and simple answer to our two initial questions about the rationale and status of Socrates' implication in *Republic* 5 and 6 that the condition of existing cities is irremediable, and of his radical solution to the problem that constitutes. What underlies Socrates' assessment will in that case have been Plato's own experience and consequent evaluation of the state of contemporary politics and political systems as irremediable, made quite explicit in the letter. And the conclusion that philosopher rulers are the only way out of the resulting cul-de-sac is then not only asserted by Plato, but asserted as what he Plato was asserting in the *Republic*. 'I was compelled to say' must mean: 'in the *Republic*', since 'say' points firmly to some publicly recognizable pronouncement of Plato's, and since the phraseology adopted here to enunciate the thesis about philosopher rulers is clearly designed to call to mind the formulations used by Socrates in the *Republic*.

Yet *did* Plato write the letter? If someone else was its author, then it is not yet excluded that the narrative passage quoted above faithfully mirrors Plato's own views and positions, but there is no a priori probability that it does. Here is not the place to develop a full treatment of the authorship question. But there are grounds for thinking that, so far as scrutiny of this passage on its own goes, the *Seventh Letter* looks more like Platonic pastiche than the genuine article.[19] Take, for example, the concluding statement on philosopher rulers, where the author—whether he is Plato or not—is deliberately adapting phraseology from all of three closely related *Republic* passages. The adaptation is a gauche performance. Expressions which work unproblematically in their original *Republic* context strike a false note as used here.[20] But there is a more fundamental problem. '*I was compelled*' to make the statement, says 'Plato'. But in the *Republic* it was *not* Plato speaking in his authorial person who said he was compelled to argue for truly philosophical rulers. It was Socrates—Plato's character 'Socrates'. If we are to believe that Plato himself wrote the *Seventh Letter*, it must follow that he is implying here that the Socrates of the *Republic is* him, or at any rate his spokesman. Is that credible? Is it credible either (a) that Plato saw Socrates as his spokesman, or even if he did (b) that he would speak as though the *Republic* were not a dialogue, but a pronouncement in his own person?

As to (b): Plato is the most reticent of philosophical writers. He might have expounded views in his own person in a continuous discourse, like the Presocratics or sophists before him. As it is, he invests huge energy and remarkable literary ingenuity in the creation of philosophical dramas—and dramatis personae to people them—in which he must in some sense be all and none of the characters whose voices are heard in the conversation. John Cooper is right to say:[21] 'It is in the entire writing that the author speaks to us, not in the remarks made by individual speakers.' It is of course true that when Socrates advocates introduction of philosopher rulers in the *Republic*, that is what Plato is saying to us (assertively, tentatively, ironically, hypothetically or whatever) in the dialogue. But the particular remark at 499B, about truth compelling the interlocutors to insist that philosopher rulers are the only solution to our political problems, is simply the way the character Socrates puts the point at that juncture in the conversation. For Plato now in the *Seventh Letter* to merge authorship with the authorial 'I', and imply that *he* made that remark, would constitute an abrupt lurch out of his own carefully constructed literary persona.[22]

With (a) we enter choppy scholarly waters. At one extreme are Platonic interpreters who do treat Socrates (or in the *Laws* the Athenian Visitor) as Plato's spokesman or representative. At the other are those who see the dialogues as entirely dialogical: there is no separate or separable authorial point of view to be communicated—only the interaction of whatever points of view are expressed in the conversation Plato is imagining. Something subtler and more flexible is needed than either of these approaches. In commenting recently on the issue, David Sedley has called attention to the analysis in several later dialogues of thinking itself as an internal dialogue of question and answer. He suggests that the question-and-answer sequences in the dialogues constitute externalizations of Plato's own thought processes. That is how Plato maintains a 'dominating and inescapable presence' in the dialogues. An answer to the question of authorial point of view suggests itself. The dialogues are to be read as 'Plato thinking aloud'.[23]

Sometimes Plato's thinking aloud can consist very largely in analytical scrutiny of ideas about courage or self-discipline or piety or poetry that turn out incapable of withstanding a Socratic examination, as in many of the earlier dialogues. On one occasion it takes the form of pastiche of the Athenian funeral oration (the *Menexenus*), on another of a systematic exercise—presented precisely *as* exercise—in the derivation of contradictory consequences from one and the same abstract hypothesis (the *Parmenides*). Even when the principal speaker in a dialogue develops a set of constructive proposals, there is often no very straightforward way in which these can be claimed without qualification to be Plato's views. Dialogues are written in a variety of registers. The *Sophist* and *Statesman*, for example, are mostly demanding, unrelenting abstract ratiocination, requiring of the reader considerable experience and skill in philosophy. The *Republic* adopts styles of presentation and argument that seem to appeal to the imagination as much as to the reasoning powers of receptive philosophical amateurs (represented by Glaucon and Adeimantus), and at critical points the provisional status of the discourse is emphasized. The *Laws* is different again. It offers an account of the transcendent moral and religious framework of political and social life, and the legal norms needed to sustain it, that is designed to be persuasive to citizens at large (and to a similarly broad readership, represented in the persons of the interlocutors Cleinias and Megillus), without any particular talent for philosophy or experience of it. Is it *Plato's* moral and religious framework? Or rather Plato's moral and religious framework presented from and for a particular point of view? On the interpretation that will be developed in this book, the viewpoint he adopts in the *Republic* is Socratic, in the *Statesman* Eleatic, and in the *Laws* Athenian—all in senses to be defined and elaborated as we progress. A preliminary word is needed in this connection, however, about the *Republic*.

It has often been claimed that after Book 1 of the *Republic*, a Socratic critique of various ideas about justice very much in the manner of the earlier dialogues, the 'Socrates' in the remainder of the dialogue sheds any distinctively Socratic beliefs or methods of argument, and mutates into a vehicle for Plato's own ideas.[24] This is too simplistic a reading of the situation. Take some of the basic unargued premises underlying the critique of Homer and the poets in Books 2 and 3. It is by no means clear that it is more Platonic than Socratic to hold that god is essentially good and cannot be the cause of anything bad, or that so far as living well is concerned the good man is maximally self-sufficient. Echoes of the *Apology* are even stronger in the way Socrates dismisses the fear of death in this same context.[25] Books 5 to 7 communicate a Platonic vision if anything in Plato does. Yet the first proposal advanced in Book 5—that there should be women 'guards' or rulers, not just men—has a clear Socratic motivation. Socratic ethics taught the radical thesis that virtue or moral excellence is one and the same thing in a man and a woman.[26] Perhaps here and elsewhere in the *Republic* it would be better to say that Plato often sees *himself* as Socrates' voice (rather than the other way around), with his 'Socrates' extrapolating implications from positions that his teacher had held. If so, we might be even more inclined to doubt the authenticity of the way the 'Plato' of the *Seventh Letter* appropriates 'Socrates'' 'truth compels us to say' from the *Republic*.

3. *Socrates: Engagement and Detachment*

We are engaged on an attempt to understand how Plato came to make his Socrates propose in the *Republic* that starting afresh with a clean slate is our only hope in politics. Section 2 has argued that if we look to the *Seventh Letter* for an explanation, we will be relying on a document of doubtful credentials. Would its inauthenticity necessarily entail its unreliability? Even if the author does not speak in a tone that is quite Platonic enough, might not the story he tells be the right story to tell? Scholars have often thought so. A common view is that if Plato did not write the letter himself, the writer must have been someone close to him, probably an associate in the Academy, so that we can trust the broad lines of his narrative.[27]

However that may be, I want to suggest that the story itself, not just its telling, strikes a note false to Plato, or at any rate to the Plato who wrote the *Apology*, *Crito*, *Gorgias* and *Republic*. The story focuses on Plato himself: his experience of politics, his views on the preconditions of successful management of affairs (reliable friends, sound laws) in a non-utopian political context, his judgement about the condition of Greece, his frustrated hopes of opportunities for political involvement and his radical conclusion about the need for philosophical rulers. The treatment of Socrates by both the thirty and the restored democracy certainly figures prominently in the account, with particular emphasis on its moral resonances. But it is there to help us understand something about Plato. This is subtly unlike the way Plato talks in writings that are unquestionably authentic. In them he is palpably a writer so obsessed with Socrates that until near the very end of his life all his dialogues are set in the imagined world of his memories of Socrates' Athens. Socrates' trial and death are built into the frame of dialogues such as the late *Sophist* and *Statesman* which otherwise contain little that is overtly or directly about Socrates. The *Apology, Crito, Gorgias* and *Republic* itself represent an evolving pattern of critical responses to something which one might call the defining cataclysm shaping Plato's whole emotional and intellectual outlook, something to which he returns again and again as he wrestles with what was evidently for him the ultimate problem for politics: its need for a rationality it rejects.

The letter communicates none of the intensity of argument that comes through so strongly in the *Apology* and the three dialogues mentioned above. Of course, if we assume the authenticity of the *Seventh Letter*, a Plato looking back in his old age on what had led him to embrace the radical political programme of the *Republic* might have recollected it all rather differently from when he was actually working out his ideas in those much earlier writings. Just as we cannot necessarily infer unreliability from inauthenticity, so conversely reliability does not follow from authenticity, contrary to what defenders of authenticity invariably assume. In what follows I shall argue that the reflection on Socrates' quietist activism in which Plato engages in *Apology, Crito, Gorgias* and *Republic* points in fact to a richer and more compelling explanation of the radical political solution proposed in the *Republic* than the narrative about his own experience of politics presented in the *Seventh Letter*—*whether he wrote that or not*.

The scholarly consensus is that *Apology* and *Crito* are probably among Plato's first literary productions, to be dated to some time in the 390s BC. In both the focus is primarily Socrates' behaviour and its motivation, in *Apology* at his trial, in *Crito* in prison awaiting death. Are *Apology* and *Crito* history or fiction? Whereas Plato may well have put a lot of his own thinking into even his earliest fictive representations of Socratic dialectic (as for example in *Ion* or *Hippias Minor*), scholars have often wanted to claim for *Apology* and *Crito* a greater historicity, or at least the intention to produce a strong impression (quite absent in *Ion* or *Hippias*) of historical realism. Yet the private conversation the *Crito* dramatizes between Socrates and his old friend Crito must be largely Plato's creation or re-creation, even if we may speculate that Crito kept some notes on what he remembered being said. There has been much debate about how far the speeches in Socrates' defence that Plato puts in his mouth in the *Apology* confine themselves to what Socrates actually said. We know that other writers circulated their own versions (Xenophon's is the only other contemporary survivor), but we do not know enough about the conventions of the genre. It is obvious, however, that even if Plato accurately reproduces the main topics covered in their original order, the detailed development each receives and its concrete literary and argumentative texture will have been at least as much Platonic as Socratic, however faithful to Socrates he intended to be.[28] This is what makes it appropriate to treat *Apology*, no less than the dialogues, as in some sense a crystallization of Platonic reflection on Socrates, not simply Socrates' self-characterization.[29]

In his main speech at the trial Socrates seems to have spent less time on the formal charges of impiety and corrupting the young (so much so that Xenophon is at pains to insist that he did make a serious attempt to deal with these) than on explaining himself and his life's work in general to the Athenians. He refused to beg the jury to acquit him, or to produce weeping children to arouse pity, as we know was a standard manoeuvre. In other respects, the speech as Plato reconstructs it employs variants of common democratic rhetorical tropes that a person appearing before the court might be expected to use to convince the judges of his probity and service to the city, and to make it clear that acquittal is in their interest as well as his. Socrates' account of *his* public service and its benefits to Athens is complex, paradoxical and extremely provocative. It gives us a first sense of the difficulties Plato is going to be exploring in the relationship between philosophy and politics.[30]

One fundamental tension in Socrates' posture is this. He does not hesitate to claim that he is a benefactor of the city. In fact he makes the extravagant assertion—no doubt perceived by many of the judges as arrogant nonsense—that the Athenians have never enjoyed a greater good in their city than his 'service to the god': his philosophical activity. He stresses his neglect in consequence of his own affairs and the absence of any financial rewards for his service, both things commonly represented as evidence of honest dedication to the public good (*Apol.* 30D–31C). On the other hand, by ordinary standards he is plainly what would be reckoned *apragmôn* (although significantly he avoids the word)—politically inactive or uninvolved or at any rate unambitious. As he himself puts it, he stays out of 'political affairs' (*politika pragmata*), and he has never had the nerve to ascend the speakers' podium and give advice to the city before a public gathering of the people (*plêthos*) (*Apol.* 31C–32A). That too is represented as being for a reason which very likely gave offence to some judges: because nobody will survive very long who gets up and opposes the Athenians or any public gathering anywhere, or tries to stop politically motivated unjust and illegal acts from occurring in the city. Here, then, is a major paradox. Socrates is the city's greatest benefactor, but avoids any part in its affairs.

There may well be a subtext to Socrates' account of himself. Like much over-used political vocabulary, the word *apragmôn* could be invested with varied evaluative colourings depending on context and point of view. There are plenty of Athenian texts from the late fifth century BC in which the politically unambitious *apragmôn* is represented in approvingly conservative terms as a citizen of sterling worth, the backbone of society. Pericles, by contrast, says famously in his funeral speech that the Athenians reckon someone who takes no part in politics not *apragmôn* but useless. But the other evidence suggests that his claim was contestable, even if it fits Thucydides' analysis of the Peloponnesian War as the conflict between Athens as an active power and Sparta as one whose posture and instincts were more *apragmôn*. Moreover, there is no clear instance of the antonym, *polupragmôn*, and its cognate expressions, being used positively at this period—they denote hyperactivity, or being a busybody. The way Pericles formulates his remark itself indicates that *apragmôn* did not automatically carry a negative charge. To get the negative evaluation he wants he has to substitute another expression.[31]

However Socrates' trial was held at a time when Athens had very recently been polarized between democratic activists and sympathizers, and those who had been implicated in the oligarchic regime of the thirty, or who had done nothing to distance themselves from it. Although a general amnesty had been declared following the restoration of democracy in 403 BC, there was evidently a climate of heightened political and religious anxiety in the years 400–399, which is precisely when the lawsuit against Socrates was brought. His confessed political inactivity would not have helped him much in resisting a prosecution whose motivation was very likely primarily political. For, although Plato represents him as studiously avoiding any mention of Critias, leader of the thirty, his association with Critias would presumably have been regarded as the principal evidence of the corrupting effect of his teaching on his associates, along with Alcibiades, the aristocratic politician who was rightly or wrongly regarded as implicated in the scandal over the Mysteries in 415 BC, and ended up going over to the Spartan enemy. As the orator Aeschines was to put it in a forensic speech delivered half a century after the event (*Against Timarchus* 173): 'Men of Athens, you executed Socrates the sophist because he was shown to have educated Critias, one of the thirty who put down the democracy.'[32]

Socrates' political inactivity, therefore, was on the face of it of no benefit to the city at all, and at that point in time might well have been regarded as a black mark against him. It is at least interesting that of the two examples he gives of incidents where he happened to get caught up in public affairs, each time resisting pressure to act illegally or unjustly, he comments that one occurred under the democracy (it can be dated to 406 BC), the other under the oligarchy of the thirty—as though to demonstrate his even-handedness, while at the same time leaving nobody in any doubt that he *did* do his bit to resist the thirty, risking his life in the process (*Apol.* 32A–E). His larger point is to suggest the irrelevance of categories like democracy and oligarchy (mentioned with calculated casualness), and (much more thematically) public and private. His behaviour—he says—demonstrates the sort of person he is and what his values are. Whether very occasionally on the public stage or in his usual mode in the private sphere, he is just the same: a fierce opponent of injustice (*Apol.* 32E–33B).[33]

Socrates does more than discount traditional political categories. In demonstrating the authenticity of the services to the city he performs, he goes out of his way to exploit and subvert the associations of the conventional vocabulary and to appropriate it for himself—or rather for his moral mission. He describes his private questioning of those he encounters as 'advice' (*sumbouleuein*, the term standardly used, as in the very next line of his speech, for political advice and in particular for contributions to debate in the assembly), and—unflatteringly—as 'busybodying' (*polupragmôn*, the expression used by critics to denigrate democratic involvement in politics as hyperactive), incidentally putting as much distance as he can between himself and the image of the *apragmôn* (*Apol.* 31C). In his second speech, delivered after the verdict, in which he himself notoriously proposes as his punishment the 'penalty' of free meals at the public expense, Socrates insists at the outset that he has never led the 'quiet life' (*hêsuchia*), and near the end that leading it would be for him an impossibility (*Apol.* 36B–E, 37E–38A). In neglect of every other possible pursuit, he has spent his time persuading people to care for their own selves before their possessions, and for the city itself before its possessions. The 'quiet life' had its own political resonances—of aristocratic restraint and decorum. It was another way of characterizing the lifestyle of the *apragmôn*, and Plato in the *Charmides* suggests that Critias and Charmides gave it a central place in their ideology if not in their political behaviour. Socrates' rejection of the quiet life demonstrates his own democratic credentials—on an understanding of what counts as democratic activity cast in terms of his own redefinition of public service, of course.[34]

In one sense the *Apology* presents a blazingly affirmative picture of the relationship between philosophy and the public sphere. Philosophy's role is to perform for the city the supreme public benefit of moral criticism: of nagging the citizens into examining themselves and their and the city's priorities for their own true good. It is summed up in Socrates' striking image of himself as a gadfly sent by the god to sting into activity a large, noble, but sluggish horse. As Josiah Ober comments, the speeches of the *Apology* perform his 'ultimate challenge' to the city. They can be regarded as 'his last, best sting'.[35] Athens through the decision of its court may have signalled that it would not tolerate philosophy on these terms. But readers of the *Apology* might wonder whether the work's final message need be the conclusion that there is, after all, no contribution that philosophy will ever be allowed to make to the public good under democracy. Socrates *had* been tolerated for seventy years. And he himself suggests, at the beginning of his second speech, that there was a lot of contingency about the verdict. Had not the powerful figures of Anytus and Lycon put their names to the charges, Meletus—the lead prosecutor—would have lost the case heavily (*Apol.* 36A–B). The warning of retribution Socrates gives the Athenians in his third and final speech—in the shape of harsher and more numerous probings from younger critics in the future—is not the talk of someone who sees his cause going down to final defeat (*Apol.* 39C–D).

The *Crito* has often been thought difficult to render consistent with the *Apology*. The Socrates of the *Apology* declares in ringing tones that he will obey the god rather than the court should it require him to stop philosophizing (*Apol.* 29B–30C). The Socrates of the *Crito* imagines the laws of Athens putting to him a powerful case for the obligation of a citizen to obey all judicial decisions that have the law's authority: in the present instance, rejecting any thought of escape from prison, and accepting the sentence of death pronounced upon him (*Crito* 50A–52A). Perhaps we are not to suppose that the laws' arguments have the standing of a piece of Socratic philosophizing or even Socratic rhetoric.[36] But Socrates does not resist them. If the consistency of *Apology* and *Crito* is debatable in this area, from another point of view the two works seem to share a common outlook. In both of them Socrates is represented as an Athenian who sees his life and work as intimately related to his citizenship of Athens. To be more precise, in *Apology* he construes his philosophizing as a public service. In *Crito*, conversely, it is he who is portrayed as the beneficiary of the city. The laws claim that he owes everything to them, in the sense that they have provided the entire framework within which he was born, raised and given the education of body and mind that his father provided for him. They go on to argue that he has rejected every conceivable opportunity to opt out and take up residence elsewhere (even though he has often expressed approval of the systems of government in Sparta and Crete), and they infer that he must be comfortable with Athens and its system of justice. In both *Apology* and *Crito* the possibility that he might go and philosophize in exile is entertained and rejected on a variety of moral and pragmatic grounds—with *Crito* giving a much fuller and seemingly more considered exploration of the issues at stake (*Apol.* 37C–D; *Crito* 53A–E).

In sum: the two works represent Socrates' philosophizing as deeply embedded in and engaged with Athens. Nothing they say about it points to its being *essentially* tied to Athens or indeed to citizenship or politics, except insofar as the moral critique to which Socrates subjects an individual may inevitably encompass his commitments and behaviour as a social and political being. There is no suggestion, for example, that philosophy can be developed and fostered as a practice only in a society which protects and fosters freedom of speech in general.[37] Socrates in the *Apology* portrays himself as a great public benefactor, but he does not claim that he is thereby fulfilling his obligations as a citizen. On the contrary, philosophy is presented as the response to a divine imperative, and its benefit to the city accordingly as a gift of god. Socrates leaves us in no doubt that its authority derives from a different and higher source than the city.[38] So the embeddedness is something contingent.

But despite contingency, embeddedness can go deep, whether we think of the commitments of (for example) a freely chosen relationship such as marriage, or of a profession conducted for years in a particular place, as it might be by a doctor or a priest or a teacher. Its depth in the case of Socrates' philosophical activity is apparent in at least two ways. We are offered the picture of a Socrates who has no interest in philosophizing elsewhere, and never has had. And there is no imaginative exploration—as, of course, there will be in the *Republic*—of a utopian alternative in which philosophy might play a different and more integrated role in the city, and in which political activity would not require (almost as a matter of course) the commission of acts in contravention of law and justice. If we look for an explanation of all this, there is one obvious answer, which comes through loud and clear in both *Apology* and *Crito*. It is that Socrates never questioned his own identity as a citizen of Athens, and never conceived that that identity could be challenged or compromised by his philosophical activity. Hence the problem his condemnation by the court posed for him. If he cannot continue philosophizing as a citizen of Athens, he cannot continue philosophizing. But if he cannot continue philosophizing, he cannot continue to live. So death is the only solution.

Embeddedness and engagement are what have disappeared in the analysis of the relationship between the philosopher and the city that Plato puts in Socrates' mouth in the *Republic*. When Adeimantus challenges Socrates' argument for the thesis that philosophers are the only people who have the qualities of mind and character needed in a ruler, with the objection that experience suggests just the opposite (they are either weird, not to say vicious, or else and at best useless), Socrates responds first with his famous ship of state analogy. The city is like a ship in which a lot of violent, quarrelling, ignorant sailors vie with each other to persuade the short-sighted and slightly deaf owner to give them control over the wheel, having no comprehension of the expertise of the one person who is really qualified to steer the boat, and regarding him as a useless stargazer (*Rep.* 6.487A–489A). The moral is then spelled out. The blame for the perceived uselessness of morally decent philosophers lies not with them, but with those who make no use of them (489A–D). Second, however, it is only too likely that those with philosophical potential will indeed have been morally corrupted, because the society around them will have warped their development (Socrates means societies in general, but all the detail indicates that he has the Athenian democracy particularly in mind). There are a tiny number of people who have actually become true philosophers (Socrates includes himself among them). Of them he says (496C–497A):

'Those who have become members of this small group have tasted how sweet and blessed a possession is philosophy. They can see that virtually nothing anyone in politics does is in any way healthy, and that they have no ally with whom they could go to the rescue of justice and live to tell the tale. The philosopher would be like a person falling into a den of wild animals, refusing to join in their vicious activities, but too weak to resist their combined ferocity single-handed. He wouldn't get a chance to help his city or his friends. He would be killed before he could be any use either to himself or to anyone else. Taking all this into his calculations, he will keep quiet, and mind his own business, like someone taking shelter behind a wall when he is caught by a storm of driving dust and rain. He sees everyone else brimful of lawlessness, and counts himself lucky if he himself can somehow live his life here pure, free from injustice and unholy actions, and depart with high hopes, in a spirit of kindness and goodwill, on his release from it.'

'Well,' he said, 'if he could have accomplished that before his departure, it would be no small achievement.'

'And yet not the greatest achievement either—not without finding a political system worthy of him. In one which *is* worthy of him his own growth will be greater, and he will be the salvation of his country as well as of himself.'[39]

There is much in this passage that self-consciously recalls the *Apology* and Socrates' statements there of his own attitude to political activity. It makes the same diagnosis of lawlessness as the prevailing tendency in public life. It sees the prospects for anyone who fights for justice surviving and achieving anything beneficial for himself or the community in the same pessimistic light. It too recognizes abstention from injustice and impiety as the philosopher's ultimate sticking point. But the attitude to the city, or rather 'the many', is very different. Whereas the Socrates of the *Apology* addressed his judges as people who might conceivably listen to him and respond intelligently to what he was saying to them, this Socrates speaks of the 'madness' of the many; and his metaphors and similes (the ferocious wild animals, the storm of driving dust and rain) negate all possibilities of rational interaction. Just as significant is what is omitted. The *Apology*'s paradoxical presentation of Socrates' philosophical activity as public service in a radically new mode simply drops from view. Socrates no longer hesitates to apply the notion of the 'quiet life'—coupled with that of 'minding one's own business' (Critias's formula for self-discipline in the *Charmides* (161B–164C) as well as the *Republic*'s formula for justice (4.433A–434D))—to the philosopher's renunciation of political activity.

It also transpires that the city of his birth no longer gives the philosopher his true identity. When Adeimantus presses Socrates to explain what he means by a political system 'suited to philosophy', Socrates replies (*Rep.* 6. 497B–C):

'None of them [i.e. the present-day systems],' I replied. 'That's precisely my complaint. There is no present-day political regime which lives up to the philosopher's nature. That's why his nature gets twisted and transformed. It's like the seed of some exotic plant. When it's sown outside its native land, it tends to lose its distinguishing properties and vigour, and degenerate into the indigenous variety. In the same way, as things stand at present, the philosophic type tends not to preserve its distinctive power. It degenerates into some other sort of character. If it ever does find the best regime—just as it is itself the best—then it will show that it was a truly divine type, whereas all other types of nature or life are merely human.'

28

The agricultural simile is highly significant, with its suggestion that the city of the philosopher's birth is actually foreign soil, alien to his nature. As Socrates cashes the comparison out, philosophers will only truly be themselves—maintain their own identity as philosophers at full strength—in another city, under the 'best political system' the *Republic* has been constructing in the imagination.

The echoes of the *Apology* suggest that Plato has reached these conclusions not (as the *Seventh Letter* implies) by reflecting on his own experience of politics, but by rethinking Socrates' relationship to Athens. He must have come to believe that it was not a matter of embeddedness and engagement, as Socrates himself may have felt it to be, but in harsh reality alienation, detachment and a degree of personal impoverishment. Support for this diagnosis comes from the *Gorgias*, a dialogue antedating the *Republic* in which we find Plato already rewriting the narrative of the *Apology* in similar terms. Towards the end of the sustained confrontation between philosophy and political rhetoric staged by the dialogue, Socrates is made to imagine himself put on trial before the Athenian people. It is as if he were a doctor required to defend the treatment he had prescribed before a jury of children, with a pastry chef for prosecutor (*Gorg.* 521E–522B):

Socrates: Ask yourself what defence such a person could make in that situation. Suppose the prosecutor said something like this: 'Children, this man here has done you many injuries—you are suffering yourselves, and he is ruining the youngest of you with the cuts and burns he inflicts, and reduces you to a state of paralysis by starving and choking you, making you take exceptionally bitter drinks and forcing hunger and thirst upon you. Not at all like me, who feasted you on all sorts of delicious things.' What do you think the doctor, caught in this predicament, would have to say? Suppose he told the truth: 'I did all these things, children, in the interests of health.' What uproar would this provoke among a jury of this nature, do you think? Pretty substantial, surely?
Callicles: Possibly.
Socrates: One has to think so. And don't you think he would be completely at a loss what to say?
Callicles: Indeed I do.

Socrates is made to conclude that he will be able to say neither what is true nor anything else. In other words, because he realizes that the Athenians are too infantile to respond to a rational concern for their true good, in this revised version of his trial he will make no mention of what the buoyant rhetoric of the *Apology* characterized as his gadfly activity. He will recognize that it would be pointless to do so even before he begins to speak—and so will be unable to say anything. That (Plato is now saying) is how a Socrates who perceived his true situation at his trial—and more generally assessed realistically the situation of philosophy—would have to have behaved. It is not until the *Republic* that Plato has him draw the utopian conclusion: Socratic philosophizing has to be moved 'out of the democratic polis-as-it-is and into the polis-as-it-should-be'.[40]

4. The Projects of the Republic

What is the main project undertaken in the *Republic*? The late Neoplatonist Proclus starts his commentary on the dialogue by reporting an ancient disagreement about the issue—which gets replayed, in one form or another, in modern scholarship also. Some (*On the Republic* 7.9–8.6) said the main project was the enquiry into justice, meaning by that the moral virtue an individual needs in order to behave properly towards others. They pointed out that this was the topic of Socrates' initial discussions with Cephalus, Polemarchus and Thrasymachus in Book 1. Then they noted that discussion of the city is initially introduced in Book 2 as a way of pursuing the more rigorous examination of the same topic demanded by Adeimantus and Glaucon, but by *analogy* and on a larger canvas. Finally, they registered Socrates' frequent reminders to his interlocutors throughout the dialogue that the justice of the individual is the object of the enquiry, and to cap it all the way he ends the whole work, with a myth picturing the rewards of a life of justice in the hereafter. Modern scholars who make these same points conclude that the *Republic* is therefore in essentials an exercise in moral, not political, philosophy.[41]

To return to Proclus, there are just as many writers, he says, who put another line of interpretation with no less warrant (*On the Republic* 8.7–11.4). They treat the initial discussions of justice in the dialogue as providing nothing more than a way in to the treatment of *politeia*, the main theme (I shall leave *politeia* untranslated for the moment).[42] *Politeia* was, after all, Plato's title for the work (much learned comment on dialogue titles follows), and the backwards references in the *Laws* and the *Timaeus* exclusively to the *Republic*'s political material confirm that Plato himself took it to be primarily a project in political philosophy. It could have been added that Books 5 to 7 are presented quite explicitly as a digression into further discussion of political questions, interrupting the next stage proposed at the end of Book 4 for the argument about justice and injustice, but not actually pursued until Books 8 and 9—yet this 'digression' turns out to be the crowning glory of the whole dialogue, opening up as it does the metaphysical vista of the Forms and the theory of the Good, together with its account of the mathematical sciences that we need to acquire if we are to achieve understanding. And, as G. R. F. Ferrari puts the argument, the *Republic*'s 'proposals for social reform—its utopian refashionings of education, of property-rights, of the very structure of the family—go well beyond what correspondence with the individual would require, and seem to be developed for their own sake'.[43]

Against the champions of the *Republic*'s claim to be read as political philosophy, it is sometimes objected that the dialogue does not offer much serious analytical treatment of constitutions or the idea of a constitution. Unfavourable comparisons are made with the *Statesman* and the *Laws*, and above all with Aristotle's *Politics*.[44] This line of objection betrays a misunderstanding of what Plato meant by *politeia*. Translators of the *Politics* have found that for Aristotle 'constitution' works fairly satisfactorily as an English equivalent for *politeia*, preoccupied as he is with the system of offices or positions of rule operative in a city.[45] The *politeia*, on his definition, is a certain ordering of positions of rule, particularly the one that is sovereign over all the others (*Pol.* 3.6, 1278b8–10, 4.1, 1289a15–18). Armed with this formulation, he is well placed to address the merits and demerits of monarchical, oligarchic and democratic forms of government and associated constitutional arrangements. In the *Republic* and much other writing on *politeia*, however, the focus is rather different.

We get a much better sense of what the word means in that tradition if we consider the issue that triggers the whole digression of Books 5 to 7 of *Republic*. Back in Book 4 Socrates has been stressing how important it is for the unity of the city he and the other interlocutors have been discussing that those with the appropriate talents are assigned to the three classes they have distinguished (producers, military, rulers), as well as that the city should not be too large. He adds that further more numerous and detailed prescriptions are not necessary, provided that one requirement is satisfied (*Rep.* 423E–424B):

'And what is that requirement?' he asked.

'Education and upbringing,' I said. 'If the guardians are well educated, and grow into men of sound judgment, they will have no difficulty in seeing all this for themselves, plus other things we are saying nothing about—such as taking wives, marriage, and having children. They will see the necessity of making everything as nearly as possible "shared among friends", in the words of the proverb.'

'Yes, that would be best,' he said.

Education, upbringing, rules governing marriage, the role of women in society: these are the subjects a contemporary reader would have expected to find discussed in a work entitled *Politeia*, as for example in Xenophon's short treatise *Politeia of the Spartans*, perhaps to be dated to around 394 BC. In his first seven chapters Xenophon covers: eugenics and the role of women; education (including diet, clothing and pederasty); the conduct of adolescents; choruses and athletic contests; public common meals and the use of drink; relations between parents and children; money and the accumulation of wealth. Virtually all of these topics are likewise attested as the main issues explored a generation after Aristotle in the *Politeia* of the Stoic Zeno of Citium. Nothing was regarded as more important than discussion of women and children. Xenophon followed Critias, author of both a prose and a verse *Politeia of the Spartans* before him (and, of course, well before Plato wrote), in beginning his substantive exposition with *teknopoiia* ('child production'), and specifically with eugenic methods for producing vigorous offspring. The first sentence of Critias' prose treatise is preserved (Fr. 32):

I will begin with the birth of a human being. How would one produce the best and strongest physique? If the father exercises, eats heartily, and demonstrates physical endurance, and if the mother of the child that is to be produced is physically robust and exercises.

Xenophon for his part reports that the Spartan system permits an aged husband to allow his young wife to have children by a more vigorous younger man, or someone who does not wish to cohabit with his wife to have children by someone else's wife if she is productive and well-born—provided the husband agrees. As for a scenario in which women share rule with men, and marriage takes the form of open and communal polygamy, we can infer that before Plato composed a word on the subject it had figured in Athenian speculation, and had caused intense public interest. For Aristophanes satirizes the idea in his *Assemblywomen* (392 BC), where he imagines women seizing power from men for themselves and instituting sexual communism.[46] No wonder that Adeimantus and Socrates' other discussants in the *Republic* are outraged and incredulous that, in a scheme for the good city so obviously Spartan in its sympathies, Socrates wants to move on to other topics when he has so far said almost nothing on this subject (5. 449A–450D).

The core meaning of *politeia* is 'citizenship', 'the condition of being a citizen'. In the literary tradition in which the *Republic* seems to belong, it has come to include the implicit or explicit idea of a *system* of laws and practices structuring the life of the citizens. A *politeia* treatise might accordingly include discussion of the appropriate stratification of society. Hippodamus of Miletus, writing perhaps some time in the mid-fifth century, had already before Plato proposed a tripartite division—into craftsmen, farmers and warriors—in a purely theoretical account of the best *politeia*.[47] But *politeia* writing did not necessarily pose the question of who should rule. It was not addressed by Hippodamus or Xenophon, or by the Stoic Zeno, so far as our evidence goes. We do find the issue of who rules, and in whose interest, clearly taken as the key issue for determining what kind of *politeia* a city has adopted in (for example) Pericles' funeral speech in Thucydides (2.37). Herodotus famously presents a debate on the comparative merits of monarchy, oligarchy and democracy as systems of rule in the improbable context of an argument within the Persian nobility in Book 3 of his *History* (3.80–2). Yet Pericles is more interested in the way of life and habits of mind and speech fostered under democracy than in its constitutional provisions, while the Persian Otanes spends much of his speech in Herodotus on analysis of the *lifestyle* of the despot. As Richard Stalley has observed, Aristotle too 'recognizes that there needs to be an agreement between a city's constitution and its general way of life, particularly so far as education is concerned'.[48] At one point he actually describes a *politeia* as in a sense 'a city's way of life' (*Pol.* 4.11, 1295a40). So when in *Republic* 8 and 9 Plato's Socrates reviews the 'degenerate' forms of constitution or political and social systems (as we might best in the end translate *politeia*), there is nothing in the least idiosyncratic in his focusing on lifestyle and patterns of personal and social motivation in the treatment of oligarchy and democracy that he offers, for example, rather than on analysis of their constitutional framework.

Proclus would not allow that the *Republic* has two projects: an enquiry into justice, and a treatment of the best *politeia*. His measured answer is that these are really just the two constituents of one and the same project, since the role justice plays in the soul or mind of the individual is exactly the same as that of the ideal political and social system in the well-governed city. He goes on to give quite an elaborate account of the isomorphisms involved in Plato's tripartite analysis of city and soul, noting among other things how Plato's Socrates treats the structure of the *politeia* as what justice in the city consists in, and conversely justice in the soul as a *politeia* within (*On the Republic* 11.5–14.14). Alexandre Koyré, the distinguished French historian of thought, took a very similar approach. But the very question made him angry:[49]

In our editions, as in our manuscripts, the *Republic* always bears a subtitle: *On Justice*. And the ancient critics of the imperial period, Plato's first editors, asked themselves in all seriousness: what is the principal subject of the book—what is it primarily about, justice or the constitution of the city? Is it moral or is it political? The question is a trifling one in my opinion; even worse, it is an absurdity. For it reveals in the consciousness of the editors a dichotomy between ethics and politics (which amounts to saying between politics and philosophy), such a dichotomy being the last thing in the world Plato wanted.[50]

He then rightly attacks the modern idea that for Plato politics was the study of the state. As a category for the historical analysis of the Athens and Sparta of Plato's time, the modern concept of state—as the impersonal sovereign power from which government and all the agencies of government derive their authority—has its uses. But 'state' does not correspond to any ancient Greek or Roman category, and it is certainly not what the word *polis* ('city') means.[51] For Plato and Aristotle (as Chapter 5 will explore) the city is simply the most complete form of community there is. The *Republic*'s analogy of individual and city is focused on the identity Plato proposes between the structure of the soul and the structure of the ideal community. For Koyré it is more than analogy:[52]

34

Because the analogy rests upon a mutual interdependence, it is impossible to study man without at the same time studying the city of which he forms a part. The psychological structure of the individual and the social structure of the city fit together perfectly, or, in modern terms, social psychology and individual psychology are mutually interdependent.

There are different ways of defending the interdependence interpretation of the *Republic*. The version of it adopted in this book will be presented in Chapter 6.[53]

Another way of looking at the question is to start from the very disparate origins of the two projects. The enquiry into justice derives from a deep-seated Socratic preoccupation, as will already be apparent from our discussion of the *Apology*. Its attempt to work out a theory of the soul and of what caring for its happiness consists is clearly (as Proclus' first group of commentators rightly argued) the dialogue's fundamental and overarching project. The discussion of the city and its political and social system draws heavily on quite different resources: on the *politeia* tradition, and especially idealization of Spartan institutions. It is as though the *Republic* says to us: we will be able to carry through the main Socratic project about justice to a successful conclusion only if we engage—with no less determination, imagination and willingness to let the argument take us where it will—in an apparently quite different kind of exercise in the *politeia* tradition. In particular, it is only by undertaking the *politeia* project that we will come to appreciate the importance of *philosophy* for the good city (including the need for the radical solution of the clean slate) and for the happiness of the individual. Only in the process of doing that will we find a perspective where by virtue of intense absorption in the eternal order of things and its unifying principles we can transcend all other concerns.

5. *Education, Sparta and the* Politeia *Tradition*

Education—interpreted in the broadest possible sense—has a claim to be considered perhaps the greatest preoccupation of both the *Republic* and the *Laws* alike. As Myles Burnyeat puts the point with regard to the *Republic*:[54]

If you are designing an ideal society, as Plato does in the *Republic*, and contrasting it with the corruptions of existing societies, as he also does in the *Republic*, then you need to think about much more than political institutions in a narrow sense. You need to think about all the influences, all the ideas, images, and practices, that make up the culture of a society.

Diskin Clay has something similar to say of the *Laws*:[55]

For Plato, written laws (*nomoi*) cannot take hold in a society without the civic education of a citizen body by custom (*nomos*). And for this reason any consideration of written statutes must take into view what the Greeks spoke of as 'unwritten laws': 'These are the bonds that keep the entire social and political order together... as ancestral customs of great antiquity (*Laws* 7.793A–B).'

The crucial role in society played by 'education and upbringing' is explicitly stated in Book 4 of the *Republic* (423E–424A). And Plato could scarcely mark the centrality of this theme in the *Republic* more emphatically than by making it the topic of the most powerfully memorable of all the images which saturate the dialogue: the allegory of the Cave at the beginning of Book 7 (whose opening sentence announces *paideia* (education, culture) and its opposite *apaideusia* (being uneducated and uncivilized) as the subject: 7.514A). Here Socrates portrays ordinary humanity[56] as chained up in a dark subterranean cavern. They live in a world of shadows, with no conception of what reality is like. They are able to see nothing—themselves and each other included—except the shadows cast by firelight on to the back of the cave by objects carried by puppeteers along a low wall behind them and by themselves, and are capable of no intellectual activity other than reminiscences and guesses about the passing scene. Burnyeat draws an inference:[57]

The Cave image shows the prisoners unaware that their values and ideas are uncritically absorbed from the surrounded culture. They are prisoners, as we all are to begin with, of their education and upbringing. When Socrates introduces the point that they have seen nothing of themselves and each other save the shadows on the back of the cave, he is explaining (515A5: *gar*) what he means by saying the prisoners are 'like us'. He means they are like us in respect of the education and culture we were brought up in.

There is a perhaps surprising connection between these Platonic ideas about *paideia* and the Spartan system of education.

As Xenophon explains it, a key difference from the practice elsewhere—where parents would make their own individual arrangements for the provision of teaching—was that at Sparta education was organized and controlled by the city, which appointed from the ruling class an official who exercised oversight of the boys under his charge as a group (*Lac. Pol.* 2.1–2). It is clear from his and other accounts that the training provided (the *agógē*, as it was known) involved a brutal and brutalizing regime of extreme physical deprivation and hardship. Its purpose was to develop resourcefulness as well as toughness and resilience, but no less importantly obedience to superiors and habituation to the militaristic values of Spartan society. Plato rejected the militaristic conception of virtue to which the Spartans, like the Cretans, seemed to be wedded. But what he found compelling was the notion that the whole nature of a society and the development of the individual alike could be transformed in tune with each other if the city itself made sure that it had not just an educational system, but an entire cultural environment designed with the single-minded aim of fostering virtue and the desire to become 'a perfect citizen'. What he wanted to put in place of the social environment he indicts elsewhere in the *Republic* is best indicated in a telling passage from Book 3 on material culture—statues, buildings and the like—quoted by Burnyeat (3.401B–D):[58]

Our aim is to prevent our guards being reared among images of vice—as it were in a pasturage of poisonous herbs where, cropping and grazing every day, they little by little and all unawares build up one huge accumulation of evil in their soul. Rather, we must seek out craftsmen with a talent for capturing what is lovely and graceful, so that our young, dwelling as it were in a salubrious region, will receive benefit from everything around them. Like a breeze bringing health from wholesome places, the impact of works of beauty on eye or ear will imperceptibly, from childhood on, guide them to likeness, to friendship, to concord with the beauty of reason.

Burnyeat emphasizes 'little by little and all unawares' and 'imperceptibly'. It is the unconscious even more than the consciousness of the young that needs to be permeated with influences making for virtue: above all with grace and beauty.

The prominence of the theme of education in *politeia* writing at Athens, and the Spartan focus of much of this literature, is already apparent. In fact the whole business of *politeia* writing before Plato and in his own time was a politically partisan activity particularly—perhaps exclusively—favoured by aristocratic admirers of Sparta: 'Laconizers'. In their eyes Sparta constituted the ideal alternative to what were perceived as the deficiencies of Athenian values and practices. Besides the writings already mentioned on the Spartan *politeia*, another notable example is the *Politeia of the Athenians*, found in manuscripts of Xenophon, but already recognized as unXenophontic in antiquity, and nowadays ascribed to an anonymous Athenian author writing perhaps somewhere between 425 and 415 BC, who has come to be known as 'the old oligarch'.[59] This Spartan sympathizer explains to others of the same mind why, although the way Athens is run is appalling, its institutions and way of life are cleverly calculated to advance and consolidate the interests of the mass of the *dêmos*, and will not easily be overthrown.[60]

Plato's attraction to this Laconizing literature was no doubt overdetermined. Critias, leader of the Spartan-instituted junta of 404–03 BC, was his mother's cousin; Critias and Xenophon were regarded by themselves and others as members of the Socratic circle; and Socrates himself frequently expressed admiration for the 'good government' (*eunomia*) at Sparta and in Crete, if we may believe Plato's *Crito* (52E).[61] Plato's ambiguous fascination with the Spartan alternative is apparent at various places in the dialogues. An early example comes in the *Protagoras*, where in a passage of outrageous insincerity Socrates is made to portray the Cretans and particularly the Spartans as closet philosophers. Spartan dedication to physical exercise is only a smokescreen designed to disguise an educational system actually focused on 'philosophy and argument', from which women profit as well as men (*Prot.* 342A–E). But the most important text for comparison with the *Republic* in this regard is the *Laws*, uniquely among the dialogues set outside Athens—in Crete. Its first book is largely taken up with a vigorous *attack* by the Athenian Visitor on Spartan and Cretan militarism and the deficient conception of virtue that goes with it, and then on Sparta's misconceived austerity where the use of strong drink and the institution of the symposium are concerned. All this adds up to a radical critique of Spartan ideas on education. In the *Critias*—also a late work[62]—criticism is left implicit. We should scarcely be surprised[63] that the representation of an uncorrupted Athens, victorious in her war with Atlantis, that Plato puts in Critias' mouth reads (as Christopher Gill has argued) like 'a picture of Sparta lodged in an Attic locale'.[64] This Athens has a much more extensive and fertile territory than in historic times; it is a land power supreme in warfare;[65] and it enjoys *eunomia*, the good government synonymous with the Spartan way of life (*Tim.* 23C–D, 25B–C; *Critias* 110C–112D). Critias presents his Athens as a living embodiment of the Platonic Socrates' *politeia* (*Tim.* 26C–D). However it is ruled not by philosophers, but by a militia living communally in isolation from the rest of the population, just as in Sparta—which is how Socrates himself had recalled his account of the ideal city at the beginning of the *Timaeus* (*Tim.* 17B–19A; *Critias* 110C–D, 112D–E).

In all this Platonic material there is a great deal of inwardness and ambivalence. It is as though an important audience for Plato's own writing on the topic must be those Athenians who (in reality or in his imagination) had like himself been profoundly impressed by the thinking of the Laconizing Socratics—and the Laconizing Socrates—of his earlier years: already in the *Republic*, but above all in the *Laws*.[66] On the one hand, he is constantly critical of Spartan and Cretan attitudes and institutions. On the other, there is a clearly a sense in which for him Sparta and Crete set the terms of reference for discussion of *politeia*, even if much of the time he wants to indicate that and how they must be transcended. In Books 2 and 3 of the *Republic* the distancing from the Spartan and Cretan model is only implicit. Nonetheless the very introduction of the topic in the first place requires to be understood against that background. There is no doubting the general Spartan character of the context. Those to be educated are a discrete class of citizen 'guards' who will give the city its capacity to wage war:[67] when Socrates proposes that, he is advocating something which was anathema at Athens and in most Greek cities, but absolutely fundamental to Spartan and Cretan political organization. For Plato's original readers this would immediately give his *politeia* an emphatically Spartan character. If the Laconophiles among them were further expecting that the guards' training would be anything like the Spartan *agôgê*, however, they were in for a rude shock.

Socrates briefly makes the argument that, as well as having the physical attributes of a pedigree guard dog, his human guards will need to be spirited by nature if they are to be courageous in soul (2.375A–B). But he then spends much more time arguing that if they are to be gentle in their dealings with their own people, they must also have a natural disposition of just the opposite sort. The disposition he identifies is one rooted in knowledge (pedigree dogs behave gently towards people when and because they know them)—which can therefore be characterized as philosophical (2.375B–376C): embryonically philosophical, we might want to say. When Socrates turns to the education appropriate for such persons, he advocates a version of what he describes as the traditional system: physical exercise for the body, education in music and poetry for the soul, with music and poetry started first. The tradition in question is *not* Spartan or Cretan at all, but Athenian practice, as described for example by Protagoras in his great speech in the dialogue Plato named after him, again with music first, then physical training (*Prot.* 325D–326C). Neither Glaucon nor Adeimantus—who takes over as interlocutor for the discussion of education—shows any signs of discomfort with this approach (2.376E, 3.410C–D), which constitutes a radical alternative to the Spartan and Cretan model, addressed to a radically different conception of the relationship appropriate between the military class and the rest of the population. Aristotle, according to Plutarch (*Lycurgus* 28), reported that at Sparta war was declared on the serfs (the 'helots') annually, in order to sanction any killings that occurred: something more or less encouraged as an exercise undertaken in the course of the *agôgê*. The *Republic*, by contrast, is determined that the education its guards receive should *not* predispose them to behave towards the other citizens as 'savage masters', more like wolves attacking the sheep than dogs looking after them (3. 416A–C).[68]

Modern readers are more often struck by the scope and vigour of the sweeping reform of music and poetry undertaken in Books 2 and 3 than by the Athenian affiliations of Socrates' conception of education. There is certainly something Spartan about the reform programme. For example, Socrates' excision of large tracts of Homeric and Hesiodic verse on moral grounds, and his reduction of musical modes to just two, selected as expressive of courage and reflective restraint (3.399A–C), represent a conception of education for virtue that has some Spartan resonances. The musical mode associated with courage is the Dorian—Spartans and Cretans were ethnic Dorians; and Megillus in the *Laws* comments that the mode of life described by Homer (he means unexpurgated Homer) is not Spartan but Ionian (*Laws* 3.680C).

Nonetheless, as in Protagoras' account of Athenian practice (*Prot.* 325D–326C), Socrates devotes much more space to music and poetry (376E–403C) than to physical training (403C–410B). Moreover, the main point he makes about physical training is that it is to be undertaken primarily for the benefit of the soul. As Socrates sums the matter up (411E–412A):

If you want my opinion, then, the two elements for which some god has given mankind two arts—one musical and poetic, the other physical exercise—seem to be not the mind and the body (or only incidentally so), but the spirited part of their nature and the philosophical part, so that these can be brought into harmony with one another through the appropriate tension and relaxation.

There seems nothing specially proprietary to a military class in this description of the virtue of a harmonious soul. Indeed, when Socrates comes to offer his general account of justice as psychic harmony at the end of Book 4 he recalls this passage when he explains the proper relationship between the rational and spirited elements in the soul (4.441E–442A). As the argument of the central Books 5 to 7 develops, it will transpire that a proper education for 'the philosophical part' will require a demanding course of study in the mathematical sciences, culminating in an understanding of their mutual relationships. That in turn will constitute the right preparation for the attempt to master dialectic, conceived as the philosophical method that will yield a grasp of eternal reality at once analytical and synoptic. Its inspiration is Pythagorean and Socratic—and owes nothing any longer either to Athenian or to Spartan models.

In the *Laws* a critical view of Crete and Sparta is made quite explicit, and in fact the Athenian Visitor launches the entire work with an argument that relates directly to it. He begins by asking for a rationale of the requirement for common messes, gymnasia and the possession of military equipment demanded by Cretan law. Cleinias responds with the claim that their lawgiver designed all their institutions with a view to victory in war, since 'peace' is no more than a name—it is simply in the nature of things that every city is always involved in undeclared war with every other. Megillus the Spartan agrees that Spartan society is organized on the same basis. Then scrutiny of Spartan and Cretan militarism begins. The Athenian Visitor elicits from Cleinias the belief that warfare—the struggle for mastery—permeates society through and through, right down to its smallest units, and indeed is echoed in the conflict internal to the psyche of the individual. He begins to dislodge Cleinias from his position by getting agreement that within a *family* a legal judgment designed to secure reconciliation and friendship would be a more desirable outcome to a dispute than a ruling that the bad elements are to be destroyed or ruled over by the good. This leads to the key move: wouldn't it be more important to organize *society at large* so as to protect it from *internal* warfare (*stasis*), by promoting friendship and peace, than with an eye to warfare against external enemies? Once Cleinias agrees to that, the way is open for argument that courage (the virtue sung by the Spartan poet Tyrtaeus) is only a small part of virtue. Even for civil strife *reliability* is more important.[69] And the union of justice, restraint, wisdom and courage would be best. That is what the lawgiver needs to consider. He will then be in a position to regulate the whole range of activities that make up the life of the society in the light of it, and so promote its well-being (*Laws* 1.625C–632D).

Accordingly, as Diskin Clay has written, 'the greatest part of the *Laws* is devoted to acculturation rather than to legislation'. He goes on to elaborate the point: 'Training, acculturation, education, persuasion, and even enchantment are Plato's means to create the model for a single city of free citizens dedicated to freedom and human excellence out of the 5,040 households of colonists that constitute the city of Magnesia.'[70] For example, most of the rest of Book 1 and of the following Book 2 are devoted to education and training in virtue, while the work will end in Book 12 with discussion of the advanced studies in theology and other subjects enabling a synoptic understanding of things that members of the Nocturnal Council—the standing body charged with review of the city's legal provisions—will have needed to pursue. The dialogue gives great attention to poetry and music. Whereas many readers remember the *Republic* for its critique of Homer and Hesiod and its expulsion of the poets, the *Laws* is more striking for the loving detail it lavishes on the forms of *mousikê* in which citizens will be expected to become experienced: 'In Magnesia there will be state choruses of Dionysos, musical competitions in the continuous calendar of festivals to honor the twelve gods, theaters, and even comic poets.'[71] This is how G. R. Morrow, most magisterial of modern commentators on the *Laws*, sums up the way Plato goes about improving upon the Spartan and Cretan approach to an education designed to promote virtue:[72]

There must be a return to the vigor and simplicity of the Dorian way if any lasting improvement is to be made in the life of the Greek city—that Plato certainly believes. But some of this simplicity is already apparent in the institutions of early Athens, and in any case the Dorian ways, if they are to serve the highest purpose, must take on some of the grace and intelligence manifested in the later developments of Ionian life. It is to Athens that Plato apparently looks to provide this necessary supplement.[73]

Is education for Plato an ethical or a political topic? Clearly both, in the *Republic* and the *Laws* alike. To return once again to the *Republic*, the dialogue argues that it is very difficult to develop into a good person, and to live as a human being should, in a corrupt society; and the good society it envisages needs good citizens and above all good rulers. The educational programme it describes is designed to turn those who are shaped by it into people who will play well the role they are allotted in the city; but that education is something that will benefit them as individuals by enabling them to make the most of their lives. As Socrates says of the philosopher: 'In a city which is worthy of him his own growth will be greater, and he will be the salvation of his country as well as of himself' (6.497A). In such a society the right education makes such persons better able than philosophers elsewhere to participate *both* in the philosophical *and* in the political life (7.520B).[74]

Notes

1. Ferrari and Griffith 2000: xi.
2. Laks 2000: 258. Laks's exposition of the *Laws* provides an excellent short introduction to the dialogue's political philosophy. In his essay 'The history of freedom in antiquity', Lord Acton wrote that the books from which he had learned 'the most about the principles of politics' were Plato's *Laws* and Aristotle's *Politics*: see Acton 1956: 74.
3. In fact (as has often been observed: e.g. Strauss 1964: 143), Thucydides actually avoids the word *historia* (enquiry) which Herodotus had used at the beginning of his *Histories* to characterize the subject matter of the work.
4. For a full discussion, see Nightingale 1995: ch. 1.
5. See especially *Symp.* 201D–212A; *Rep.* 5.474B–6.487A.
6. For a sustained development of this point of view, see Waldron 1995: 138–78.

7. Main passages referred to: *Rep.* 5.472A–473B; *Laws* 5.739A–E; *Tim.* 17A–26E; *Ep.* 7.326A–B, 327D–328A.

8. See Aristotle *Pol.* 2.1–6 (main treatment of *Republic* and *Laws*). Also e.g.: *Pol.* 1.1, 3.15, 4.2 (pivotal chapters where Aristotle engages with key ideas from the *Statesman*); 4.4 (discussion of the *Republic*'s account of an 'economic' city (2.369E–371E)); 5.12 (on the treatment of transformations in political systems in the *Republic*); 8.7 (criticism of the *Republic* on music). Aristotle's conception of an ideal city in Book 7 of the *Politics* has many affinities with Magnesia in the *Laws*.

9. For the evidence, see Schofield 1991: chs 1 and 2.

10. See Hahm 1995.

11. 'Don't hope for Plato's *Republic*', says Marcus Aurelius of its utopian vision two and a half centuries later (*Meditations* 9.29): For discussion of related texts by mostly Roman authors, see Reydams-Schils 2005: 84–9.

12. See Zetzel 1999.

13. Translation adapted from Trapp 2000: 220.

14. Translation adapted from Wilson 1983: 115.

15. See Popper 1961 [1945]; Strauss 1964. These and other nineteenth- and twentieth-century responses to Plato's political philosophy are surveyed in Lane 2002.

16. See, for example, Turner 1981.

17. So Burnyeat 2001: 22. For a narrative based on a full review of the ancient evidence, see, for example, Guthrie 1975: ch. II. The evidence for Plato's date of birth is not very secure: for discussion, see Nails 2002: 243–50, where it is put at 424/3 BC.

18. For orientation on the issues of authenticity, see, for example, Morrow 1962; Gulley 1972; Aalders 1972; Brisson 1987. Stylometric evidence: Brandwood 1969; Deane 1973; Ledger 1989. My own general views on the *Seventh Letter*: Schofield 2000b.

19. For the approach taken in what follows I am much indebted to an unpublished MS of Myles Burnyeat: 'The second prose tragedy: a literary analysis of the pseudo-Platonic *Epistle VII*'.

20. Briefly: (1) 'I was compelled to say' seems to echo Socrates' 'compelled by truth' at *Rep.* 6.499B. In that context use of the word 'compelled' had a clear rationale. Socrates meant: 'Despite general dispiriting experience of what nowadays passes for philosophy or a philosopher, truth compels us to insist that having *genuine* philosophers in power is the solution to our political problems.' Here by contrast 'compelled' looks as though it represents 'Plato's' reaction to something altogether different: the dire condition of contemporary cities—a general thesis very abruptly introduced following the reflections on the recent history of Athens. (2) Nor is there anything in the context to motivate the punch that 'genuine' carries in the *Republic* passages. 'Right' sounds as though it should contrast with something—but what? 'The right philosophy' is not in fact a Platonic locution. For the *Republic* philosophy is invariably an activity. In 'the right philosophy' the word must mean something closer to 'philosophical system'. Authentic Platonic usage may be illustrated from the *Phaedo*, where Socrates talks about 'those who do philosophy in the right way' (*Phd.*

67D–E) or 'those who do get a grip on philosophy in the right way' (64A) or 'those who are philosophers in the right way' (82C). (3) The *Republic* would agree that philosophy gives insight into political and individual justice. But philosophy's importance for politics was represented there as a function of philosophers' understanding of ethical truth in general and of its influence on their moral character. (4) Perhaps most strikingly odd is the curious phrase: 'the classes [*genê*] of mankind'. The author seems to have taken from *Rep.* 5.473D the phrase 'the human race [*genos*]', and from *Rep.* 6.501E 'the class [*genos*] of philosophers'. It is as if he then decided that in order to register recognition that the human *genos* is of a different order from that of either philosophers or rulers, the singular noun *genos* had better be replaced by the plural *genê*.

21. Cooper 1997b: xxiii.
22. On the literary tact of Plato's occasional self-references in the dialogues, see e.g. Most 1993 (on *Phd.* 59B, 116A); Sedley 2004: 35–7 (on *Tht.* 150D).
23. See Sedley 2003: 1–2, which also gives references to further literature. For nuanced statements of the view that Plato characteristically maintains a distance between his own perspective and the position taken by the main speaker in a dialogue, see e.g. M. Frede 1992: 201–19; Cooper 1997b: xviii–xxv; Blondell 2002: ch. 1. The contrary view is put by Kraut 1992a: 25–30.
24. For a classic presentation of this view, which advances the thesis that Book 1 was originally an early dialogue complete in itself and written significantly earlier than the rest of the work, see Vlastos 1991: ch. 2. For a critique: Kahn 1992.
25. See *Rep.* 2.379A–380C, 3.386A–388E. Vlastos himself concedes the point with respect to the first of these passages: Vlastos 1991: 162–3, with n. 27.
26. Evidence: Plato *Meno* 72D–73C; Arist. *Pol.* 1.13, 1260a20–2; Xen. *Symp.* 2.9; D.L. 6.12 [Antisthenes]. The thesis was also held by the Stoics (D.L.7.175 [Cleanthes]), I take it as part of their Socratic inheritance.
27. So e.g. Guthrie 1975: 8.
28. Here there is perhaps a comparison to be made with Thucydides' famous remark that he would make his speakers say what was needed while keeping so far as possible to the general sense of what was actually said (*History* 1.22).
29. For the general view advanced here of Plato's representation of Socrates in dialogues usually considered early, see e.g. Kahn 1996, with the earlier article Kahn 1981; Cooper 1997b: Introduction. The contrasting view that these writings constitute a historically reliable Platonic recreation of the philosophy of Socrates is defended by Vlastos 1991. For discussion of the particular issue of the broad historicity of Plato's account in the *Apology* of Socrates' speeches at his trial before the Athenian jury, see the judicious discussion in Guthrie 1975: 70–80, and the more recent pamphlet Hansen 1995.
30. On Socrates' speeches considered in their rhetorical context as well as in their philosophical import, see Ober 1998: 166–79.
31. For a review of the relevant evidence, see Carter 1986.
32. For the evidence referred to in this paragraph, see e.g Hansen 1995.

33. This is what George Kateb describes as Socrates' 'negative citizenship'—motivated by his refusal to be 'an instrument of wronging others': see Kateb 1998: 85, 82. As Kateb says (1998: 86), it seems to reflect 'hopeless resignation' to wrongdoing on a grand scale, particularly by one city against another: 'The wrongdoing is systemic; it is almost unconscious, so ingrained and inveterate are the cultural causes of it. To be aggressive, predatory; to act to the limit of one's capacity and to attempt to act beyond it; to desire to possess more than one's share, as if true satisfaction exists beyond mere satisfaction; to see in one's power not so much as a stake to defend as a precondition for transgressive adventure; and to thrive on risk, especially to one's continued existence—all this is the product of individual and group masculinity, the project of hubris and pleonexia, of rejecting the very idea of limits. This project is so driven that it cannot be withstood. But there is no excuse for base small-minded horrors; people know better, or ought to; no imagination is required to see the wrong. People should not be carried away and in a real or manufactured passion initiate or sanction an atrocity or profound evil of detail.' Here Kateb portrays a Thucydidean version of the conception of politics ascribed to Thrasymachus by Plato in Book 1 of the *Republic* as the backcloth against which Socrates' stance needs to be understood.

34. For the argument of this paragraph, see Reeve 1989:155–60; cf. also Carter 1986; North 1966: ch. III.

35. Ober 1998: 178.

36. On the *Crito*, see the major study of Kraut 1984; also Weiss 1998, who argues against taking the laws' arguments as representing a Socratic viewpoint (the usual interpretation, espoused by Kraut).

37. A version of this interpretation of Socrates' attachment to Athens can be found, e.g. in Kraut 1984: ch. VII.

38. Kateb (1998: 84–5) suggests that while religion (but not of any conventional sort) may fortify Socrates, he is motivated by something 'purely secular': his 'one, if only one, positivity ... a positive commitment to others' (1998: 108). But the text of the *Apology* makes it hard to doubt that Socrates could only conceive that 'positive commitment to others' in terms of a divine command. Cf. Nehamas 1998: 163–8: reflections on Foucault's treatment of Socratic *parrhêsia* (p. 248 n. 18 incorporates what Nehamas nicely describes as an 'intriguing' passage of Nietzsche on Socrates as 'divine missionary'—where Nietzsche speaks of 'one of the subtlest compromises between piety and freedom of spirit ever devised').

39. Ober (1998: 237) translates the last sentence here: 'For in a suitable one, he himself will expand his capacity in that he will preserve communal as well as private affairs.' He interprets accordingly (ibid.): 'a man who lives only for himself, taking care of his own soul, minding only his own private business, and ignoring the realm of communal interaction, fails to achieve his fullest capacity. His full potential to do good, for himself and for others, can only be achieved through a sort of "political" activism.' But the Greek connects the two clauses of the sentence simply with 'and', not anything corresponding to 'in that'. There is no suggestion that the second explains or supports the second. As Dominic Scott has helped me to appreciate, the

point Socrates makes is this: in the right kind of *politeia* a philosopher will *both* flourish much more as person (because *this* is a city which will provide the educational and cultural environment needed for his proper development as a philosopher) *and* contribute to public affairs (as *this* city will want him to do, having educated him precisely for that purpose). It is recapitulated in different terms at *Rep.* 7.520B–C, when Socrates explains to philosophers imagined as brought up in this way why they owe it to their country to take their turn in government.

40. Ober 1998: 212. My argument in this section is much indebted to the long ch. 4 of Ober's 1998 book, *Political Dissent in Democratic Athens: Intellectual Critics of Popular Rule*. It offers a rich and powerful account of the whole topic of Plato's evolving treatment of the possibilities for accommodating the values of Socratic philosophy within the democratic *polis* from the *Apology* and *Crito* through the *Gorgias* to the *Republic*.

41. For a recent statement of this standpoint see Annas 1999: ch. IV.

42. Modern scholars point out that the very first page of the dialogue—at least as read in retrospect—is heavy with political resonances: Polemarchus, the leading participant in the scene near the Piraeus it depicts, was like his friend Niceratus (also mentioned as present) to be put to death by the thirty at the end of the Peloponnesian War. He had funded the democratic resistance to the junta, which was based in the Piraeus. 'The decisive battle—the conflict in which Critias lost his life—took place by the temple of Bendis, the goddess whose inaugural festival gave Socrates ... a reason to come to the Piraeus in the first place' (Ferrari and Griffith 2000: xii). For a full discussion, see Gifford 2001: 35–106.

43. Ferrari and Griffith 2000: xxiii.

44. See e.g. Annas 1999: 91–2, with nn. 49 and 50.

45. But this preoccupation is not original with Aristotle. See e.g. Xen. *Mem.* 4.6.12. And at various points in the *Laws* (e.g. 5.735A; cf. 4.712B–713A) Plato takes a similar view of *politeia*.

46. The relationship between the ideas about women in Book 5 of the *Republic* and in Aristophanes' *Assemblywomen*, and their conceivable debt to earlier sophistic or satirical writing (but Aristotle said that Plato was the only thinker to propose having women and children in common: *Pol.* 2.7, 1266a34–6), is much controverted. For a sage assessment, see Dawson 1992: 37–40; the presentation and discussion of the evidence, in Adam 1902: I.345–55, remains authoritative.

47. Nonetheless his tripartite division of the citizenry evidently draws some of its inspiration from the Spartan system, with its warrior class of citizen 'peers', non-citizen artisans living outside the main settlement, and the rural serf population engaged in farming. According to Aristotle he wore his hair long, an affectation of Laconizing Athenians—though we do not know how far his association with Athens extended beyond responsibility for laying out the street plan of the Piraeus. (For all this information, see Aristotle, *Politics* 2.8, 1267b22–37, and for a general treatment of Hippodamus, see Shipley 2005.)

48. See Barker 1995: 354.

49. Koyré 1945: 71.

50. But at every stage in the argument of this book it will be apparent that tension between philosophy and politics, if not between ethics and politics, permeates Plato's thought.
51. See the classic study of Skinner 1989; cf. Schofield 1995.
52. Koyré 1945: 72.
53. A notable presentation of an interdependence interpretation is Lear 1992; for a critique, see Ferrari 2003.
54. Burnyeat 1999: 217.
55. Clay 2000: 274–5.
56. At least this is the usual interpretation. J. Wilderbing works out an ingenious case for the thesis that it is politicians, sophists and artists who are the prisoners (Wilderbing 2004: 128). A key consideration he advances is the competition for justice in the courts and political honours in which the prisoners engage (*Rep.* 7.517D–E, 520C–D; cf. 516C–E). But when Socrates tells Glaucon that the prisoners are 'like us' (7.515A), he surely has in mind precisely people like Glaucon, identified by Adeimantus in the next book as a competitive spirit (8.548D).
57. Burnyeat 1999: 240.
58. Burnyeat 1999: 219.
59. This short essay is most conveniently available in the expanded edition of *Xenophon: Scripta Minora* in the Loeb Classical Library (Marchant and Bowersock 1968); see also Osborne 2004 (which includes bibliography). There is much debate about the point of the work and the genre to which it belongs. The best discussion of this question is still Gomme 1962. As Gomme says, the tract is an 'academic' work, using techniques of argument we associate particularly with the Greek sophists to sustain a paradox, 'making the worse case the better'—but without the stylistic polish one might expect of a sophist. To my mind its opening paragraph is designed to make crystal clear that it is a quizzical contribution to the *politeia* literature: quizzical, since it is not Sparta that the author will hold up for admiration, as was usual in the genre, but—with pitch-black humour—Athens.
60. For more on the Laconizing literature, see Ferrari and Griffith 2000: xiv–xvii; Dawson 1992: ch. 1; Schofield 1999b; Menn 2005; Hodkinson 2005. Interesting connections between Critias' ideas and projects and themes in the Old Oligarch are proposed in Canfora 1988.
61. The Spartans were thought to have modelled their *politeia* on the Cretan system: e.g. Herodotus 1.65.4–5; Aristotle *Pol.* 2.10, 1271b20–32.
62. Named after the grandfather of the leader of the thirty tyrants, who is the dialogue's principal speaker. Or so I think. Christopher Gill—see below, n.64—takes a different view. For more on this contested issue, see Ch. 5, p. 243 n. 47.
63. At any rate on the assumption that admiration for Sparta had a long history in Plato's family: see n. 62 above.
64. Gill 1977: 295.
65. There is no mention of any Athenian interest in the sea or in naval warfare (in this version of 'prehistory', that is associated with the rival power of Atlantis). Critias implies that Athens relied on traditional hoplite infantry.

66. Isocrates in his *Panathenaicus* of 342–39 still waxes sarcastic about Lac-
onists (*Panath.* 41). And a generation or two later the early Stoics were
championing Laconism *against* Plato: see Schofield 1999b. For speculation
on the Athenian dissident 'critical community', see Ober 1998: 43–51; and
for a fuller discussion of Spartan parallels with the institutions and ideology
of the *Laws*, with speculations on the dialogue's message for a Spartan or
Laconophile readership, see Powell 1994.

67. The word I render 'guards' (*phulakes*) is more usually translated 'guardians'.
Probably the principal associations of 'guards' are nowadays, on both sides
of the Atlantic, those conveyed (for example) by 'security guards' (who
protect a company's property and employees from external dangers). This
function parallels pretty exactly the prime function of Plato's *phulakes*, at
least as originally articulated in his comparison with guard dogs (see e.g.
2.375A–D), although 'prison guard' is the association that may be conjured
up by Socrates' remark that locating the guards in their own garrison will
best enable them to 'control [lit. 'hold down'] those within, if any of them
refuse to obey the laws' (3.415D–E).

68. In the *Laws* Plato incorporates a reference to the *krupteia*, that element in
the *agôgê* which required adolescents to go into the mountains for a full year,
and making themselves invisible (*kruptoi*, 'hidden') live by theft and worse.
This is apparently to be prescribed for new recruits to the magistracy known
as *agronomoi*, 'country-wardens' (*Laws* 6.760A–763C): for discussion, see
Brisson 2005: 113–14. But it is given no prominence nor indeed place in the
dialogue's general educational prospectus.

69. Reliability (being *pistos*) is later given (5.730C) as a main reason why truth-
telling is first of all the excellences of character that citizens should develop
and respect (you can trust people who are committed to telling the truth).

70. Clay 2000 : 275–6.

71. Clay 2000: 276. For comedy, see *Laws* 7.816D: 'It is impossible to know
serious things without becoming acquainted with the ridiculous, or to know
any one of two contraries without knowing the other.' But performances
will be by slaves or foreigners.

72. Morrow 1960: 92. Chapter VII of his book—running to one hundred pages—
is devoted to the dialogue's treatment of education.

73. In his old age Plato has not lost a capacity to surprise and disconcert. The
first ingredient in citizen training to be recommended is encouragement of
drunkenness at parties—properly regulated parties, of course. Discussion
of the virtue of courage that his Spartan and Cretan interlocutors so prize
has led to the question: is it to be conceived as involving a battle just
against fears and pains, or against desires and pleasures too? In which case
shouldn't we be trained to resist pleasure and desire, in the same sort of
way as the Spartan and Cretan lawgivers have provided in the *agôgê* a
training to cope with pain and fear? In other words, shouldn't the virtue
of restraint be developed, as well as the virtue of courage more narrowly
defined? As it is, the Spartans simply prohibit occasions when people
might be tempted to excessive pleasures, particularly in drink—as Megillus

reports with approval, and as Critias celebrates in verses contrasting Spartan moderation with Athenian abandon. Plato therefore devotes the rest of Book I to defence by the Athenian Visitor of the educational value of a properly conducted symposium—a thoroughly Athenian practice—as a method of training people to deal with exposure to extremes of pleasure and desire, and so enabling acquisition of the virtue of restraint. Morrow's 'grace and intelligence' will presumably be more evident in the outcome than in the process of reaching it (*Laws* 1.633C–650B).

74. See also p. 46, n. 39 above.

2

Athens, Democracy and Freedom

1. Democratic Entanglements

1.1 Plato's contexts

In Karl Popper's famous book *The Open Society and its Enemies*, Plato figures not as the earliest architect of an anti-democratic ideology (that accolade went to Heraclitus), but as the most influential of all anti-democratic thinkers in the Western tradition. Hence the title of Popper's first volume: *The Spell of Plato*. His interpretation of the *Republic* was highly controversial, and in some respects demonstrably mistaken. But although there are lines of thought worked out in the *Republic* that need not in themselves be regarded as incompatible with democracy, few readers would deny that its main political argument is profoundly undemocratic in basic direction. The contemporary political theorist John Dunn puts the point nicely:[1]

The *Republic* is a book with many morals. It is also a deliberately teasing book, and open to an endless range of interpretations. But no serious reader could fail to recognize that it comes down firmly against democracy.

There is a curious paradox here. The invention of the idea and practice of democracy[2] is perhaps the greatest legacy of ancient Greece to modern political thought and practice. Yet most of the theoretical and argumentative reflection on their politics and political systems in surviving writings of the ancient Greeks themselves is developed from perspectives that are either acutely critical of democracy, or compare its strengths and weaknesses with those of other forms of constitution with more or less cool detachment.[3]

It is not that the intensely argumentative Athenians of the fifth and fourth centuries BC had nothing to say in recommendation of democracy and its values. Especially in the speeches for the assembly and the popular courts that are preserved in the corpus of the Athenian orators,[4] quite complex arguments about citizenship, freedom and the public good were often developed. No surprise, however, that the main object was to persuade an audience how they should vote on a specific practical proposition. Democracy constituted the *context* in which the public activities of litigation and politics were conducted. So appeals by speakers to its values, as common ground confidently shared by all right-thinking people, were unsurprisingly much more in evidence than attempts to give them a fully articulated expression or defence. The sophisticated analysis of Athenian political values worked out in the funeral oration Thucydides represents Pericles as delivering in honour of the Athenian war dead is exceptional. At the same time, there is a case for suggesting that democracy was also the matrix of theoretical debate—often hostile to democracy—about different political systems.[5]

The major surviving fifth- and fourth-century contributors to that debate were all Athenian writers: as well as Plato himself, Thucydides, Isocrates and—by virtue of his long-term residence in the city—Aristotle. The *politieia* tradition with its focus on Sparta as model of an alternative form of society, developed (as we saw in the last chapter) by two more Athenian authors, Critias and Xenophon, seems to get its point from an implicit negation of Athenian democracy. One might in fact describe the literary activity of all these thinkers, transacted in a range of different genres (history, deliberative oratory, *politeia* pamphleteering, philosophical dialogue, philosophical treatise), as an exercise in the imagination of alternatives—alternatives to the Athenian democratic way of doing things. The Greeks had long been intensely self-conscious about the difference between their own way of life, in the self-governing *polis*, and the absolute monarchy of the Great King of Persia, as is especially clear from Herodotus' narrative in the *Histories*. For disaffected Athenian writers working out their ideas during or under the baleful tutelage of the Peloponnesian War, it seems likely enough that it was the events of those years—the horrors and privations of war itself, conflict with an adversary whose political arrangements were quite different from their own, and the sequence of internal revolutions and counter-revolutions Athens experienced in its later phases—which constituted circumstances prompting a more intense and general preoccupation with alternative *politeiai*.

All the same, it is also hard to think that such a preoccupation would have so engrossed so many major thinkers if the democratic society which fostered them had not encouraged open debate on themes like these. In fact we can infer from surviving examples of yet two more genres, Euripidean tragedy and Aristophanic comedy—composed as they were for the civic institutions of public festivals—that the Athenians relished it. Among the many debates on fundamental moral and social themes staged by Euripides in his wartime plays are two set-pieces, admittedly of no great profundity, in which the merits and demerits of democracy are argued out by protagonists of democracy and absolute monarchy (*Phoenician Women*, lines 503–85; *Suppliants*, lines 301–19, 399–466). Aristophanes' *Birds* (415 BC) is wholly devoted to construction of a fantastic alternative to Athens, in fact the original Cloudcuckooland. The critique of democracy conveyed by the *Republic*'s ship of state analogy has affinities with the satire on Athenian public decision-making presented on the comic stage in Aristophanes' *Knights* (424 BC). In particular, the Platonic Socrates' deaf, short-sighted, ignorant ship-owner echoes Aristophanes' portrayal of the sovereign Athenian *demos* as a 'stupid, gullible, overindulgent old man'.[6] 'Demos', the chorus of knights observes at one point (in a passage that might have been taken from Plato's *Gorgias*), 'your rule is glorious indeed, seeing that all men fear you like a tyrant. But you are easily led astray, you enjoy being flattered and deceived, and you gape open-mouthed at whoever happens to be speaking—and your mind, though present, is absent.'[7] More generally, there is a broad persuasiveness in Sara Monoson's argument that among the historical circumstances favouring the very existence of the

Platonic dialogue as a vehicle for criticism is the democracy's attachment to *parrhêsia*, frank speaking, in the theatre, in the assembly, in the courts.[8]

Given this background, it is hardly surprising if Plato's intellectual negotiations with democracy turn out on further inspection to be various and quite complicated. Chapter 1 already drew attention to the range of different registers in which the Platonic dialogue itself is composed. Where Plato's attitude to democracy is concerned, the very different philosophical projects undertaken in the *Republic* and the *Laws* (to take the examples which will most preoccupy us) make comparison and evaluation of what they say on the topic particularly tricky. And from our review of other Athenian writing critical of democracy, it looks as though another consideration that may be useful to bear in mind is a distinction (particularly associated with the political philosopher Michael Walzer) between *immanent* or *connected* and *rejectionist* or *disconnected* critique: criticism working from a position within or detached from a society, and with or against the system it questions.[9] Thus Critias and Xenophon can usefully be seen as writing in rejectionist mode, and Aristophanes in the immanent. I will be suggesting that some of Plato's complexity comes from his writing now in one mode, now in the other, and sometimes in a style which simultaneously reflects *both* perspectives.[10]

Christopher Rowe says of the Socrates of the *Apology*, *Crito* and other early dialogues:[11]

To ask whether Plato's Socrates is a democrat or an antidemocrat is perhaps not a useful question. He is an otherwise loyal member of the citizen community who nevertheless has some fundamental criticisms to make of the system under which he lives—and the system is such as to permit him to do that.

As Rowe points out, Richard Kraut's book *Socrates and the State* makes much of the preference for Athens over all other cities that the *Crito* attributes to Socrates (*Crito* 51C–53A). Kraut takes that preference to be not just a matter of his loyalty in practice, but principled recognition on his part of the freedom of enquiry he and all other citizens enjoyed under democracy. On his reconstruction, Socrates appreciates 'the system' precisely because it promotes the freedom it claims to promote.[12] However that may be, Socrates is certainly a thoroughly embedded critic of democracy, as Chapter 1 has argued. His fundamental idea that in every field we should look to the wisdom of the one, not the opinion of the many, cohabits uneasily with democracy's commitment to rule by the people gathered in the assembly or as judges in a court. Yet he articulates it as something applicable here and now, not as a utopian project.

How different from this was Plato's stance? How far did Plato's unembedded utopianism and his anti-democratic satire coexist with commitments that are best understood as democratic? Christopher Rowe follows his remarks about Socrates with the observation that we know very little about Plato as citizen, especially by comparison with Socrates, although we have no reason to think he was not a loyal Athenian. Profitable debate about a democratic Plato—or about signs of inclination to democratic values in Plato—has therefore consisted in argument over what can or cannot be inferred from the dialogues themselves. In recent years this has been pursued in a variety of ways. I begin by examination of these by considering two very different areas of controversy. One concerns the actual form and texture of the Socratic dialogue. The second relates to the evaluation of the treatment of democracy offered in two late writings—*Statesman* and *Laws*. A third—what we may or may not infer from the satire on the democratic city in Book 8 of the *Republic*—I shall defer for briefer discussion in Chapter 3.

1.2 Platonic dialogue and democratic discourse

One school of thought on the first of these two issues claims that the very form of the Socratic dialogue reveals it to be a democratic, anti-authoritarian mode of discourse.[13] There are different ways of articulating this approach to the dialogues, but two ingredients emerge as particularly salient in some of the contributions to the topic made by Peter Euben, one of its most eloquent representatives. The first reflects rising interest in the notion of *deliberative democracy*. This is the idea that what legitimates democratic decision-making is not (as in liberal theories of the state) the way the rights of citizens are protected and their interests negotiated. Nor (as in republican theories) is it the way decisions express the participation of free and equal citizens in the process, as part of something that matters more: the shared form of life that constitutes society. Instead, democratic legitimation turns on the extent to which decisions are the transparent results of fair and reasoned deliberation, conducted within a whole network of processes—both institutional and informal—of different kinds. On this view, what counts is the quality of the deliberative procedure.[14] (Not everyone agrees. For some a focus on deliberation simply fails to capture too much that is intrinsic to the actualities of politics and democratic process.[15])

It has been claimed that both the idea and the practice of deliberative democracy 'are as old as democracy itself'. Jon Elster quotes Pericles in the funeral speech saying of the Athenians that 'instead of looking on discussion as a stumbling-block in the way of action, we think it an indispensable preliminary to any wise action at all' (Thucydides, *History of the Peloponnesian War* 2.40).[16] Theorists of deliberative democracy have drawn particular inspiration from the work of Jürgen Habermas on critical rationality, especially from the 1960s and 1970s. In writings of this period Habermas worked out an ideal model of what unconstrained dialogue or 'communicative reason' would be like. This (rather than later and less idealized treatments of communication he has proposed) is what Euben has in mind when he speaks of the 'Habermasian dimension' in Socratic dialogues.[17] He suggests that a Platonic text such as the *Gorgias* reflects 'a Habermasian ideal of a communicative reason in which dialogue and deliberation are governed by ideas of frankness, mutuality, consensus and rational argument derived from the formal structure of communication itself'.[18]

Supposing we ask what is there that is specifically democratic about that very general conception of critical rationality. Would it be sufficient to reiterate the attractive proposal that among the historical circumstances favouring its embodiment in the Socratic dialogue, high importance must be accorded to the Athenian democracy's attachment to *parrhêsia*, frank speaking? I think not. We might agree that the very existence of Plato's oeuvre should be seen as something *made possible* by the Athenians' practice and conception of *parrhêsia* as the *sine qua non* of democratic social and political culture.[19] But that would not show that Habermasian dialogue itself has any democratic potential. In explaining how it might have, Euben proposes that philosophical dialogue contains the possibility of functioning 'as an idealized analogue for democratic deliberation'.[20]

The point of the Habermasian ideal of dialogue is precisely to articulate what political deliberation *needs* to be like if it is to be properly political. It has to be capable of transforming participants' existing preferences and beliefs through public and rational discussion so that they converge on a shared conception of the common interest.[21] Habermas's ideal offers a way of giving substance to a conception of the 'political' that is sharply and properly distinguished from 'politics', interpreted as the arena in which politicians compete for power and the control over management of public resources that it brings.[22] On that assumption, the reasoned cooperative search for truth that the Platonic Socrates often professes he is engaged in with his discussants does indeed look more like a paradigm for political discourse as Pericles characterizes it in the funeral speech.[23] In one dialogue at least, moreover, Socrates actually uses the political vocabulary of 'decision' and 'common deliberation' to explain to his interlocutor—his old friend Crito—the sort of argumentative enterprise the two of them are engaged in (see *Crito* 49C–E). Here, as Socratic conversation itself turns deliberative, Plato chooses to describe it in terms which serve to emphasize its similarities with its political analogue. To do that, however, he has to downplay its characteristic procedure of question and answer (which is *not* readily usable as a paradigm for political discourse, even if witnesses in the courts were subjected to it).[24]

At the other end of his life as a writer, we find Plato developing a piece of actual theorizing about the foundations of a good society which incorporates something rather like the Habermasian ideal. In a key passage of the *Laws*, the leader of the conversation—an 'Athenian Visitor' (to Crete)—suggests that its citizens would be entitled to something more than peremptory imposition of a legal system to shape their communal life. Legislation should involve a form of persuasion that is compared to philosophical discussion. This is because citizens are free persons, not slaves (*Laws* 4.719E–723D, 9.857B–E). But the need to enshrine respect for freedom in the society's social and political system is something the Visitor associates with the notion of democracy (3.693D–E). Here are just the materials—philosophical dialogue conducted by free persons as an analogue for democracy—that Euben built into his Habermasian story. Of course, all the elements in the text of the *Laws* I have mentioned in such quick succession—philosophy, dialogue, freedom, democracy—will need a good deal of unpacking before we are in a position to understand quite what Plato is proposing. We shall undertake that in the third section of this chapter.

The *deliberative democracy* approach to the conversation of a Platonic dialogue runs the danger of depoliticizing politics in assimilating it to the frankness and mutuality of genuinely critical philosophical conversation. The other approach Euben advocates is in extreme tension with the appeal to a Habermasian ideal. It runs the opposite risk: of politicizing philosophy. It is governed by the idea that Plato's dialogues are *polyphonic*, dialogical. That is to say, in the conversations they represent, many voices expressing different and sometimes irreconcilable and even incommensurable points of view are heard, but no one voice among them—not even Socrates'—carries any ultimate authority.[25] This view of dialogue often draws inspiration from the work of Mikhail Bakhtin, and indeed Euben quotes him on the difficulty polyphony creates for the very communication of meaning by one speaker to another:[26]

The word, directed towards its object, enters a dialogically agitated and tension-filled environment of alien words, value judgments and accents, weaves in and out of complex interrelationships, merges with some, recoils from others, intersects with yet a third group: and all this may crucially shape discourse, may leave a trace in all its semantic layers.

On this interpretation, engagement in dialogue involves not just contested negotiations of belief, but something agonistic: manipulations of power exercised through the language and the rhetorical techniques employed by the different parties to the discussion—and also resistance to manipulation. This is philosophy politicized. Even if what Socrates may be questioning—as in *Gorgias* or *Republic*—is democracy, the dialogical mode and context of his questioning are themselves, Euben argues, 'democratic'.[27]

'Democratic' is how Euben himself puts the point. The warning quotation marks alert us to the metaphorical status of the notion as deployed in the *polyphony* approach. Josiah Ober comments drily that Euben seems to be operating with 'a modern (or postmodern) vision of democratic discourse (a conversational willingness to contest meanings)'—something very different from the democracy of fourth-century Athens.[28] Plato's own distinction between philosophy and rhetoric (examined in Section 2 of this chapter) warns us against collapsing the difference. His Socrates is at pains to insist on the huge *difference* between the private conversation of philosophy and the forms of public speech that went with the rule of the *dêmos*, which he sees as vehicles of competition for power before mass gatherings indulging themselves as collectivities. The conversation with Polus in the *Gorgias* contains a particularly memorable articulation of this theme (474A–B):

So please don't tell me to call for a vote from the people present here. If you have no better 'refutations' than these to offer, do as I suggested just now: let me have my turn, and you try the kind of refutation I think is called for. For I do know how to produce one witness to whatever I'm saying, and that's the person I'm having the discussion with. The many I disregard. And I do know how to call for a vote from one person, but I don't even discuss things with the many.[29]

It is not in any case clear why philosophical dialogue itself should be described as even metaphorically 'democratic', even assuming—something many readers would contest—the politicized polyphony of the dialogue form as interpreted on Bakhtinian lines. Dialogues such as the *Protagoras* and the *Gorgias* are perhaps the most promising specimens Euben could (and in the case of *Gorgias* does at length) select. For example, we might want to say that Socrates and Protagoras,[30] or again Socrates and Callicles, try to outmanoeuvre each other into speaking each other's languages and so into each other's valuations of things and claims to authority: 'the will to power', not disinterested immersion in truthful conversation, is what gives their argumentation much of its impetus. That phenomenon might indeed be conceived as a form of politicization of discourse—but hardly of its 'democratization' (contestation of other points of view is not something that only democracy can accommodate).[31] Euben argues that some of the substantive criticisms which Socrates levels against the claims the other speakers in the *Gorgias* make for rhetoric expose their *anti*democratic potential. And he suggests that Socrates is represented as sympathetic to a democratic culture in which citizens take responsibility for themselves and their own political thinking. The next section of this chapter will support Euben on these points. But they are not points that emerge just from the *form* of the dialogue.

1.3 Deathbed conversion to democracy?

With mention of the *Laws* in the previous section, we have already put one foot into the second area of controversy over Plato's attitude to democracy. The late dialogues *Statesman* and *Laws* certainly say some things about it that are very different from the damning treatment it gets in *Gorgias* and *Republic*. Did Plato's outlook change? Or is it rather—as I shall be arguing—that the projects he engages on in the later works are new projects necessitating other emphases, not incompatible evaluations? These are topics I shall be pursuing from different viewpoints in the next two chapters, as well as in Section 3 below. For the moment, a few quotations from recent writing on the subject will give a flavour of some of the things at stake. First, taking an unashamedly developmentalist perspective, is Julia Annas, discussing the treatment of democracy in the *Statesman*.[32] She says: 'In the *Statesman* we see him [i.e. Plato] for the first time realizing the advantages of democracy from the viewpoint of a realistic assessment of how political institutions actually function.' What she has principally in mind is 'his newly sensible evaluation of democracy' as a system which 'makes it difficult'—because it parcels out authority more widely than other forms of government—'for the vicious and selfish to take control and impose their own views and interests' (as well as for the virtuous to take control and impose their expertise).[33] Above all, she sees a new respect on Plato's part for established law as the repository of collective wisdom. I shall be rejecting every one of these claims.

For the *Laws*, I quote from Thanassis Samaras' book *Plato on Democracy*. He sums up a long discussion of the dialogue as follows:[34]

In the *Republic*, democracy is a politically inefficient and morally destructive form of government, straightforwardly and unreservedly rejected. In the *Laws*, this changes. Democracy is now elevated to a position where it can contribute, at least to some degree, towards the best humanly achievable Greek city, the city that Magnesia [i.e. the settlement imagined as being founded on Platonic principles] purports to be.

But is the meaning or reference of 'democracy' still the same? If it is not, the kind of change at stake becomes debatable.

On the other side are scholars who find an essential unity to the thinking about democracy in all Plato's writing on the subject. For example, in a number of publications over the last decade Christopher Rowe has strongly contested the supposed evidence for a change of outlook in the later works. In later dialogues the Athenian form of democracy 'remains firmly out in the cold'.[35] On the other hand:[36]

Underlying both the *Republic* and the *Laws*—and also the *Politicus* [i.e. *Statesman*] there is a single preferred model for constitutions, with the essential features (1) that its laws and institutions are rationally based (and that there is a part of the population, however small, that can understand the reasonings of the original lawgivers); (2) that it promotes the common good of all the citizens, which consists of a life informed by virtue, if not necessarily by knowledge; (3) that such a life, for all the citizens, includes ruling as well as being ruled; and (4) that anyone prevented from living such a life, by their occupation and/or their character and temperament, is excluded from full membership of that community. It seems clear to me that this model, when all four features are taken in combination, has considerably more in common with the democratic idea than it has with oligarchy, or with the usual varieties of autocracy (though it has certain features that we, and Plato, might want to treat as 'autocratic'), and certainly more than it has with the sort of autocracy—of the intellect—with which Plato is usually associated.... Plato's 'best constitution', in fact, bids fair to be a paradigm of what democracy should have been but in his view was not: in the words of Socrates in the *Menexenus*, 'an aristocracy ... which has the approval of the many'.

I think this is much closer to the truth.[37] But it is not quite how I would have put it—for a reason I now discuss.

Rowe and the developmentalists share a premise that I questioned in Chapter 1. Both assume that reflection on democracy as a *constitution* was or eventually became an important preoccupation of Plato's philosophizing about politics. I beg to differ. As I read the dialogues, he shows comparatively little interest in constitutional theory or practice at any stage in his life. Even in the *Laws* detailed constitutional arrangements are not accorded much space, as Aristotle observed in the *Politics* (*Pol.* 2.6, 1265a1–2).[38] Plato is not on that account a lesser political theorist. Tocqueville's *Democracy in America* is valued at least as much for the penetration of his account of American society and the American way of life as for his analysis of the Constitution.

The argument of John Dunn's *Setting the People Free* turns on the observation that for us democracy 'has come to name not merely a form of government, but also, and every bit as much, a political value'.[39] Democratization means not just the ability of an equal electorate to vote a government in or out, but the impact of that on social, cultural and economic life—and the recasting of the terms on which political authority is recognized and exercised, creating 'a world from which faith, deference and even loyalty have largely passed away' despite the great inequalities of power and resources produced by capitalism, or what Dunn calls the order of egoism.[40]

On the interpretation offered in this book, what above all permeates Plato's political philosophy is not any interest in constitutions as such, but a constant preoccupation with the need for wisdom or expertise in government, a vision of what constitutes a true community, and ongoing engagement with the challenge of developing an ideology which will secure the commitment of citizens to a social and political order which will embody reason and genuine community. These will accordingly be the main themes taken up in Chapters 4 to 7. As for his intense engagement with democracy, Plato's *writing* about it undoubtedly conveys a much more varied and indeed opportunistic impression than Rowe's suggestion of an underlying model might have led one to expect. For better or worse, nowhere in the dialogues is there a magisterial final statement. Brilliant forays into the territory—mostly critical rather than constructive—are more the order of the day.

1.4 Prospect

Our analysis of Plato's thinking about Athens and democracy will begin with a closer look at the relevant dimensions of the two dialogues—written decades apart—that have figured most prominently in this and the previous section: the *Gorgias* (together with the *Menexenus*) and the *Laws*. Section 2 will examine his own exploration, principally in 'Plato's manifesto for philosophy',[41] the *Gorgias*, of something which also fascinated Aristophanes and Thucydides, democracy's love affair with political rhetoric, after introducing the Beast: the most memorable of all his images of the *dêmos*. Section 3 will turn to consider the very different perspective and associated tone of voice he adopts in talking about democracy in the *Laws*, and the no less different political climate in which the dialogue was composed. It will pay particular attention to his decision to recognize the importance of freedom as a basic ingredient needed in any good political and social system. A brief conclusion is added as Section 4.

One thing that will be emerging is the essentially fluid and contested character of the concept of democracy in fourth-century Athens, as well as Plato's own adaptability in exploiting that fluidity. This finding will put us in a position to explore (in Chapter 3) Plato's only sustained explicit treatment of democracy, in Book 8 of the *Republic*: which is sometimes written off as a caricature that bears too little relation to the realities of the Athenian or indeed any conceivable system of government. I shall argue it to be a brilliant piece of theory—focused on democracy as an ideal, but cast in the form of satire. Four main features will emerge: egalitarianism, freedom, pluralism, anarchy. Finally, I shall turn to Plato's fundamental charge against democracy: its failure, as (following Socrates) he saw it, to provide a role for knowledge or expertise in government. In arguing this case (principally in the early dialogue *Protagoras* and the late dialogue *Statesman*), Plato nonetheless worked at constructing for critical purposes an alternative conception of 'democratic knowledge'—whose inadequacies it is left mostly for the reader to infer.

2. Democracy and Rhetoric

2.1 The power of the people

When in the *Meno* Socrates puts it to Anytus that there are people who advertise themselves as teachers of virtue, the so-called sophists,[42] he elicits a vigorous reaction from his future prosecutor (*Men.* 91C):

Heracles, watch your tongue, Socrates! I hope no relative or friend of mine, whether Athenian or from elsewhere, would be so mad as to go to those people and end up ruined by them. Those people are the manifest ruin and corruption of all who associate with them.

Plato has Socrates question this claim. He represents Anytus as having to concede that it is based on no experiential evidence whatever. In the *Republic*, too, Plato makes Socrates dismissive of the idea that the prime responsibility for the corruption of the young rests with the sophists. That must be laid at the door of those who complain about sophists: the people as a whole—particularly 'when they're all sitting together in large numbers, in the assembly, or in the lawcourts, the theatre, or on active service, or any other general gathering of a large number of people' (6.492B). Socrates goes on to explain what he takes to be the actual role of sophists a page or so later, in the second of what we might call his analogies of democracy. As the Ship analogy addresses the issue of the apparent uselessness of true philosophers in politics, so the Beast analogy explains the real relationship between sophists and the society in which they operate (6.493A–C):

All the mercenary individuals the public call sophists, and think of as competitors, are teaching exactly the same convictions as those expressed by the general public in its gatherings. Those are what they call wisdom. It's rather like someone keeping a large, powerful animal, getting to know its passions and appetites, how to approach it, how to handle it, when and why it is most awkward and most amenable, and what makes it so; and what is more, the various sounds it is in the habit of making in different situations, and the sounds which soothe it or infuriate it when someone else makes them. Imagine he'd learnt all this as a result of being with the animal over a long period of time. He might then call what he had learnt wisdom, might organize his findings into an art or science, and take up teaching, though in truth he would have no knowledge whatsoever of which of these convictions and desires was fine or ugly, good or bad, just or unjust, and would assign all these names in accordance with the opinions of the huge animal. Things which gave the animal pleasure he would call good. Things which annoyed it he would call bad. He would have no other account of them available, and so he would call things just and fine when they were merely necessary. He would never have seen, nor would he be capable of explaining to anyone else, the vast difference which in fact exists between the nature of what is necessary and the nature of what is good. If that were how he behaved, don't you think he would be a pretty odd teacher?

The image of the Beast conveys a great deal of what Plato wanted to say about democracy. Fundamental is the thought that in a political system of direct popular rule, where key decisions are taken not by an individual or a body with restricted membership, but by the assembled populace itself, the people become the source of all values in the society. As we might put it, democracy is in this regard a totalitarian system. More specifically, the power of public opinion generates a radically corrupt system of values. This is because it is the passions and appetites of the populace which in the end dictate the content of what passes for wisdom. If they like something, that counts as good (i.e. as what we should truly want), in the teaching of the sophists as for everyone else; if they dislike it, the opposite. Necessity—that is (presumably), political expediency—is what gets dignified by the language of moral approbation: 'just', 'fine'. What has happened to reason as the basis on which judgements are made? An animal has no reason, but simply passions and appetites. You might think that the sophist—a practitioner of wisdom, someone dedicated to education—would as animal-keeper bring independent reason to bear on the business of ethics. But not so. The message is that the Beast controls him, not the other way around.[43]

So much for sophists—for those who, like Protagoras, under-took to produce 'good citizens' by their teaching. Might things be different for a teacher of rhetoric like Gorgias?[44] Plato ascribes to him the claim that rhetoric bestows on its practitioners the ability to persuade large gatherings like those Socrates lists in the first of the two *Republic* passages just quoted, and thereby enables them to exercise rule over other citizens and to achieve freedom for themselves.[45] Followers of Gorgias like Meno and Polus are represented by Plato as admiring him (and despising sophists), precisely because his conception of rhetoric was, as they interpreted it, intrinsically amoral: he made no promises about teaching virtue, only about equipping people to speak.[46] Whether or not they would have agreed with Socrates' account in the *Republic* of the subservience of sophists to the populace, they would insist that politicians who command the skills of rhetoric stand in a quite different relationship with their audi-ences from the one predicated of sophists in the Beast analogy. The contention they advance is that rhetoric puts the politician in the driving seat.

Plato subjects this thesis to a sustained and complex examina-tion in the *Gorgias*. The dialogue falls into two unequal parts.[47] In the first, Socrates teases out of Gorgias the key features of his idea of rhetoric (447–461). He develops a critique—fundamental to the philosophical position he advocates in the dialogue—of the conception of power inherent in that idea, principally in conversation with Gorgias' acolyte, Polus (461–481).[48] And he pulls apart the terms in which the aspiring Athenian politician

Callicles then presents a rhetorical restatement of the same notion of power (481–500). The second part of the dialogue (from 500 on) proceeds on the assumption that a new definition and evaluation of rhetoric is needed. It sets that issue in the context of a decision between the political life (as currently conceived) and the life of philosophy (which contains within itself the possibility of a radical transformation of politics—politics as it might be). Rhetoric—Socrates now proposes (502D–503B)—might be either a manipulative technique designed to achieve the gratification of an audience (on the first option), or a mode of discourse employed to promote their well-being (on the second).[49] He endeavours to make it clear that the choice between these turns in the end on a more fundamental ethical question (507C–509C). Is the worst thing that can happen to a person being on the receiving end of wrongdoing without redress against it (as Callicles holds)? Or is it committing injustice and not being punished for it (Socrates' view)?

Much of what Socrates says in this second part of the dialogue consists in argument against the option of manipulative rhetoric for which Callicles now elects. That option is attractive above all because it might seem to constitute the only reliable way of securing power, and with it the ability to avoid becoming the victim of others' wrongdoing. Socrates rejects it, first because it offers no protection against what *he* sees as the worst possible moral scenario—committing injustice with impunity (510E–512B); but second, and more soberingly for Callicles, because it *actually* involves subservience to the populace, not power over them (512D–513C), and so in the end loses its *raison d'être* because it affords no protection even against *being* harmed. The upshot is one in line after all with the picture of democracy drawn in the Beast analogy of Book 6 of the *Republic*. The Athenian politicians who are practitioners of rhetoric as the art of manipulation turn out to be no different from the sophists. For all their ambitions and delusions of power, they too dance to the popular tunes, and are out on their ear when the people tire of them (515C–516E). Josiah Ober comments: 'The dialogue . . . exposes the reality that lies at the heart of the democracy: that in Athens, the demos really does rule. It reveals that the instrument of demotic rule is an ideological hegemony over each citizen, and especially over would-be leaders.'[50]

2.2 The contradictions of rhetoric

There prove to be multiple ambiguities in the symbiosis of rhetoric and democracy as we see it examined in the pages of the *Gorgias*. To start with, there are the strikingly anti-democratic ambitions of rhetoric as articulated by its advocates. Perhaps it is significant that the dialogue's proceedings are conducted—as in the case of the encounter with sophists in the *Protagoras*—behind the doors of a private house, with Socrates and his friend Chaerephon, a well-known democrat, missing out on Gorgias' demonstration of his art because, like good Athenians, they have been spending time in the *agora*, the city's prime public space.[51] Gorgias claims that rhetoric will enable its practitioner to rule over others in the city by dint of its power of persuasion; to make other experts that Socrates has mentioned (doctors, trainers) his slaves; and to ensure by his hold over the people that businessmen make money for him, not themselves (452D–E). In other words, the power of persuasion is a means to securing the more fundamentally important power to achieve whatever you like, as Polus argues explicitly when he enters the discussion—and offers as an immediate comparison the power of a tyrant over life, death and property (466B–C). Callicles' ideal of the superior person—the real *man*—is someone who has the natural capacity to throw off the shackles of the unnatural laws and conventions imposed by the majority, and who reveals himself as their master (483E–484A). The insouciance with which all three champions of rhetoric manage to sustain a silence on the contradiction with democracy's own aspiration to give its citizens the freedom of self-determination individually and collectively, is quite breathtaking.[52]

From the outset Socrates questions rhetoric's self-portrait. The reality—he will argue—is that it is a device for flattering or sucking up to people. Socrates locates rhetoric within an elaborate taxonomy of professional practices. Genuine forms of expertise like medicine and legislation which can explain themselves and how they promote a person's good are paired with techniques devised solely for popular gratification which cannot, but which impersonate those which can: such as cookery or the performances of sophists (462B–466A). So far from bestowing real freedom on its possessor, rhetoric on this reckoning turns out to be something thoroughly servile (521A; cf. 518A). At the very outset of his conversation with Callicles, Socrates accuses him of being unable to oppose the *dêmos*, just as a lover changes what he says to agree with whatever his beloved wants (481D–E). One particularly interesting section of argument in this connection is a passage later in the discussion where Socrates starts with a point thoroughly acceptable to him (510A–E). In order to secure the means to avoid having wrong done to them so far as possible, and to exercise great power in the city, then, as Callicles agrees, people will need to be on terms of friendship with the ruler. That involves developing the same character, the same likes and dislikes as the ruler (Socrates very significantly fastens on the example of a savage and uneducated tyrant),[53] since otherwise the ruler will not be comfortable with a person he has as a friend. Then comes the crunch. Socrates goes on to apply this principle to the circumstances of *democracy* (*Gorg.* 513A–C):

If you think that anyone in the world is going to pass on to you some art or science which will make it so that you have great power in this city, but yet stay unassimilated—whether for better or for worse—to its political character, then in my view, Callicles, you are making a big mistake. It's not just a question of mimicking this people. You have to be like them in your very nature, if you are to make any real progress towards friendship with the Athenian demos... That's why it's the person who will make you most like these people, it's that person who will make you into a politician and rhetorician in the way you want to be a politician. All groups of people take pleasure in speeches made in their own spirit, and are offended by speeches made in one that isn't theirs.

Callicles does not like this conclusion—cannot believe it is right. But Plato makes him a living example of its truth. For, in representing him as someone who thinks happiness consists in the freedom to assert oneself without restraint, taking pleasure in the satisfaction of whatever desires one may have (491E–492C), Plato treats Callicles as already assimilated at least in his wishes to the lifestyle Book 8 of the *Republic* will judge characteristic of democracy. Callicles' ideal is close to Socrates' description there of the 'democratic' soul, which contains no order or necessity, but takes all its desires to be on an equality and in pursuing all indiscriminately calls the life so lived 'pleasurable and free and blessed' (*Rep.* 8.561D).

Yet there are further ironies here. From Callicles' first intervention in the argument, Socrates has saluted his *parrhêsia*, the outspokenness or frankness with which he has expressed himself (487A–D; cf. 491E). *Parrhêsia* was celebrated by the Athenians as a performance of the freedom that their democratic institutions fostered.[54] There is an obvious appropriateness in its adoption by Callicles. He is an Athenian who values above all else the idea of a world in which those who have the capacity to exercise rule over their inferiors should be in a position to 'give voice to something free and great and effective' (485E). So, in asking him whether in view of the argument in the quotation above he recommends the aspirant politician to become a *servant* to the Athenians, Socrates means to touch a raw nerve. The pain can only be intensified when he couples with that question a reminder that Callicles began by being outspoken, and should now continue in the same style (521A): 'speak well and nobly now too!' Democracy demands of those who advise it *both* flattery *and* frankness: hardly a comfortable or stable combination. This diagnosis is echoed in modern historical analysis:[55]

The Athenian system for controlling elite politicians worked precisely because it was based on a series of contradictions. The orator had simultaneously to be of the elite and of the mass, and he was expected to prove his membership in both on a regular basis.... The wealthy orator gave material gifts to the people, protected them by attacking their enemies, worked hard to provide them with good advice, and hence they were grateful to him. But he was also grateful to them every time they gave him their attention when he spoke in public, voted for him in a political trial or for a proposal he supported in the Assembly, or allowed him to profit materially by his political position, the orator was put in the demos' debt. *Charis* [i.e. generosity/gratitude] bound orator and audience together by reciprocal ties of obligation. But *charis* and the bonds it engendered could be dangerous. The orator who spoke only in order to please and win *charis* betrayed his function and *harmed* the people by binding them to himself.... The contrariness of the expectations placed on the orator clearly benefited the demos.... The masses set the rules and always acted as combined referee and scorekeeper; the vague and internally contradictory rules they devised for those who would play the game of political influence allowed the demos to reserve for itself the right to cast its own judgments according to its own lights—and hence to keep control of the state.

E. R. Dodds, in the great modern edition of the Greek text of the *Gorgias*, notes Socrates' warning to Callicles of a page or two before (519A–B, in the context of comment on the Athenians' tendency to bite the hands of their politicians):

It may be that they will seize upon you, if you're not careful, and my friend Alcibiades, when they lose what they had to start with as well as the gains they have made since—though you're not responsible for their ills (even if you've perhaps contributed to them).

Dodds makes an attractive if inevitably speculative suggestion:[56]

In the desperate last years of the Peloponnesian War, and still more in the revolutions which followed its close, a man so ambitious and so dangerously frank about it may well have forfeited his life. I suspect that Callicles, who in the dialogue is just embarking on an active career (515a), died too young to be remembered—if Plato had not remembered him.

Whether the Callicles of history himself finally opted for frankness or flattery, Plato's readers are left reflecting that one Athenian who stuck true to his democratic *parrhêsia* to the end was Socrates himself (as the trial before a jury of children imagined at 521E–522B reminds us). Plato never lost sight of this theme. As Sara Monoson comments, in the *Laws* 'we find a dramatic appropriation of the ideal of parrhesia for philosophy'.[57] The context is the difficult business of regulating sacrifices and festivals. Divine guidance is needed—but failing that, the Athenian Visitor sighs longingly for a Socrates (*Laws* 8.835C):

As things stand now, it looks as though what is required is some bold person who will set exceptional value on *parrhêsia*, and say what he thinks best for city and citizens. Speaking before an audience of those whose souls have been corrupted, he will recommend what is fitting and in line with the whole social and political system. He will be up against gargantuan appetites, and he will find no human ally. He will be alone in following reason alone.

2.3 Rhetoric and the history of Athens

But back to the *Gorgias*: to understand Socrates' remark that Callicles and Alcibiades are not the cause of the Athenians' political problems, we have to fit it into the entire immediate context. It belongs within a sequence of argument prompted by Callicles' claim that there *were* once politicians in Athens who did not flatter the populace, but made the citizens better people: Pericles, Cimon, Miltiades, Themistocles (503B–C). Socrates attacks this thesis with gusto. The people eventually turned against each and every one of these leaders: not the treatment you would expect, he argues unpersuasively, from citizens who had truly been improved by them. He mentions the complaint against Pericles that he made the Athenians 'idlers, cowards, chatterboxes, and scroungers' (515E), by being the first to make them dependent on payment for attendance at the assembly and as jurors. Socrates will allow that these venerated figures serviced the Athenians' appetites better than the present generation of politicians. That simply means they brought about more harm, but because its effects have taken time to work through they escape the blame for it. As Socrates puts it to Callicles (518E–519B):

You are praising to the skies people who have feasted the Athenians, giving them an abundance of what they desired. People say they made the city great. They don't realize that the city is now a festering sore because of those figures of the past. They have filled the city with harbours and dockyards and walls and tribute and rubbish of that kind, without a thought for restraint or justice. And when the crisis of infirmity comes, they will blame their present advisers, and praise Themistocles and Cimon and Pericles, the ones responsible for their ills. It may be that they will seize upon you, if you're not careful, and my friend Alcibiades, when they lose what they had to start with as well as the gains they have made since—though you're not responsible for their ills (even if you've perhaps contributed to them).

Plato is taking issue here with a version of Athenian history known to us principally from Thucydides.[58] In fact Socrates' indictment of the politicians he mentions 'could hardly be more anti-Thucydidean'.[59] For Thucydides, Themistocles was a truly great statesman, distinguished particularly by acute political judgement (1.138.3), while Pericles was thoroughly justified in boasting that he not only understood policy, but instructed the people, for love of the city—and was above trying to make money from it. The rot set in after him (2.65.8–10):[60]

The reason [for Athens' decline following Pericles] was that Pericles, who owed his power to public esteem and to intelligence and had proved himself clearly incorruptible in the highest degree, for his part restrained the populace freely, and led them rather than was led by them, because he did not speak with a view to pleasing them, getting power by improper means, but was able on the strength of public esteem to speak against them even so as to provoke their anger. At any rate, whenever he saw them unwarrantably confident and arrogant, his words would cow them into fear; and when he saw them unreasonably afraid, he would restore them to confidence again. Democracy existed in theory, but in fact it was rule by the leading citizen. Pericles' successors, by contrast, being more on a level with each other and yet striving each to be first, began to surrender the conduct of affairs to the people on the basis of pleasure.

Plato and Thucydides are in fact agreed that where there really is full-blown democracy, politics and political oratory will inevitably consist in flattery and deception of the populace. What Plato resists is the Thucydidean story of a gradual degeneration in politics and political discourse, reaching its nadir in the debates of the Assembly in 414 BC which led to the decision to undertake the disastrous Sicilian expedition. As Plato sees it, there was no really significant difference between democratic politics in the times of Themistocles and Pericles and in the period after Pericles.[61]

He gives oblique expression to the assessment in his handling of Pericles' funeral oration of 431 BC in honour of the war dead. The speech is presented by Thucydides as a masterly testament to the liberality of public life and the rationality of political decision-making under Periclean leadership (2.35–46). Plato evidently regarded it as an exercise in popular gratification as gross as any other example of democratic rhetoric. He makes his view crystal clear in the short dialogue *Menexenus*, a sort of companion piece to the *Gorgias*. Socrates is full of sarcasm about such performances (*Menex.* 234C):

My dear Menexenus, dying in battle has to be a fine thing many times over. The deceased gets a fine and splendid funeral, even if he was a poor man. Again, he will have his praises sung, though he may be no good, by men of wisdom, who deliver not random words of praise but long-prepared speeches.[62]

Moreover, because the speakers include the city and the citizens in their speeches, 'their praises make me feel very grand, and I am always carried out of myself as I listen and am bewitched by their charms, and all in a moment I think myself to have grown bigger and grander and finer than I was' (235A–B).[63] Plato then has Socrates deliver a pastiche funeral oration himself:[64] a eulogy of Athens and its history, employing the full range of stock tropes of the genre. Its opening is clearly designed to echo the beginning of the Thucydidean speech, if only to assert (what Thucydides' Pericles denies) the wisdom of the practice of delivering such orations[65]—which, as Nicole Loraux has shown, were central showpieces for the expression of democratic self-identity.[66] No less significant is Socrates' claim about its authorship. It was written, he says, by Aspasia, the courtesan who was Pericles' mistress—and what is more, she is the real author of Pericles' own funeral speech, and has included in her present oration material she prepared when writing that (236A–C). In other words, on the assessment implicit in this outrageous suggestion, Periclean rhetoric was designed (like his mistress's professional activities) to give its audience one thing only: pleasure, albeit in style.[67]

Perhaps the most extraordinary feature of this extraordinary exercise is its flagrant disregard of chronology. Socrates' historical narrative ends with a long passage (244D–246A) on international politics since the end of the Peloponnesian War, down to the treaty of 386 BC known as the King's Peace, which terminated hostilities between the Greeks and the Persians, on terms highly favourable to Persia and demeaning for Athens. Socrates and Aspasia had both been long dead by then. The anachronism serves to highlight the account of recent events that Plato puts in Socrates' mouth. It is a persuasive conjecture that what prompted Plato to write the dialogue at just the time he did—presumably soon after the conclusion of the treaty—was a sense that its outcome confirmed everything he believed about the disastrous consequences of democracy and of the complicit political rhetoric which helped to sustain it.[68] What is most striking about the detailed content of Socrates' oration is its consistent suppression of uncomfortable truths. For example, the disastrous Sicilian expedition of 415–13 BC is portrayed as a highly principled—and nearly successful—war of liberation; the excesses of the junta of the Thirty Tyrants are passed over in total silence; and the account of recent events does its best to represent the Athenians as standing alone against the Persians, when in reality their conduct during this period exhibited a pattern of self-interested compromises with them and most of the other parties to the conflicts. 'There is no parallel in his [i.e. Plato's] other works for the distortions and falsifications we get here, some of them involving events so well-known and recent that

---

their misinterpretation could only have been willful; and being so patent, it could not have been made with the intention to deceive.'[69] This is Plato *engagé*: the connected, internal critic at work, writing an occasional piece designed to comment and reflect on a particular political event. [70] In its consistent idealization of Athenian history, Socrates' speech becomes intelligible as a working demonstration of the kind of flattery of the *dêmos* by which politicians feed the popular illusion that failure is really success.

3. The Laws on Democracy and Freedom

3.1 Situating the *Laws*

If we wind the clock forwards thirty years or so—to the late 350s BC—we find ourselves in the very different world of the *Laws*.[71] For one thing, the conversation takes place not in Athens (as in every other of Plato's dialogues), but in Crete. For another, and again uniquely, the interlocutors do not include Socrates. Even in dialogues where he is not the main speaker—like the *Timaeus*, or the *Sophist* and *Statesman*, for example—he makes some contribution, and in one way or another the importance of his presence is flagged up. So his absence in the *Laws* is remarkable. This is clearly to be a very different kind of dialogue. Socrates' place is taken (as it were) by an anonymous Athenian Visitor, the guest, along with a Spartan named Megillus, of the Cretan Cleinias. At the beginning of the *Laws* these three elderly men are portrayed as toiling through the summer heat on an ascent, for unspecified religious purposes, to the cave of Zeus on Mt Ida, where, according to Homer, the great Minos—mythic Cretan lawgiver—conversed with the god. 'God' is the first word in the entire dialogue, indicating the foundation and ultimate focus of all the theorizing about law that will follow: is it god, asks the Visitor, or a human who is responsible for the way the laws are in Crete (1.624A)?[72]

'*Politeia* and laws' is the way the Visitor expressly describes the subject of the conversation they will be having, a few lines further on (1.625A).[73] The *Laws* does indeed discuss *politeia*, social and political system, as well as the nature of *nomos*, law, before it gets down to the business of working out a legal code for the

settlement Cleinias imagines himself and his guests to be theor-
etically constructing (3.702B–D). The topic is first introduced at
the beginning of Book 3, which starts with the origins of civilization and then offers a reflective history of political systems,
giving prominence to Sparta, and finally moving on to Persia
and Athens. After specifying various preconditions needing to
be satisfied if the enterprise is to have the chance of success, at
the beginning of Book 4 (4.704A–712A), the first question the
Athenian Visitor asks when he turns to the business of legislation is the prior one: 'Well now, what political system (politeia)
do we have it in mind to prescribe for the city?' (4.712B–C).
His answer will be: none of the existing forms (democracy, oligarchy, aristocracy and kingship are listed), but one in which law
is the master of those in office, and they are slaves of the law
(4.712C–715D). In due course it will transpire that the system he
devises in line with this principle is designed as an approximation
to the ideal city of the *Republic* (5.739A–E): indeed, the approximation the *Republic* had already foreshadowed in its treatment
of the problem of whether its ideal could ever be realized (*Rep.*
5.471E–473B).[74] So, for example, as in the *Republic*, women are
in theory to be as much of a resource for the city as men, with all
the educational and other institutional provision appropriate for
that (6.780E–781D). But very early on it is made clear that the
nuclear family will not now be abolished (4.720E–721A). Private
property—something else denied to the *Republic*'s guards—will
be reinstated on a highly restrictive basis, but holdings are to be
regarded as common to the entire city (5.739E–740B; 'how can
I use it to benefit the city?' is the question citizens need to ask
with regard to the land allocated to their families).

The dialogue is not, however, entitled *Politeia/Republic 2*. In
calling it *Laws* Plato indicated not only its main topic, but the
vantage point from which it is written. We have no evidence of
any prior history of theoretical writings going under that title,
comparable with the *politeia* tradition to which the *Republic*
belongs. The associations called up by the word 'laws' are quite
different. The Athenian Visitor is not an anonymized Socrates,
but a successor to wise lawgivers like Solon (at Athens) and Lycurgus (at Sparta).[75] The very designation 'Athenian Visitor' is doubtless meant to bring Solon to mind. Herodotus has Solon greeted
on his arrival in Sardis by the Lydian king Croesus with the
following words (1.30): 'Athenian visitor, a great deal of talk has

reached us about you, on account of your wisdom and your travelling. You have traversed much of the earth in your philosophical efforts to contemplate things.' Just so the *Laws'* Athenian has a wide experience of a range of different social and political institutions (1.639D), unlike his Spartan and Cretan interlocutors. He comes to Crete not just to give of his wisdom, but to learn: this time like Lycurgus, of whom Herodotus reports that he borrowed the Spartan social and political system from Crete, according to the Spartans' own version of the matter (1.65). Or rather, not to learn, but first to symbolize recognition of the debt which the *Laws'* vision of a closed political and social system, regulated at every point by public law, owes to the Doric (that is, Spartan/Cretan) model—despite much borrowing and adaptation of Athenian law in the detail of the code;[76] and second, to indicate that, like Solon, the Visitor is both Athenian and yet in his breadth of knowledge and understanding detached from Athens.[77]

Athenians of the fourth century believed that Solon was not only responsible for most of their laws, but author of their democratic *politeia*.[78] Historians differ over whether it is likely that by the middle of the fourth century any hard information was still available about what Solon's constitutional reforms actually consisted in, although a consolidated account purporting to be historical survives in the *Politeia of the Athenians* that was produced in Aristotle's school (*Ath. Pol.* 5–12).[79] What is clear is that, in appealing to Solon's authority, writers and speakers in the courts with different agenda of their own, and of varying political persuasions, used whatever they thought they knew of his reforms to suit their own purposes. The fiercely democratic orator Demosthenes, for example, who not infrequently invokes Solon's name, is sure that Solon gave the courts (i.e. the popular courts) unfettered authority (*Against Timocrates* 148); and certainly many other sources convey a similar impression.[80] Increase in the powers and scope of the courts is seen as the most strikingly democratic element in his reforms—to the extent of giving the *dêmos* the authoritative voice in the entire political system, according to the *Politeia of the Athenians* (*Ath. Pol.* 9.1). Contrast Plato's rival, the teacher of rhetoric Isocrates, who shared Plato's stance on contemporary democracy, and argued for the reintroduction of what he called 'the democracy bequeathed by our ancestors' (*Areop.* 15). His *Areopagiticus*, written (probably in 355 BC) as a wake-up call to Athens in the aftermath of the collapse of its second brief attempt to sustain an empire, attributes to Solon and Cleisthenes the institution of this ancestral form of democracy (*Areop.* 16). Nothing here about the popular courts. Much emphasis, rather, on the balance struck between the people's power of appointing magistrates and calling them to account, and the responsibility for governing vested in office holders (by implication there is no role here for a popular assembly), who were selected on merit, not (as with the vast majority of magistracies in contemporary Athens) by lottery (*Areop.* 21–7).[81] Much emphasis, too, on the role assigned in the ancestral democracy to the Council of the Areopagus in supervising 'good order' in the city, e.g., by supervising the way young men spent their time—on horsemanship, athletics, hunting and philosophy, not gambling and flute-girls (*Areop.* 36–55).

The *Laws* was being composed at the same time as the *Areopagiticus* appeared. Its agenda is different, but it breathes the same air. It locates its approach to *politeia* design within the same broad context of images and uses of history, and its outlook has clear affinities with that apparent in the *Areopagiticus*. This is the context we need to appreciate when we consider the final section of Book 3 ('The Lessons of History', in Trevor Saunders' Penguin translation, which he entitles 'Monarchy and Democracy').[82]

3.2 Democracy and freedom

The Athenian Visitor has just articulated the thesis that in legislating for a city's political system, there are three main things a lawgiver should be aiming to secure for it: freedom (i.e. political freedom), wisdom (i.e. political judgement) and friendship (i.e. consensus within the society). He now explains further (693D–694A):

Athenian: There are two mother-systems, so to speak, which you could fairly say have given birth to all the others. Monarchy is the proper name for the first, and democracy for the second. The former has been taken to extreme lengths by the Persians, the latter by my country; virtually all the others, as I said, are varieties of these two. It is absolutely vital for a political system to combine them, *if* (and this is of course the point of our advice, when we insist that no city formed without these two elements can be constituted properly)—*if* it is to enjoy freedom and friendship allied with good judgment.

Cleinias: Of course.

Athenian: One of the two was over-eager in embracing only the principle of monarchy, the other in embracing only the ideal of freedom; neither has achieved a balance between the two. Your cities, in Sparta and Crete, have done better, and time was when you could say much the same for the Athenians and Persians, but things are worse now. Let's run through the reasons for this, shall we?

Cleinias: Yes, of course—if, that is, we mean to finish what we have set out to do.

And with this encouragement the Visitor launches into his lesson.

'Things are worse now': this phrase contains the clue to understanding how Plato can now make an element of democracy indispensable for any good political system, despite all he had said to condemn democracy explicitly in *Gorgias* and implicitly in *Menexenus*—not to mention *Republic*, to which we shall return at greater length in Chapter 3. Plato's Athenian Visitor will go on to tell the same kind of story of decline from *true* freedom to the degenerate version dominant in contemporary Athens as Isocrates tells in the *Areopagiticus*. 'Those who ran the city in those times' did not introduce the sort of political and social system now in place, which has 'educated the citizens to regard licentiousness as democracy, lawlessness as freedom, outspokenness as equality, and the license to do these things as happiness' (*Areop.* 20). In the history lesson that follows the extract from Book 3 quoted above, Plato for his part makes the Athenian Visitor explain how 'complete freedom from all authority is infinitely worse than submitting to a moderate form of rule by others' (698A–B). He maps the distinction between the two on to a narrative of Athenian decline from the latter—represented as the Solonian system of government still in force at the time of the Persian invasions in the early fifth century BC—to the extreme liberty represented as prevailing or at least looming in present-day Athens. There is no doubt that Plato has a specifically Solonian *politeia* in mind. The key passage runs as follows (698B):

At the time of the Persian attack on the Greeks—on virtually everyone living in Europe, is perhaps a better way of putting it—we had an ancient *politeia*, in which a number of offices were held on the basis of four property-classes. We also had a sort of master:[83] respect (*aidôs*);[84] and because of that we were willing to live in servitude to the laws then in force.

As Glenn Morrow pointed out, the four property classes were 'a well-known feature of Solon's constitution', whether they were instituted by him or taken over and adapted to his purposes.[85] Interestingly, however, the Visitor does not call his *politeia* a democracy, as do both Isocrates (*Areop.* 16) and Aristotle (*Pol.* 2.12, 1273b38). Plato evidently wants his account of the ancestral Persian and Athenian constitutions to do nothing to appear to compromise the earlier claim that any sound system will combine elements of both monarchy and democracy—as he will explicitly elaborate later, in spelling out rules for election to the Council (the body responsible for conducting the day to day business of the city) in his own ideal *politeia* (*Laws* 6.756E–758A).[86]

This story about Athens matches a parallel narrative of the decline of Persia from the wise and moderate monarchy of Cyrus (mid-sixth century BC), in which freedom was respected and social harmony fostered, to its present parlous condition. In their excessive enthusiasm for depriving the people of freedom and introducing despotism, the Persians have destroyed friendship and common interest. Their rulers formulate policy in their own interest, not to benefit those they govern and the people. In consequence, 'when they come to need the people to fight for them, they discover that there is no common cause, and no eagerness to face danger and fight: they have millions and millions of soldiers—all useless for war' (697D–E).

In the Athenians' case, what the Visitor stresses is not political and military decline, but a comprehensive degeneracy consisting in the prospective collapse of all forms of respect for authority. The freedom which brings that about is broadly distinguished from 'moderate' freedom (as we might call it) by reference to the popular attitude to the law. 'Under the old laws', says the Visitor, 'it was not the people that had authority over things—they lived in a kind of voluntary slavery to the laws' (700A). The rot began not in the political or social domain, but with cultural change. More specifically, it was abandonment of objective rules and standards controlling musical performance that led to a free-for-all in that sphere, or to what might be called 'theatocracy' in place of 'musical aristocracy'. Just as Pericles' teacher Damon the musician predicted (according to the *Republic* (4.424C)), that triggered disregard for law in general—and the onset of the pursuit of freedom.[87] When freedom becomes the dominant value, we can expect people to refuse to be subject to their rulers, and then to their parents and elders; next to try to escape the authority of the laws; and finally to disregard oaths, promises and the gods. In short, we can anticipate just the same kinds of consequences as Socrates itemizes more discursively in his discussion of the anarchy bred by freedom in Book 8 of the *Republic* (8.562C–564A).

What does the 'moderate' freedom endorsed by the Visitor consist in? He never articulates any explicit answer. Two things at least seem to be envisaged. First, voluntary acceptance of the rule of law—a *politeia* doesn't count as a *politeia* if this is not the case (3.690C, 8.832B–C). Second, the freedom of participation in the political system that citizens must enjoy if they are to be proper citizens, and not simply the slaves of their rulers. In its first two books the *Laws* begins with an explanation of the need for a city to make its citizens virtuous, and with a lengthy discussion of the kind of education appropriate for this purpose. One general formulation of the objective is that it should be to 'make a person desire passionately to become a perfect citizen, who knows how to rule and to be ruled as justice requires' (1.643E)—with the practice of justice in all things 'willingly and without constraint' emphasized in a subsequent passage (2.663E). This is freedom wearing a very different face from the license for anarchy satirized in Book 8 of the *Republic*.

Not that the *Republic* is without its own rhetoric of freedom. Socrates talks positively of freedom in connection with the ideal city in various places. Sometimes he has its political independence mostly in mind—for example, when he describes the guards as 'craftsmen of freedom for the city' (*Rep.* 3.395C). But even there other connotations are in the offing. He goes on at once to talk of the models the guards should be imitating from their earliest childhood: 'people who are brave, self-disciplined, god-fearing, free, that sort of thing'. He means by 'free' persons of independent spirit, just as he does shortly before when he says (of the guards themselves again) that they must be 'free, fearing slavery rather than death' (387B). Like the *Laws*, the *Republic* attaches special importance to a non-slavish style of education in marking out the free person as an independent spirit. Ordinary people, says Socrates in Book 6, 'have not spent enough time listening to the fine, free talk which adopts every means at its disposal to achieve knowledge in its strenuous search for the truth' (6.499B). This is an aristocratic conception of freedom, whose appearances in the dialogue—unsurprisingly—are confined to discussions of the elite.[88] What the *Republic* does not do, by contrast, is accord any explicit recognition to freedom as a fundamental value needing to be built into the basic design of the *politeia* of the good city.

Why should the *Laws* emphasize freedom (of any kind) as well as wisdom in its formal recipe for a sound political system, when the *Republic* does not? Is there an implicit criticism of the *Republic* here—and a change in Plato's views? In the first instance, the reason for the *Laws'* explicitness on the issue is to be sought in its distinctive way of doing political philosophy. The *Republic* develops a utopian ideal, and then from that loftily radical perspective rejects all alternative systems and their characteristic schemes of values, democracy and freedom among them. Contemporary Athens (as Plato decides to represent it) sinks with democracy, Sparta with timarchy. This is criticism primarily in what Michael Walzer calls *rejectionist* mode. The *Laws* proceeds in a quite different way. As Saunders indicated, it approaches the business of articulating principles for the construction of a good political system historically—or rather, by appealing to myths of history. The assumption is that our job is to learn from the best in our history as much as from the worst: *immanent* criticism in Walzer's terminology. For his Athenian readers that history was a democratic history. That does not necessarily mean that in the interval since the composition of the *Gorgias* and *Menexenus* Plato has acquired a greatly enhanced respect for history as a mode of intellectual enquiry,[89] although Book 3 of the *Laws* certainly exhibits a relish in telling his version of it. Ultimately the point is one about the dialogue's rhetorical register. In the *Laws*, Plato has elected to talk to his readers in language that (unlike the *Republic*) offers no challenge to the conceptual framework with which they are antecedently familiar.

One consequence is that when it talks about Athens and democracy and freedom, the *Laws* sounds like a lot of other texts of the fifth and fourth centuries BC. Most famous of all is the remark Herodotus attributes to the deposed Spartan king Demaratus, when he says to Xerxes (on the eve of the Persian expedition against Greece of 480 BC (7. 164.4)):

When the Spartans fight individually, they are second to none, but when they fight in a body they are best of all. The reason is that though they are free, they are not completely so, because they have a master over them—the law—which they fear more than your subjects fear you.

Plato's paradox of 'voluntary slavery' to the laws simply transfers Demaratus' maxim from Sparta to Solon's Athens. He is buying into popular ideology about Greek freedom and Persian tyranny, with his implicit contrast between different uses of the metaphor of slavery: enslavement to a ruler (which negates any freedom worth having) and enslavement to law (which is a discipline reinforcing and enhancing the sense of responsibility engendered by political freedom). Rousseau, that great admirer of ancient Sparta, famously wrote (*Le Contrat Social* 1.7): 'Whoever refuses to obey the general will shall be constrained to do so by the whole body, which means nothing other than that he shall be forced to be free.' The alternative is not an illusory absolute freedom, but exploitation and tyranny. Demaratus would have been puzzled by the formulation, but the basic sentiment is the one he too expresses. Democratic ideology tended to avoid paradoxes such as these. But in a speech delivered probably in 353 BC, at just the time Plato was writing the *Laws*, Demosthenes could still say (*Against Timocrates* 5): 'I suppose that no man living will attribute the prosperity of Athens, her freedom, her democratic system, to anything rather than the laws.'[90] Indeed, 'democrats, in open polemic against supporters of the other two types of constitution [i.e. oligarchy and monarchy] tried to monopolize that particular high ground'.[91]

Where freedom is concerned, therefore, we clearly have evidence of different rhetorical preoccupations from the *Republic* in the *Laws*. But is there also a change in philosophical view? Development rather than change, perhaps. The 'knowing how to rule and to be ruled as justice requires' (*Laws* 1.643E), that goes with the political freedom citizens enjoy, is something fundamental for the ruling and military classes in the *Republic* too. It is true that the *Republic*'s economic class has no part in rule; but there is no real contrast here with the *Laws*, since those who engage in menial occupations or the crafts or (something 'not very appropriate for free persons': 8. 842D; cf. 11. 919D–E) in trade are now excluded from the ranks of the citizens altogether, as in the ideal city of Books 7 and 8 of Aristotle's *Politics*.[92] And what the *Laws*'

Solonian version of democracy and freedom entails—voluntary enslavement to laws, not enforced enslavement to a despot—has at least some affinity with the agreement all classes in the *Republic*'s ideal city make to respect the political settlement that its legislators (i.e. Socrates and his discussants) work out in Books 2 to 4. 'The need for consent to laws', writes George Klosko, 'sets the *Laws* apart from Plato's other political works.'[93] Where comparison with the *Republic* is concerned, this is an understandable but misleading reaction.[94] The *Republic* refuses to provide many details of the legislation it thinks may (or may not) be needed for the *politeia* it sketches (4.425A–427A), and does not comment specifically on consent to law. There is no denying that the *Laws*—as its title indicates—develops Plato's thinking on both heads, even if there is no fundamental change in his views. But the *Republic* has its own version of consent. It makes consensus within the good society a function of 'natural attunement of worse and better as to which element should rule, both in city and in each individual' (4.432A–B), subsequently described as 'the shared opinion of rulers and ruled' (4.433C).[95]

How truly voluntary is the consent of the ruled in either *Republic* or *Laws*? Does it fail the test of the Critical Principle? This is the principle that 'the acceptance of a justification does not count if the acceptance itself is produced'—however much that is concealed by the operation of false consciousness—'by the coercive power which is supposedly being justified'.[96] Establishing that what gets people to hold a belief is not its truth or goodness (as in sound education), but really the authority of power, sounds as if it should indeed be an essential tool of social and political criticism. But proving a causal connection of that sort could never be straightforward or uncontroversial. So as a test of legitimacy the Critical Principle is problematic. Critical theorists have not been daunted. Jürgen Habermas tried to develop the resources of the theory further to meet the difficulty. He offered 'a thought-experiment in terms of a space that is *herrschaftsfrei*, free from improper normative power, and the idea is that if a belief is sound, then it could have been accepted in those circumstances'.[97] In the next section, I shall suggest that the theory of legislative 'preludes' which Plato develops in the *Laws* offers something similar to the Habermasian thought-experiment, and presupposes a notion of fully rational freedom which would support the legitimacy of the consent the dialogue envisages.[98]

3.3 Rational freedom

Perhaps the most interesting—and according to the Visitor innovative (4.722B–C)—of all the ideas developed in the *Laws* is the distinction between two sorts of law, or rather two approaches to lawgiving. Undiluted, law is dictatorial prescription: 'Do this, or that will be done to you.' Better for a legislator dealing with free people, not slaves, to proceed more gently, and preface law with a *prelude*. The idea of a prelude bears further examination. Some of the issues it raises I discuss here. Others I explore later in Chapter 7.

Preludes do not prescribe—if successful they put people in a favourable state of mind, more apt for learning, and so make them more amenable to accepting the legal prescriptions with which preludes are coupled in what the Visitor calls the 'double' method of legislation. The sort of persuasion envisaged is illustrated by a comparison with doctors who are slaves and doctors who are free men.[99] Slave doctors just give the patient orders. This by contrast is what the Visitor says about free doctors (4.720D–E):

The visits of the free doctor are mostly concerned with treating the illnesses of free persons. He examines their origins and he appeals to nature, sharing his thoughts with the sick person and his friends. In this way he learns something himself from those who are ill, and at the same time he teaches the invalid all that he can. He gives no prescription until he has somehow succeeded in persuading the patient of it. Then, coaxing the sick person into continued cooperation, he tries to complete his restoration to health.

In a reprise of this passage in Book 9, the Visitor compares the discourse of a free doctor with a free man to philosophy (857D): 'He will be close to philosophizing in the way he argues, getting hold of the origin of the condition, and taking the problem back to the whole nature of the body.'[100]

As is the way with analogies, this one has its potentially misleading aspects.[101] From the many examples of legislative preludes in formulated the *Laws*,[102] it is clear that they are one-way traffic from the legislator as legislator to the citizens at large, not (as the quotation above suggests) dialogue between two individuals. They function more like preventative medicine than the discussion you have with your doctor when you are already ill: designed to make punishment—the analogue of medical intervention—unnecessary. The aim is to persuade citizens that it will be better for them or for the city or for both if they refrain from the undesirable activities prohibited by the law in question. If they *don't* refrain (i.e. if they *are* 'sick'), then willy nilly they will be punished as the law prescribes—quite the opposite of what happens if a patient is not persuaded by the doctor. Legislation remains at its core a threat, and at this point the threat kicks in.[103]

Plato could hardly have been unaware of these points. Is there a way of construing the doctor analogy that renders them inapposite? A strategy for making better sense of the analogy is to take it *hypothetically* and as bearing on the citizens' *entitlement* to persuasion, not as indicating (unconvincingly) the manner in which persuasive preludes actually function as instruments of social control. On this interpretation, we are invited to suppose for the sake of argument that a particular citizen *has* done something detrimental to their own or the city's good, or both: i.e. that he or she *is* 'sick'. The hypothetical encounter such a person consequently engages in with the legislator is then to be understood as educative in something like a Socratic mode (this is educating the citizens, not legislating for them, the Visitor says: 9.857D–E). In other words, it is a conversation in which a person with expert understanding (the 'doctor') extracts from someone with less (the 'patient') information about the latter's moral condition, until two things are achieved: (i) the 'doctor' is clear on the basis of a scientific diagnosis how improvement in it can be achieved; and (ii) the 'patient' comes to accept that the means and the end identified in (i) on the basis of the diagnosis are appropriate to his or her case. The moral content of a prelude is necessarily expressed in general terms. But it should be understood from this point of view as supplying the *kinds* of consideration that an individual in an unsatisfactory moral condition will be likely to need to take on board: if the cap fits, he or she should wear it.

The legislation of the *Laws*, including its preludes, is on this reading *actually* (for the citizens) an instrument of social control. But it is *justified* (to us, the critics, complicit in the design of the system) as encapsulating the voluntary outcomes that *would* be achieved by innumerable exercises in Socratic dialogue: a dialogue always conducted between a person with expert moral understanding and someone with less, and focused deliberatively on the need to improve the latter's moral condition. In short, it is justified on classic paternalist lines. The justification (to revert to a question left hanging at the end of Section 1.2) bears some affinity to Habermasian principles. But the affinity is rather weaker than the theory of deliberative democracy would require, in that citizens are not in a position of intellectual and therefore deliberative equality with the legislator, and indeed have no democratic part in whatever deliberative processes actually generate legislation.[104] What makes Plato think nonetheless that some such justification is needed is presumably (as the analogy stresses) the fact that legislation is addressed to *free citizens*. As he unpacks the idea, that means addressing responsible participants in a community that is principally designed with a view to enabling them to become morally good people (*Laws* 1.630C; 4.705D–706A, 707D; 12.963A).[105] Without their consent to the legislative framework within which their lives are led, enslavement to the laws could not be voluntary, but slavery without qualification. But to repeat: the doctor analogy implies that consent here is the consent a rational person of lesser understanding *would* give, following Socratic deliberation with another rational person of more expert understanding. Preludes simply embody the *outcomes* of such deliberations, and as such are regarded as satisfying the citizens' entitlement to persuasion. It can be more precisely formulated as the stipulation that citizens are entitled to the opportunity to be persuaded—and the claim that they *will* consent if they are reasonable.

So construed, Plato's requirement that laws be prefaced by preludes bears some affinities with the notion of a hypothetical agreement explicitly employed by Rawls (in his idea of an agreement reached by persons in what he calls 'the original position' of ignorance concerning what any of their actual interests are),[106] and widely taken to be what Hobbes, for example, must rely on in his hypothesis of the covenant men have to make if they are to leave the state of nature. Generally, criticism of Rawls has not focused on the propriety of the notion of a hypothetical agreement itself.[107] What more often gets questioned is whether the fiction is any more than dramatization of the way any one individual would exercise rational choice regarding his or her self-interest. But the contract surely does presuppose something further: that members of a political community have an equal right to rational justification of the principles that will govern their lives as partners in a cooperative enterprise.[108] Whether that presupposition really invites or demands expression in terms of mutual agreement might still be doubted. It is interesting that neither here in the *Laws*, nor earlier in his introduction of the idea of political obligation as founded on a contract not explicit but 'in effect' between city and citizen in the *Crito* (*Crito* 51C-52C),[109] does Plato himself make any use of mutual agreement *between individuals*—although he was certainly aware of its currency in the social contract theory developed among the Sophists.[110]

We may conclude that underlying the entitlement to persuasion deriving from political freedom is the potentiality citizens have for what we might call *rational freedom*.[111] Plato nowhere enunciates in so many words the principle the Stoics would express in the paradox that only the wise person (i.e. the perfectly rational person) is free—as they held, because only the wise person is not enslaved to the passions which prevent us from identifying what is truly good and successfully pursuing it. But the rule of reason over emotion and appetite in the souls of the *Republic*'s philosophers is precisely what gives them the power to achieve the good that (as the *Gorgias* would put it) everyone really wants but few think they do (e.g. 4.441E-442C). And the cave analogy of Book 7 (7.515C-D) represents this achievement unforgettably as liberation from the bondage of illusion.[112] By the same token, the condition of the person whose soul is wholly dominated by the motivations of appetite is described as true slavery (9.577C-579E). And for those who cannot themselves exercise rational control over their appetites, persuasion is to consist in bringing it home to them that 'hope of salvation', as Gregory Vlastos put it,[113] 'lies only in living under another's moral tutelage'. The moral tutelage envisaged is in fact their enslavement to the best person—the person in whom reason *does* rule (9.589B-591A, a passage shot through with the vocabulary of freedom and slavery). They have no claim on the respect for other persons as minds which underlies the Platonic idea of rational freedom.

The rule of reason in the soul is a major preoccupation of the *Laws'* conception of virtue, too (the fundamental text is 1.644D-645B). Just as in the *Republic*, Plato throughout assumes not a merely instrumental but a substantive conception of reason, which takes it to be capable of a true grasp of reality, of desiring the good in accord with that, and of governing our dispositions and behaviour in consequence.[114] In the *Laws* it is this capacity to recognize truth (rather than the full achievement ascribed to philosophers in the *Republic*) which equips someone to exercise the freedom of a citizen. Christopher Bobonich argues convincingly that the capacity in question encompasses more than true belief about good and bad, but is represented by the Visitor as constituting a form of wisdom. It is an understanding of why things are right and wrong or good and bad, even if (for example) a philosophical account of the unity and plurality of virtue is beyond those who possess it.[115] We may draw an inference. The freedom Plato associates with reason 'is not an all-or-nothing matter. The more we willingly allow our lives to be governed by reason the more free we are.'[116] Nonetheless it is the philosopher who achieves that freedom in the highest degree. Plato never wrote more eloquently on this theme than in the 'digression' of the *Theaetetus*. There the slavishness of the petty concerns of those who spend their lives in litigation is contrasted with the large view taken by philosophers. Philosophers 'have truly been brought up in freedom and leisure', can 'look to the whole', and 'attaining harmony in their speech, know how to hymn the life of gods and humans who are blessed' (*Tht.* 175A, 175E–176A).

4. Conclusion

This chapter has been preoccupied throughout with Plato the Athenian. When Plato reflected on democracy, Athens was never far from his thoughts. Dialogue after dialogue mingles critique of the key commitments of contemporary democracy with successive attempts—each in an entirely different mode—to rewrite Athenian history. Plato seems to have thought of history as a form of rhetoric. His rewritings of it are part and parcel of his critique of rhetoric: demonstrations of a rhetoric alternative to Thucydidean narrative (in the case of the *Menexenus* alternative by exaggeration). It is only in the *Laws* that he articulates at all explicitly more positive thoughts about the way the political freedom that Athenians trumpeted *should* be understood and valued, as one of the indispensable foundations of any true *politeia*. But before we explore further Plato's own ideas about rationality and the best city, we need to dig deeper into his analysis of democracy. Here the principal texts with which we shall be concerned are Book 8 of the *Republic*, the *Statesman*, and the *Protagoras*.

Notes

1. Dunn 2005: 44–5. The endnote (n. 68) that he attaches to his last sentence reads as follows (ibid. p. 198): 'Just what practical conclusions to draw from this (or even what practical conclusions Plato himself went on to draw from it) remains far from obvious—far enough from obvious to provide the main stock in trade for an entire school of political thought, the extended *clientela* of Leo Strauss, an important element in American (and hence world) politics over the last three decades: Anne Norton, *Leo Strauss and the Politics of American Empire* (New Haven: Yale University Press, 2004).'
2. There is an excellent source book: Robinson 2004.
3. It is a commonplace that in the fifth century 'comprehensive and systematic discussions and justifications of democracy on a theoretical level have not survived and probably never existed': Raaflaub, 1990: 34. Often it is supposed that the speech Plato puts in the mouth of Protagoras in the *Protagoras* (discussed in Ch. 3), represents the sophist's own theory, and so constitutes an exception to that generalization: see Farrar 1988. I am sceptical of this view. Other candidates for democratic 'theory' might be the pamphlet by the 'old oligarch' (briefly discussed in Ch. 1, Section 5, and Ch. 3, Section 1), and the remarks on politics surviving in the fragments of Democritus: on which, see Taylor 2000.
4. But not only there: for a review of other material—mostly in Herodotus, Thucydides, and Attic tragedy—see Raaflaub 1990.
5. See above all Ober 1998.
6. Yunis 1996: 51; the translation of *Knights* 1111–20 that follows is borrowed from him.
7. Ancient Greek representations of the *dêmos* as a tyrant are interestingly discussed in a number of the essays collected in Morgan 2003. Plato's development of the theme is examined in Section 2 of this chapter.
8. See Monoson 2000. Her title (*Plato's Democratic Entanglements*) is borrowed for this section of the chapter. My agreement with the general thrust of her argument—particularly as it relates to *parrhêsia*—is flagged in the sentence to which this note is attached (see also Section 2 below). On the other hand I subscribe to some of the 'orthodoxies' representing Plato as a 'notorious antidemocrat' (ibid. p. 115) or as 'democracy's most determined enemy' (Vidal-Naquet 1995: 79) which she questions. I agree rather with Vidal-Naquet's subsequent comment: 'Everything [i.e. key features of modern totalitarian regimes] is to be found here, from history rewritten to serve ideology to the establishment of concentration camps known as "places of reflection" (*sôphronistêria, Laws* 908A), where the wrong-headed and the

ill-behaved have all the time in the world to meditate upon the best of constitutions.'

9. See Walzer 1987.

10. See Sections 2 and 3 of this chapter, and also Section 1 of Ch. 3 for further 'democratic entanglements'.

11. Rowe 1998: 245.

12. See Kraut 1984: ch. VII.

13. Representative statements may be found in Euben 1994 and 1996; Monoson 1994 and 2000.

14. Here I am drawing on one of Jürgen Habermas's more recent and most accessible accounts of what he calls the proceduralist model of democracy: Habermas 1996. A good introduction to debates about the idea of deliberative democracy is Bohman and Rehg 1997: see especially the Editors' introduction (pp.ix–xxx).

15. See e.g. Walzer 2004b; Anderson 2005: ch. 5. Walzer identifies as 'the central problem' for the idea the fact that 'deliberation in itself is not an activity for the demos'. He goes on (2004b: 109): 'I don't mean that ordinary men and women don't have the capacity to reason, only that 300 million of them, or even one million or a hundred thousand, can't plausibly reason together. And it would be a great mistake to turn them away from the things they can do together. For there would then be no effective, organized opposition to the established hierarchies of wealth and power. The political outcome of such a turning is readily predictable: the citizens who turned away would lose the fights they probably want, and might well need, to win.'

16. Elster 1998: 1.

17. For a helpful brief account of Habermas's model, see Benhabib 1986: 279–97.

18. Euben 1996: 338. It seems improbable that such ideals could be deduced from the formal structure of communication: for criticism of the claim, see Williams 2002: 225–32 (cf. 100–10).

19. So Monoson 1994: 172–97.

20. Euben 1994: 222; 1996: 343.

21. See Elster 1997.

22. Cf. Wolin 1996.

23. It is a paradigm consonant with the picture painted by Nicole Loraux of the democratic ideology of the Athenians in the fourth century BC, following the political amnesty they declared at the end of the Peloponnesian War. She argues that the distinctly unHabermasian connotations of *kratos*—'force', 'control'—were such as to encourage a preference for talking about *politeia* or the *polis* rather than *dêmokratia*, or to talk up the 'mildness' of *dêmokratia*. See Loraux 2002: 68–71, 245–64. (But her argument is heavily dependent on evidence from Isocrates, who has his own distinctive agenda: see e.g. Ober 1998: ch. 5.)

24. On the *Crito*'s deliberative dimension, see Lane 1998b; Harte 1999. Very shortly after the passage referred to (*Crito* 49C–E), the dialogue abandons its Socratic mode of conversation entirely, and imagines the laws of Athens as engaging in a full-blown exercise in political rhetoric, designed to persuade Socrates not to commit the injustice of civic disobedience.

25. For a clear statement of this viewpoint, see Blondell 2002: ch. 1.
26. Bakhtin 1981: 276.
27. Euben 1996: 331, 338, 342–3; cf. Euben 1994: 223. See also Nightingale 1995: ch. 4. Euben himself invoked the name of Michel Foucault in this context (as well as Bakhtin's), but not at all convincingly. As Michael Walzer says, 'Foucault desensitizes his readers to the importance of politics' (Walzer 1988: 204).
28. Ober 1998: 159.
29. Socrates has just given an example: his helplessness on the occasion when as president of the Council he had to put a matter to the vote (473E–474A).
30. See Schofield 1992.
31. Demosthenes can say that 'in an oligarchy harmony is obtained by the equality of those who control the city, but the freedom of a democracy is guarded by the rivalry with which good citizens compete for the rewards offered by the people' (20.108). But in Herodotus' constitutional debate, oligarchy is portrayed as a regime fraught with strong private hatreds which fuel the growth of factions who sooner or later engage in bloodletting (3.82.3); and Plato's Athenian Visitor in the *Laws* says that there are more rulers in an oligarchy than under any other system (3.710E).
32. Annas and Waterfield 1995: xvii–xx.
33. But the Eleatic Visitor is explicit that while democracy may for that reason be the best of regimes if law and order has broken down, under systems in which respect for the law is enshrined 'life is *least* liveable' (my emphasis) in a democracy (*Plt.* 303A–B).
34. Samaras 2002: 349.
35. Rowe 2001: 73. A convincing articulation of this view so far as concerns the *Laws* is offered in Brisson 2005: 106–9.
36. Rowe 1998: 251–2.
37. Some of what Rowe claims in detail seems not right. So far as concerns participation (4), he must presumably be assuming that the *Republic*'s business class does not enjoy 'full membership' of the society, since it certainly takes no part in rule (cf. (3)). But this assumption is at odds at any rate with the way Socrates sets up his good city and the political settlement he bases on its class system. In the *Laws* those involved in business activity are excluded from citizenship altogether, but the extent of political participation allowed to the generality of those who *are* citizens is questionable.
38. The main discussion of the Magnesian constitution takes up under twenty pages in Book 6 (751A–768E; but the discussion of systems of government in the second half of Book 3 (689E–702E) is of greater general importance). It is indicative that only one of the sixteen chapters in Stalley 1983 is devoted to the topic. Morrow 1960 has as an entry in its analytical table of contents: 'Possible explanation for the incompleteness of his constitutional law', p. xi. Brunt 1993: 272 endorses Morrow's view that when Plato bracketed Crete with Sparta, what he had in mind was the similarity in social and educational practices. He says of the Cretans: 'I suspect that he knew and cared little about their political arrangements.' See also Perlman 2005.
39. Dunn 2005: 130. The debt to Tocqueville is acknowledged on p. 162.

40. See Dunn 2005: 130–8, 160–72; quotation from p. 184. He borrows the expression 'order of egoism' from the account of the plot against Robespierre's successors to restore the revolution, written by one of its participants, Filippo Michele Buonarroti, in his *Conspiration pour l'égalité, dite de Babeuf.*

41. Kahn 1996: 125.

42. On sophists—the itinerant intellectuals, active in the later years of the fifth century BC, who offered teaching in 'wisdom' (*sophia*) for a fee, and are thought to have been particularly successful in attracting young Athenians aspiring to success in politics—see above all the witty and malicious group portrait in Plato's *Protagoras*. They are the subject of Guthrie 1969.

43. Here—as often in the *Gorgias*—Plato's treatment of the *dêmos* is convergent with its portrayal as tyrant in fifth-century Attic literature: see the essays in Morgan 2003; note, too, that the critique of democracy by Megabyxus in Herodotus' debate of the Persian nobles explicitly compares its excesses with those attributed to tyranny by Otanes (3.81.1–2). But the tyranny of the majority is a recurrent theme. 'Others may pretend to direct the vulgar, but that is not my way: I always let the vulgar direct me; wherever popular clamour arises, I always echo the million.' So Mr Fudge, in Oliver Goldsmith's *The Citizen of the World* (1761), quoted at Raven 1992: 66. 'When a man or a party suffers from an injustice in the United States, whom do you want him to address? Public opinion? That is what forms the majority. The legislative body? It represents the majority and obeys it blindly. The executive power? It is named by the majority and serves as its passive instrument. The public forces? The public forces are nothing other than the majority in arms. The jury? The jury is the majority vested with the right to pronounce decrees: in certain states, the judges themselves are elected by the majority. Therefore, however iniquitous or unreasonable is the measure that strikes you, you must submit to it.' The verdict of Tocqueville 2000: 241.

44. For discussion of the historical Gorgias and of Plato's treatment of him in the *Gorgias*, see Wardy 1996: chs 1–3.

45. See *Gorg*.452D–E. I follow the standard interpretation of 452D6–7, in taking it that 'freedom for the people themselves' means freedom for the potential orators who are the recipients of Gorgias' teaching. Against this, John Cooper has argued that it means 'freedom for humankind itself' (Cooper 1999: 33 n. 5). This seems unlikely, given that Gorgias is made to go on at once to say that with the ability he imparts the orator will make practitioners of other arts—the doctor or the athletic trainer—his slaves. The ideal he adumbrates is not very different from Thrasymachus' picture of injustice as 'stronger and freer and more despotic' than justice (*Rep.* 1.344E), nor from Pericles' representation of imperial Athens (Thucydides 2.63).

46. See especially *Men*. 95C. In the *Gorgias* Socrates nonetheless manoeuvres Gorgias into agreeing that he will teach his pupils the truth about the good, the just and the fine if they don't know it already (459C–460A). With most scholars, but against Cooper (1999: 33–51), I take it that the reader

is meant to suppose that Polus is quite right in insisting that this is a misrepresentation of Gorgias' position (461B–C).

47. In making 500A a turning point I follow Dodds 1959: 318, although my division of the discussion is based on a different contrast.

48. For discussion, see e.g. Penner 1991; Segvic 2000; Doyle 2007, forthcoming.

49. Socrates comes back to the idea of a proper use of rhetoric—to promote justice—at the end of the eschatological myth which ends the *Gorgias*, as the final item in his review of the main philosophical theses he has argued earlier (527C): see Sedley 2007b, forthcoming. It is debatable whether the true politics in which he goes on to imagine himself and Callicles alike engaging (527D) is an anticipation of the rule of the philosophers in the *Republic*, or rather (as in the *Apology*) a way of representing his own philosophical activity as a moral mission for the *public* good—despite the confession a few pages earlier in the jury passage (521E–522B) that in a city like Athens there is nothing he could say, and a fortiori no rhetoric he could use, that could persuade his audience (see Ch. 1, Section 3). I agree with Sedley that the second option fits better with the overall argument and conceptual framework of the *Gorgias* itself. But Ober may be right to see the *Gorgias* as poised on a cusp at this point (Ober 1998: 206–13).

50. Ober 1998: 190; cf. also Ober 1989: 335–6.

51. *Gorg.*447A–C. It is tempting to go a little further, and say (with Ober 1998: 194): 'Socrates is thus initially identified as the critical citizen, duty-bound to improve his fellows, who has been carrying out his mission openly in the public square.' For more on Socrates' demotic intellectual style, see Blondell 2002: 75–80.

52. For a fuller presentation of the argument of this paragraph, see Euben 1994. On the other hand, the plays of Aristophanes—not to mention Pericles' famous treatment of the Athenian empire as a tyranny—suggest that tyranny might well appeal to the *dêmos* as the pleasure of a forbidden fruit: see e.g. Henderson 2003. From the 430s BC the comic playwright Cratinus more than once lampooned Pericles for himself behaving like a tyrant: Henderson 2003: 162–3. Nor should we forget Plato's claim that 'being a tyrant and doing whatever you desire' is generally held to be one of the good things in life (*Laws* 2.661A–B).

53. As is noted in Ober 2003: 230–2.

54. See again Monoson 1994.

55. Ober 1989: 335–6.

56. Dodds 1959: 13. On the other hand, as Nicholas Denyer suggests to me, an alternative explanation for the absence of any other information about Callicles whatever might be that he was an utterly insignificant figure: who was all bombast but totally ineffective in action—and conceivably lived in obscurity to a ripe old age.

57. Monoson 2000: 179–80.

58. Plato's response in the *Gorgias* (and to a minor extent the *Menexenus*) to Thucydides' account of Periclean rhetoric is much more fully examined in Yunis 1996: 136–56.

59. So Yunis 1996: 142.

60. Translation adapted from Yunis 1996: 67.

61. One way in which Plato seems to mark his disenchantment with historical narrative as the means for capturing the truth about politics is through the notorious indifference to chronology exhibited in the *Gorgias*. Pericles has only just died (503C), and that, together with Gorgias' presence in Athens, suggests a date of 427 BC. But other details require a much later date: for example, Socrates served 'last year' as a member of the Council (473E)—an allusion to the trial of the generals after the battle of Arginusae (cf. *Apol.* 32B)—which must be 406 BC (see Dodds 1959: 17–18 for more details). Vidal-Naquet speculates about the point of these 'chronological fantasies' (1995: 23–8).

62. The reference to 'long-prepared speeches' implies a criticism of speech-writers like Lysias, a fervent democrat, and author of a surviving funeral oration. Many details in the speech Socrates delivers seem designed to contradict the Lysian oration: e.g. his praise of the sea-battle at Salamis as the greatest of Athenian victories (*Epit.* 48), relegated to second place after Marathon in the *Menexenus* (241A). See Kahn 1963: 230–2.

63. As is pointed out in Loraux 1986: 311, this piece of comic insincerity is simply lifted by Plato from Aristophanes: see *Wasps* 636–42.

64. A pastiche, not a parody: there is no humour, black or otherwise, *in* the speech (only in Socrates' comments *on* it). Readers who take it as parody find themselves disconcerted by the moving concluding words of the speech, initially addressed by the dead to their children (*Menex.* 246B–249C); and they sometimes conclude that here Plato has finished with satire, and conveys serious thoughts of his own (so e.g. Monoson 2000: 199–202). What is needed is a right appreciation of pastiche: if a pastiche of a funeral speech is to be a good one, of course it will have to move us, and make us swell with those sentiments typically evoked by such performances which Socrates described at the outset.

65. See e.g. Kahn 1963: 221–4.

66. See Loraux 1986.

67. On erotic themes in the *Menexenus*, see Monoson 2000: 193–6.

68. This conjecture is the main thesis of Kahn 1963.

69. Vlastos 1973: 190–1. For a list of the distortions and falsifications, see Méridier 1931: 59–64.

70. Even if the evidence does not permit us to do more than glimpse the cultural and political circumstances that prompted its production. It does seem likely that Plato was truly affronted by the shabby compromise with Persia represented by the train of events that culminated in the King's Peace. A striking Panhellenist passage in Book 5 of the *Republic*—striking because it is gratuitous so far as concerns the main line of argument Socrates is pursuing at that point—treats Greeks and 'barbarians' as natural enemies (5.469E–471B). And as Yunis says: 'War was a fact of life Plato never failed to recognize and accommodate' (1996: 144).

71. For introductions to the *Laws*, see Laks 2000; also Stalley 1983. The major study of Morrow 1960 remains indispensable.

72. For further discussion of the significance of the setting and *dramatis personae* in the *Laws*, see Schofield 2003.

73. There are sage comments on the language of *politeia* and *nomoi*, and their interchangeability in contexts relevant to our enquiry, in Finley 1975a: 37–8.

74. See Laks 1990: 213–17; also Laks 2000: 267–75.

75. Cf. *Phdr.* 278C; *Laws* 9.858C–E. Lycurgus is a shadowy figure, perhaps more myth than history. As to Solon, M. H. Hansen writes (1991: 299): 'Most Athenians in Demosthenes' time [i.e. the middle fifty years or so of the fourth century BC] no doubt genuinely believed that their democracy went back to Solon (or even to Theseus); for they made no distinction—as we pride ourselves on doing—between history and myth. Nowadays we put Solon in history books and Theseus in books about mythology, but to the ordinary Athenian they were part of the same story; and that made Theseus more historical than we can accept—and Solon more mythical.'

76. See Morrow 1960; Saunders 1991.

77. For Solon, see Ker 2000; more briefly, Nightingale 2004: 63–4.

78. Solon, as author of Athens' 'ancestral constitution', first comes into view at the end of the fifth century: certainly in 403 BC, at the restoration of democracy after the collapse of the junta of the Thirty Tyrants, and probably in 411, when an oligarchic regime was briefly in control. For a lucid account, see Finley 1975a: 34–40; also (more sanguine about the evidence in 411) Hansen 1990: 88–90.

79. For a recent summary and discussion of the issues, see Rhodes 2006; and for all questions to do with the Aristotelian *Politeia of the Athenians* Rhodes's magnum opus: *A Commentary on the Aristotelian Athenaion Politeia* (Rhodes 1981).

80. See Rhodes 1981: 162, on *Ath. Pol.* 9.1, and citing principally Aristotle *Pol.* 2.12, 1274a27; Plutarch *Solon* 18.3.

81. Aristotle tells a similar story in the *Politics* (2.12, 1274a15–21)— perhaps reflecting a common view among 'dissident intellectuals' (for the term and the concept, see Ober 1998). This Solon has in fact become 'the grand old man of the moderates': so Vidal-Naquet 1986b: 270.

82. Saunders 1970: 143.

83. The Greek has 'a sort of mistress' (*despotis tis*): but 'mistress' nowadays conjures up thoughts of sex, not despotism.

84. *Aidôs*, here translated as 'respect', is a powerful motif throughout the *Laws* (see Cairns 1993: 373–8). Plato treats it (1.646E–650B) as originating in a fear of disgrace at the thought of breaching social norms, that is then internalized and when habituated forms the basis of the virtue of *sôphrosunê* (restraint). His handling of *aidôs* is traditional—indeed 'archaizing', as Cairns comments (1993: 375 n. 95)—and reinforces the climate of 'conformity rather than commitment' (1993: 376) that permeates the ideal society the Visitor imagines. In the account he gives of Athenian history, *aidôs* towards the Solonian laws still inspired those who fought against the Persians at Salamis, although even so the city and its sacred places would never have been defended had it not been for the solidarity engendered by fear of the enemy, including the fear felt by cowards quite lacking in *aidôs* (on this point, see Rowe 2007). Its departure—a deeply traditional theme

(as in Hesiod, *Works and Days* 197-200; Theognis 289-92; Euripides, *Medea*: 439-40)—is what powers the city's decline (3.699A-701A).

85. Morrow 1960: 84; relevant texts are *Ath. Pol.* 7.3; Aristotle *Pol.* 2.12, 1274a19-21; Plutarch *Solon* 18.1-2. Morrow argues that the other main elements in the Visitor's description of the *politeia*—eligibility of citizens for office tied to property qualifications and respect for the laws—also evoke Solonian legislation.

86. As Richard Stalley says (Stalley 1983: 119), these are 'peculiarly complicated', with twice the required number of candidates in each class chosen by vote following elaborate nomination procedures, from whom just half make it to final selection—by the operation of a lottery. The point of the system is to combine use of the democratic principle of randomness—'to avoid the anger of the man in the street'—and a monarchic or meritocratic principle, ensuring that greater virtue gets greater recognition. But as is obvious enough, use of the lot is secondary, and to be employed 'as little as possible': it imports a spurious equality, at odds with the genuine equality that assigns much to the great and less to the less great (6.756E-758A). This arrangement typifies the spirit of the constitutional provisions of the *Laws* in general. The popular assembly is to have none of the powers to make policy enjoyed by the Athenian *dêmos* (it seems restricted mostly to electing officials and members of the council), and the role of the popular courts similarly appears much reduced. By contrast, magistrates are to have much greater powers than in contemporary Athens, albeit subject to audit of various sorts, and placed more generally 'in slavery to the laws' (4.715D). The balance struck is highly reminiscent of the Solonian *politeia* as described by Aristotle (*Pol.* 2.12, 1274a15-21), and also by Isocrates (*Areop.* 21-7), who even makes the same point about equality. See further Harvey 1965.

87. Plato's specification of changes in musical performance as catalyst for political degeneration sounds prima facie far-fetched. However, the Old Oligarch is also alarmed by democratic undermining of 'those practised in music' (*Ath. Pol.* 1.13); and Damon was thought a sufficiently sinister figure that he was ostracized, i.e. driven into exile by popular referendum (Plutarch, *Pericles* 4). It may well be that the subversion of elite hegemony in the cultural as well as the directly political sphere in the fifth and early fourth centuries was itself perceived—by *dêmos* and elite alike—as politically significant. For evidence and discussion, see Csapo 2004; Wallace 2004; Wilson 2003, 2004.

88. This aristocratic interpretation of what it means to be a free citizen is discussed e.g. in Raaflaub 1983: 527-36. For its use to characterize the freedom of the philosopher (on which see Section 3.3 below), see Nightingale 2004: 118-27.

89. The claim that he has is a principal thesis of Samaras 2002. For a review of the question, with references to the relevant literature, see Nightingale 1999 (who likewise gives it a positive answer).

90. See Cohen 1995: 52-7. This book provides an illuminating commentary on the differences between the way the rule of law was conceived in the Athenian democracy and in the political philosophies of Plato and

Aristotle, and also on the way the appeal to the law was manipulated in the actual conduct of litigation in Athens, playing out the logic and dynamics of conflict characteristic of a feuding society (cf. also e.g. Todd and Millett 1990; Carey 1994). Scholars diverge in their assessment of the society imagined in the *Laws*. Thus P. Vidal-Naquet comments (1986c: 296): 'In the *Laws*, the city-state, which is a theocracy "in the etymological sense of the word", only has the appearance, although it is reproduced down to the minutest detail, of a classical city, that is to say, of a group based on the responsibility of each citizen. The traditional institutions and magistratures perform only more or less fictional functions; sovereignty is elsewhere.' On the other hand, Cohen writes (1993: 313): 'The sovereign "rule" of the laws is merely a fiction designed to persuade citizens to pursue civic virtue in a certain way. That is, because the continuing authority of the law depends *solely* upon the willingness of the citizens to live by its precepts, the sovereignty of the law is embodied in its citizens.'

91. Hansen 1991: 74 (citing the orator Aeschines 1.4–5, who talks of tyranny rather than monarchy).

92. Bobonich 2002: 417 agrees that 'a producer class of citizens simply no longer exists in the city of the *Laws*', but seems not to see that this fact jeopardizes many of the contrasts he wants to make between the political philosophies of the *Republic* and the *Laws* (e.g. in that context, whether or not the city is conceived as a community of the virtuous—no, on his view, in *Republic*; yes, in the *Laws*). Like is not being compared with like. On the other hand, we should note with Vidal-Naquet (1986a: 232–4) the extraordinary passage in Book 11 where the Athenian Visitor speaks of the class of artisans 'who have together furnished our lives with the useful objects they produce by their skills' as dedicated to Athena and Hephaestus, and then defines military engineers as those 'who, by means of other skills focused on defence, ensure the safety of the products made by the artisans' (11.920D–E; they are dedicated to Athena and Ares).

93. Klosko 1986: 227.

94. For discussion of the comparison with the *Statesman*, see Section 5 of Ch. 3.

95. For further discussion of consent in the *Republic*, see Section 5 of Ch. 6 below; also Kamtekar 2004.

96. Williams 2005: 6. See also his fuller discussion of the principle and of its defence by Habermas in Williams 2002: 219–32.

97. Williams 2002: 225. For Habermas's thought-experiment—the 'ideal speech situation'—he refers to Geuss 1981: 65 ff. (see also Section 1.2 above). Williams, too, thinks that the test needs to be formulated in hypothetical terms (2002: 227): 'If they were to understand properly how they came to hold this belief, would they give it up?'

98. For a brief discussion of the difficulties facing the very idea of the legitimacy of the state—including reliance on the appeal to consent—see Geuss 2001: 57–68.

99. In discussion Geoffrey Lloyd has pointed out that the distinction between slave and free doctors made here by Plato is almost certainly a construction of his own. It starts off with the anodyne observation that doctors have

assistants, and then the further suggestion that while doctors have a knowledge based on 'nature', their assistants simply pick up expertise by observing and obeying their masters (4.720A–B). Both points are accepted readily enough by Cleinias: there is no reason to doubt their historicity, though the second suggestion presumably generalizes and oversimplifies. But the slave/free polarity and the contrast between two different forms of treatment are not attested in other evidence on Greek medical practice, and—interestingly—are not endorsed as fact by Cleinias.

100. For discussion of these passages (and of preludes more generally), see Bobonich 1991; also Bobonich 2002: 97–119.

101. The Visitor does not claim (as readers of the Loeb translation are led to believe) that it is 'a very exact analogy' (4.722B). The Greek says rather that the case of the two doctors was 'very correctly placed in comparison' with the two possible modes of legislation (persuasion and force)—'an extremely apt parallel', as Saunders puts it in the Penguin edition.

102. For discussion, see Ch. 7, Section 3.2.

103. See Stalley 1994: 170. I am grateful to André Laks for correspondence on this issue.

104. Nonetheless it could be argued that Plato's provisions satisfy the principle 'that a regulation may claim legitimacy only if all those possibly affected by it could consent to it after participating in rational discourses': Habermas 1995: 16 (depending on how 'could...after participating' is taken). Cohen 1993: 312–13 argues that his citizens do have an *actual* deliberative role, citing in particular *Laws* 5.745E–746D. But all this text says is (i) that implementation of the legislator's provisions will depend on a willingness on the part of the citizens 'not to refuse to tolerate' the arrangements, but to 'put up' with them (the division and disposition of inalienable land holdings, limits on property holdings, prohibition of gold and silver, trading and banking, etc.). This is followed by an admission (ii) that there may be a reasonable concern that the legislator is dealing in dreams and fictive models only. The legislator responds by proposing (iii) that whoever 'demonstrates the paradigm' should reproduce all the finest and truest elements, but where anything is impossible to execute omit that, and for the rest achieve the best approximation he can. Finally, and most significantly of all for the point presently at issue, he suggests (iv) that then the 'demonstrator' and the legislator should consider together what in the scheme is advantageous and what too demanding, in the interests of internal consistency. No role at all here (particularly in the crucial discussion between demonstrator and legislator) for deliberation by the citizen body. Frederick the Great seems to have done rather better. In 1784 'he took the remarkable step of allowing extracts from a draft of the General Law Code (*Allgemeines Landrecht*) to be discussed in public. Only experts were to be involved and only certain aspects of the Code were affected, but it aroused much enthusiasm among the Prussian intelligentsia (as did, *mutatis mutandis*, Catherine the Great's exposure of her *Nakaz* to the Legislative Commission)' (Blanning 2002: 228).

105. See Stalley 1983, ch. 4; Bobonich 2002: 119–23.

106. See Rawls 1972: 21–2.

107. R. Dworkin objected: 'A hypothetical contract is not simply a pale form of an actual contract; it is no contract at all' (Dworkin 1977: 151). But Dworkin's point seems to have been that we should therefore not take the idea literally. In the rest of the discussion, at any rate, he went on to give a sympathetic reading of the real philosophical work it does in *A Theory of Justice*.

108. For discussion, see (besides Dworkin 1977: ch. 6) Freeman 1990 (for contemporary theorists); and for Hobbes e.g. Harrison 2003: ch. 4.

109. For discussion of the idea in general and its status as 'tacit' contract in particular, see Kraut 1984: ch. VI.

110. As evidenced in the use he has Glaucon make of it in his challenge to Socrates at the beginning of Book 2 of the *Republic* (2.358E–360D): on which, see e.g. Schofield 2000a: 203–7, with further references.

111. This is what C. D. C. Reeve calls *critical freedom* (in an echo of Habermas, whom he does not mention, and Hegel, whom he does), defining it as the freedom to have and to satisfy desires sanctioned by the critical theory of rationality—see Reeve 1988: 233.

112. See e.g. Moravcsik 1983: 8–9.

113. Vlastos 1995: II. 94.

114. On this conception of reason, widely shared by Greek philosophers, see M. Frede 1996.

115. Bobonich 2002: 194–200.

116. Stalley 1997–8: 157. The freedom of the rational person will not resemble the equal pursuit of any and every pleasure Plato imagines as characteristic of his 'democratic' person (*Rep.* 8.561A–E). As Geoffrey Lloyd suggests to me, it will presumably be closer to what Aristotle describes as the condition of the free members of a household in *Metaph.* 12.10, 1075b19–23: 'Those who are free are least at liberty to act as they will, but all or most things are already ordained for them, whereas the slaves and the beasts do little for the common good, and for the most part live at random. For this is the sort of principle that constitutes the nature of each.' I am grateful to Michael Pakaluk for comments on political vs. rational freedom.

3

Problematizing Democracy

---

1. *From Polarity to Complexity*

On 28 August 2005 the Iraqi parliament finally approved a new constitution, after months of negotiation and debate. It failed to win the support of Sunni representatives; Arab nations feared for the security of the region; and many political commentators foresaw a future grimmer than the grim present. President Bush, on the other hand, congratulated the Iraqi people on a further step in the transition from dictatorship to democracy. He commented on the freedoms of expression and association and on other liberties recognized in the document. And he spoke of a free people finding self-expression at the ballot box under freely enacted laws. In short, he summoned a whole battery of polarities. As freedom (and freedoms), law, self-determination and self-expression were ranged with democracy, so oppression and disempowerment were associated by dark implication with the arbitrariness of dictatorship and the violence of those who were now afraid of losing out with its demise.

Democracy has always been held up for admiration or disfavour by comparison with some alternative.[1] In much of the evidence which survives from fifth-century Athens,[2] the issue was represented as a choice between democracy and dictatorship's ancient predecessor: tyranny or absolute monarchy.[3] The clash of Eastern despotism and Greek freedom is one that structures the entire conception of Herodotus' *Histories*. The Athenian tyrannicides Harmodius and Aristogeiton (responsible for the assassination of Hipparchus in 514 BC) loomed large in Athenian democratic ideology—although the credit for liberating Athens was contested by the powerful Alcmaeonid family, whose best known members were to be Pericles and Alcibiades. As Thucydides represents a renegade Alcibiades telling the Spartans in the winter of 415/414 (6.89.4): 'My family has always been opposed to tyranny (any force that opposes those exercising absolute power (*dunasteuomenoi*) gets called democracy),[4] and that is why our leadership of the masses has been continuous.' But by now Alcibiades had notoriously been suspected by the Athenians of aiming at tyranny himself, not least on account of some involvement in two violations of religious sensibilities: the parodying of the Mysteries and the mutilation of the Herms. Aristophanes' *Wasps* and *Knights*, plays of the late 420s, are already drenched in obsession with supposed conspiracies against the *dêmos* on the part of politicians with tyrannical ambitions.[5]

It is true that in the poet Pindar a tripartite division of *politeiai* or political systems is presupposed (the rule of one vs. the best vs. the many: *Pythian* 2.86–8, perhaps 468 BC). The percolation of this analysis into popular consciousness is suggested by Thucydides' report of the Athenian *dêmos*'s conclusion that the affair of the Mysteries 'was all the work of an oligarchic or tyrannical conspiracy' (6.60.1).[6] Yet it is striking that in the earliest full-scale presentation of the analysis (in Herodotus), the lion's share of the argument between the Persian nobles who debate the issue is taken up with the merits and demerits of democracy as an alternative to monarchy, reflecting the preoccupations of the *Histories* as a whole. Oligarchy is by comparison decidedly undertheorized in this text (3.80–2).[7]

There are two late fifth-century Athenian writers with theoretical ambitions, however, in whom oligarchy is something much more salient. When Thucydides and the 'Old Oligarch' discuss democracy, there is still a polarity taking centre stage. But now it is the opposition between democracy and oligarchy. 'The antithesis between the rule of the few and the rule of the many', as Roger Brock and Stephen Hodkinson observe, 'runs throughout Thucydides' accounts and analyses of political activity in the later fifth century.'[8] Exactly the same is true of the

Old Oligarch's short tract, although he prefers to contrast the 'valuable' (*chrêstoi*), well-born and rich with the poor, degraded (*ponêroi*) and 'vulgar' (*dêmotikoi*) element in the population: 'in every country the best element is opposed to democracy' (*Ath. Pol.* 1.5; for his use of the terminology of oligarchy vs. democracy see 2.20). By the time Aristotle writes his *Politics* nearly a century later, most people suppose (he says) that there *are* only two constitutions, oligarchy and democracy; and for most practical purposes he thinks this adequate enough (*Pol.* 4.3, 1290a13–19; 5.1, 1301b39–1302a2). The Old Oligarch, of course, is at odds with democratic ideology in general, and does not share its particular and distinctive concern with the spectre of tyranny. His own outlook seems to be that of an aristocratic Athenian dissident of Spartan sympathies. Thucydides' consuming interest in the oligarchy/democracy polarity is born above all of his reflection on *stasis*, the internal civil conflicts endemic in Greece during the Peloponnesian War, fanned by Athens and Sparta to further their own interests (3.82.1–2), and on the banners of democracy and oligarchy under which they were fought (or rather under the decent-sounding slogans of 'equal rights for ordinary citizens' and 'moderate aristocracy' (3.82.8)). But it may also have been shaped by the interest in constitutional reform and the debates generated by it which were part and parcel of the short-lived oligarchic revolutions in Athens of 411 and 404 BC.[9]

By comparison with all that had gone before, the complexity and sophistication exhibited in the identification and analysis of *politeiai* in Books 8 and 9 of the *Republic* are of an altogether different order of magnitude. Instead of a single polarity—democracy or ...—Plato contrasts with the good city he has constructed in Books 2 to 4, and further elaborated in Books 5 to 7, a sequence of four bad or flawed systems (and corresponding conditions of the soul). He indicates that this is only a selection from an infinite number of possibilities (*Rep.* 4.445C–E; cf. 8.544D). Those he does select he exhibits *as* flawed—by identifying both the centrifugal forces within each social and psychological structure and the dynamic that makes one structure transmute into another. The four sample *politeiai* chosen are timarchy or timocracy (modelled on Crete and Sparta), oligarchy, democracy and tyranny.[10] Matching these are specimens of what it is to have a timocratic or oligarchic or democratic or tyrannical personality. Plato has Socrates suggest the way a city or a soul might easily degenerate from one condition to the next, moving on eventually to the limiting case (tyranny or the tyrant), which is portrayed as the paradigm of injustice and misery. His account not only complements the discussion of Books 2 to 4, but relies for its explanations of political and psychological structures alike on the analysis of the soul there into three elements or sources of motivation: reason, spirit, appetite.

So *all* the options over which people fought in the fifth century—in argument or on the streets or on the field of battle—are rejected from the vantage point of the ideal as inferior political and social systems, echoed in more or less damaged individual personalities. In mounting his critique of them, Plato does not rely solely on the psychology worked out at the end of Book 4 of the dialogue. He also exploits for his own ends a considerable stock of current historical and political lore. A famous example is the evident use of Peisistratus (the Athenian sixth-century tyrant) and Dionysius I of Syracuse in Sicily as models for the account of tyranny (at *Rep.* 8.565D–569C).[11] I shall illustrate the point from Plato's treatment of timarchy and oligarchy.

In the first place, Plato has no truck with any claim or implication that these regimes might be forms of aristocracy: rule by the best people, as in the self-image commented on by Thucydides (3.82.8) and evidenced in (for example) the Old Oligarch (*Ath. Pol.* 1.2–9), or by Megabyxus in Herodotus' debate of the Persian nobles (3.81.3). He reserves the term 'aristocracy' for rule by the truly virtuous: the good and wise guards of his own ideal city (*Rep.* 4.445D, 8.544E). In a timarchy the rulers tend to be drawn not from the ranks of the wise and truly virtuous, but from people of a competitive type; and timarchy 'has one striking characteristic, which comes from the dominance of the spirited element: love of victory and honour (*philotimia*)' (*Rep.* 8.548C). This diagnosis of the transparently militaristic character of Spartan society[12] is an obvious application of the social psychology Plato has already adumbrated in Book 4 (4.435E–436A) and will elaborate in more detail subsequently (9.580D–581E). But in his explanation of how the good city might degenerate into a timarchy, he has posited not just an honour-loving but a money-loving strain in the psychological make-up of the ruling class. That is why they allow themselves private property (contrary to the regime imposed on the guards of the ideal city), and why they will develop a secret passion for gold and silver, hoarded in treasuries and strongrooms, that will in due course sow the seeds of oligarchy (8.548A–B, 550C–551B). There are two things worth noting here about this characterization of timarchy. First, it plainly embodies awareness that accumulation of private wealth was a fundamental ingredient of the classical Spartan social system;[13] and it recalls in particular Herodotus' talk of the treasuries of the Spartan king Ariston (6.62.2). It also reflects the common perception that Spartan kings and other members of this elite were notably susceptible to bribery.[14] In fact, in wartime plays, Aristophanes and Euripides treat it as common knowledge that the Spartans that the Athenians and others have to deal with are not only treacherous (the prime complaint)[15] but sordid profiteers (*aiskhrokerdeis*: Ar. *Peace* 619–27; Eur. *Andromache* 445–52). Second, even if the causes of change from timarchy to what Plato calls oligarchy were more complex and structural than emerge in his account, 'it is evident that, by the fourth century, Sparta was rapidly becoming a plutocracy—a society dominated by the rich, whose ambitions increasingly distanced them from ordinary Spartiates'.[16]

Plato takes oligarchy to be a form of society and a system of government in which wealth is the be-all and end-all (*Rep.* 8.554A).[17] It will by now be apparent that this is not the way oligarchs themselves saw oligarchy. They would not have objected to Plato's claim that what defines oligarchy is introduction of a wealth *qualification* for anyone who is to be eligible to participate in rule (8.551A–B, 553A). But their argument was that the wealthy were better able to contribute to the commonwealth with 'persons and resources'.[18] It was not hard for democrats to counter this claim. Here, for example, is the Syracusan Athenagoras (Thucydides 6.39.1–2):

Some will say that democracy is neither intelligent nor fair, and that the wealthy are best able to rule. But I answer first that the *dêmos* is the name of the whole people, while oligarchy names only a part. Second, though the rich are indeed the best guardians of the city's money, the best at deliberation are the intelligent, and the best judges of what they hear are the many. Now in a democracy there are fair shares in all these things, both globally and for each particular sector of the population. But while an oligarchy allows the many their share of dangers, it takes more than its fair share of the benefits—in fact it takes the lot.

On two points at least Plato sees eye to eye with Athenagoras. For him, the first main failing of oligarchy is the way it ties eligibility for rule to a property qualification (*Rep.* 8.551C): 'Think what it would be like if you appointed ships' captains in this way, on the basis of a property qualification, and refused a command to a poor man even if he was better qualified.' The second is that such a society is deeply divided between the haves and have-nots: 'a city of the poor and a city of the rich, living in the same place, but constantly scheming against one another' (*Rep.* 8.551D). Athenagoras charges oligarchs with greed (*pleonektein*, 'taking more than their fair share'). Plato makes this the force that motivates and explains the entire oligarchic system: the paradigm of an oligarchic system, if you like,[19] but one doubtless shaped in his mind as such by the behaviour of the oligarchy of the Thirty Tyrants at Athens in 404 BC,[20] which was agreed by observers from very different points on the political spectrum to have been driven by greed.[21] As becomes crystal clear when Plato turns to consider the oligarchic personality, oligarchic behaviour for him reflects the dominance in the soul not of reason or spirit, but of 'the appetitive and money-loving element' (8.553C).[22]

In the narrative of Book 8 of the *Republic* oligarchy meets a sticky end. In due course the wealthy lose all capacity for self-discipline and indulge in idle luxury, while the poor become disenfranchised or get into debt and grow more and more disaffected. The body politic is now thoroughly unhealthy, and may become actually ill and openly conflicted at the slightest provocation. These are circumstances in which the poor, sensing weakness in the ruling oligarchy, may well overthrow the regime and institute *democracy* with its egalitarian institutions. As Socrates explains the matter (8.557A):

Presumably it turns into a democracy when the poor are victorious, when they kill some of their opponents and send others into exile, and give an equal share in the political system and in access to public office to those who remain, and when offices in the city are allocated mostly by a lottery.

But that does not put an end to divisions between rich and poor. As a materialistic citizenry comes to relish its anarchic freedom to do as it chooses, the rich have their property confiscated, which after democratic politicians have taken the lion's share is redistributed to the poor. Mutual suspicion and hostility grow, more virulently than in an oligarchy, until the poor look for a champion who becomes 'the architect of civil war against those who own property' (*Rep.* 8.566A). This strongman then inevitably requests and acquires a bodyguard—and conditions are ripe for *tyranny* and enslavement of the populace.

In this narrative of decline, the catalyst for the downfall of each successive regime in the sequence is the ruling class's increasingly aggressive pursuit of greater wealth. In what modality is the story written? Aristotle assumed that Plato was suggesting that oligarchy, for example, changes into democracy *generally if not always*, and similarly democracy in its turn into tyranny (*Pol.* 5.12). Followed by some modern scholarship, he criticized him on that account (*Pol.* 5.12, 1316a23–4): 'The very reverse may happen. Democracy, for example, can change into oligarchy, and indeed it can do so more easily than it can change into monarchy.' It is hard to believe that Plato can have thought very differently. What he has Socrates actually say avoids any suggestion of a law governing the direction of change, notably in his statement (*Rep.* 8.556E): 'An unhealthy city needs only the slightest pretext—one side appealing for outside help to an oligarchy, or the other to a democracy—to become ill and start fighting against itself.'[23] Socrates goes on to say that a democracy comes into being when the poor emerge victorious from civil conflict, and institute a system offering equal political participation and equal access (mostly through the lot) to public offices. He does not say that this is the *only* way democracy is originated; he does not even say that when it comes about in this way oligarchy has to be what it replaces.[24] He does commit himself to the generalizing proposition that when the poor majority are campaigning against the few, they always set up a single champion. But Plato is careful *not* to claim that such champions *inevitably* turn into tyrants, only that 'this position of champion is the sole root from which the tyrant springs', and that once such a person begins killing and exiling people and hinting at general cancellation of debts and redistribution of land, *then* there is an inevitability: either he will be killed by his enemies or he will become tyrant, 'turning from human into wolf' (*Rep.* 8.565E–566A).[25]

So, for all its symbolic and exemplary importance, the sequence of regime changes traced in *Republic* 8 is not depicted in deterministic terms. Christopher Gill catches the spirit of Plato's enterprise when he writes:[26]

The survey of degenerate constitutions in Book 8, while presented in apparently temporal sequence (and heralded as a kind of epic-history in a way similar to *Critias*), is in fact arranged on purely theoretical principles.

What principles are those? Here is Dorothea Frede's attractive suggestion:[27]

His intention is to depict model-states that *truly* deserve their names because each of them is exclusively governed by its characteristic value (cf. 548B–C). Thus in his timocracy, valour is the only acknowledged value, oligarchy is driven by wealth as its only aim, in democracy freedom reigns supreme, and tyranny means slavery to the tyrant's worst desires.

She then asks:[28] 'If Plato aims for a demonstration of the ills of each of the model-states that result from the monopoly of their basic values, why does he give it in the form of a story of decline?' The answer, as she goes on to bring out, must be one to do with the inevitable destabilization of a society in which reason is no longer in control of spirit and appetite. The real threat comes from appetite, already exercising an insidious power under timarchy, but increasingly assertive in the other three degenerate systems. Once reason loses its grip on society, appetite moves into the driving seat, with ever more destructive and self-destructive consequences. And those can best be dramatized in terms of a temporal sequence.

2. *Democracy, Equality and Freedom*

In his diagnosis of oligarchy as driven by nothing but greed, Plato simply ignores its pretensions to virtue, competence and concern for the public good. This is rejectionist criticism in a style any democrat might applaud.[29] With democracy things are quite different. Plato accepts what democracy claims for itself. Equality and freedom *do* flourish under democracy. But they are a recipe for chaos, not for the good life. The logic of democracy is self-destructive.

Something needs to be said right away about the differing roles of equality and freedom in Plato's account of democracy.

Socrates starts by identifying democracy *as* democracy in terms of equal political participation and equal access to public office (8.557A). As the account develops he comes back to the theme of equality. He concludes the section on the democratic life-style (8.557A–558C) with the verdict: 'You'd expect it to be an enjoyable kind of regime—anarchic, colourful, and granting equality of a sort to equals and unequals alike.' This diagnosis then becomes the mainspring of the detailed description Socrates gives subsequently of the way this form of equality—extended to every area of life, not just politics—leads to an anarchy which ultimately destroys democracy (8.562E–563E). But *freedom*, not equality, is what he fastens on as the hallmark of life under a democracy (8.557A–558C). 'This', says Socrates a bit further on (8.562B–C), 'is what you hear said in a city under demo-cratic rule—that in freedom it has the finest of possessions, and for those whose nature it is to be free a democracy is on that account the only place to live.' What does he understand here by 'freedom'? Not the rational freedom that represents the Platonic ideal,[30] but the freedom of a person who has license 'to do what he wants' (8.557B). *Why*, under a political system with demo-cracy's origins and constitutional arrangements, there should be a distinctive celebration of freedom so understood is something Socrates does not attempt to explain—although once freedom is understood as unfettered freedom for everybody, it is easy enough to see why anarchic equality might be the consequence.

In fact it is not hard to understand why both equality and freedom get woven—in different ways—into Plato's discussion of democracy. It is very probable that equality, or rather *iso-nomia* (equality under the law, understood broadly as political equality), was the name the Greeks first gave to democracy.[31] In the debate Herodotus stages between advocates of different *politeiai*, such equality is associated with the use of the lot, accountability and decision-making by the whole community (3.80.6). Elsewhere he associates Athens' rise to power after the fall of the Peisistratid tyranny at the end of the sixth century BC with the introduction of equality of speech (*isêgoria*) under Cleis-thenes' constitution (5.78). Other fifth-century writers provide further evidence of how the Athenians understood their demo-cratic equality. Kurt Raaflaub cites passages from Euripides and Thucydides in particular:[32]

In the *Suppliants* Euripides stresses equality of vote, equality of justice guaranteed by common control over the laws and publication of the laws, equality of shared power provided by the principle of ruling in annual turns, and the supreme realization of equality, freedom of speech. In the Funeral Oration, Thucydides focuses on equality before the law in private disputes and on equality of chances and participation in politics.

As Raaflaub concludes after reviewing quite a range of less direct evidence, 'fifth-century literature reflects all the main elements occurring in Aristotle's discussion of democratic equality'.[33] Plato assumes a reader who already commands all this knowledge. Hence one reason at least for the brevity of his reference at 557A to the equal share in both the political system and the access to public office which is what makes democracy.

Celebration of freedom as the principal achievement of democracy was perhaps something that developed later at Athens than recognition of equality as its defining attribute, perhaps only in the mid-fifth century.[34] Of the evidence from the fifth-century, Raaflaub says:[35] 'The focus always remains the same: the demos rules (i.e., all the citizens are involved in governing the city), therefore the city is free.' In other words, democratic freedom is something intimately related to equality. The point of political equality is that it supplies the conditions for freedom and its exercise. By freedom two things were meant above all: the political freedom for the citizens collectively to manage their city's affairs themselves (in contrast to the position under oligarchy or tyranny); and social freedom for each citizen to live his life as he pleased. Pericles' funeral speech in Thucydides gives classic expression to the Athenian ideology of freedom (2.37.2–3):

The political life of our community is marked by freedom; and as for suspicion of one another in our daily pursuits, we do not frown on our neighbour if he behaves to please himself, or set our faces in those expressions of disapproval that are so disagreeable, however harmless.

These are the two dimensions of freedom Aristotle confirms in his analysis of democracy (*Pol.* 6.2, 1317a40–b17). And it is worth reminding ourselves again of John Dunn's argument in *Setting the People Free* that democratization signifies not just a political order built on principles of equality, but the impact of that on social, cultural and economic life—leading to creation of 'a world from which faith, deference and even loyalty have largely passed away'.[36]

None of the first readers of Book 8 of the *Republic*, therefore, would have seen anything needing explanation when the Platonic Socrates moves from talk of an equal share in the political system to talk of freedom as the keynote of life in a democracy. What must surely have struck them, however, is that his treatment of the democratic lifestyle focuses entirely on *social* freedom, to the exclusion of any discussion of the way they 'want to be free *and to rule*' (as the Old Oligarch put it: *Ath.Pol.* 1.8)—in sharpest contrast with the picture of Athens drawn by Aristophanes in play after play, where the political dimensions of democracy give him most of his opportunities for entertainment. The democratic city, Socrates tells us, is 'full of freedom and outspokenness (*parrhêsia*)', and a person has license 'to do what he wants' (8.557B). The consequences of these opening formulations are then spelled out. In what follows, both in this passage (8.557A–558C) and in the further account of the consequences of defining freedom as the good (562A–563E), the discussion spells out a whole variety of ways in which acceptance of the idea that anyone can do what he or she likes generates a permissive—but in the end highly *in*tolerant—society. These include the manner in which the permissive ethos results in what one might call the *internalization* of the constitutional principle of equality. Hence the terms of Socrates' summing-up at 558C, where he says of democracy: 'It will be an agreeable kind of regime—anarchic, colourful, and granting equality of a sort to equals and unequals alike.'[37]

The expression 'anarchic' shows that it would be wrong to imply that Plato leaves Socrates entirely silent in this context on the political aspects of the democratic way of life. In one of the more outrageous passages in this section of Book 8, Socrates envisages the social freedom to do what one pleases as *engulfing* the realm of the political (8.557E–558A):

'There is no compulsion to hold office in this city,' I said, 'even if you're well qualified to hold office, nor to obey those who do hold office, if you don't feel like it, nor to go to war when the city is at war, nor to be at peace when everyone else is, unless peace is what you want. Then again, even if there's a law stopping you holding office or being a member of a jury, there's nothing to stop you holding office and being a member of a jury anyway, if that's how the mood takes you. Isn't this, in the short term, a delightful and heaven-sent way of life?'

'It probably is, in the short term.'

Some of this sounds more like Aristophanic fantasy than Athenian reality (e.g., the efforts of the anti-hero Dicaeopolis in the *Acharnians* to make a private peace while the city remains at war). But Plato is killing two birds with one stone: articulating the logical consequences of pushing freedom to extremes with a strong undertow of contemporary satire.[38] He continues in this vein: along with liberty for oneself goes tolerance of others, similarly caricatured (558A). Plato is at once very close to democracy and very distant from it. He talks like an Athenian grumbling and caricaturing, adopting the immanentist critical tropes of a comic playwright. But comments of this sort are set within the overarching frame of a rejectionist critique of *all* existing political systems.

In this narrative and satirical mode Plato is spelling out a paradox of democracy. Democracy depends on citizens' availing themselves of the freedom to participate in rule, and on respect for a legal and constitutional framework which governs the exercise of their freedoms. But if the freedom to do as one pleases also enshrined in democracy is pushed to its limits, people will regard themselves as entitled to ignore that legal and constitutional framework, and to participate in rule or not just as they like, *not* as the law provides. Note the 'if' in my formulation. In Plato's text there is no 'if'. It is presented as what *does* happen. This is not mere whimsy or insouciance on his part. Plato's narrative takes the form it does because it functions within the overarching context of an account of the destructive effects of the grip exercised on society by appetite. Money has been the obsession of oligarchic society. When oligarchy is overthrown, the desire for it remains rampant, even if it is no longer obsessive. As is clear from a later passage in Book 9 (580D–581A), Plato's theory is that one reason people love money is because it provides the means to satisfy all their other appetites. Satisfaction of all the appetites is the stage in the downward spiral powered by materialism that is reached with democracy.[39]

So, before all else, given the social freedom to do as one likes, what people in general *will* do under a democracy is the thing money gives them the *capacity* to do—satisfy their appetites.

It is because democracy is a society governed by appetite that Plato thinks himself entitled to assume that exercise of social freedom will inevitably win out in the end over respect for the framework that supports it and political freedom alike. When he turns next to consider the *individual* he describes as democratic, Plato quite explicitly identifies his characteristic lifestyle with the equal and indeed anarchic pursuit of any and every desire he conceives. This makes him 'fine and colourful, just like the democratic city' (8.561A–E).

3. Democracy and Pluralism

The dominant human type in a timocracy is the competitor. In an oligarchy it is the obsessive wealth accumulator. Given the premium set on freedom in a democracy, it might have been expected that Plato would have identified the dominant type in such societies as what we might call libertarians: people who treat personal freedom as their highest priority, and thereby shape the democratic lifestyle. This is not what happens. One reason why it does not has to do with Plato's overall philosophical strategy for explaining the differences between societies and their political systems. At the end of the day such differences were evidently, in his view, rooted in human psychology—in intellect, emotion and appetite. Hence not merely his hypothesis of three basic human types (philosophical, competitive, materialistic), but a strong presumption that it will be possible to explain the characteristic features of *any* society—including therefore democracy—by reference to that hypothesis. Another reason has to do with the way freedom functions as a good in shaping behaviour. If someone makes honour and victory or money and profit their goal, a great deal of their behaviour is likely to be structured in such a way as to achieve it—paradigmatically in the lives of the soldier and the businessman. But freedom (like the modern idea of a right) is what one might call an enabling good. It is freedom *to*—'to do what a person wants', to recapitulate the formula Socrates reproduces. In a society which makes freedom its good, lifestyles will be structured principally by pursuit not of freedom but of what that freedom enables people to pursue: 'what a person wants'. Or, as Socrates spells out the point (8.557B): 'Where there is license [to do that], then obviously each person can arrange his own life within the city in whatever way each person pleases.'

Socrates now draws the consequence (557C): 'So it is above all in this social and political system that there would be found people of the most varied human types.' In a democracy there is no *one* dominant type, as under timocracy or oligarchy or as in the good city Socrates and his interlocutors have constructed. What gives democracy the character it has is the *diversity* of lifestyles it enables. In his diagnosis of diversity Plato articulates the penetrating insight that a democracy is an essentially pluralist society (to put the point in contemporary terms).[40] In a system where the highest store is set on positive freedom, then given diversity within the population of beliefs or culture or (as Plato is proposing) psychological types, a diversity of lifestyles can be expected to flourish. Plato goes so far as to have Socrates make the striking and strikingly *un*expected claim that democracy contains 'all kinds of political system because of the license' to do what one likes (8.557D):

'Anyone wanting to found a city, as we have just been doing, will probably find he has to go to a city with a democratic regime, and there choose whatever political arrangements he fancies. Like shopping for constitutions in a bazaar. Then, when he has made his choice, he can found a city along those lines.'

'Yes,' he said, 'he's not likely to find any shortage of models to choose from.'

The implicit logic here, I suggest, goes as follows. The lifestyle of a particular social and political system is a sort of projection on to the society as a whole of the human character-type that predominates within it. Now in a democracy *every* human character-type flourishes (this is the profusion of models Adeimantus must be taking Socrates to have in mind). So from *any* such type we can project the lifestyle which *would be* characteristic of the corresponding social and political system—where that character-type predominates in the ordering of society, its arrangements for government and the good it takes as it highest value. That is the sense in which democracy is a sort of constitutional bazaar. It would doubtless not have been too difficult to find human models in Athens for timocracy or oligarchy—but for the ideal society delineated in the *Republic* Socrates would presumably be just about the only potential paradigm.

Some recent commentators propose a different reading of the text just quoted. They want Plato to be introducing an ambitious thesis in the sociology of knowledge: only in a free-speaking democracy is there the possibility for the fundamental self-criticism (as well as the knowledge of human diversity) needed 'to imagine a regime that runs entirely against the grain of the one in which it is imagined'.[41] That would make democracy, for all the inherent drawbacks Plato identifies in the immediate context, a system in which he finds unique intellectual merit. But his Socrates is not at this point in the passage discussing freedom of speech. He is doing something quite different: reinforcing in a highly dramatic fashion the message that the variety of human character you can find in a democracy is truly remarkable.

My account of Book 8's treatment of democracy diverges sharply from the influential and highly critical interpretation propounded by Bernard Williams.[42] Despite acknowledging that Plato's Socrates characterizes democracy as a system 'in which one finds men of every sort', and which is 'decorated with every sort of character' like a garment of many colours, Williams held that on account of the predominance principle Plato had to say (i) that democracy gets its character from the majority who are its rulers, and (ii) that the majority must therefore themselves be 'democratic' in character. And he observed that by an application of his city-soul analogy, Plato has Socrates propose (iii) that the democratic character is 'always shifting, without expertise in anything, prepared to indulge any *epithumia*, etc.' Williams notoriously concluded:[43]

Moving between the social and the individual level once more, Plato seems disposed to confound two very different things: a state in which there are various characters among the people, and a state in which most of the people have a various character, that is to say, a very shifting and unsteady character.

The first thing to question here is (i). Williams thought Plato was committed to (i) and (ii) because he took the most plausible reading of Socrates' remarks about the way a city derives its character from the characters of the people living in it to be the 'predominant section' rule:

(P) A city is F if and only if its leading, most influential, or predominant citizens are F.

(P) is an attempt to articulate Socrates' very much less precise statement that (S) the different kinds of *politeia* don't come from nowhere (or rather—proverbially—'from oak or from stone'), but from 'the characters in the cities' (*Rep.* 8.544D–E). How do we test whether (P) is a helpful formulation of what Socrates says? One obvious tactic is to see whether it makes good sense of the detailed discussions of particular *politeiai* which Book 8 goes on to give. Even for timarchy, where spirited people dedicated to the pursuit of honour and victory are the leading citizens, (P) does not capture the way Socrates explains the character of the society. What he actually says is (8.548C): 'It has one striking characteristic, which comes from the dominance of the spirited element: love of victory and honour.' In other words, he has Socrates refer to the prominence of a particular sort of *motivation*, and accounts for that in turn by reference to the part of the soul that is in control. In the case of democracy (P) yet more clearly fails to express what Plato has in mind.

He shows no interest in explaining 'democratic' as applied to the city by reference to its application to citizens. What does emerge clearly from the text is the idea that (V) the democratic city has a variegated character because the human types that flourish within it exhibit great variety. (V)—which affirms the pluralism entailed by the freedom to which democracy is committed—cannot be expressed in terms of Williams's (P), but its wording is very close to Socrates' own phrasing in (S). Perhaps one reason it did not occur to Williams that (V) is what Socrates meant is because (V) neither says nor implies anything about the identity of rulers in a democracy. Here we simply need to recall the point that Plato, like Tocqueville, is interested as much (if not more) in the whole style of life and scheme of values in a social and political system as in its arrangements for government. So there is no need to accept that he would have wanted to assert Williams's (i) (democracy gets its character from the majority who are its rulers), nor therefore (ii) (the majority must therefore themselves be 'democratic' in character) either.

Williams might still have wished to argue that his main objection to Plato's treatment of democracy still stands: the proposition that variety in the city is due to variety *among* the characters of its citizens is confused with the proposition that it is due to variety *within* the character of each of its citizens. It has been easy to show that it is only the first of these propositions, not the second, that expresses what Plato wanted to say about democracy. At the same time it is not hard to see why someone might suspect that some of his programmatic statements about city and soul *commit* him to asserting the second, too. The reason for the suspicion is that Socrates enunciates (S) at the beginning of Book 8 in order to buttress the proposal that the enquiry should consider not just flawed social and political systems, but flawed dispositions of the soul in individuals that correspond to them. What is more, back in Book 4, after his initial introduction of the analogy of city and soul, Socrates makes some remarks designed to support the project of exploring it that are close in spirit to (S)—for example, the observation that the spiritedness of the Thracians and Scyths can hardly be due to anything except spiritedness in individual Thracians and Scyths.

These moves on Socrates' part might suggest that the right explanation of the spiritedness that is the hallmark of timocracy, for example, would be something potentially to be worked out in terms of the spiritedness of the 'timocratic soul', which he goes on to discuss immediately following his account in Book 8 of the timarchic *politeia*; and the same *mutatis mutandis* with the materialism of oligarchy. On the other hand, what Socrates expressly claims is strictly speaking only that (a) the types of political -ocracy must be expected to have their counterparts in human -ocracies (which in the event turn out to be highly complex), and (b) this is because political systems are derived from the psychological tendencies of its members (i.e. their leading character traits). And as G. R. F. Ferrari has recently argued at length, his principal *point* in picturing and analysing the individual with a timocratic soul in parallel with timocracy, and the individual with an oligarchic soul in parallel with oligarchy, is *not* to promote further understanding of the society in question. As the main moral agenda of the *Republic* dictates, it is primarily to illuminate the psychology of the individual, and more particularly the degeneration and instability that result once reason is no longer in control.[44]

In the case of the democratic soul too, this is again the primary purpose. As we have seen, what gives a democracy the character it has is not the dominance of 'democratic souls' (however they might be defined), but the flourishing presence within it of every kind of soul. Nonetheless, the general expectation of a parallelism between city and soul makes it likely that there will be a particular kind of individual who paradigmatically encapsulates within himself a psychological structure mirroring the variety of democratic society: someone from whose behaviour you could, as it were, read off that variety all at one go—in short, a versatile and superficially attractive Alcibiades or indeed Calliclean figure whose soul leaps in an egalitarian spirit from philosophical to competitive to materialistic enthusiasms. That is what Socrates describes as the fully developed democratic soul, which—as we might say—sums up democracy as a bazaar. This image is not meant to present us with a *typical* example of life under a democracy.[45] In that it does not differ from Socrates' images of a timocratic individual (whose circumstances are in fact so described as to be compatible with virtually any society 'not well governed' (549C)) and an oligarchic individual (too miserly to get very far in politics). They are not designed to be generalizable, but to give a vivid illustration of what it might be like for the inevitably complex life of the soul to be dominated by competitiveness or materialism or a passion for variety.[46]

4. *Democracy and Anarchy*

In his penetrating study of the theory of democracy, Ross Harrison has this to say about a fundamental tension between the idea of government and belief in inalienable individual rights:[47]

If individuals really possess rights upon which no other person or body may legitimately encroach, then it seems that there cannot be any legitimate form of absolute, or sovereign, power. For whether this power be a democracy or a dictatorship, there are still going to be certain things which it may now not legitimately do. Hence it would seem that it is not an absolute power at all; hence the question arises of whether it could be a government.

In his portrayal of democracy in *Republic* 8, Plato seems to have drawn a similar conclusion. If a society really does make freedom for its members the supreme good, so that everyone has license to do what they want (as we saw Socrates explaining above), the society itself will be unable to exercise any authority.[48] It cannot make its citizens hold office, obey officials, perform military service, serve on a jury—or stop them from doing all these things—without abandoning or qualifying its commitment to freedom. So freedom means 'a permissive free-for-all'.[49] Its consequence is anarchy, as Socrates indicates in the summing-up quoted in Section 2: democracy will be 'an agreeable kind of regime—anarchic, colourful, and granting equality of a sort to equals and unequals alike' (*Rep.* 8.558C).

As I have presented Plato's analysis, that is just what it is: a theoretical analysis of what a political system dedicated to maximizing personal freedom would be like. At the same time, we are obviously meant to think of Athens. Indeed Socrates explicitly appeals to experience, confirmed in Adeimantus' reply (8.558A):

'And what about the relaxed attitude of those sentenced by the courts? Isn't it civilized? Or have you never seen people who have been condemned to death or exile in a regime of this kind, who nonetheless remain in person, hanging about at the centre of things, and haunting the place like the spirit of a departed hero, without anyone caring or noticing?'

'I've seen plenty,' he said.

Some commentators take this to be caricature so far-fetched that it misses its target completely. Julia Annas, for example, simply explodes at this point: 'Plato knew that Athenians were not free to disobey the law (Socrates could hardly ignore his death-sentence!).'[50] She continues with fierce strictures on the portrayal of the social position of women at Athens implied a little later in the text. The fact is, however, that as Adam pointed out in his magisterial commentary on the Greek text of the dialogue, the conversation Socrates has with Crito in the *Crito* as he awaits death in his prison cell is throughout conducted on the assumption by both parties that if he wanted to escape, that could be arranged without much difficulty—for him as presumably for others in the same situation.[51] Not for nothing do historians of fifth- and fourth-century Greece discuss as a problem the Athenian state's limited capacity for law enforcement. And there is no doubt that an image of a distinctive easy-going tolerance figured prominently both in Athenian ideology (as in Pericles' funeral speech), and in more hostile or satirical portrayals of Athenian mores (as in Aristophanes and the pamphleteer known as the 'Old Oligarch').[52] On the other hand, Athenian ideology did also set high store by the sovereignty of law. The reality was of course complex, as it would have to be in any actual society.

The question for us is not whether there was more tolerance in Athens than in other contemporary Greek societies, but how far Plato's analysis of democracy as anarchy can accommodate anything but tolerance. In fact there soon emerges a recipe for intolerance.

Socrates develops the theme of anarchy in the passage which introduces the transition from democracy to tyranny. What interests him is freedom's self-destructive dynamic if it is pursued with an insatiable desire, and to the neglect of everything else. He argues that when that happens, respect for rulers, parents or teachers is lost as assertion of freedom and equality takes its place, embracing immigrants, women, slaves, even domestic animals too. What this breeds is no longer the tolerance described earlier, but on one side aggression and contempt, on the other fear and ingratiating behaviour. Socrates sums up (8.563D–E):

'To generalize, then, from all these collected observations, have you noticed how sensitive it makes the souls of the citizens, so that if anyone seeks to impose the slightest degree of slavery, they grow angry and cannot tolerate it? In the end, as I imagine you are aware, they take no notice even of the laws—written or unwritten—in their determination that no one shall be master over them in any way at all.'

'Yes, I am well aware of that,' he said.

Socrates reserves a crucial analytical point to the end (again he represents it as coinciding with Athenian reality). Insistence that freedom should be subject to no restrictions of any kind means that laws and conventions are inevitably regarded (as by Callicles in the *Gorgias*) as the imposition of slavery.

Plato next makes Socrates go on to argue that this state of affairs is unstable, and in particular that conditions are now ripe for the transformation of democracy into tyranny, with 'excessive freedom' being transformed into 'excessive slavery' (*Rep.* 8.564A). The key idea is that civil conflict is becoming inescapable. Socrates suggests that it will be triggered by appropriations of the property of the rich—presumably in consequence of collapse of respect for laws of property. The rich will strike back ('they really do then become oligarchical in outlook, although not intentionally'),[53] with 'impeachments, trials, and legal vendettas', prompting the advent of a strongman as champion of the people (*Rep.* 8.565B–C). It is hard to think that this is the only scenario that could develop from the initial conditions (Plato's thoughts at this point were apparently preoccupied with the rise to power of Peisistratus, and even more of Dionysius I in Sicily).[54] But if elevation of freedom to supreme good means that everyone is entitled to assert themselves without legal or other restrictions, some version of the war of all against all surely is inevitable.

What appears to be left out of Plato's account of democratic freedom as anarchy is the very idea of democracy, i.e. rule *by the people*. The emphasis of the treatment of democracy in Book 8 is on its ambitions and successes in promoting the personal freedom of individuals, not (as in the *Gorgias* and the analogies of Book 6) on the *dêmos* in assembly as a mass audience requiring the servile attention of political orators. The idea that the people in democratic assemblies and courts could indeed make momentous and effective decisions on war and peace, life and death, seems in danger of being forgotten. Socrates does in fact have something to say on the topic, in the course of his description of the onset of class conflict. He remarks that the largest section of the *dêmos*—manual labourers who are politically inactive and own little property—are the biggest and most important group in a democracy when it assembles. But he and Adeimantus agree that it has little incentive to meet provided the politicians ensure as they do that some of the pickings from their depredations of the wealthy come its way (*Rep.* 8.565A–B). So the issue is raised—tangentially, and without any theoretical engagement—only to be consigned to relative insignificance. It is not readily accommodated within Plato's project here: of demonstrating the consequences of making freedom the supreme value. He does seem to have taken the view that democracy was intrinsically weak when considered simply as a *form* of government (however monstrous its totalitarian potential as a force for moral corruption in practice, a vision reiterated in a dialogue as late as the *Laws*).[55]

That is the position explicitly adopted in the taxonomy of political systems in the *Statesman* (*Plt.* 303A): 'The rule of the mass we may suppose to be weak in all respects, and capable of nothing of any importance either for good or for bad as judged in relation to the other systems, because of the fact that under democracy offices are distributed in small portions among many people.' The Eleatic Visitor—with an appetite for classification, not apparent in the *Republic*, that is wholly characteristic of him

and the dialogues in which he appears (*Sophist* and *Statesman*)—
has taken over the traditional division into three types of regime
familiar from Herodotus' debate of the Persian nobles (3.80–2),
and has divided each into two: a better and a worse form,
depending on whether rule is in accordance with law or not
(*Plt.* 302B–E).[56] On this basis kingship—as ordinarily experienced, not the rule of the expert statesman—is distinguished
from tyranny, aristocracy from oligarchy, and a better from a
worse form of democracy.[57] The better form of democracy is
declared the worst of the law-governed systems and the best
of the lawless ones—precisely because democracy is relatively
weak as a system. That puts it at a disadvantage when compared
with kingship or aristocracy, but makes it less unattractive than
oligarchy or tyranny (*Plt.* 302A–B). This decidedly schematic
way of looking at politics hardly gives very much cause for any
greater enthusiasm about democracy than is communicated by
the *Gorgias* or the *Republic*.[58]

5. *Democracy and Knowledge*

5.1 The *Statesman*

The *Gorgias* had argued that rhetoric—perceived as something
woven inextricably into the conduct of democratic politics—is
no form of knowledge or expertise.[59] Is there however a form
of knowledge which *could* underpin democratic government?
The *Republic* assumes not. Nothing is said on the matter in the
discussion of democracy in Book 8—another issue not readily
assimilated in its agenda. But Book 6—particularly in the ship
of state analogy (487A–489A)—is clear that a regime without
philosophy deprives itself of any access to real knowledge.[60] A
more searching examination of the question is undertaken in
two dialogues which explicitly consider the role of knowledge
in ruling: the late *Statesman* and the much earlier *Protagoras*.
The final verdict is both times in the negative—but not before
Plato has considered the possibility of a specifically 'democratic' knowledge.

The main point Plato makes in the *Statesman* about all the
'not correct' forms of constitution that it classifies—including
democracy (whether in a law-governed or a lawless version)—is

their incommensurability with the one 'right' system: rule by someone who commands political knowledge or statesmanship. Of all Plato's charges against democracy, its inability to accommodate true political knowledge is the most fundamental as well as the most Socratic. To press it home with maximum force and vividness, he reuses the *Republic*'s ship of state analogy. Having proposed that 'the truest criterion of right management of a city—the one according to which the wise and the good man will manage what belongs to those being ruled'—is whether it is or is not advantageous to them, the principal participant in the discussion (the Eleatic Visitor) spells out the conception of wisdom he has in mind (*Plt.* 296E–297B):

A navigator, always watching out for what is to the benefit of the ship and the sailors, preserves his fellow-sailors not by putting things down in writing but providing his expertise as law. So too in the same fashion a political system would be right, would it not, if it issued from those who are able to rule like that, providing in the strength of their expertise something more powerful than the laws? And in all they do wise rulers will make no mistake, provided they keep their eye on one great thing: if they always follow justice in making distributions to those in the city by intelligent application of their expertise, they will then be able both to preserve them and to turn them from worse into better people so far as is possible.

But (*Plt.* 297B–C):

No collection whatever of people en masse would ever be able to acquire this kind of expert knowledge and manage a city with intelligence. We must look instead within a small element in the population—to a few or to the one—to find the one right system. And we must count the other systems as imitations, some imitating it for the better, some for the worse.

This is an old Socratic theme. Way back in the *Laches* Socrates was saying (184C): 'What is going to be decided well must, I think, be decided on the basis of knowledge not numbers.' And in *Crito* he had memorably propounded the thesis that, as in matters of physical health we consult a doctor, so in regard to what is just and admirable and good and their opposites we must pay no attention to what the many say, but look to the person 'who knows about justice and injustice—the one and the truth itself' (*Crito* 48A). We shall be considering Plato's treatment of the topic of political knowledge much more fully in Chapter 4.

Whether democracy could rescue any conception of political knowledge for itself is the question to be pursued here.

The *Statesman* explores the issue of political knowledge and democracy in a further elaboration of the ship and doctor analogies (in the interests of simplicity I shall mostly stick to the ship in what follows).[61] In the *Republic* version of the ship all that matters to the ignorant sailors—i.e. democratic politicians—who contend with each other for control of the vessel is *getting* control. How to steer it once they have control is not anything that figures in their concerns, and they have no conception of what expertise in navigation might be like. They would regard anyone who really had the knowledge of winds, seasons and stars needed for it as useless, a 'stargazer', just 'babbling away' (*Rep.* 6.488D–489A). The *Statesman*, by contrast, imagines a scenario designed to capture the best that either democracy or oligarchy is capable of. This time the sailors, though no less ignorant, *are* properly preoccupied with the problem of actually steering the boat, and they try to tackle it on a rational basis. But expertise in navigation is once again not what they think is needed. Having lost confidence in the navigators they have had in the past, they will have recourse to *rules*, arrived at by a process that has little if anything to do with knowledge or expertise (*Plt.* 298C–E):

Visitor: We should call together an assembly consisting of ourselves— either the people as a whole or only the rich. There should be license both for laymen and craftsmen in general to contribute an opinion on sailing, and on ships and the tackle and instruments and weapons sailors should use both in handling a ship and in coping with the dangers that may confront them, whether it be wind and sea threatening the actual sailing, or encounters with pirates, or if there perhaps had to be a sea battle between triremes. Then whatever view the assembled mass decided on, whether it was navigators or laymen advising them, we should write it down on columns or stone blocks. And we should also agree on some unwritten ancestral customs. These would now be the basis on which we did all our seafaring for all future time.
Young Socrates: What you've said is distinctly odd.

One assumption the Visitor makes is that in the absence of expertise, people are likely to think the nearest they can get to reason or knowledge is by reliance on rules.

One reason young Socrates (no relation) evidently finds the scenario painted by the Visitor odd is that the idea of relying on rules for success in navigation—or politics—is hard to square with what the two of them agreed some pages before (294A–B):

Law could never accurately embrace what is best and most just for all at the same time, and so prescribe the most beneficial course. The dissimilarities between human beings and their behaviour, and the fact that practically nothing in human affairs ever remains stable, prevent any kind of expertise whatsoever from making any simple decision in any sphere that covers all cases and will stay valid for all time.

The truth, as the two interlocutors take to be obvious, is that to keep the ship afloat and on course the ability to improvise is essential. To do that there is no substitute for expertise. But the Visitor argues that in a political system in which it has been agreed to allow no place for expertise in government, only for rules and rule-following, anyone 'found looking into navigation and seafaring over and beyond the written rules' would be called a 'stargazer, a sort of babbling sophist', and brought to court for corrupting young people, to face the extreme penalty if found guilty (*Plt.* 299B–C; the less principled sailors of the *Republic* version of the analogy considered such people simply useless eccentrics). Then follows an observation indicating nonetheless that democracies or oligarchies which take this attitude to expertise might make their own alternative claim to knowledge (299C–D):

For it will be laid down that there must be nothing wiser than the laws—on the basis that no one is ignorant of medicine and health, or navigation and seafaring, since it is open to anyone who wants it to understand written rules and established ancestral customs.

In other words, and to cash out the analogies, knowledge of the relevant rules—laws and customs—is all the knowledge there is to be had so far as politics is concerned.

That is presented as the closest a democracy or an oligarchy could ever get to acknowledging the existence of any such thing as political knowledge. Plato doubtless thinks its absurd inadequacy will be obvious. But he goes on to represent the Visitor as imagining a world in which *all* areas of knowledge were conceived in this way, and the younger Socrates brings the absurdity out explicitly. In that case, he says, all forms of expertise would be lost irretrievably, and 'life, which even now is difficult, would then be altogether unlivable' (*Plt.* 299E–300A). This goes too far, in the Visitor's opinion. He responds (a) that things would be even worse if those elected or appointed to jobs by lot simply *ignored* the rules, for mercenary motives of one sort or another. At least the rules will have been established through trial and error, deliberation and popular consent (300A–B). A little later, he suggests (b) that in the political realm, while the troubles suffered by cities which operate 'according to written rules and customs without knowledge' are remarkable, it is no less remarkable that though ships sailed on similar principles would sink, some cities governed that way have a sort of natural resilience that enables them to survive indefinitely (301E–302A).[62] Ignoring all this would be a massive mistake (300B). But it is what happens often enough in the politics of existing oligarchies and democracies—depraved and hugely ignorant politicians destroy their cities because they think they have true political knowledge (302A–B).[63]

It is clear from Plato's handling of the issue that laws and customs established by trial and error, deliberation and popular consent are not what *he* would regard as knowledge. At the same time he appears to concede that in a democracy or oligarchy they might be regarded as constituting a body of wisdom and expertise. There is an interesting affinity here with the idea of 'democratic knowledge' that Josiah Ober has recently proposed in his interpretation of Athenian ideology of the late fifth and fourth centuries BC.[64] Ober identifies as central elements in the ideology: (1) the innate superiority of the Athenians; (2) the ideal of political equality; (3) the desirability of consensus and freedom of public speech; (4) the superior wisdom of collective decisions; (5) the threat that elite citizens pose to democracy (even though they are regarded as indispensable participants in its processes). And he suggests that this ideology operated as a socially and politically constructed Foucauldian 'regime of truth'—providing the basis on which the city decided what was true and false, how that was determined and sanctioned, and who had what authority to determine it. Hence in the Athenian democracy it had achieved the status of knowledge.

The overlap with what Plato in the *Statesman* takes to be 'wisdom' in an oligarchy or democracy is obviously not total (indeed items (1), (2) and (5) on Ober's list are specific to Athens and to democracy). But the coincidences are significant enough. In particular, items (3) to (5)—if we interpreted 'elite' as 'intellectual elite'—map well enough on to Plato's analysis. Plato stresses the empiricist underpinning of this 'wisdom'—not its social construction. This is only superficially at odds with Ober's approach. Ober allows that the Athenians themselves would have supposed that 'democratic knowledge' was in large measure discovered and validated by performative experience, and sustained by their own willingness to defend it in practice.

5.2 The *Protagoras*

In a much earlier dialogue Plato had seriously explored a notion comparable with 'democratic knowledge' or with a wisdom rooted in norms acquired by experience—in the *Protagoras*. The *Protagoras* stages a confrontation between Socrates and the leading sophist Protagoras. After some preliminaries, discussion focuses on Protagoras' claim to be a teacher of virtue. Like other sophists, in the intellectual climate of the late fifth century his credentials as one of the new educators of Greece depended on its being accepted that virtue is a field of *technê* or expertise like any other (from mathematics and medicine to navigation), and on agreement that it is not just a gift of nature or something acquired by practice, but knowledge you can learn from a teacher. The virtue he himself undertook to impart is described more specifically as 'wisdom in dealing with one's own affairs, so as to manage one's own household to best advantage, and also with the city's affairs, so as to become a real power in the city, in the spheres of speech and action alike' (*Prot.* 318E–319A). Socrates disputes the claim in the first instance by arguing that experience of the way politics is conducted in democratic Athens implies that such wisdom *cannot* be taught, at any rate as the Athenians think. In short, democratic practice poses a serious question mark over Protagoras' entire educational prospectus.

Protagoras' answer to it constitutes a remarkable if implicit articulation of a concept of democratic knowledge. Before we can consider that answer, however, we need to spend some time on the question. The issue turns on the notion of *technê* (expertise). Socrates gets Protagoras first to agree that what he has in mind by wisdom here is a sort of political *technê*, which is then spelled out as the capacity to make men 'good citizens'. His main counter-argument (A) consists in pointing out the huge difference between the way the popular assembly behaves when it wants advice on some specialist topic (such as the construction of buildings or ships), and how it deliberates on the management of the city's affairs. In the one case, the Athenians call on craftsmen (builders, shipwrights), and howl down non-experts. In the other, they allow anyone at all to advise them—rich or poor, of good family or none—and nobody objects that the speaker hasn't learned or had a teacher. We have to infer, says Socrates, that they do not consider the giving of political advice a subject for expertise, and that they think the ability to give it cannot therefore be learned or taught (*Prot.* 319A–D).

He adds a supplementary argument (B), which seems to have been something of a commonplace of controversy at the time. The best and wisest politicians—he mentions Pericles here (in a very different tone of voice from the *Gorgias*); in the *Meno*, Themistocles, Aristides and Thucydides, son of Melesias, as well[65]—have their sons well educated in activities for which teachers are available (*Meno* 93A–94E). But Pericles doesn't himself educate his sons in his own field of political wisdom, nor does he send them to anyone else for this purpose. The obvious inference from this and argument (B) is that virtue *cannot* be taught (319D–320C).

Interestingly enough, the whole issue is recapitulated in the *Republic*'s version of the ship analogy. Of the sailors who correspond to democratic politicians, Socrates says four things relating to the art of navigation, i.e. expertise in ruling: (1) they have never learned the skill; (2) they cannot point to anybody as their teacher, nor to any period of time when they were learning it; (3) they say the skill cannot be taught; and (4) they are ready to tear into anyone who says it can. This goes further than the argument put by Socrates in the *Protagoras*. The unteachability of the skill of politics is no longer something just inferred from the way democracy and its politicians operate. The ship analogy attributes to the politicians what they would have had to say about themselves if they had drawn that inference themselves. In that sense it strips away the illusions, and reveals them as hungry only for power. At the same time, it is obvious that in contrasting them with the true navigator, i.e. the philosopher who really does understand what ruling consists in, Plato's Socrates takes it for granted that the knowledge the philosopher commands *can* be taught. The educational programme in mathematics and dialectic sketched in Books 6 and 7 of the *Republic*, and the celebrated images of the line and the cave, will provide some of the underpinning supporting that assumption.

———

127

In other words, on the teachability issue, the Socrates of the *Republic* is in the same camp as Protagoras. This lends colour to the suspicion that Socrates' arguments in the *Protagoras against* the thesis that virtue can be taught represent a debating posture, not his or Plato's own considered view. Already by the end of the dialogue he will have established a theoretical basis of his own for concluding that virtue is nothing other than a form of knowledge. And at that point he acknowledges that it looks after all as though he ought to agree that it is teachable. In which case he would also need to go back and question the arguments—(A) and (B)—which led to the opposite conclusion. It is easy enough to imagine how a Socratic or Platonic reconsideration of (A) and (B) might go. These arguments are premised explicitly (if doubtless ironically) on the hypotheses that the Athenian democracy conducts its politics wisely, and that Pericles is a good and wise politician. The *Gorgias* and *Republic* supply plenty of evidence that Plato took both of these propositions to be false.[66]

In the *Protagoras*, Protagoras is represented as offering a way of resisting (A) and (B) that leaves democratic assumptions about politics intact. Discussion of (A) is more relevant to our purposes in this chapter, so I shall focus solely on the response Protagoras makes to (A). In taking on this challenge, he first tells a myth of the origins of civilization. Natural abilities and various acquired competences and skills were bestowed on humans, but it subsequently transpired that they could not live together in the cities they built for protection against wild beasts, because they had no expertise in politics. Zeus asks Hermes to distribute justice and respect among them, for otherwise their survival is in jeopardy. Hermes is told to make the distribution not as though these were specialist skills (like medicine), where a single doctor will be adequate for a particular community, but universally. These are attributes *everyone* must have if there are to be cities. The moral is that goodness in a citizen (which is what Protagoras has promised to teach) is at its core justice—proper social behaviour—and everybody in the society has to have acquired a measure of it if the society is to survive.

How, then, is it acquired? Protagoras turns from myth to commentary on it. He now argues that the whole society inculcates virtue in people from childhood up, by a combination of habituation and instruction supported by punishments and rewards (he himself simply has a particular facility in this regard, not specialist knowledge of a different kind). *Everyone* is a teacher of virtue, just as everyone in the society teaches Greek by talking it all the time—Socrates has missed this, because he assumes it is a specialist skill needing to be taught by a specialist. That being so, then contrary to (A) the Athenians are right to think that virtue is teachable, and to assume that since everybody is taught it, everybody has what it takes to give political advice.

The argument Plato puts in Protagoras' mouth here has been much discussed and long admired as in effect the most penetrating theoretical defence of democracy to survive in ancient Greek literature.[67] Its strength lies in its strategy of rooting democracy in the basic conditions that have to be satisfied if there are to be communities of any size and complexity at all. The social virtue necessary for the existence of a political system is the social virtue sufficient for active participation in its decision processes. What *must* be universally distributed to satisfy the existence condition is for that very reason universally *available* for purposes of decision-making. It follows that if it is to be taught as knowledge, non-specialist conceptions of both teaching and knowledge have to be developed to account for that. We might describe these as performative: teaching is effected mostly by a range of basic methods universally employed for influencing *behaviour*, and what someone educated in this way knows is *how to behave*.

Particularly in passages devoted to description of the detail of the operation of these educational methods, and the effects they are intended to achieve, there is material which Plato will exploit elsewhere, notably in Socrates' account in *Republic* 2 and 3 of the education in poetry, music and gymnastics that the guards are to receive. Plato clearly thinks that basic character training has to take the form Protagoras describes. But it needs little reflection to see why he could not have thought Protagoras' argument an adequate defence of democratic politics. There is simply more to political decision-making than elementary justice and respect for others, even if (as passages quoted above from the *Statesman* make clear) justice is the ultimate criterion of a right decision. Ruling—navigation, in the ship of state analogy—requires a theoretical and practical understanding far beyond the basics of morality. It is simply a fudge on Protagoras' part to proceed as though, in demonstrating a universal capacity for justice, he has shown ability to participate also in 'the rest of political virtue'.

This is no doubt why, in the long cross-examination he now has to undergo, Socrates presses him so hard on what precisely he counts as virtue, on the interrelation between its different ingredients and, above all, on the place of knowledge in virtue.

6. Conclusion

In Book 8 of the *Republic* Plato reveals himself as a writer and thinker who sees democracy from the inside as well as from the elevated standpoint of his philosophical ideals. While he does not like what he sees, his insight into the pluralism of democracy and its potential for anarchy generates a powerful and original piece of socio-political analysis, which owes something of its energy and wit to democracy itself.[68] His picture of oligarchy is a glummer affair, as its subject matter dictated. His perspective here (as in aspects of his treatment of timarchy) incorporates views that had long been current—not least in Athenian democratic discourse. In the *Statesman* and *Protagoras* we seem to catch a glimpse of democracy trying to argue back at him. But as soon as the incipient argument pretends that democracy is underpinned by knowledge, its limitations are represented as palpable.

If democratic knowledge turns out to be an illusion, what exactly is Plato's alternative? So far we have seen him sketching an answer primarily by means of analogy between the navigator (or the doctor) and the statesman or the philosopher. But is statesmanship the same thing as philosophy? Or is it a form of expertise in its own right? This is the principal question to be explored in Chapter 4.

Notes

1. Throughout much of the history of Western civilization disfavour was dominant: see Roberts 1994.
2. As indeed in Book 3 of Plato's *Laws*: see Section 3 of Ch. 2.
3. See in general Lanza 1977; Giorgini 1993; Morgan 2003.
4. In attempting to ingratiate himself with the Spartans, here Alcibiades distances himself from democracy. He will describe it a few lines later as 'acknowledged folly' (6.89.6).
5. See Raaflaub 2003.

6. There will be some comments in Section 4 of the chapter on Plato's appropriation and elaboration of the tripartite scheme of one/few/many in the *Statesman*.
7. See Raaflaub 1990: 41–5; Pelling 2003.
8. Brock and Hodkinson 2000: 17.
9. See Osborne 2003.
10. Readers would not have been surprised to find oligarchy, democracy and tyranny listed: as we have seen, the triadic scheme was already familiar, as shown by its use in Pindar and Herodotus. But the identification of a fourth category—timarchy—is an original move on Plato's part, no doubt born of conviction that the very distinctive form of society found in Crete and (especially) Sparta could not easily be accommodated within the scheme, as well as from the need of his overall project for an analogue of the rule of the spirited element in the soul. Plato's scheme has some affinities with that offered in Xenophon, *Memorabilia* 4.6.12, inasmuch as Xenophon too recognizes five *politeiai*: kingship, tyranny, aristocracy, plutocracy (another name for Plato's oligarchy) and democracy. But Xenophon distinguishes between his five in terms (law and consent or their absence, and eligibility for office) much more consistently constitutional than does Plato. For discussion see Sinclair 1951: 169–71.
11. The parallels with Dionysius are usefully assembled in Adam's commentary: Adam 1902: II.257–61.
12. As has often been noted, Plato makes no attempt here to describe the unique and highly complicated Spartan constitutional system. For discussion of the point, see D. Frede 1996: 260–2. She comments aptly that Plato is not doing political science or empirical sociology but genealogy of morals.
13. See Hodkinson 2000: ch. 13.
14. 'Herodotus attaches more stories (eight in total) of potential, alleged and actual gift or receipt of bribes to Sparta than any other Greek state' (namely, at 3.56, 3.148, 5.51, 6.50, 6.66, 6.72, 6.82, 8.5): Hodkinson 1994: 185.
15. See Bradford 1994: 59–85; Hesk 2000: ch. 1.
16. So Hodkinson 2000: 432; cf. 31–2. Xenophon is a notable proponent of this point of view: see *Lac. Pol.* 14.
17. Aristotle reiterates the claim at *Pol.* 5.10, 1311a9–11. But as W. L. Newman points out (1887–1902: 4.xxxiv), he sometimes treats the pursuit of gain as more characteristic of 'the many' (*Pol.* 2.7, 1266b38–1267a1, 6.3, 1318b16–17); and he objects against Plato that it is absurd to think that oligarchies come into being because those in office are money-lovers (*Pol.* 5.12, 1316a39–b6).
18. See Thucydides 8.65.3, on the oligarchic party's claim at the time of the revolution of 411 BC (also the Aristotelian *Ath. Pol.* 29.5). For discussion of oligarchic ideology, see Brock and Hodkinson 2000: 16–20.
19. See here the analysis offered by D. Frede 1996: 262, 266–9.
20. The *Seventh Letter* (324D–325A) represents the episode of the thirty as particularly traumatic and formative for Plato. This is likely enough to be true whether or not Plato was himself the author of the letter.
21. For the evidence, see Balot 2001: 219–24.
22. For fuller exploration of Plato's psychology of money, see Ch. 6 below.

23. This sentence is strikingly reminiscent of what Thucydides famously says about *stasis* during the Peloponnesian War (where there is no presumption that change between oligarchy and democracy was in only one direction): see 3.82.1.
24. As Dorothea Frede points out, Plato could hardly have expected his readers to believe that this is how democracy at Athens emerged (D. Frede 1996: 262–3).
25. Machiavelli thought very similarly (*Discorsi*, 1.40): 'When a people is induced to make the mistake of holding someone in high esteem because he is down on those whom they hold in detestation, and *that* someone has his wits about him, it will always happen that a tyranny will arise in that city. For he will wait until, with the support of the populace, he has got rid of the nobility, and will not begin to oppress the people until he has got rid of it, by which time the populace will have come to realize that it is a slave and will have no way to escape.'
26. Gill 1977: 300. He compares *Rep.* 8.545D–E, 547A–B, with *Critias* 108C. See also Adam 1902: II.195–6, whose balanced treatment of the issues can seldom have been bettered.
27. D. Frede 1996: 266–7.
28. D. Frede 1996: 268.
29. The concepts of rejectionist and immanent critique were introduced in Ch. 2, Section 1.1, with acknowledgement to Walzer 1987.
30. See Section 3.3 of Ch. 2 for discussion of manifestations of this idea in Platonic dialogues.
31. See, for example, Ostwald 1969; Vlastos 1964; Raaflaub 1996.
32. Raaflaub 1996: 141.
33. Raaflaub 1996: 142. He is referring to the claim in *Pol.* 3.13, 1284a19, that 'cities with a democratic regime are thought to aim at equality above everything else', as elaborated at *Pol.* 6.2, 1317b17–1318a10.
34. Here I am following Raaflaub 1983 rather than Hansen 1996 (on which, see Raaflaub 1996: 162 n. 27, 163 n. 44).
35. Raaflaub 1983: 521.
36. See Dunn 2005: 130–8, 160–72; quotation from p. 184, repeated from Ch. 2, Section 1.3. The demise of deference is precisely what Plato highlights when he visualizes not just sons treating their fathers and pupils their teachers with contempt, but even horses and donkeys when they barge into passers-by who fail to get out of their way (*Rep.* 8.562E–563D).
37. Notice the consequences for deference already implicit in the formula: 'granting equality of a sort to equals and unequals alike'.
38. This assessment is close to that offered by D. Frede 1996: 263–5, 267–8, although she does not think anyone in Athens would have been persuaded by the satire as satire (as distinct from the argument's force as *reductio ad absurdum* of the democratic ideal). Perhaps Plato (like Aristophanes) was hoping to amuse, not persuade people that Athens really was like that. However I suspect that he would have found quite a bit of agreement with the main thrust of the satire: that there was no longer enough deference in Athens, nor the cultural basis for inculcating it effectively.

39. It is simply taken for granted that in a democracy virtually everyone is making money (8.564E). For further discussion of money and desire, see Ch. 6, especially Sections 2 and 3.
40. This point is well taken by Mitchell and Lucas 2003, who entitle their chapter on the *Republic*'s treatment of democracy 'Plato and Pluralism'.
41. Roochnik 2003: 79. Cf. e.g. Griswold 1999: 116; Monoson 2000: 166–8.
42. Williams 1973: 201–3. I am responsible for the representation of his interpretation in terms of an argument via steps (1) to (iii) below to his conclusion.
43. Williams 1973: 201.
44. See Ferrari 2003: chs 2 and 3; cf. also D. Frede 1996: 269–74—although she posits a stronger link between individual characterizations and the corresponding societies than does Ferrari.
45. This point is well made by D. Frede 1996: 271. Her interesting suggestion that Plato is meaning to portray a typical member of the elite in a democratic society (ibid. pp. 271–2) is more debatable. Nobody but a member of the elite would have the leisure and resources for the democratic man's lifestyle. But what is 'typical' about him is the way the pluralism of democratic society is mirrored in his personality.
46. For puzzles about the source of the passion for variety within the structure of the soul, see Cooper 1984: 10–12; Scott 2000: 22–6. The issue is briefly discussed below, in Section 3 of Ch. 6.
47. Harrison 1993: 141.
48. This analysis is endorsed as the basis for a critique of contemporary pluralism by Mitchell and Lucas 2003: ch. 9. They argue that various features of a more mature democracy—such as the need for a common morality with an authority independent of the law of the state, or for accepted canons of rational debate and criticism through the operation of a free press—'depend fundamentally upon a "platonic" conception of an objective good together with a human capacity to recognise it' (ibid. pp. 123–4).
49. Annas 1981: 300.
50. Annas 1981: 300.
51. Adam 1902: II.236 (on 558A3).
52. Plato has Socrates join in the fun (8.563C–D): 'You wouldn't believe, without seeing it for yourself, how much more free domestic animals are here than in other cities. Dogs really *are* like the women who own them, as the proverb says. And horses and donkeys are in the habit of wandering the streets with total freedom, noses in the air, barging into any passer-by who fails to get out of their way. It's all like that—all full of freedom.' Adeimantus says he's often experienced just that on his way out of the city.
53. A revealing remark and an even more revealing qualification, confirming Dorothea Frede's contention (D. Frede 1996: 266–9) that Plato's account of oligarchy (as of the other regimes) and the oligarchic personality delineates an ideal type, which actual oligarchs are not necessarily focused or consistent enough to exemplify.
54. See Adam 1902: II.257, on 566D.
55. See *Laws* 3.700A–701D, with its famous description of the extreme democracy Athens has become as a 'depraved theatocracy': discussed in Ch. 2, Section 3.2, above.

56. For him these are all 'incorrect' forms of constitution (302B) by comparison to the only correct form: rule by someone with *expertise* in statesmanship (*Plt.* 291D–293E; cf. e.g. 301C–D)—on which see Section 5.1 and Ch. 4 below. Aristotle presents a different but similar bipartition of the tripartite scheme in *Politics* 3.7. This is just one of a number of affinities between the *Statesman* and Aristotle's *Ethics* and *Politics* which make it tempting to sense in them differing reflections of debates within the early Academy.

57. Aristotle distinguishes better from worse according as rule is in the common interest or in that of the ruling individual or faction. Cf. *Laws* 4.715B.

58. C. Griswold has more than once suggested that Plato is pointing us 'to constitutional democracy composed of free citizens as the "best" regime for the current cycle of the cosmos'. See e.g. Griswold 1999: 123; cf. e.g. Versenyi 1971: 234–6; and Monoson 2000: 120. This suggestion assumes that the Visitor does not consider kingship or aristocracy—as just defined—practicable options, with consequent damage to his entire analysis, as T. Samaras points out: see Samaras 2002: 196 n. 19. Resentment at the thought that there could ever be someone willing and able to rule with virtue and expert knowledge is what explains the actual situation (*gegone* vs. *genomenon an*), as the Visitor sees it: rule by tyrants, kings, oligarchy, aristocracy, democracy—all are listed without distinctions between them (301C–D).

59. See Ch. 2, Section 2.

60. See the brief discussion in Section 3 of Ch. 1, pp. 29–30.

61. The Visitor does not explicitly state that he has democracy in particular in his sights, but the cumulation of references to political institutions and processes which were highly characteristic of democratic Athens, if not unique to it, makes it clear enough what moral the reader should draw. See e.g. Dusanic 1995.

62. Sparta—famous in antiquity for the durability of its political system (see e.g. Polybius, *Histories* 6.10)—is probably the example uppermost in Plato's mind. As his explicit discussion of contemporary democratic Athens in the *Laws* makes crystal clear (3.700A–701E), he continued to regard his own city as well on the way to extreme lawlessness and terminal disaster.

63. Plato's view of democracy therefore remains critical in the extreme in the *Statesman*. The best to be hoped for is that if it operated 'according to written rules and customs without knowledge', it might survive bloodied but unbowed indefinitely. Operating in that way is the nearest it could get—clearly not near at all—to 'imitating well that true constitution of the person ruling with expertise' (300E–301A). For difficulties in interpreting the text of *Plt.* 300–303, and for the approach taken to them here, see Rowe 2001. For another treatment (and criticism of earlier studies on *Plt.* 291–303 by Rowe), see Michelini 2000.

64. Ober 1998: 33–6.

65. A politician contemporary with Pericles, and his main adversary before his period of total dominance; not the author of the *History of the Peloponnesian War*.

66. A similar assessment is probably appropriate for the *Meno*, which has often been read as a sequel to the *Protagoras*. To its main question—can virtue be taught?—Plato's Socrates ends up returning the answer that it is not

knowledge and therefore not anything taught, but 'a gift from the gods that is not accompanied by understanding, unless there is someone among our statesmen who can make another into a statesman' (99E–100A). This verdict is compatible with the view that the best of the statesmen we actually have—Themistocles and Pericles have again been discussed—have no knowledge and therefore no *real* virtue, but that if there *were* someone possessed of true virtue, that virtue would be a knowledge that is teachable. For further discussion, see e.g. Guthrie 1975: 236–65.

67. See e.g. Prior 2002, which provides a selective review of the literature. Prior holds that the argument is probably Plato's work, not Protagoras'. But many scholars think otherwise: see e.g. Guthrie 1969: 63–8, 265–6; Kerferd 1981: chs 11 and 12. I incline to the view that while Protagorean material may underlie the myth in particular, its use by Plato to provide democracy with a theoretical basis is Plato's own idea. In any event, Plato represents the speech as a sophistic performance by a thinker who himself had only contempt for the intelligence of 'the many': see *Prot.* 317A, 352D–353A.

68. J. Adam went so far as to claim that 'Plato's whole account of democracy and the democratical man (557A–565C), in spite of manifest exaggerations, brings Athens nearer to us than almost any monument of ancient literature, Aristophanes alone excepted': see Adam 1902: II.234. He added sagely: 'We can see that Plato was fully alive to the wonderful variety and colour of Athenian life; but even on this ground democracy did not appear to him worthy of praise. Multiplicity and variety are the offspring of that fatal *anhomoiotês* [unlikeness: 547C; cf. 4.444B] which works ruin alike in the city and the soul.'

4

The Rule of Knowledge

1. Philosophy or Political Expertise?

'Understanding the world in which we live', wrote John Dunn in 1992,[1] 'requires an extravagantly complicated division of cognitive labour—perhaps a more complicated division than human beings are capable of creating, and certainly one far more complicated and trustworthy than they have yet contrived to create.' The experience of the intervening years has only served to confirm the assessment. The global scale of the challenges to understanding—whether we think of the economic system, or climate change, or terrorism—is apparent in every news bulletin every day of the week. Getting that understanding and putting it to effective use is a political necessity of increasing urgency.

Dunn went on to formulate one fundamental aspect of the problem in decidedly Platonic terms:[2] 'How exactly should we see the relation between science or knowledge and the claims of different human beings to be equipped to rule, or even to decide between the merits of different possible rulers?' He commented: 'It is a singularly difficult question, and we do not as yet have any coherent idea of how to answer it with the slightest authority.' He added that it is 'a question that has largely been stricken from the public record of modern democratic life'. Democracy was devised to secure 'the avoidance of direct subjugation', not 'the steady genesis of valid understanding'. But Plato's insistent question—in one form or another—demands an answer.

His own answer to it, of course, is unlikely to find acceptance anywhere today, even if it were adequate. Plato himself was only too well aware that the *Republic*'s hypothesis—a ruler with the requisite knowledge, legitimated as ruler precisely on account of that knowledge—was utopian: a possibility not likely to be realized.[3] Nonetheless reading him may still be illuminating, not for grappling with the problem of how to bring it about that knowledge is effective in government, but for engaging with the prior question of what kind or kinds of knowledge or understanding are needed. Two answers, not one, seem to recur in Plato's writings. One is the idea of a specifically political expertise, managing the knowledge and skills of other experts. The other is the idea of philosophical wisdom, particularly moral wisdom.

Both ideas have contemporary resonances. A significant element in President G. W. Bush's attractiveness to the American electorate[4] has arguably been the belief that he represented an ideal of leadership rooted in a sound moral and religious philosophy.[5] At the same time he has been perceived as taking a stance against big government, i.e. against extensive management of the economy and civil society on the part of the state, and unenthusiastic about policies that are 'science-led'. On the other hand, once societies as different as Spain and Russia liberated themselves from the ideologies of conservative authoritarian regimes, the changes introduced by or under the successor regimes have often been spearheaded by 'technocrats', usually free-market economists. The assumption here is that the pace and complexity of the world in which these states now aspire to flourish are such that management of change based on expertise is indispensable.

These beliefs are only the latest incarnations of ideas that have been current for much longer. In this chapter they will be explored initially (Section 2) in the writings of two British thinkers—J. S. Mill and Benjamin Jowett—who epitomize high Victorian confidence in the power of reason and its prospects for shaping society. Both draw inspiration from Plato: Mill primarily from the concept of 'scientific' management of government in the *Statesman*; Jowett from the ideal of the philosopher as true statesman in *Gorgias* and *Republic*.[6] Sections 3 and 4 then turn to the text of Plato himself. Section 3 examines the earliest and heavily problematized appearances of the political expert in the dialogues: in *Charmides* and *Euthydemus*. Section 4 considers what precisely it is about philosophy as conceived in *Republic* that equips a philosopher to be a ruler. It has not always been appreciated that two very different conceptions of knowledge in politics are in play in these different contexts. How Plato conceives their relationship—whether he even considers them compatible—is the issue addressed in Sections 5 and 6, which are devoted to a treatment of the *Statesman* (Section 5) in relation to *Republic* and *Laws* (Section 6). Finally, Section 7 attempts to sum up some key differences in the treatment of knowledge in the political projects of these three dialogues.

2. *Mill and Jowett on Plato*

2.1 Mill's 'scientific governor'

In 1866 John Stuart Mill, whose reading of Plato in Greek had begun in early boyhood, published a long review in the *Edinburgh Review* of the three volumes of *Plato and the other Companions of Socrates* (which had appeared the previous year) by his friend and fellow radical George Grote.[7] Mill reread the entire Platonic corpus, in Greek again, in preparation for the task. He found himself, he said, in almost total agreement with the interpretation and assessment given in Grote's work, which was the first serious presentation of Plato ever offered to an English readership. It remains a classic treatment still repaying study—one of the 'few indestructibles', as Guthrie's *History of Greek Philosophy* put it a century later.[8] What Mill himself provided in the review has been aptly described as 'a majestic survey' of Plato's philosophical oeuvre[9] along largely Grotean lines: combining deep admiration for the Socratic method with a warier attitude to Platonic metaphysics. Whereas Grote highlighted Plato's rejection of the sophists and all their works, Mill made 'commonplace'—'the acceptance of traditional opinions and current sentiments as an ultimate fact'—his chief enemy.[10] And the one point on which he explicitly flagged divergence was over Grote's endorsement of Protagorean relativism. 'Each man', Grote had said, 'has a standard, an ideal of truth in his own mind; but different men have different standards.'[11] To which Mill replied: 'Of the proof of truth, yes; but not, we apprehend, of truth itself. No one means anything by truth, but the agreement of a belief with the fact which it purports to represent.'[12]

After wrestling with Plato's own epistemology, the review moved to its climax with Mill's discussion of Plato's ethical and political doctrines—'really the only ones which can be regarded as serious and deeply-rooted convictions'—in contrast, for example, with the theory of Ideas and the doctrine of Reminiscence which in due course 'drop[s] out of his speculations'.[13] Mill focuses on just one element in those 'serious' doctrines: something that he evidently found powerfully attractive. This is the role Plato assigns to knowledge in ethics and especially politics. Mill sees Plato as exalting knowledge, 'not Intellect, or mere mental ability, of which there is no idolatry at all in Plato, but scientific knowledge, and scientifically-acquired craftsmanship, as the one thing needful in every concern of life, and pre-eminently in government'. It is for him 'the pervading idea in Plato's practical doctrines'.[14]

For Mill, the Platonic theory of moral and political knowledge has its strong and weak sides. He starts with the strong side:[15]

First, the vigorous assertion of a truth, of transcendent importance and universal application—that the work of government is a Skilled Employment; that governing is not a thing which can be done at odd times, or by the way, in conjunction with a hundred other pursuits, nor to which a person can be competent without a large and liberal general education, followed by special and professional study, laborious and of long duration, directed to acquiring, not mere practical dexterity, but a scientific mastery of the subject.

Where Plato went wrong was in postulating 'infallibility, or something near it, in rulers thus prepared', and in ascribing 'such a depth of comparative imbecility to the rest of mankind, as to unfit them for any voice whether in their own government, or any power of calling their scientific rulers to account'. But Mill clearly thought that if the balance is redressed to accommodate these criticisms, the basic idea of the professionalization of government survives intact as a valid principle of highest significance.

Mill's endorsement of 'the demand for a Scientific Governor'[16] could not have pleased Grote, who, as a champion of Athenian democracy and a subscriber to Protagorean relativism about knowledge and truth, thoroughly disliked this dimension of Platonism, and compared the proposal for a 'scientific dictator' responsible for legislation in the *Laws* to 'the persecuting spirit of self-satisfied infallibility of medieval Catholicism and the Inquisition'.[17] Nonetheless, in articulating his conception of the science Plato had in mind, Mill was clearly inspired by Grote's eloquent account of the relevant sequence of argument in the *Statesman*[18]—it is the longest quotation he makes from *Plato and the other Companions of Socrates*.[19] Of particular interest is his own definition (prefaced to the quotation) of what he took the *Statesman* to mean by science: 'a philosophic and reasoned knowledge of human affairs—of what is best for mankind'.[20] Mill's formulation suggests one reason why in the first instance he chose this dialogue rather than the *Republic* to explain the way knowledge figured in Plato's thinking about politics. The knowledge discussed in the *Statesman* can indeed be seen as focused on human affairs. In the *Republic*, by contrast, the knowledge that distinguishes philosophers (and so philosopher rulers) from non-philosophers is undeniably metaphysical knowledge of the eternal and changeless reality of the Ideas.

Mill would have been hard pressed to represent *that* as the science of human affairs he thought indispensable to government. To be sure, he sees the *Republic* as developing the same ideal of government as the *Statesman*. When in the passage quoted above he speaks of it as 'not a thing which can be done at odd times, or by the way, in conjunction with a hundred other pursuits, nor to which a person can be competent without a large and liberal general education, followed by special and professional study, laborious and of long duration', he is clearly summarizing the *Republic*. Mill stresses his admiration for the *Republic*'s recognition of the corrupting influence society can exercise on those with the requisite gifts for the task of government, and for the way the scheme of education and training is designed to counteract it by withdrawing them from other occupations and interests.[21] In short, it is as though the *Statesman* explains what scientific government *is*, but the *Republic* that tells us the social and educational arrangements we need if we are to produce people qualified for the job of government. What is missing is any sense of the way in which the *Republic*'s distinctive conception of philosophy, and the associated metaphysics, feed into its theory of the ideal ruler. For that we can turn to another great Victorian Platonist.

2.2 Jowett's 'true statesman'

Benjamin Jowett's translation of Plato's dialogues—which did even more than Grote's *Plato* to make them known to English-speaking readers—was first published in 1871. For the second edition of 1875 he expanded the section of the introduction to the *Gorgias* devoted to critical reflections of his own, and among other issues took up the question: 'Who is the true and who the false statesman?' His answer weaves reminiscences of Plato into his own contemporary thoughts. The *Republic*, not the *Statesman*, is the main source of inspiration, and the differences that result from engaging less selectively than did Mill with the *Republic*'s approach to government are immediately apparent. Here is an extract from Jowett's initial characterization of the true statesman:[22]

He is not a mere theorist, nor yet a dealer in expedients; the whole and the parts grow together in his mind; while the head is conceiving, the hand is executing. Although obliged to descend to the world, he is not of the world. His thoughts are fixed not on power or riches or extension of territory, but on an ideal state, in which all the citizens have an equal chance of health and life, and the highest education is within reach of all, and the moral and intellectual qualities of every individual are freely developed, and 'the idea of the good' is the animating principle of the whole. Not the attainment of freedom alone, or of order alone, but how to unite freedom with order is the problem he has to solve.

What shapes Jowett's account is the *Republic*'s treatment of the philosopher—particularly (1) the conception of the philosopher statesman as 'not of the world' but 'descending' to it; (2) the philosopher's holistic approach to the problems of government; (3) the role of the 'idea of the good' in informing that approach; and (4) the concern with an ideal state (albeit described in terms more Kantian than Platonic) as setting the parameters for his political objectives. Jowett is no keener than was Mill to tie himself to the metaphysics of Platonic Ideas or Forms. That does not prevent him from doing justice to the *Republic*'s insistence on the need for statesmanship to adopt the perspective of the ideal.

In the pages that follow Jowett has a good number of shrewd things to say about the pragmatism and sense of his own limitations which the statesman will be well advised to develop if he is to achieve anything. He appreciates that such pragmatism is not very Socratic. 'Socrates,' he says, 'who is not a politician at all, tells us [*Gorg.* 521D] that he is the only real politician of his time.' This thought leads Jowett to some concluding reflections that probe some of the difficulties in the *Republic*'s idea of a philosopher ruler:[23]

We may imagine with Plato an ideal statesman in whom practice and speculation are perfectly harmonized; for there is no necessary opposition between them. But experience shows that they are commonly divorced—the ordinary politician is the interpreter or executor of the thoughts of others, and hardly ever brings to birth a new political conception. One or two only in modern times, like the Italian statesman Cavour, have created the world in which they moved. The philosopher is naturally unfitted for political life; his great ideas are not understood by the many; he is a thousand miles away from the questions of the day.

Yet in the end, Jowett thinks (a Socratic thought, as he represents it), the philosopher who never enters the political arena may have a profound impact on the world. He cites Locke, Hume and Bentham, among others, as private persons who 'sowed in the minds of men seeds which in the next generation have become an irresistible power'. We might think of Locke's influence on the founding fathers of the American Republic and the Declaration of Independence, or the adoption of Bentham's utilitarian principles in the planning processes supporting decisions across whole swathes of public policy over the last two centuries.

2.3 Divergent visions

One thing Jowett captures in these observations is the tension between philosophy and politics that *Gorgias* and *Republic* both in different ways make a major theme and take to be a critical problem. That tension is absent from Mill's account of the 'scientific governor', as it is from the *Statesman* itself. The fact is that despite some points of similarity in outlook, Mill and Jowett are talking about two quite different intellectual animals. There is a sense in which the science of Mill's scientific governor is not and cannot be in tension with politics, because—'philosophic' as it may be—it is *defined* as the science of *human affairs*, and it is a body of knowledge *geared to practice*. Mill suggests that Plato derived the idea of it from Socrates, 'who (says Xenophon) "considered as kings and rulers not those who wield the sceptre, or those who have been chosen by the incompetent (*hupo tôn tuchontôn*), nor those who have drawn the successful lot, or who by force or deceit have got into the highest place, but those who *know how* to rule"' (*Mem.* 3.9.10; Mill's italics).[24] And the *Statesman* is then introduced as the dialogue Plato devotes to the topic of 'what constitutes the man who knows how to rule'.

The philosophers Jowett describes, by contrast, are preoccupied primarily with the ideal, with what is *'not of the world'*. They are engaged in theory which they may never even attempt to put into practice. Indeed, philosophers are *'naturally unfitted for political life'*. There may well be tension between their philosophical vision and the exigencies of political practice. Admittedly, there is 'no necessary opposition' between the two; and the Platonic statesman Jowett imagines (in line with the *Republic*) would be a successful practitioner of politics ('a task which will call forth all his powers',[25] running against the grain of his philosophical nature and outlook as it will). So the *Republic*'s attempt to marry philosophy with politics is not inevitably doomed. But experience is mostly against it. The Socratic idea of the 'true politician' in the *Gorgias* (as Jowett seems to interpret it)—of the philosopher who will in due course change the world simply by his ideas, not by his own direct intervention in it—is a better guide to the way philosophy, with rare exceptions, can and actually does impact on practice. I think Jowett is saying that there is more wisdom on that question implicit in the *Gorgias*—the dialogue on which at this point he was commenting—than in the *Republic*.

In my assessment, each of the two readings we have been considering is in broad outlines faithful to the spirit and core ideas of its text. Departures from Plato are products not of inaccuracy but of convictions about which of those ideas are still valid. Yet the *Statesman*, as interpreted by Mill, and the *Republic*, as read by Jowett, yield incompatible pictures of what qualifies someone to be the person we might neutrally describe as 'the ideal ruler'. In Mill it is a knowledge of human affairs geared to practice; in Jowett theoretical speculation not naturally fitting anyone for politics, directed as it is away from the world to the realm of the ideal. This divergence no doubt reflects two different Victorian casts of mind. But the fact is that the intellectual universes of the *Republic* and the *Statesman* are very different. Much modern scholarship has treated them as complementary, not divergent—let alone incompatible. Trying to get this issue straight will preoccupy us for much of the rest of this chapter.

3. *Architectonic Knowledge*

3.1 Political knowledge and the good

Mill was quite right to find in Plato's preoccupation with knowledge 'the pervading idea' in his reflections on practice in general and politics in particular. Mill talked of 'deeply-rooted convictions' and 'doctrines' in this connection. But while the *Statesman*'s handling of the topic is undoubtedly didactic, there are other dialogues in which Socrates is represented as *wrestling* with the problem of giving an adequate account of what political knowledge or expertise might be. Of the two dialogues in question—*Charmides* and *Euthydemus*—the first is set in the wrestling school of Taureas, and the second in the gymnasium at the Lyceum. Even the locations suggest a strenuous workout, as well as a homoerotic atmosphere (especially pronounced in *Euthydemus*). It is difficult to be confident of the relative date of either work, although nobody doubts that they are both earlier than the *Statesman*.[26] Stylistically they belong with the dialogues of the first main group (most of them usually known as 'Socratic' dialogues).[27] As in other such dialogues, Socrates—the dominant figure in each—spends much of his time cross-examining other participants in the discussion on his favourite ethical themes (although in *Charmides* knowledge as much as virtue is what preoccupies him, and in *Euthydemus* he also undergoes questioning by the sophists Euthydemus and Dionysodorus on *their* favourite themes). Nor, as with other Socratic dialogues, is there much to show by way of positive results. But each exhibits a methodological sophistication, and explores or at least touches on a range of themes, that between them lead some scholars to suspect a closer connection with dialogues of the second main group such as *Republic* and *Theaetetus*.[28]

Charmides and *Euthydemus* come closer than any other among Plato's writings, including the *Republic*, to anticipating the treatment of the topic presented in the opening pages of the *Statesman*. Here the Eleatic Visitor compares political knowledge with the expertise of an *architectôn* or master-builder.

Master-builders 'don't act as workers themselves, but manage workers', by dint of the understanding at their command. Political knowledge is similarly architectonic, achieving its objectives principally by ruling or controlling subordinate forms of expertise (*Plt.* 259E–260C).[29] In both the earlier texts Plato works out an ambitious but very formal specification of knowledge of just this kind—and then gestures towards a contrast with something undoubtedly more substantive, but apparently quite different: the knowledge of what is good and bad. In fact, in *Charmides* and *Euthydemus*, the attempts to articulate an architectonic conception of political knowledge *founder*, not least because they cannot say what relationship there might be between the technocratic knowledge they are trying to specify and knowledge of the good. On this crucial issue of knowledge of the good, neither dialogue has any clarification to offer.

It seems that we are being invited by Plato to draw an inference. The idea of an architectonic political knowledge as key to general happiness may or may not be a mirage. But the fundamental task for *philosophy*, and the ultimate target of Socratic enquiry, is something different: the nature of the good, and what knowledge of that would consist in. If this is indeed the implicit message that Plato intends to convey in the *Charmides* and the *Euthydemus*, then it becomes inviting to construe these dialogues as in some sense asking to be read with the *Republic*. For it is in the *Republic* that Plato's Socrates explicitly acknowledges the question of the good as 'the most important thing to study, as you have often heard me say' (*Rep.* 6.505A). And then he engages at once with the *Euthydemus*'s problematic—before launching out on the analogies of the Sun, Line and Cave, offered as substitutes for the authoritative argumentative explanation of the good that he confesses is beyond him. One option for interpretation might be that, among their other purposes, *Charmides* and *Euthydemus* were written specifically to set puzzles that Plato was already intending to deal with later in a less quizzical mode elsewhere. In the case of the *Euthydemus* the references to themes specific to *Republic*—an example follows in Section 3.3 below—are in fact so pronounced that instead of 'elsewhere' we should substitute 'in the *Republic*'.[30] Another option might be that either or both of these dialogues presuppose a reader already familiar with the *Republic*, and are intent on showing what problems arise if its proposals about the relationship between knowledge and the good are ignored. On that view, *Charmides* and *Euthydemus* will be dialogues belonging chronologically with those stylistically assigned to the middle group, written to substantiate the teaching of *Republic*, but by means of examination of alternatives conducted in characteristically Socratic style.[31] But other options are of course conceivable.[32]

What our consideration of Mill's account of the 'scientific governor' and Jowett's presentation of the 'true statesman' threw up was a sense of potential conflict between the *Statesman* and the *Republic* regarding the knowledge required by the ideal ruler. It now transpires that in dialogues such as *Charmides* and *Euthydemus* Plato himself flags up a difficulty in reconciling a technocratic idea of political knowledge that anticipates the *Statesman*, and the need for moral knowledge—the knowledge of the good, above all other objects of enquiry, that will be the focus of the crowning moment in the philosophizing of the *Republic*. Of course, the difficulty raised in these dialogues is not necessarily connected (let alone identical) with the problem we identified in discussing Mill and Jowett. To try to get clearer about what is at stake, we need now to take a close look at the relevant stretches first of the *Charmides*, then the *Euthydemus*.

3.2 The *Charmides*

The *Charmides* is a fairly short work. Like many 'Socratic' dialogues, it ends 'without any definite result' regarding the topic of its enquiry, to quote the judgement Mill appended to his unpublished translation.[33] As we have noted, it is usually considered as belonging to the earliest group of Platonic dialogues, although readers have often thought that its epistemological preoccupations and methodological sophistication set it apart from (for instance) the *Laches* (on courage), which in some ways reads like its companion piece. Socrates' principal interlocutors are Charmides and Critias, relatives of Plato's, and later leading lights in the junta of the Thirty Tyrants. 'The choice of these interlocutors', as Charles Kahn points out,[34] 'permits Plato to elaborate on the fame and distinction of his own family and its connections by marriage.' He suggests that this 'conspicuous self-reference' in the elaborately constructed prologue indicates a dialogue in which the author takes 'an unusually personal interest'.

The topic is the virtue of *sôphrosunê*—a truly untranslatable word (Mill offered five alternatives), whose core meaning is 'soundness of mind' or (as Mill said) 'good sense', but then in different contexts 'prudence', 'moderation' or 'self-control', with connotations of intellectual or moral sobriety variously uppermost.[35] I shall opt for 'measured judgement'.[36] The second half of the dialogue is devoted to sustained examination of a single proposal about its identity: that it is equivalent to self-knowledge. Here Socrates works through a nested sequence of hypotheses about self-knowledge: (i) that it is a form of knowledge that is self-reflexive and second-order—knowledge of all forms of knowledge, itself included; assuming (i), (ii) that in virtue of such knowledge a person will know what he himself knows and does not know, and similarly in the case of other people will know that they know or do not know what they claim to know—for example, one will be able to discriminate between the true doctor and the quack; assuming (ii), (iii) that such knowledge is beneficial.

It is in attempting to make a case for (iii) that Socrates investigates the possibility that measured judgement is an architectonic form of knowledge, which in controlling the administration of household and city constitutes a great good (*Charm.* 172D). The case for (iii) goes like this (171D–172A):

'Those of us who possessed measured judgement, and all the other people who were ruled by us, would live our life free from error. We would not ourselves attempt to do what we did not understand, but we would find those who did and hand it over to them. As for those over whom we ruled, we would not entrust them with any task except one that they would perform correctly if they undertook it—that is, one where they possessed knowledge. That way, by means of measured judgement the running of the household would be well managed, and similarly the running of the city, and so with everything else where measured judgement was in charge. With error eliminated and correctness in control, people so circumstanced would be bound to do admirably and well in all their doings, and in virtue of doing well achieve happiness. Isn't that what we meant about good sense, Critias', I said, 'when we spoke of the great good constituted by knowing what a person knows and does not know?'

'That is certainly what we meant,' he said.

In other words, on the assumption (A) of the possibility of an architectonic form of knowledge which can have at its command a whole range of subordinate bodies of knowledge and expertise, there is in principle available to us just the knowledge needed for government. For (B) the deployment of such knowledge in ruling will produce a great benefit that we look for from the proper conduct of government: happiness.[37]

Unfortunately—according to arguments Socrates now presents—(A) is insecure, and (B) false. The reason he gives for suggesting that (A) is insecure is actually just a reminder of the way earlier stretches of argument have gone (Charm. 175B–C). On examination Socrates had ended up unable to determine whether self-reflexive capacities were a real possibility or not (169A–B). And he had concluded that nobody except a doctor can know whether a claim to medical knowledge is well founded or not (171B–C). However, even given assumption (A), he represents the inference to (B) as fatally flawed. An architectonic political knowledge could through its control of subordinate disciplines ensure that our physical health improved, and that we could have greater security at sea and in battle. But it could not guarantee us more happiness. That, Socrates argues, is because whereas medicine can make people healthy, it cannot make them happy. To which Critias volunteers that only knowledge of good and bad can do that (174A–B). When he tries to suggest that knowledge of good and bad, too, might be subordinate to architectonic knowledge, Socrates points out that it would however be from knowledge of good and bad that we got the benefit of happiness, *not* from architectonic knowledge (174D–175A).

One thing that is clear from the *Charmides* is the intensity of Plato's fascination with the idea of an architectonic 'knowledge of knowledge(s)' as the basis for an ideal politics. It is not presented as a Socratic idea.[38] The original proposal for identifying measured judgement with self-knowledge comes from Critias. He makes it in a moralizing speech that is his longest and most eloquent contribution to the conversation (Charm. 164C–165B)—although we have been given to understand that Critias' 'official' definition of *sôphrosunê* was 'doing one's own thing' (161B–162E).[39] Following some leading questions from Socrates, it is again Critias who elaborates the proposal as the highly abstract thesis that measured judgement is knowledge both of all other forms of knowledge and of itself (166B–C). Finally, Socrates is made to repeat its attribution to him quite emphatically following scrutiny of the notion of self-reflexive capacities, and Plato represents his reaction to Socrates' critique as the behaviour of someone feeling a strong sense of ownership and pride in the interpretation (169B–D).

We need not doubt that in making the original proposal about self-knowledge (at 164D–165B), Critias expresses a view to which Socrates is likely to be genuinely and indeed extremely sympathetic. After all, the whole point of the practice of Socratic questioning is portrayed in the *Apology* as getting people to question their own lives by finding out whether they really know what they think they know. But the consequent introduction of the abstract formula, making self-knowledge knowledge of itself and of other forms of knowledge, looks distinctly *un*Socratic. It turns self-knowledge away from individuals, their souls and their lives, and transforms it into something like an impersonal science. Presumably, there must have been something about the historical Critias' intellectual style which made Plato use him to convert Socratic self-knowledge into abstractions of this kind.[40] But there is no independent evidence that he actually proposed the idea of a knowledge of knowledge. So conceivably Plato is its real author. The extent and complexity of Plato's treatment of this notion of an architectonic knowledge can hardly be explained except as evidence of his own absorption in its possibilities, including in due course its political possibilities. At the same time, it is tempting to think Critias might well have found congenial the vision 'of a managerial élite, who without special knowledge of the domains in which their underlings are experts, nevertheless know who to deploy in what role and where, and what their capacities and weaknesses are.' Perhaps, and again there is no concrete historical evidence for the guess, 'it was among the ideas that inspired the Thirty—those of them, at least, who like Critias had pretensions to intellectual attainment'.[41]

Nonetheless, the question of the benefit or good of *sôphrosunê* is insistently pressed throughout the dialogue, as the crucial test of any proposal for its definition under examination, at any rate once Charmides' first shot at an answer is dispensed with (*Charm.* 160B–D). In the last two or three pages of the work, Socrates is portrayed as receptive to the thought that what produces the benefit of happiness is knowledge. But this has to be understood not simply as 'living knowledgeably', nor as Critias' architectonic knowledge, but as 'only this single form of knowledge—knowledge with regard to good and bad' (174B–C). The

Charmides therefore leaves us not just with a tension between the rival claims of the architectonic knowledge it explores and moral knowledge, but with a bare, unelaborated conclusion as to what matters most (in spite of Mill's verdict, there *is*—in this limited sense—a definite conclusion, though not about *sôphrosunê*). What really counts is the knowledge of good and bad, 'which has the function of benefiting us' (174D).

It is sometimes suggested that in the *Republic* Plato dissolves this tension by making knowledge of the Form of the good the 'most important thing to study' (*Rep.* 6.504D–E)—because it 'has all the other arts as its content'.[42] On the contrary: its *content* is simply the good. One thing that marks out its pre-eminence as an object of knowledge is that the good (*not* knowledge of it) makes whatever else is useful and beneficial useful and beneficial—including other arts and forms of expertise. So if we commanded other forms of knowledge, but not knowledge of the good, we would not know what it is about the things that they study or produce that is beneficial and useful (6.505A–B). This much is no more than an elaboration of the *Charmides'* conclusion about what matters most,[43] not a solution to its difficulties.

3.3 The *Euthydemus*

The *Euthydemus* is not so much a Socratic dialogue as a dialogue that plays with Socratic and non-Socratic ideas, and with Socratic and non-Socratic methodology. It contains anticipations or echoes of other Platonic writings (notably the *Meno* and the *Republic*). That above all is what makes it so hard to place within any chronological or developmental scheme, though it certainly has none of the stylistic peculiarities of the latest group of dialogues. It might be called an exhibition piece: interweaving into a satirical presentation of 'eristic', purely combative sophistical logic-chopping (demonstrated by the brothers Euthydemus and Dionysodorus), two episodes of no less teasing philosophical questioning conducted by Socrates. Both the eristic and the philosophical conversation tie themselves in knots—for very different reasons in the two cases.

At the beginning of the second Socratic episode, the dialogue takes up the question of the identity of the knowledge needed for happiness. This is the context in which the *Euthydemus* introduces the notion of political expertise as an architectonic form of knowledge. Socrates prepares the ground with a distinction between the knowledge required for making something (e.g. lyre making) and the knowledge required for using it (e.g. lyre playing), subsequently developed into a contrast between making or hunting down (including discovering) and using. What prompts the distinction is the thought that we only get benefit from things we make or discover if we know how to use them. The consequent proposal is that political expertise will make us happy by its architectonic use of subordinate skills like those of the general—who 'hunts down' the enemy and delivers this 'product' of his generalship to be ruled over by a king or statesman who commands that expertise (*Euthd.* 288E–291D).

But whose proposal is it? Just as in the *Charmides*, so here Plato goes out of his way to avoid putting the hypothesis of an architectonic knowledge in Socrates' mouth. Actually that is something of an understatement. To achieve this object, Plato writes one of the most extraordinary stretches of dialogue in the entire corpus. It can be analysed into three progressively deconstructive stages.

(A) First comes a passage in which Socrates offers spoof answers to the question of the identity of the expertise that brings about happiness. He suggests the expertise of first the speech-writer, and second the general.[44] His interlocutor—a callow teenager called Cleinias, hitherto an ingenuous and entirely passive respondent—has no difficulty in disposing of these suggestions by invoking Socrates' distinction between making and using. The speech-writer is a maker (as indeed is shown by the very construction of the Greek expression *logopoios*), not a user. In the case of the general, Cleinias improvises a bit: the general is something analogous to a maker—a hunter—but, again, not a user (*Euthd.* 289C–290B).

(B) Second, in elaborating his thoughts about generalship Cleinias becomes increasingly and improbably creative and sophisticated. He illustrates his distinction between hunters and the users to whom they hand over their catches not just with fishermen and cooks, but with a reference to mathematicians and dialecticians. This reference only makes sense as an allusion to the epistemology and metaphysics of Books 6 and 7 of the *Republic* (to the theory, whether or not the text of the *Republic* was already composed by the time the *Euthydemus* was written). Cleinias suggests that as mathematicians make their discoveries available to dialecticians since it is the dialecticians who know how to use them,[45] so generals similarly hand over the cities of armies they capture to politicians.[46] Therefore it can't be generalship that is the user expertise which will make us happy (290B–D). Attribution of all this material to Cleinias advertises its non-attribution to Socrates in flashing lights, but at the price of losing any pretence of verisimilitude.

(C) The point about verisimilitude is now made by Plato himself. The third phase in the sequence is initiated by an interruption of the reported speech of the main conversation on the part of Crito, the old friend to whom Socrates is recounting it. Crito simply cannot believe Cleinias said anything like what he is reported to have said. Socrates at once backs down from the claim that he did—insisting that at any rate it wasn't Euthydemus or Dionysodorus. And, in explaining to Crito how the argument *subsequently* developed, he represents the conclusions reached as the outcome of joint enquiry by himself and one or more unnamed participants (*Euthd.* 290E–291C). Here, there is doubtless the implication of a Socratic point about philosophical argument—familiar, but timely, in a context highlighting differences between Socratic method and the competitiveness of the sophists. What matters is the *argument*, not what you or I think, even though you and your views will be put under scrutiny by the argument (*Prot.* 333C); and argument is typically *shared enquiry*, as is insisted upon above all in the *Laches* (e.g. *Lach.* 187B–D, 196C–D, 197E, 201A–B).[47] But that cannot be the only or the most important point. Why with Crito's intervention—quite unparalleled elsewhere in the dialogues—does Plato at this juncture simply abandon the illusion of authenticity conveyed by the conventions of the dialogue form? He seems to be writing 'in code'.[48] What message or messages are being encrypted Plato leaves as matter for speculation. The main thing must be to announce abandonment of the pretence that readers are any longer in (or just in) the *Euthydemus*, and to acknowledge that this is the *Republic* (so to speak). In other words, Plato is saying to us: 'This is not life but a text—and here not just text but intertextuality.'

According to Socrates, the further conclusions that emerged from joint enquiry include his mention of the insouciant equation of kingship with political expertise, to be repeated in the *Statesman*, and its consequential identification as the user expertise that brings happiness. We may find the equation more unexpected in a conversation in democratic Athens than did Plato's Athenian readers. The fact is that many Athenian texts of the fifth and fourth centuries, especially by writers of aristocratic tendency, treat kingship as the default system when it comes to conceptualizing the idea of the exercise of rule over others. This is one index of the extent to which democratic society was able to accommodate the perspectives of alternative political frameworks.[49] Similarly, the way Plato introduces the proposal of philosopher *kings* in the *Republic* suggests that he did not expect that element in the hypothesis to be particularly disturbing. The idea that philosopher kings should be *philosophers*, or *queens* as well as kings, was what he expected to be found provocative. On the other hand, when Plato reiterates the equation of kingship and political knowledge in the *Statesman*, the notion of kingship is subjected to some thoroughgoing deconstruction (see Section 5 below). So the suspicion of insouciance remains.

To return to the *Euthydemus*, the next twist in the argument of the dialogue is by contrast thoroughly Socratic. Its general character is foreshadowed by Socrates when he says to Crito (*Euthd.* 291B):

When we got to the expertise of kingship, and were giving it a thorough inspection to see whether it might be the one that provided happiness as the outcome of its function, just then we got into a sort of labyrinth.

In fact the notion that an architectonic form of political expertise might be what would bring people happiness fares no better here than in the *Charmides*. In dialogue with Crito, Socrates subjects it to a typically Socratic cross-examination, starting with the observation that if it is the expertise they are looking for, it must be something beneficial. Now he and Cleinias had concluded at the end of the first Socratic episode that wisdom or knowledge is the only good.[50] So if the knowledge that constitutes kingship is to confer a benefit on people, it will have to do so by making them wise—making the citizens rich or free or rid of factional strife would be to supply them with things that are neither good nor bad. But since the only way in which wisdom is a good is that it is knowledge, knowledge confers no benefit but itself—and we can apparently say nothing more except that anyone in possession of it will convey it to others in turn. In particular, *what* it is about knowledge that makes it good, or that makes someone who possesses it good, seems totally obscure (*Euthd.* 291B–292E). We have ended up with a reflexivity in knowledge different from that explored in the *Charmides*, but no less sterile.

The root of the problem here is evidently the earlier admission that wisdom is the only good (*Euthd.* 281E). This had been agreed on the strength of an elaborate argument to the effect that unless knowledge controls them, 'not only all the external things we value, such as health, strength, and pecuniary means, but all that we regard as virtues—courage, temperance, and the rest—may be so used as to do harm instead of good' (I quote Mill's report of what he regarded as the best argument in Plato for the proposition that virtue is a form of knowledge).[51] The very formulation of this conclusion shows that it presupposes the existence of something good other than knowledge after all. There is a further connection here with the *Republic*. When Socrates there summarily rejects the proposal that understanding (*phronêsis*) is the good, he has in mind something very close to the objection to the proposal constituted by the 'labyrinthine' train of thought in the *Euthydemus*. Anyone pressed on what sort of understanding is envisaged in the proposal will in the end have to say: 'understanding of the good'. Which is ridiculous—because that answer either makes understanding its own eternally regressive object or leaves the notion of good wholly mysterious (*Rep.* 6.505B–C).[52]

To sum up, in both *Charmides* and *Euthydemus* Plato signals his attraction to the idea of an architectonic form of knowledge as the basis for good government that will produce general happiness. In both, Plato takes care to distance Socrates himself from the idea. In the *Charmides* it derives from a proposal made by Critias (who seems to have been a figure of sufficient intellectual weight for this to be credible). In its different guise in the *Euthydemus* it is presented at a moment when thoughts about users and producers intrude from the *Republic*. Each time the excessive formalism of the way the idea is articulated prevents its acceptance as the key to the good life it purports to constitute. 'Living knowledgeably'—even if we understand by that an architectonic political form of knowledge—does not on its own give us the recipe for the good on which happiness must depend. And in both dialogues there seems to be an implicit suggestion that something else instead holds out the best hope for achieving the wisdom needed for happiness: the preoccupation of the deeply *un*political Socrates with a more substantive knowledge of the good. Which sets at least one agenda for the *Republic*.

4. *Philosopher Rulers*

How might politics become a domain where knowledge rules? This is the underlying question, I suggest, fuelling Plato's interest in the idea of architectonic knowledge that is explored in the *Charmides* and the *Euthydemus*. If that idea could be made to work as a coherent idea, then there opens up the prospect of a genuine form of expertise in politics—something sophists like Protagoras and Prodicus or exponents of rhetoric like Gorgias had professed to teach, but (on Plato's assessment) without being able to substantiate their claims to knowledge or wisdom; and something Socrates himself had pointed towards, if we may rely on his talk of preference for one person who is expert over the opinions of the many in early dialogues like *Crito* (48A) and *Laches* (184C), or his claim in *Gorgias* to be the only Athenian alive making the attempt at true expertise in politics (521D). What would qualify people to be kings or statesmen on this scenario would be their command of the true knowledge of how to rule, i.e. architectonic knowledge. There would be nothing in the least paradoxical in envisaging a political system in which government was entrusted to those who satisfied this qualification, as the attested experts in the business of ruling.

The rule of knowledge is fundamental to the political project of the *Republic*. Yet the terms in which the idea of it is articulated are paradoxical in the extreme; and the dialogue's most famous statement on the issue is explicitly presented as a paradox (*Rep.* 5.473C–E):

'Unless', I said, 'either philosophers become kings in our cities, or those who are now called kings or the powers that be engage genuinely and successfully in philosophy—unless there is this convergence of political power and philosophy, with all those people whose present natural inclination is to pursue one or the other exclusively being forcibly prevented from doing so—there is no end to troubles for our cities,

Glaucon, nor yet, I suspect, for the human race. Unless that happens, there is no chance that the political system we have just expounded in our discussion will grow into a possibility and see the light of day. This is what I was so hesitant about putting forward, because I could see that it would be a very paradoxical claim. It is hard for people to see that there is no other route to happiness for a city in its arrangements for the private or public life of its inhabitants.'

The paradox is simply that, on the usual view (as Adeimantus will object a few pages further on), philosophers are most of them oddballs, at worst utter scoundrels and at best useless to society: in other words, the last people to put in power if you want an improvement in the condition of people's lives (*Rep.* 6.487C–D). The hypothesis of a king or a statesman endowed with the expertise in politics constituted by architectonic knowledge, on the *Charmides* or *Euthydemus* model, would be a quite different proposition, at any rate if we assumed Socrates' difficulties with it—especially about its relationship to the good—had been overcome. But the *Republic*'s philosopher ruler is simply a version of something more familiar—a philosopher. There is no mention of anything resembling the architectonic knowledge that the *Euthydemus* passage associated with kingship. It looks as though the philosopher is to be made into a king without possessing or acquiring expertise in kingship.

So it looks, unless Socrates is simply *redefining* kingship—and expertise in kingship—as philosophy, or as philosophical understanding of the good. This is the way he is taken by Charles Kahn, for example, who suggests that in Book 6 of the *Republic* Plato is now offering his own specification of the architectonic political knowledge that eluded satisfactory definition in the *Euthydemus*:[53]

In Plato's view it is the Good itself, the good as such, that must be the object for royal knowledge, for the art of the philosopher-kings. And such knowledge will be useful precisely because, in the hands of the rulers, it will guide the right use of the workings and products of all the other arts, as it governs the whole of society in the light of what is genuinely good, including the right use of those prima-facie goods, such as prosperity, freedom, and civic harmony, which were rejected in the argument of the *Euthydemus* as capable of being misused.

This is partly right, partly wrong. Throughout his exploration in Book 6 of the idea that philosophers should become kings (or vice versa), Socrates treats kingship simply as the possession and exercise of supreme power, not as a form of expertise. Nonetheless the analogy of the philosopher with the stargazing navigator (6.488D–489C) clearly implies that philosophy supplies the true expertise needed for political rule. So the intuition that kingship as a form of expertise is implicitly being redefined as philosophy is surely correct. However, there is no hint in the text of Plato construing philosophy or philosophical understanding of the good as the architectonic knowledge which uses all the other arts.[54] As we shall see, he makes Socrates go out of his way to stress the otherworldliness of philosophy here, not its practicality. In his first introduction of the Form of the Good, Socrates does state that use of the good makes what is just (and everything else) useful and beneficial (6.505A–B). But this thought is not developed in what follows, and certainly not given the explication and elaboration in architectonic terms that Kahn supplies.

G. R. F. Ferrari claims that 'Plato is exaggerating when he allows the prospect of philosophers in power to seem as preposterous and laughable as ever Aristophanes did the spectacle of the rule of women.'[55] He argues:[56]

Historically, the coincidence of philosophic ability and political power in notable individuals was by no means unprecedented. One intellectual who drafted a code of law has already been mentioned: Solon, Plato's sixth-century ancestor, who not only brought social reform to Athens but composed poetry on the political issues he was responsible for resolving. Another example is furnished by the 'sophist' (itinerant professor) Protagoras, who wrote the laws for Thurii, and is mentioned in the *Republic* (600C). We have seen that Critias too could have been thought himself, at first, something of a philosopher-king. More generally, philosophers of the sixth to fifth centuries tended to belong to the upper echelon of their communities and for that reason alone would have been called upon for political office—a duty not a few of them are reported to have fulfilled.

Ferrari cites in particular the Pythagoreans, notably Plato's friend Archytas of Tarentum.

It would be easy enough to reply to Ferrari that there is little reason to think Solon or Protagoras or Critias would have been the first candidates for the title of 'philosopher' to spring to the minds of Plato's Athenian readership (thoughts would surely have turned in the first instance to the apolitical Socrates himself). The Greeks spoke of Solon as a *sophos*, 'wise person' or 'sage' (indeed 'the wisest of the seven' legendary sages: *Tim.* 20D–E), someone endowed above all with reflective practical judgement of a high order. That is the reputation that attached to the name of Protagoras, too, as a glance at the opening pages of Plato's *Protagoras* will confirm. Critias' intellectual interests were probably not what made most people remember him: 'Critias, one of the Thirty who put down the democracy' is how the orator Aeschines referred to him fifty years after his death (*Against Timarchus* 173). Archytas the Pythagorean, on the other hand, was indeed a philosopher statesman. Yet his dominance at Tarentum was exercised not as king but—like Pericles in Athens—as general, apparently under a democratic constitution.[57]

Quite apart from all that, in Plato's time the word *philosophos* was still an expression probably only just gaining general currency, with its proper scope still contested (as Chapter 1 pointed out).[58] Plato's own use of it is clearly governed by its Socratic associations. His representation of the idea of philosopher kings as a paradox should be seen as a further product of the *Gorgias*'s meditation on the starkness of the choice between the political life (as articulated and exemplified by Callicles) and the life of the Socratic philosopher. Indeed, Adeimantus' subsequent characterization of philosophers as useless oddballs is virtually a reprise of Callicles on the same subject—even down to his clarification that he means 'not the ones who dabble with it as part of their education, and then give it up at an early age, but the ones who spend much longer on it' (*Rep.* 6.487D; cf. *Gorg.* 484C–D, 485A–E).[59] The meditation was to continue, with another memorable instalment in the digression of the *Theaetetus* on the unworldliness of philosophers, as compared with the slavish small-mindedness of habitués of the law courts (*Tht.* 172C–177C).

The paradox in the hypothesis of philosopher rulers remains even when Socrates has first explained at length what he means by a philosopher, and has then devoted equal space to dealing with Adeimantus' difficulties with the proposal. The nub of the matter is what Jowett recognized as the otherworldiness of Plato's 'true statesman'. Plato's argument is not that philosophers are not useless because not unworldly. The logic goes in the opposite direction. Otherworldliness is precisely what makes philosophers and only philosophers the right people to establish the ideal city and to govern it once established. Only they have the moral and metaphysical understanding and sharpness of vision, and the virtues of character required, to give appropriate shape to the institutions of the city and the characters of the other citizens. Only they will have struggled out of the imprisonment of the common illusions symbolized by the image of the prisoners in the Cave, chained to the unthinking assumption that the world of the senses is the only world there is. 'Blinding oneself to the world is a precondition for seeing the Forms, and contemplating the Forms is a precondition for seeing clearly and acting virtuously in the human realm.'[60]

In the ideal city Plato imagines, the unworldly philosopher is not so ill-equipped for ruling as one might antecedently suppose. A combination of rigid social stratification, effective propaganda, and intensive education and training for the warrior class, should ensure that there will be no need for anything like democratic politics or political arts in Plato's city. Of course, philosopher rulers will need to have some experience of how to take decisions, but Socrates is made to stress that they will not be lacking in experience of the world (*Rep.* 6.484D–485A). They will acquire it through holding military commands and 'any other position which is suitable for the young' (7.539E). Then they will be on *trial*, but (540A) it's a trial not of intellect or skill but of *character*, 'to see if they will stand firm when pulled in different directions'. This is all a long way from politics as ordinarily understood. Its abolition—because the need for it no longer exists—is in fact the tacit presupposition underpinning the idea that philosophers and only philosophers will be suitable rulers for the city. Once the presupposition is registered, the idea of philosopher rulers starts to make more sense.

The Platonic Socrates' explanation of what a philosopher is appeals to the two elements in the construction of the word *philosophos*—*philos*, sometimes 'friend', but here 'lover', and *sophia*, 'wisdom'—and their interrelation. The basis of the whole argument is a point about lovers. Properly speaking, lovers don't count as real lovers unless they love everything about the object of their affections—not cherishing one kind, but rejecting another. True lovers of wine, for example, will find something to attract them in *every* kind of wine. By the same token, philosophers are those who have a passionate desire for every kind of wisdom: they want to know anything and everything that can be known (*Rep.* 5.474C–475C). Socrates will soon describe that desire not merely as *philia* but as *erôs*, erotic passion. The philosopher will not cease to feel its pangs or desist from it 'until he grasps the nature of each thing—what it is in itself—with the part of the soul that is akin to it'. That involves 'approaching and joining in intercourse with what is really real, and so giving birth to understanding and truth' (6.490B).[61]

His conclusions about the love of knowledge lead Socrates to make a famously tricky distinction between knowledge and mere opinion, evidently inspired ultimately by the distinction between truth and mortal opinion forged by the Presocratic philosopher Parmenides. The main thing Socrates wants to extract from it is a contrast between conventional standards of beauty, justice and so on, which sometimes enable correct identification of beautiful things, just behaviour and the like, but sometimes not, and actual knowledge, which securely grasps what beauty or justice really *is*—since only what really *is* is really knowable (*Rep.* 5.475D–478E). The only viable candidates for objects of true knowledge turn out, therefore, to be Platonic Forms or Ideas (*Rep.* 5.478E–479E), since it is only Beauty, Justice and the rest that are as they are always and unchangeably, in being 'what beautiful or just is' (*Rep.* 6.507B). The hypothesis of Forms is intimately related to the pursuit of definitions so characteristic of Socrates in 'Socratic' dialogues like *Euthyphro* or *Laches* or *Charmides*. Forms are simply the objectively and eternally existing entities we are talking about when we raise questions like 'What is the beautiful?' or 'What is the just?' They do not themselves constitute or supply definitions. They are what it is we will have defined once we have achieved understanding of the beautiful and the just.[62]

So philosophers are preoccupied as philosophers with the eternal. Their passionate desire for wisdom is expressed as love of 'any study that would help to reveal to them the reality which always is, and is not driven this way and that by becoming and ceasing to be'—and by reality is meant 'the whole of reality': they don't readily pick and choose between the more and less important (*Rep.* 6.485D). Such persons can be expected to be large-minded, disciplined, and, in their roles as social animals, just and gentle. They will also be likely to have the intellectual capacities needed for philosophical understanding since, over the long haul, enthusiasm without the ability required for success is generally unsustainable as an enterprise. This combination of will, character and intellect is Plato's latest explication of the core Socratic idea that if you truly know what is good, that will be enough to make you perform it in all you do. It is what qualifies philosophers to be statesmen, 'always reaching out for the wholeness and totality of things—divine and human' (*Rep.* 6.486A). The demanding education in mathematics and dialectic that they are to follow is geared precisely to the job of equipping them with synoptic understanding of the connections between the sciences and of their relation with the nature of reality (7.537B–C).[63] Socrates does not call it architectonic. Nor has it any intrinsically practical orientation like the architectonic political knowledge sketched in *Charmides* and *Euthydemus*, and (subsequently) in the *Statesman*. In particular, there is no focus on its *use* of other forms of expertise. The similarity is simply that understanding of the good constitutes a single, ultimate vantage point on everything in the theoretical domain, corresponding to that claimed for architectonic political knowledge in the practical.

How a philosopher's theoretical understanding of the eternal will convert into something of practical benefit to society is the subject of a passage later in Book 6, near the end of Socrates' reply to Adeimantus' objections to the account I have just summarized. This is what Socrates gives us (*Rep.* 6.500B–D):

'I don't imagine, Adeimantus, that there's time for the person who truly has his mind fixed on reality to glance down at the affairs of men, or compete with them, and be filled with envy and ill-will. No, he fixes his view and his gaze on those things which are properly arranged, which are always the same, which neither wrong one another nor are wronged by one another, and which are all ordered according to a rational plan. These are what he imitates, and tries, so far as possible, to resemble. Do you think it is at all possible to admire something, and spend time with it, without wanting to imitate it?'

'No, that's impossible,' he said.

'So the philosopher, spending his time with what is divine and ordered, in fact becomes as ordered and divine as it is possible for a human being to be. Though mind you, there's always plenty of prejudice around, wherever you look.'

'Precisely.'

'And if there were some compulsion on him to put what he sees there into effect in human behaviour, both in private and public, and not just moulding himself, do you think there will be anything wrong with him as the craftsman of the self-discipline, justice and general excellence we need in the general population?'

'Certainly not.'

In other words, it is because the moral order of eternal reality has shaped the philosophers' own characters that they are equipped for statesmanship: it is their goodness as much as their wisdom that counts. There follows a notorious remark about the 'clean slate' philosophers will need if they are to succeed in their work, and the recipe for a political and social system which will produce 'a godlike form and likeness' in human characters. Philosophers will look to 'what is by nature just and noble and disciplined and everything of that sort' (501B).

By this point the philosopher has turned into a figure of sacral authority: a divine incarnation, a lawgiving prophet like Moses. Already a few pages earlier Socrates had claimed that the sort of human character that will flourish in the ideal political system will be seen to be 'divine' (497B–C). And when the *Laws* looks back to the *Republic*, it describes its ideal city as a home for 'gods or children of gods' (*Laws* 5.739D). The religious rhetoric indicates Plato's recognition of the degree of idealization that has now engulfed the philosopher's identity and function. It might be thought to be in some tension with the rhetoric of expertise in the ship of state passage. There the suggestion was that the philosopher's suitability for government derived from expertise. Like the navigator, his expertise was informed first and foremost by study of things above—in his case the eternal Forms, not the heavens and the seasons. But the implication was that, just as with the navigator, his expertise was not simply reducible to the knowledge won through theoretical study.

That implication, however, is not in fact abandoned in the passage we have just been reviewing. Socrates describes the philosopher explicitly as an artist working on the slate of the *politeia*, and as 'rubbing one bit out and drawing another bit in to replace it' within the outline of the constitution—a process of trial and error, with his eye moving back and forth between his model and the human characters he is drawing through the medium of the varied practices that constitute his palette (501A–C; cf. 484C–D). This is presumably intended as a metaphor for the expertise in applying knowledge of eternal Forms to the human sphere that the philosopher will utilize in setting up the ideal city (as distinct from steering its course like a navigator once it is a going concern). So it is imagined that, as well as knowledge of moral truth, the philosopher will have practical expertise too: not the architectonic knowledge speculatively associated with expertise in politics or kingship in the *Charmides* and *Euthydemus*, but something altogether more modest—the experimental methods of the artist.[64]

Shortly thereafter Socrates proposes that, as well as being the city's original legislators, philosophers should be made its guards or rulers too. He turns accordingly to consider whether they would require further education beyond the character training already described in Books 2 and 3, before it was envisaged that guards would need a philosophical understanding of things. This is the context in which he introduces the important thesis that 'the most important thing to study, as you have often heard me say, is the form of the good' (*Rep.* 6.505A), and then at once adverts to the problematic of the *Euthydemus*, or more precisely to sophisticated people who identify the good with wisdom (*phronêsis*). Socrates objects that those who take this view cannot show what wisdom is (that certainly fits the 'labyrinthine' predicament described in the *Euthydemus*). They are forced in the end to say that it is knowledge of the good—as though without further clarification we knew what *that* was.[65]

Plato could scarcely say more clearly that the rule of knowledge envisaged in the *Republic* is thoroughly Socratic, and *not* what was contemplated in the *Euthydemus* or (in a different version) in the *Charmides*: the hypothesis that political salvation turns on a special form of knowledge that is describable only in self-reflexive terms. It is Socratic above all because it is a function of knowledge of the good, here explicitly claimed to be a habitual Socratic preoccupation; to be guaranteed as knowledge by the ability to give an account of the matter that will withstand thorough cross-examination (*Rep.* 7.534B–C). Of course, the philosopher as imagined in the *Republic* is credited with an understanding of eternal moral truths that Socrates never claimed to possess. And Plato accordingly makes him apologize that he is not himself capable of giving the kind of account of the good that the enquiry really requires (*Rep.* 6.506D–E). But Plato would not have put either claim or disclaimer in his mouth unless he had wanted to emphasize the continuity between Socrates' philosophical project and (different though it is) the *Republic*'s vision of the ideal philosopher shaping the good city.

The *Republic*'s philosopher ruler is therefore no political manager or 'scientific governor' on the model desired by John Stuart Mill. Plato is imagining something quite different. He is considering what society would be like if its values were shaped by a Socrates, and then embedded as an overriding respect for knowledge and virtue in the structures and institutions of the city (6.484B–D, 500D–501A). Jowett was right to compare the impact made by a philosopher ruler, or by the 'true statesman' that Socrates claims to be in the *Gorgias*, with the influence of a Locke on the fundamental principles of the American Declaration of Independence.

5. *Architectonic Knowledge Revisited*

5.1 The *Statesman*

Plato did not abandon interest in the prospects for architectonic political knowledge. This is the topic which the *Statesman*, one of the very late group of Platonic dialogues, takes as its principal substantive theme.[66] The dialogue's leading speaker—not Socrates, but an unnamed visitor from Elea in southern Italy— accords the idea a treatment which avoids many of the problems it encounters in *Charmides* and *Euthydemus*. He makes no attempt to conceptualize it as knowledge *of* knowledge, so preempting many of the difficulties raised in the *Charmides*. And there is no suggestion that knowledge is itself the good, or the only good: the position that led to the labyrinthine problem of the *Euthydemus*. It is assumed that in exercising his political expertise, the statesman will do so *with a view to* the good, the noble and the just, conceived as independent values (e.g. 295E–297B). That does not necessarily mean that all the difficulties articulated in the two earlier dialogues are solved. For example, in taking political knowledge as (in effect) knowledge of how to *use* other knowledge, the Eleatic Visitor never addresses one of the key questions put in the *Charmides*. He does not ask how the person who possesses it will know *whether* others—such as generals or judges—command the expertise that would qualify them to be generals or judges.

164

At the core of the substantive political philosophy of the *Statesman* is a radical revaluation of the traditional notion of kingship (conceived as the paradigm of political rule). The old idea of the king as shepherd of his flock is successively defended, criticized and then abandoned for a new model: the statesman as weaver.[67] The main trajectory of the dialogue's argument for the revaluation can be quickly summarized.[68] The Eleatic Visitor begins by applying a method of iterated classificatory division to the concept of knowledge, to produce a definition of kingship as expertise in the rearing or nurture of humans, distinguished rather bizarrely from other animals as a herd of hornless two-footed animals (258B–267C). This constitutes something of a deliberate false start (more on false starts later: see Section 6 below). A new approach is needed. It is prefaced by a strange, elaborate and unusually obscure cosmological myth (marked in advance as playful), followed by criticisms of it and by lessons for the enquiry that might be drawn from it (268D–277A). The rest of the dialogue (277A–311C) interweaves passages of methodological reflection with identification and subsequent exploration of weaving as the model needed to understand what is at stake in political knowledge. In particular, it is this model which enables the *Statesman* to flesh out the architectonic function specified for it in the opening page or so of the discussion (259C–260C).

Methodological reflection is by no means an incidental feature of the argument of the *Statesman*. The dialogue is in fact as much about division, myth and models as about politics. The key central passage, set *at* its centre, is a set of reflections on what it is for any discussion, or for the exercise of any form of expertise, to be properly measured. The fundamental importance of this treatment of measure is flagged by a comparison between its significance for the enquiry into statesmanship and kingship and the role of the examination of non-being in the companion dialogue *Sophist* (283B–287B). Some readers have even been tempted to see methodology as the real subject of the *Statesman*.[69] At one point the *Statesman* itself endorses that kind of evaluation, when in the course of a key methodological passage placed at the mid-point of the dialogue the Visitor asks (285C–D):

Visitor: The next point we take up is relevant not just to our immediate enquiry, but to the whole business of discussions of this sort.

Young Socrates: What is it?
Visitor: Here's a question we might be asked about students learning at school: 'When a student is asked to spell some word or other, is the main point of the test the particular word the student has been set, or is it for him to become better at spelling all the words he's ever set?
Young Socrates: Obviously all of them.
Visitor: And what about our enquiry into the statesman? Is the main point of it just the particular subject at hand, or is it for us to become better at handling all subjects dialectically?
Young Socrates: That's obvious too—all of them.[70]

This preoccupation with method seems to go a long way to explain why Plato makes his principal speaker in *Sophist* and *Statesman* a visitor from Elea. Elea was the city of Parmenides and his younger associate, the paradox-monger Zeno. But the Visitor is not portrayed as someone who subscribes to Parmenides' metaphysical monism. At the beginning of the *Sophist* Socrates is made to refer to an encounter of his own with Parmenides (*Sph.* 217C), and this gives us a better clue as to what is Eleatic in the Visitor's philosophizing. The reference is actually a cross-reference to Plato's *Parmenides*: the dialogue in which Parmenides mounts a famous critique of the theory of Ideas, and then offers Socrates a formidable demonstration of systematic philosophical method—an exhaustive derivation of antinomies from the highly abstract hypothesis 'one is' and its contradictory. As with Parmenides in the *Parmenides*, so in the *Sophist* and *Statesman* Plato treats the Eleatic Visitor as first and foremost an exponent of abstract, systematic, expository method.[71] Systematic exposition is an essentially monological activity. The problem of accommodating monological discourse within the dialogue form is deftly dealt with (as again in the *Parmenides*) by adroit choice of discussant.[72] The main speaker is supplied—at his explicit request—with a young and docile interlocutor, although Theaetetus in the *Sophist* and the younger Socrates[73] in the *Statesman* make a bit more of a contribution than does Aristoteles[74] in the second part of the *Parmenides*.

5.2 Politics as management

The Eleatic Visitor makes the assumption that kingship is the real subject of the enquiry. Yet Socrates—the Socrates we usually think of, not yet the Visitor's young discussant—has requested an account of the statesman or politician (*politikos*) (*Sph.* 216A–217A, *Plt.* 257A–C). The Visitor has a justification for this: so far as the relevant knowledge goes, all forms of rule—whether in the household or the city—are the same. Whether one talks of king or statesman, therefore, is neither here nor there. John Cooper has pointed out that the Visitor's arguments for this thesis are extremely weak.[75] And the tortuous course taken by the trajectory of the dialogue can be attributed to the lazy assumption in the first section—exposed as wrongheaded in the second—that thinking specifically about kingship in the light of the untested analogy of the herdsman, traditional from Homer on, will be the right way to identify what form of knowledge is involved (it is striking that after the initial equation the argument of the first section is couched exclusively in terms of kingship). At crucial points in the subsequent discussion, however, the Visitor makes it clear enough that the way actually to achieve progress in the enquiry is to conceptualize the expertise in question as essentially *political*—in a sense we will need to try and explicate.

When first proposing the weaver analogy (279A–B), he switches from talk of kings to ask for something that is involved in the same kind of activity as political expertise or statesmanship (*politikê*). When commenting later on the consequences of neglecting due measure, he makes a palpable distinction between statesmanship and kingship (284B):

If we make the expertise of statesmanship disappear [i.e. in consequence of such neglect], our search after that for the knowledge which constitutes kingship will be without any prospect of moving forward.

In going on to apply the weaving example to statesmanship, he indicates that what now need to be investigated are the analogous contributory and component activities *in the city itself* (287A–B). And when finally a satisfactory definition is formulated—presented as a definition of statesmanship (*politikê*)—the Visitor relates its function to the common focus of its care for everything in the city (*polis*) (305E).[76]

These points are all made implicitly or unemphatically, without any of the pointed stage directions that highlight key moves in the argument of the *Republic*. But the moral is obvious: if you want to think about kingship, think mostly about political expertise; if you want to think about that, think mostly about the city, and all the things that make it function. In the concluding section of the dialogue, where the Visitor at last brings out the bearing of the weaving model for politics (287B–311C), he mostly talks of king and statesman more or less indifferently. But in effect the reader is offered a thoroughly *politicized* conception of kingship (as John Cooper again has argued).[77] Its theocratic associations are jettisoned, and it is converted into the idea of the supreme orchestrator—someone who will make use of the full range of roles and associated forms of expertise available in a Greek city. Readers of the *Republic* will be surprised to find that these are made to include even those of the speakers or orators most Athenians would have regarded as the real politicians.

I said 'orchestrator'. What Plato says is 'weaver'. He was not the first Greek writer to introduce weaving as a political metaphor.[78] Its use by Aristophanes in his comedy *Lysistrata* (of 411 BC) not only constitutes a striking precedent, but poses an intriguing if unanswerable question about Plato's intentions in the *Statesman*. The *Lysistrata* imagines an Athens where the women decide they have had enough of the war, and conspire against the men with the aim of forcing a peace settlement with Sparta. Under their leader, Lysistrata, they seize the Acropolis and the public funds in the treasury. When the men of the city send an envoy to ask the women to explain how they will sort out the city's confused affairs, Lysistrata launches into a brilliant speech demonstrating that their expertise in weaving is the perfect preparation for the radical political programme they will need to put in place (*Lys.* 574–87):

First of all, just like washing out a raw fleece, you should wash the sheep-dung out of the body politic in a bath, then put it on a bed, beat out the villains with a stick and pick off the burrs; and as for those people who combine and mat themselves together to gain office, you should card them out and pluck off the heads. Then card in the wool into the work-basket of union and concord, mixing in everyone; and the immigrants, and any foreigner who's friendly to you, and anyone who's in debt to the treasury, they should be mixed in as well. And yes, there are also the cities which are colonies of this land: you should recognize how you now have them lying around like little flocks of wool, each one by itself; so then you should take the human flock from all of them, bring them together here and join them into one, and then make a great ball of wool, and from that weave a warm cloak for the people to wear. (Trans. A. H. Sommerstein)

In Aristophanes' hands, this image is heavily gendered. Melissa Lane comments that throughout the play, 'the domestic agility of women is celebrated and mockingly compared with the public incompetence of men'.[79] There may have been male weavers in ancient Greece, but Aristophanes capitalizes on the overwhelmingly female associations of the craft, which stretch back to Penelope in the *Odyssey*. Yet, as Lane notes, these seem to 'cast no shadow on the *Statesman*'.[80] Why not? Perhaps the Visitor operates at such a level of abstraction that weaving is simply 'neutered' (this explanation certainly fits the general intellectual profile of the dialogue, as we shall see further in the next section of the chapter). Perhaps—additionally or alternatively—Plato is silently meaning us to take the point that statesmen could just as well be female as male (as with philosopher rulers in the *Republic*), without raising the issue explicitly, still less insisting that they will be. Or perhaps, on the contrary, he is blatantly appropriating for philosophy a characteristically female function, while more insidiously excluding women—as it will transpire—from the 'social fabric woven by his statesman'.[81] What is explicit in the text is a rather different point: as is appropriate generally with examples or models, weaving is something small-scale and well understood (279A–B; cf. *Soph.* 218E), to be favourably contrasted in its unpretentiousness and familiarity with the grandiose theological and cosmological framework of the myth (277B).

Melissa Lane also draws attention to another major difference between *Lysistrata* and *Statesman*. 'All the emphasis' in Lysistrata's speech 'technically *and* politically falls on the preparatory stages—what we may call collectively the cleansing, culling, carding and collecting.' By contrast, 'the final stage of the process, the stage of "weaving" proper—the interweaving of warp and woof on the loom—gets scarcely a sentence, essentially stated as the outcome of the People's Cloak'.[82] The *Statesman*'s discussion of weaving (279B–283B) reads almost like a critical commentary on Lysistrata's treatment of it. It lists a whole range of contributory activities Lysistrata does not mention at all: the arts that produce the tools (spindles, shuttles, etc.) used by those involved in the actual business of preparing and weaving wool. These will turn out to correspond in the political context to a huge range of mostly economic functions, from the manufacture of tools, clothes, houses, city walls and so on, to farming, cooking and trading. All are needed to sustain the life of the city (but the Visitor adds in some others too, notably the activities of musicians and painters, and again priests and seers).

More important, however, is to distinguish from weaving itself, and from its key function of *intertwining* warp and woof, other crafts which might well claim equal involvement in the production of clothes. Washing and carding are given special attention (280E–281B)—in fact just the activities Lysistrata highlights as analogues of political purge and political inclusion. In working out *his* political parallel, the Visitor identifies rather different activities, which because of their genuine kinship with statesmanship might be confused with it: principally those of the general, the political orator and the judge. What he insists is that these must be *subordinate* to statesmanship (303D–305E). In an Athenian context, this is decidedly pointed. The Athenian *dêmos* exercised its own sovereignty by membership of the juries of the popular courts, and the popular assembly was dominated by the generals and the orators.[83]

In dealing with the relationship between statesmanship and these subordinate forms of expertise, mostly Plato actually uses other resources than his weaving analogy. He has recourse to the general character of kingship as that was agreed upon at the very beginning of the whole discussion, and to the notion of measured judgement introduced in the central passage on measure. What Plato associates above all with kingship is the idea of sovereign authority, and it is this idea which is worked out in terms of architectonic knowledge in the opening pages of the dialogue. Kingship is much more a matter of understanding than practical expertise. But understanding comes in two forms: one concerned simply with pure reasoning and assessment of the findings of reason; the other with the practical business of giving directions, in the manner of a master-craftsman such as an architect—who does not engage in the manual crafts himself, but supervises those who do. The king, of course, takes no direction from anyone else (in contrast to others whose job is to give directions, like heralds or announcers): his knowledge is *self*-directing (259C–260E).

This all sounds very Aristotelian, and may indeed have been influenced by discussion in the Academy with the young Aristotle among others.[84] Most of the key ideas recur in the treatment of practical wisdom in the *Nicomachean Ethics*. There too we find the comparison with the master-craftsman and his architectonic understanding, the distinction between practical wisdom as directive (*epitaktikê*) and understanding that is concerned with assessment or discrimination only (*kritikê*) (*EN* 1.1, 1094a14–16; 1.2, 1094a18–b7; 6.10, 1143a6–10). There is also something very reminiscent of Aristotle in the political application of this conceptual apparatus, as eventually made by the Visitor in his discussion of the general and the political orator (305C–D):

If then one looks at all the kinds of expert knowledge that have been discussed, it must be observed that none of them has turned out to be statesmanship. For the one that really is kingship must not perform functions itself, but rule over those with the capacity to perform them, because it knows the right and the wrong time to begin and set in motion the most important undertakings in cities. It is for the rest to do what has been delegated to them.

Generals should have the expertise needed to fight a war. But *whether* to go to war or to resolve the dispute by peaceful means is a matter for statesmanship. Similarly political orators know how to persuade a large gathering, but whether now is the right moment for persuasion or the use of some kind of force is a matter for the expert knowledge that needs to govern the use of expertise in persuasion. The key role of judgement of the right moment in this account is directly comparable to Aristotle's treatment of knowledge of the mean. Aristotelian virtue needs the judgement of practical wisdom if it is to be in a mean. Only then will we be in a state of mind where we act or feel emotion 'at the right times, with reference to the right objects, towards the right people, with the right motives, and in the right manner'—which is what is 'intermediate and best' (*EN* 2.6, 1106b21–3).[85]

Plato's reference to the right and wrong time for action is no less theorized than Aristotle's. Here the Visitor is drawing on his treatment of the proper measure between excess and deficiency, worked out in the core discussion at *Statesman* 283–7. His governing thought is that measured judgement is indispensable if there is to be any expertise or knowledge relating to coming into being, or in other words to the realm of change in which human activities have to be conducted. Without expertise in judging what is the measured, appropriate, timely, right thing to do, there could not be anything such as statesmanship (284A–285C). And it is the use of this expertise which is given prominence in what is said about the relationship between kingship and the subordinate activities of generals, orators and the like, and in the further development of the weaving analogy at the very end of the dialogue. Nowhere do we get a sharper sense of the gulf separating the philosopher of the *Republic*, his thoughts focused on the eternal, and the statesman of the *Statesman*, in his preoccupation with the flux of human affairs where 'practically nothing ever remains stable' (294B).[86]

The full appropriateness of the weaving analogy is finally confirmed when the Visitor turns to what he represents as the fundamental challenge confronting politics: a cleavage in human nature itself. In terms reminiscent of Thucydides' analysis of the differing character of Athenian and Spartan political behaviour, he proposes that there are really two quite different sorts of people: those who are temperamentally vigorous and quick to act, and those who are no less temperamentally easy-going and slow to act—with the behaviour of the one called 'courageous' when it is timely, 'violent' or 'frantic' when it isn't, and in the other case 'restrained' when timely, 'cowardly' or 'lethargic' when not. The mutual hostility this divergence generates constitutes the worst of political diseases, as the Visitor argues (307E–308B):

Visitor: Those who are particularly orderly are always ready to live the quiet life, carrying on their private business on their own by themselves, both associating with everyone in their own city on this basis, and similarly with cities outside their own, being ready in any way to preserve peace of some kind. And because of this passion of theirs, which is less timely than it should be, when they do what they want nobody notices that they are being unwarlike and making the young men the same, and that they are perpetually at the mercy of those who attack them. The result is that within a few years they themselves, their children, and the whole city together often become slaves instead of free men before they have noticed it.
Young Socrates: You describe a painful and terrifying experience.
Visitor: But what about those who incline more towards courage? Isn't it the case that they are always drawing their cities into some war or other because of their desire for a life of this sort, which is more vigorous than it should be? And that they make enemies of people who are both numerous and powerful, and so either completely destroy their fatherlands or else make them slaves and subjects of their enemies?
Young Socrates: This too is true.
Visitor: How then can we deny that in all this both of these kinds of people are always involved in much mutual hostility and dissent, in fact on a grand scale?
Young Socrates: There's no way we shall deny it.

So the problem of opposite temperaments makes for bitter civil conflict at home, and in foreign relations either passivity or adventurism, and on both scenarios ultimate disaster.

The remedy proposed has two phases. First, it will be the job of those with a subordinate expertise in education to develop the potential that humans have for courage or restraint.[87] Then the statesman himself—by means of the legislation he promotes (309D; cf. 305E, 310A)—will take over, to perform his own distinctive function of intertwining those inclining to courage and those inclining to restraint by two bonding devices. One is moral and spiritual: the inculcation of a securely based true belief about what is good and noble and just, so that temperaments turn into real virtues (with the courageous knowing when to be active, and the restrained when to hold back). The other is eugenic: the encouragement of intermarriage between persons of opposite temperament, to ensure that over the generations those with the temperaments for courage or restraint do not get *more* extreme (not—apparently—to produce a population in which most citizens exemplify *both* courage *and* restraint).[88] The outcome would be a city marked by consensus and friendship in its common life, and as much happiness as any city could have (308B–311C).[89] In short, managerial expertise will have realized the utopian hope so pervasive in Greek political speculation: abolition of *stasis* and the causes of *stasis*, and the achievement of *homonoia*.[90]

6. *The Limitations of Management*

Is Plato now unequivocally commending to his reader the idea that the application of architectonic political knowledge is the ideal recipe for producing a flourishing human society? There are strong reasons for answering the question in the negative. The problem is not that the *Statesman*'s account of political expertise as such in the end goes astray. Quite the contrary: it offers an extraordinarily rich and penetrating analysis of the notion of political management and of the political benefits it could deliver—little wonder that John Stuart Mill found it so compelling.[91] The difficulty lies elsewhere. The Eleatic Visitor's methodological sophistication is not in doubt. What prompts more questions is the appropriateness to politics of the abstractness of his theoretical approach to it.

Two quick contrasts with the *Republic* will suffice to characterize the sense of abstractness. First, the *Republic* begins with arguments about justice, and only starts its treatment of political issues in earnest with the introduction of the city-soul analogy in Book 2. It takes its task then to be the construction of the good city, or the best scheme of political order, with a radically reformed educational system for its ruling 'guards'—concentrated on proper development of moral character—taking the lion's share of the discussion. And it introduces philosopher kings within the context of an answer to the question of how political order so conceived might be brought into being in the first place. When it is decided that philosophers should also be the 'guards' who constitute the city's ruling class, the issue of an appropriate *higher* education for philosopher rulers is then accorded huge importance.[92] By contrast, the *Statesman* addresses in the first instance the question: 'What is political expertise?' (or: 'What would it be if anyone were to have such a thing?'), and only subsequently and indirectly works out a consequential story about the way society would be managed—including the education of its citizens—if it were governed by someone with that expertise. *How* someone might *acquire* political knowledge is never discussed, nor what education would be appropriate for someone who is to acquire it. Nor is there any treatment or even mention of the moral character of the person who is imagined as possessing it. The *Statesman* develops a complex account of political knowledge. But that account is sparer and more purely hypothetical than the project of the *Republic* (or the *Laws*).[93]

Second, the impression of abstractness is intensified by the Visitor's anonymity, which serves as a metonym for his general colourlessness.[94] As Leo Strauss brought out, here in the *Statesman* is a thinker with a purely fictional identity who has no known political responsibilities or commitments. He is represented as coolly developing his arguments with a passive young interlocutor in the presence of a silent Socrates, and in a city to which he has no attachments. The *Republic*, by contrast, has a cast of historical characters who were embroiled in the social and political life of Athens. Some of them for certain figured in key events in Athenian political history,[95] including of course Socrates himself, whose deeply embedded commitment to Athens brought him—as the *Apology* represents it—to his death.[96] There is not much that is cool about his dispute over justice with Thrasymachus in the first book of the *Republic*.[97]

Abstractness comes at a price. In the rest of this section I argue that the price is a degree of impoverishment. I take three specific and fundamental issues where the *Statesman*'s thinking about politics—for all its brilliant intensity—is from other points of view more impoverished than what we are offered in *Republic* and *Laws*. In succession, these concern its conception of: *politeia* (the social and political system); the *politikos* (the political expert or statesman); and *politikê* (political knowledge or statesmanship).

(A) *Politeia* (the social and political system). The *Republic*, like the *Laws*, has as its political project the construction of the good city or the best *politeia*, or social and political system. It works out its answer in terms of a structure of three classes rigidly separated according to social function, whose members will agree on the question of who should rule and who should be ruled (4.432A). The idea of philosopher kings and queens is introduced initially as the device needed to enable this antecedently constructed system to become so far as possible a reality (5.473B–E). In the *Laws* a different answer is given. The best *politeia* is in a sense a theocracy, since it is a city governed by law, interpreted as public reason—and as such something that rises above ordinary human passions and appetites (4.713C–714B). But it is envisaged that the legislator responsible for introducing laws will proceed only by persuading the citizens at large to accede voluntarily to their establishment as laws (4.719E–723B; cf. 3.693B–E, 700A).[98]

The *Statesman*'s approach is quite different. It argues from the analogy of the statesman and the doctor that the right *politeia* simply *consists* in one person ruling with expertise (301A; cf. 293C–E), acting with justice to improve things for the city so far as he can. How society ought to be organized for unity and happiness is not even a consideration in this connection, let alone the overriding concern it was in *Republic* and *Laws*. The question of consent *is* raised, notably in the stretch of text (considered in Chapter 3, Section 5.1) dealing with the contrast between government by someone commanding true political expertise, and the recourse to law that is the inadequate best an oligarchy or a democracy could achieve.[99] Pursuing the parallel with the doctor, the Eleatic Visitor argues that what matters in a doctor is that he is knowledgeable, not whether his patients are willing or unwilling, rich or poor; not what methods he uses, or whether he follows written rules or not. So all that matters in a statesman is that he rules with expertise, whether or not those ruled accept his rule willingly or unwillingly, are rich or poor, and whether or not he governs in accordance with laws or otherwise. That is 'the only correct criterion' in the case of medicine or any other form of rule. And it follows that it is the unique basis for judging a *politeia* correct or indeed for deeming it to be a *politeia* at all—there is absolutely no principle of correctness allowing one to take any of these other considerations into account (292C–293D).

In short, the *Statesman's* conclusion is that the only thing that matters is that we should have what Mill would call 'Scientific Government'—and that for government to be scientific it is immaterial how society is organized, or whether the governed consent or not.[100] There is clear conflict between the Visitor's insistence that what matters in a doctor or a statesman is simply that his practice be informed by the appropriate expertise, not that he win his patient's or his subject's consent, and the view of the matter taken in the *Laws* (and indeed the *Republic*, too). John Cooper quotes from the *Laws* the statement that a doctor who is a free person, when dealing with patients who are likewise of free status, 'gives no prescription until he has somehow gained the patient's consent, and continually uses persuasion to gain his cooperation as he tries to complete his restoration to health' (4.720D–E).[101] Cooper rightly notes that if the Visitor had been attentive to this line of reflection, 'he could not have insisted so blankly as he does on the total disconnection of the physician's expertise from the use of persuasion'—or, one might add, the importance of consent, here and (*mutatis mutandis*) in the political sphere too.[102]

(B) The *politikos* (the political expert or statesman). The *Republic* makes one of its insistent themes the idea that those best qualified to rule will be reluctant to do so. In Socrates' conversation with Thrasymachus in Book I these are identified as the morally good, who have no interest in financial gain or honour, evidently taken to be the incentives which generally attract people into politics. Necessity—pressure—will have to be applied to force them to agree to accept office. The penalty held over them if they refuse is the prospect of being ruled by people with less moral integrity. So they will take it on as a necessity, not as a good thing or anything likely to be a good experience, since they know that a genuine ruler puts himself out to promote the advantage of others, not his own. In a city of good men, people would fight over the prize of *not* ruling, in the way they now vie to obtain office (*Rep.* 1.346E–347D).

In the central books of the dialogue exactly the same assessment is made of the philosophers whose role in the ideal city is to exercise rule. Socrates imagines it likely that there would have to be 'some compulsion' on the philosopher to put his otherworldly vision of the divine order of the eternal Forms into effect 'in human behaviour, both in private and in public', not just 'moulding himself' (*Rep.* 6.500D; cf. 499C). This line of thought is famously elaborated at the end of the Cave analogy in Book 7. There Socrates puts it to Glaucon that in compelling philosophers who have attained the vision of the Good to leave their study of it and 'look after and guard' the other citizens, or in using a combination of 'persuasion and necessity' to make them participate in the exchanges that constitute the operation of society, no injustice will be done to them. Having heard Socrates' explanation of how they will thereby be repaying the city for their education and upbringing with the contribution they are uniquely qualified to make, Glaucon agrees that there is no injustice in that—though they will treat ruling as a necessity only (the opposite from the attitude now current in politics everywhere). This time Socrates advances as a truth the general proposition that the city where those who are to rule are least keen to do so will inevitably be best governed and enjoy maximal freedom from civil conflict. In fact the best recipe for good government is the availability to the rulers of a life—the philosophical life—better than ruling (*Rep.* 7.519C–521B). It is significant that the summing up at the end of the book includes a brief reprise of the main point: philosophers will treat ruling as a necessity only (7.540A–B).[103]

There is no philosopher ruler in the *Laws*. But the *Laws* recycles some of the same thoughts about ruling. The *Republic* itself rates the chances of 'the muse' (of philosophy) controlling a city very low (e.g. *Rep.* 6.499C–D). The Athenian Visitor takes the view that it would require a miracle ('divine dispensation') for someone with the right understanding of the paramount importance of action for the common good to assume absolute power without disastrous consequences for himself and the city as a whole. Inevitably he would succumb to the human temptation to pursue his own interests and go after pleasure (*Laws* 9.875A–C; cf. 3.691C–D, 4.713C–D). Hence the *Laws'* decision to make the rule of law the basis for its choice of the best social and political system humans can realistically hope for (9.875D; cf. 4.713E–714A).

Plato's argument that the best people to exercise power are those who least want it has profound attractions, for all its utter impracticality. It embodies a reasoned response to the perception that what is most dangerous about power is the moral and political havoc wrought by its abuse. Anyone who shares that perception is likely to be sympathetic to Plato's recommendation that we should make avoidance of abuse a priority when thinking about who or what should rule. This motif dominates the whole approach to politics adopted in *Republic* and *Laws*. In the *Statesman*, by contrast, it is almost invisible. The Eleatic Visitor has little to say about the moral *dangers* of rule by a single individual, however great his political expertise. When he does advert to the issue, he expresses it as an apprehension in the popular mind, not as a basic problem he himself needs to engage with (*Plt.* 301C–D). He is content to leave it that the statesman—'superior in body and mind'—will be a rare bird (301D–E; cf. 297B–C, where the emphasis is on the difficulty most people would have in acquiring the requisite *knowledge*).

Crucial to the *Republic's* treatment of ruling is the thought that the reason that a good person or the philosopher will rule only reluctantly is awareness of a *better* life than politics. The *Statesman* gives us no reason to suppose that anyone who commanded the political knowledge it describes would feel the least reluctance about exercising rule. Its statesman is identified not as a philosopher (who would rather be doing philosophy), but as a political manager (whose expertise consists precisely in the ability to orchestrate the activities of a whole range of other experts, all contributing to the life and prosperity of the city). The philosophers of the *Republic* have to escape from the city—imaged by Socrates as the Cave—if they are ever to be able to rule it as it should be ruled. The *Statesman's* statesman 'is defined in terms of his relation to the city'.[104]

As with the science of Mill's Scientific Governor, there is no tension between politics and the knowledge the statesman commands, because it is a knowledge—unlike philosophy—geared to practice from the outset. That knowledge is certainly exercised in the light of a concern with the good, the noble and the just (see e.g. *Plt.* 295E–297B). There is no suggestion, however, that purely philosophical contemplation of the good, the noble and the just is something which might hold greater attractions for the statesman than the practice of politics for which his distinctive expertise equips him. The dialogue begins with a reference to the problem (introduced in the opening pages of the companion dialogue *Sophist*) of distinguishing between the sophist, the statesman and the philosopher (*Plt.* 257A–258B). But thereafter there is no mention of even so fundamental a topic—prominent in *Apology, Gorgias* and *Republic* alike—as the choice between the *life* of politics and the *life* of philosophy, nor indeed any explicit discussion of philosophy as such at all. The fact is that talk of the 'statesman' is no more than a way of expressing the idea of the exercise of architectonic political knowledge.

Some discussions of the *Statesman*'s statesman end up virtually assimilating him to the philosopher ruler of the *Republic*. 'The heart of the matter', writes Thanassis Samaras, 'remains that the Scientific Ruler has absolute knowledge of the same kind and calibre with the philosopher-rulers of the *Republic*.' Like them, he 'places the interests of his subjects beyond his own personal interest'. Although like them he constitutes an ideal of what a ruler should be, he is unlike them in operating within a *non*-ideal context. He has to exercise his art 'on ordinary people'. Plato has accordingly revised his ontology and epistemology 'to accommodate "the concrete historical context" of human action'.[105] The *Republic* had not had a great deal to offer by way of explaining *how* philosopher rulers apply their knowledge and wisdom to government. Other than the analogy with the navigator (*Rep.* 6.488C–489C), the brief passage comparing them with artists working with a model was Socrates' main explicit attempt at an answer (6.501A–C).[106] The *Statesman*'s development and application of the weaving analogy, together with its theory of expertise in judging what is the measured, appropriate, timely thing to do in concrete contingent circumstances, might reasonably be perceived as supplying something deficient in the *Republic*. 'The philosopher-kings of the *Republic* may seem to

lack concern with the minutiae of everyday life in the city...,
where the statesman needs to concern himself with individual
cases and their equity, but here—it could be said—the *Politicus*
merely clarifies and brings down to earth the *Republic*'s grand
view.'[107]

That would mean not simply revising the *Republic*'s conception of what the rule of knowledge consists in, but abandoning
the vision which sustains it. The nub of the issue can be defined
by considering the question: 'Is the *Statesman*'s statesman in
any sense a philosopher as the *Republic* conceives of the philosopher?' Plato certainly means its statesman to remind us of
the philosopher and indeed Socrates himself. As we saw in
Section 5.1 of Chapter 3, he recycles the ship of state analogy in
the *Statesman* (*Plt.* 297E–299D). The expert navigator is called a
'stargazer' and a 'babbler' by the ignorant, just as in the *Republic*
(*Rep.* 6.488E–489A; *Plt.* 299B). And like Socrates he is taken to
court for corrupting the youth (*Plt.* 299B–C). But these similarities do not make an identity. I cannot improve on the answer to
our question given by Melissa Lane:[108]

The correct answer is both yes and no. 'Yes,' in the sense that the
statesman does have to share in at least the most important part
of the philosopher's knowledge (the definition of the good and the
virtues)...But 'No,' in the sense that the *Statesman* precisely defines
the statesman...by his knowledge of *ruling* and whose relationship to
ruling therefore differs from that of the pure philosopher....In serving as
(and so becoming) a statesman, the philosopher does not merely apply
his knowledge when forced by necessity to do so. Rather, a central
element of his nature and education is transformed by this new role
definition...Statecraft is not just a day job for a philosopher. It is a
profession, (re)defining the philosopher who undertakes it according to
its own requirements and persona, to the extent of earning him, rightly,
a new name.

(C) *Politikê* (political knowledge, or statesmanship). The most
important remark about statesmanship in the *Laws* comes in the
treatment of legislative principle at the end of the work. This
is where the Athenian Visitor discusses the body (known as the
'nocturnal council', because it will assemble at the first glim-
mers of light before dawn) which is to be charged with reviewing
the city's laws and keeping them in a sound state of preserva-
tion (12.960B–969D).[109] In explaining the role of the nocturnal
council, the Visitor stresses the importance of enshrining in the

city's constitutional arrangements a locus of understanding of the whole rationale of its legislation (just as was argued in the *Republic*: 6.497C–D), if it is to avoid simply reacting to circumstances. He supplies the council with a mission statement. It has to know (*Laws* 12.962B–C):

First (what we are discussing) the target—whatever it might be—of statesmanship. Then how to achieve it, and which of the laws themselves (principally) and then which persons have good advice on this to give, and which not.

Just as with medicine or generalship, it is essential that statesmanship have a single overall aim. In the immediate context the interlocutors agree that it should be identified as the promotion of virtue in the city. But although this thesis recapitulates earlier formulations to the same effect about the aim of legislation and statesmanship (indeed from the very start of the dialogue: e.g. *Laws* 1.630C–631A),[110] a passage in Book 3 indicates that the issue is in fact less straightforward than one might infer from that (3.693B–C):

One should always remember that a city ought to be free and wise and to enjoy friendship with itself, and that this is what the lawgiver should concentrate on in his legislation. It ought not to surprise us if several times before now we have decided on a number of other aims, and said *they* were what a lawgiver should concentrate on, so that the aims proposed never seemed to be the same from minute to minute. When we say that the legislator should keep self-control or good judgment or friendship in view, we should bear in mind that all these aims are the same, not different. Nor should we be disconcerted if we find a lot of other expressions of which the same is true.

There are two morals we can draw. First, if the goal of the statesman's activity is the promotion of virtue, he has to bear in mind that he operates within a highly complex moral and political context. Not only is moral virtue a matter of properly controlled emotions and appetites as well as the proper use of reason, but it is best developed within a framework of social harmony that results from balancing respect for the freedom of citizens on the one side and exercise of intelligent authority on the other. There is just one goal, but not one capable of simplistic articulation. Second, as Aristotle would have agreed, we cannot begin to understand political knowledge or statesmanship unless we ask at the outset what that goal is.

The *Statesman* proceeds very differently in its analysis of statesmanship. For all their sophistication, its methods of classificatory definition and controlled use of example do not characteristically involve a reasoned specification of a goal. In fact at no stage in his methodologically self-conscious sequence of discussions of the topic does the Eleatic Visitor explicitly raise and debate the question: what is the goal of statesmanship? It is only in his very last contribution to the dialogue that he spells out what the 'fabric which is the product of political knowledge or statesmanship' consists in (*Plt.* 311B–C). What he begins with is an assumption about the *form* of political knowledge: that it is architectonic or managerial. More specific assumptions are then made: it is a sort of care for a herd; it is like weaving. One of these ideas turns out to be more apposite and illuminating than the other. Reflection on the dialogue's cosmological myth is represented as forcing more adequate consideration of what human nurture of humans has to be like (*Plt.* 274E–276C). But the Visitor never acknowledges that their freedom as citizens should be regarded as one of the parameters within which political expertise will need to be exercised. In other words, one of the two ingredients the *Laws* takes to be indispensable in a good *politeia*—the wisdom of monarchy, the freedom of democracy—is left out of the picture.

7. *Conclusion*

The *Statesman* is Plato's final testament to his fascination with the idea of architectonic political knowledge. He must have been hugely attracted to it to devote so much energy and ingenuity late in his life to its articulation and analysis. The dialogue's key central passage on measure (*Plt.* 283–7) indicates what is to be the new political perspective it offers, so different from the *Republic*'s: 'the authority of political expertise (considered a form of knowledge) in a dynamic temporal context'.[111] It is hard to doubt that Plato saw his identification of the notion of the proper mean between excess and deficiency as a lasting and fundamental contribution to the understanding of political judgement. It resonates with other pivotal statements on right measure in other late dialogues (e.g. *Philebus* 26C–D, 64D–E, 66A; *Laws* 3.691C–692C, 4.716C, 718A).

At the same time, the *Statesman's* treatment of political knowledge has quizzical elements. The decision to make Socrates listen, but not speak, seems once again to confirm the ambiguous indications of *Charmides* and *Euthydemus*. It perhaps implies that the concept grows from a Socratic thought about heeding the one expert, not the ignorant many—but one that was never elaborated into a Socratic 'doctrine' like the unity of virtue. It is as though Plato is engaged in the *Statesman* on an essentially exploratory exercise. Let's take the idea of political knowledge as the key to a proper politics, it says. Let's see how far the attempt to analyse it can take us in our exploration of what sound dialectical method consists in. And let's find out how far it really does open the door to an understanding of politics. In the course of the enterprise some false moves are subsequently flagged up as such. The *Statesman* is a *lesson* in method and in politics. But (as elsewhere in Plato)[112] there are some false moves we are left to spot for ourselves—that is part of the lesson.[113] Above all (but Plato's message, rather than the Visitor's), the dialogue does not reflect as widely as it might have done on the framework of politics and the role political knowledge might play within it. In particular, it is entirely silent on the question of how the statesman it describes could ever be produced and then installed in a city, with the powers to shape its entire social and political life in the way the Visitor envisages.

These are precisely issues to which *Republic* and *Laws* devote attention. The *Laws*, for example, discusses once again the *Republic's* question of how the ideal society might be brought into being, here as elsewhere replaying ideas and themes and preoccupations from the *Republic* in its own distinctive mode. The pages it devotes to the topic (4.709D–712A)—dense as they are in echoes of the *Republic*—are apparently designed as much as anything to indicate a basic difference in the approach the *Laws* will take to political theory. The dialogue's position on the issue is at one point summed up in its most general terms as follows (4.710E–711A):

We are saying, then, that this comes about [i.e. change to the best form of political and social system] when nature supplies a true legislator and he joins forces with those who wield the greatest power in the city. And wherever power takes its strongest form in the fewest possible hands, as in a tyranny, it is there and then that changes of system happen quickly and easily.

183

What is much more difficult and unusual is to find a powerful ruler who has a 'divine passion for restraint and justice in the pursuits he engages in' (4.711D–E).[114]

Apart from the disconcerting reference to tyranny, the most significant divergence here from the *Republic* is the substitution of the legislator for the philosopher in this recipe for regime change. This is coupled with the expectation that legislator and ruler will form a duo—in contrast to the *Republic's* proposal that philosophers should themselves *become* kings (or kings become philosophers). There is no doubt a connection with a further divergence. Whereas the *Republic* will involve philosopher kings not only in the original foundation of the good city, but in ruling it once it has been established, the *Laws* gives the political strongman envisaged in the quotation a role *only* in regime change, not in the ongoing rule and management of the city. In fact, the dialogue contains a number of passages insisting that it is not in human nature to exercise absolute power in the management of political affairs without succumbing to corruption (3.691C–D, 4.713C–D, 9.875A).[115] If by some divine dispensation some human were born with the capacity for knowledge of the common good *and* the willingness and ability to promote it, then 'he would have no need of laws to rule him'. But as things are, 'we must choose the second best, law and regulation' (9.875C–D). It is law, not any human authority, that is to be sovereign.[116]

The 'second best' of law is treated with a fair degree of disdain in the *Statesman* (see Chapter 3, Section 5.1). The *Laws* represents it as public reason, which if heeded will bring 'salvation and all the good things gods bestow on cities' (4.715D). The main basis for the difference presumably lies in two related contrasts between the different circumstances in which Plato imagines legislative activity as taking place. In the *Statesman* the main hypothesis he considers is legislation by an assembly—whether democratic (the whole *dêmos*) or oligarchic (the rich)—who must take advice from anybody: experts or non-experts (*Plt.* 298B–E). In the *Laws*, by contrast, establishing a system of laws in the first instance is the job of a philosophical legislator—for whom the Athenian Visitor stands as proxy. In other words, the *Laws'* discussion operates on something much closer to utopian assumptions than does the section on law in the *Statesman*. A second difference is that on the scenario the *Statesman* has painted, enquiry by someone with genuine expertise in politics that might lead to suggestions for the improvement of the law will be outlawed: that, in particular, is what would threaten to make life under such a regime unliveable (*Plt.* 299B–300A). But the need for review of legislation is emphasized at the start of the *Laws'* concrete legislative programme (6.768E–770B). And it is to be entrusted not to an individual, but to a body (much less likely to succumb to corruption). That body is the Nocturnal Council, whose members are to be educated so as to acquire a theologically rooted understanding of the unity of virtue that equips them for statesmanship (12.963A–969D), and whose job it is to preserve the city's legislation in the best possible condition (12.960B–962E). By this mechanism, Plato in the *Laws* makes law approximate the very different functions Mill (through the Scientific Governor) and Jowett (through the philosopher statesman) had wanted a political leader to perform. Law is both the principal instrument of expert government and the society's standing repository of moral wisdom.

Notes

1. In a collection of essays commissioned to mark the elapse of 2,500 years since Cleisthenes' reform of the Athenian constitution: Dunn 1992: 257.
2. Dunn 1992: 260.
3. 'Utopian' is a term deployed with a variety of implications. Ch. 5 presents a fuller discussion: there I opt for a use of it more open so far as concerns the practicability of utopian visions.
4. That is, to that sector of the electorate that has found him attractive.
5. 'Philosophy' in the sense of a coherent set of fundamental moral and religious beliefs, rather than in Plato's more demanding interpretation.
6. For a more general introduction to the topic, accessible and learned, see Burnyeat 1998.
7. Mill 1978.
8. Guthrie 1975: xv.
9. By F. E. Sparshott, in Mill 1978: xxxviii.
10. Mill 1978: 403.
11. Grote 1865: II.512.
12. Mill 1978: 427.
13. Mill 1978: 431, 423.
14. Mill 1978: 432.
15. Mill 1978: 436.
16. Mill 1978: 439. In this chapter I have tried only to present Mill as interpreter of Plato. For discussion of his attempts to build the principle of guidance

by 'the acquired knowledge and practised intelligence of a specially trained and experienced Few' into the theory of democracy ('No progress at all can be made towards obtaining a skilled democracy unless the democracy are willing that the work which requires skill should be done by those who possess it') in *Considerations on Representative Government* (1861) and elsewhere, see e.g. Holmes 1989.

17. Grote 1865: III.409–19, with Turner 1981: 395, 402–3.
18. See Section 5.1 of Ch. 3 above.
19. Grote 1865: II.483–6, quoted in Mill 1978: 433–4.
20. Mill 1978: 433.
21. Mill 1978: 436–9.
22. Jowett 1875: II.307–8.
23. Jowett 1875: II.311.
24. Mill 1978: 432.
25. Jowett 1875: II.308.
26. It is perhaps symptomatic that Gregory Vlastos, who had no qualms about dating them with other Socratic dialogues, regarded *Euthydemus* as 'transitional' between the early and the middle dialogues, and in his writings on Socrates seldom referred to the *Charmides*: see, above all, Vlastos 1991. So far as I know, he only once offered any analysis of an argument in the *Charmides*: in the posthumously published paper on *Protagoras* and *Laches* in Vlastos 1994: ch. 5—a brief discussion at pp. 114–16 of *Charmides* 173A–174B, the dialogue's concluding argument which we shall be discussing below. Barker 1995: 18–33 comments on Vlastos's relative silence about the dialogue. Barker's paper constitutes a deft critique of Vlastos's construction of a Socratic ethics without a significant and self-conscious epistemological dimension.
27. See e.g. Kahn 1996: ch. 2.
28. For *Charmides* see e.g. Schmid 1998: viii. For *Euthydemus* see e.g. McCabe 2002a: 363–6. Both are more concerned to emphasize morals about how we should read Plato than to propose alternative datings.
29. The Visitor only fills out the details of this model for political knowledge much later in the dialogue: see, in particular, 305C–E, with my discussion in Section 5 of this chapter, pp. 170–1 above.
30. This is the approach taken by C. H. Kahn in his hypothesis of 'proleptic' composition or 'progressive disclosure' in the Platonic corpus: for discussion of the topic of the present section, see Kahn 1996: 206–9. Kahn takes it that the less quizzical treatment will in fact have been composed later in the sequence than the puzzle-setting discussion, but he stresses that the crux of the matter is the right order for *reading* (ibid. 41–2, 48).
31. As such they would be comparable with the *Hippias Major*, on the interpretation of Palmer 1999: 59–66.
32. For further debate regarding the *Euthydemus*, see McCabe 2002b.
33. Mill 1978: 186. He added that it 'can only be considered, like so many other works of Plato, to be a mere dialectical exercise, in which various ideas are thrown out, but no opinion definitely adhered to or maintained'.
34. Kahn 1996: 187. For further reflections on Plato's family references, see Michelini 2003: 59–60.

35. Mill 1978: 407.
36. Noting the stress on measure in connection with *sôphrosunê* in Critias' poetic *Politeia of the Spartans* (Fr.6.22 Diels-Kranz, with ibid. 17, 23, 26, 28): see Wilson 2003: 206 n. 107. The prominence of *sôphrosunê* in oligarchic and Spartan ideology has often been noted in discussion of the *Charmides*: see e.g. Notomi 2000: 245.
37. There is an interesting discussion of this political application of Critias' notion of an architectonic form of knowledge in Schmid 1998: ch. 7.
38. This point—often neglected or underplayed—is well made by Schmid 1998: ch. 3, who then attempts a distinction between the sound ideal of a properly Socratic knowledge of one's own ignorance, and the suspect idea of a master or ruling science associated with Critias. While this proposal has its attractions, notice that the stretch of argument specified under (ii) in the summary above (169E–171C) appears to cut as much against Socrates' claim about the limits of what he knows (and his own practice of the elenchus) as against any position to which Critias gets committed: McKim 1985; Barker 1995; Kahn 1996: 197–203.
39. A. N. Michelini, recalling that *Republic* (4.443E–444C) uses the same formula to define justice, sees 'a strong hint that the strikingly anti-egalitarian definition of Justice promulgated in *Republic* was derived from the writings of Critias'. See Michelini 2003: 63.
40. Just as there was presumably something about Nicias' intellectualism that led Plato to make him volunteer a highly Socratic definition of courage (*Laches* 194E–195A), but then prove quite incapable of defending it under questioning from Socrates. See e.g. O'Brien 1967: 110–17.
41. So Barker 1995: 31. Thomas Schmid offers a more highly coloured version of the same thought: the ideology of the thirty tyrants 'may have been partly inspired by the Socratic "dream" of wise rule: a strangely decadent, quasi-fascist synthesis of aristocratic/Laconophilic and epistemic/sophistic presumption': Schmid 1998: 129.
42. Sprague 1976: 91.
43. So e.g. Kahn 1996: 209.
44. Tongue in cheek though both these suggestions are, as often in Plato there is a barbed subtext. The speech-writer who cannot himself make use of his productions is surely meant to put us in mind of Plato's rival Isocrates, who notoriously never himself spoke in public (allegedly on account of his weak voice), and who is very probably the target of the attack in the epilogue to the dialogue (*Euthd.* 304C–306D) on people—again identified as speech-writers—who dabble in both philosophy and politics and fall between two stools (see especially 305C). By comparison the proposal about generals is rather underplayed: perhaps we are to think of Pericles, whose dominance of Athenian politics was associated with a long sequence of re-elections to the office of general.
45. We can presumably infer that dialectic, as defined in the *Republic*, is an architectonic science, inasmuch as it knows how to use the discoveries made in mathematics (*Euthd.* 290C).
46. The vocabulary of 'handing over' is one of the commonalities between the *Charmides* and *Euthydemus* passages, whose close interconnection

has always been recognized. In the *Charmides* statesmen hand over other functions to the experts they know to have the expertise to perform them correctly (*Charm.* 171E); in the *Euthydemus* makers and hunters hand over the things they produce or discover to those who have the expertise required to use them properly (*Euthd.* 290B–D).

47. So Gill 2000: 140.
48. So McCabe 2005: 207.
49. See e.g. Gray 2000: 146–51.
50. The interpretation of this thesis has been much discussed. See e.g. McCabe 2002a: 380–6.
51. Mill 1978: 432.
52. So e.g. Striker 1994: 248. See further p. 163 above.
53. Kahn 1996: 209.
54. So far as concerns the relation of the mathematical sciences to dialectic, it is striking that unlike the geometricians and astronomers of the *Euthydemus*, who hand over their discoveries to the dialecticians to use (*Euthd.* 290B–C), those Socrates talks about in the *Republic* are content to leave their assumptions unquestioned, without feeling any need to subject them to dialectical examination (*Rep.* 6.511A, 7.533B–C). The *Euthydemus'* mathematicians are mathematicians as they might be; the *Republic* mathematicians as they are. This only highlights the very different agendas being pursued at comparable junctures in the two dialogues.
55. Ferrari and Griffith 2000: xxi.
56. Ferrari and Griffith 2000: xx.
57. See Diogenes Laertius 8.79, 82; Strabo, *Geography* 6.280. He is sometimes thought to be the model for the figure of Timaeus in Plato's dialogue and to have inspired some of its ideas. And the *Seventh Letter* makes Archytas' good offices crucial in extricating Plato from the clutches of Dionysius II on his final visit to Sicily. How far he might have approximated to Plato's ideal of a philosopher ruler is uncertain. For a judicious review of the evidence relating to Archytas, see Huffman 2005.
58. See Nightingale 1995: ch. 1.
59. See the note on *Rep.* 6.487C in Adam 1902: II.8.
60. Nightingale 2004: 127.
61. For more on philosophical *erôs*, see Kahn 1996: 271–81; cf. also Ferrari 1992.
62. For more on Platonic Forms, see e.g. White 1992; Kahn 1996: ch. 11.
63. See Burnyeat 2000: 1–81. Burnyeat sees Plato as pointing the reader to an understanding that the good is a function of unity. This is a theme taken up in its own terms in the *Laws*. What is needed above all in legislation and statesmanship, according to the Athenian Visitor (*Laws* 12.963A–964A), is synoptic understanding of what makes the goal of the enterprise a single thing: in short, the grasp of the one in the many that is precisely what the *Republic* saw as the distinctive achievement of philosophy (*Rep.* 5.475E–476D; cf. 6.507A–B). That means seeing exactly what the four virtues have in common, but also (the Visitor proposes) what make the good and the noble or beautiful one—exactly as the *Republic* had insisted (*Laws* 12.965B–966B).

64. For further discussion of the artist model, see Nightingale 2004: 127–31; more speculative is Reeve 1988: 82–6. There are excellent remarks on philosophy, not a special *technê* or expertise, as what equips philosophers to rule, in Cambiano 1988: 55–7.

65. The *Euthydemus* ended up talking of a knowledge that provides us with something good (*Euthd.* 292A), but could not explain what that meant or how it could be true (292D–E). Similarly, the *coup de grâce* for Critias comes with his admission that the knowledge that can make us happy will have to have good and bad as its subject matter (*Charm.* 174B). See pp. 148, 149 above.

66. The most accessible and stimulating monograph on the rather inaccessible *Statesman* is Lane 1998a. See also the old translation with long introduction of Skemp 1952. There is a more recent and reliable translation: Rowe 1995a; available also in Cooper 1997b. Rowe 1995b offers a representative sample of recent scholarship.

67. There had already been disparagement of the herdsman analogy in the *Theaetetus* (see Lane 2005: 330). Socrates says there of the philosopher that 'when he hears the praises of a despot or a king being sung, it sounds to his ears as if some stock-breeder were being congratulated'. But he thinks rulers have a 'more difficult and treacherous animal to rear and milk', and having no leisure will inevitably become 'as coarse and uncultivated as the stock-farmer' (*Tht.* 174D–E).

68. It is sometimes represented that the *Statesman* is a poorly constructed dialogue: see e.g. Annas and Waterfield 1995: ix–xii. For an exposition and defence of its structure, see Rowe 1996: 159–71.

69. See e.g. Diès 1935: ix: 'Tel est donc, en définitive, l'objet de notre dialogue: un problème politique servant de matière à des exercices dialectiques et à des considérations de méthode.' This interpretation has recently been elaborated at length in Delcomminette 2000.

70. Julia Annas aptly comments (Annas and Waterfield 1995: 45 n. 43): 'It need not be, as sometimes thought, that the point of the dialogue is to develop a topic-neutral ability that could just as well have been practised on something else. Rather, getting an adequate account of the expertise of ruling is not philosophically self-contained: in deepening our understanding of one area of philosophy we thereby improve the philosophical skills that will also be employed elsewhere.'

71. As Section 6 will argue, abstraction will turn out to be a particularly salient feature of the *Statesman* when comparison is made with the *Republic* and the *Laws*.

72. Some scholars see the dialogue form as still alive and well in the *Statesman*: see e.g. Miller 1980; Gill 1995. For the case against, see Rowe 1996: 171–8. What can be said is that in all his recantations and sidetracking, the Eleatic Visitor conveys the impression—for all his systematic ambitions—of a thinker arguing *with himself*.

73. There is no evidence that 'the younger Socrates' had any family connection with his more famous namesake. His identity is uncertain: no less than eighteen persons bearing the name 'are apparently of the right age to be the younger Socrates' (Nails 2002: 269).

74. Later one of the thirty tyrants (*Parm.* 127D). Perhaps Aristoteles of Thorae, son of Timocrates, who was to become an Athenian general in the Peloponnesian War: see Nails 2002: 57–8. It is hard to avoid the suspicion that his choice as interlocutor is a Platonic joke. Does Plato mean his name to call to mind *his* more famous and much more argumentative and independent-minded namesake, already by the time *Parmenides* was composed a member of the Academy, and doubtless already given to contesting Platonic theses with vigour?

75. Cooper 1997a: 73–8. As he points out, the thesis is criticized in the first chapter of Aristotle's *Politics* (*Pol.* 1.1, 1252a8–16), and the rest of the first book is shaped by a determination to bring out the significant differences between the various forms of rule. On this, see Schofield 1990: 16–20.

76. The Visitor draws attention to the word play (see Rowe 1995a: 239).

77. Cooper 1997a: 90–102.

78. See Scheid and Svenbro 1996; and on its use in the *Statesman* the comprehensive essay of Blondell 2005.

79. Lane 1998a: 166.

80. Lane 1998a: 167.

81. See Blondell 2005: 67–71 (quotation from p. 68).

82. Lane 1998a: 169.

83. See Hansen 1991: 268–77, on *rhetores kai strategoi*, 'the speakers and the generals', as the expression in ancient Greek most nearly corresponding to our 'politicians'.

84. I develop a fuller version of the argument of this paragraph in Schofield 1997: 224–30.

85. On the comparison (and contrast) with Aristotle, see Lane 1998a: 182–9.

86. Lane 1998a: 145–6 observes that the notion of judgement of the right time for action is not absent from the *Republic*: 'What originates the degeneration of the ideal city in *Republic* VIII is the philosopher-guardians' misjudgment of the *kairos*' (i.e. the right moment). But as she goes on to comment, 'calculation of the *kairos* is not part of the philosopher-rulers' mathematical studies which are purely theoretical. It belongs rather to the domain of application, applying mathematics to the seasonal demands of determining the right moment for sexual intercourse.'

87. Anyone who has failed a test for suitability for education will have been weeded out beforehand and marked down for slavery (if stupid) or elimination of one sort or another (if vicious). This is a problem briefly addressed also at the beginning of Book 5 of the *Laws* (5.735A–736C).

88. The *Republic* had already registered the problem diagnosed by the *Statesman*, which is that such traits are naturally at odds with each other (see e.g. *Rep.* 2.375B, 3.410C–411A). It also recognizes that in some people one naturally dominates, in some the other (*Rep.* 3.411B–C, 6.503B–D). The *Laws*—which gives provisions governing marriage great prominence in its presentation of a legal code—agrees with the *Statesman* in wanting eugenics to play an important role in addressing the issue (*Laws* 6.772E–773E). For discussion of the relationship between the Visitor's treatment of courage and restraint and the Socratic conception of virtue (and the unity of virtue), see Mishima 1995 and Bobonich 1995.

89. The *Statesman*'s overall objectives of a virtuous citizenry united in consensus, friendship and happiness are shared with the *Republic* (e.g. 4.420B–421C, 432A) and the *Laws* (e.g. 1.631B, 3.693B–E, 5.743C).

90. To the ears of some scholars, there are various features of the society envisaged in this account of the fabric woven by the statesman that sound broadly democratic in flavour. These include, for example, the provision of a role in it for orators and political persuasion, provisions for the appointment of office-holders, and the apparent absence of hierarchical social and political stratification: see e.g. Samaras 2002: ch. 10. But the dialogue makes no attempt to etch the form political life will take. All the features just mentioned reappear in the constitution of the ideal city of the *Laws*, which has some affinities with what dissident intellectuals conceived of as Solonian democracy, but little resemblance to the Athenian democracy of Plato's own day. One may recall that Homer represents the assemblies of the voteless Greek army before Troy as a forum for oratory (cf. Schofield 1986). See further Ch. 2, Section 3.2 (especially n. 83).

91. I make no apology for using 'management' to identify the sort of expertise delineated by the *Statesman*'s *politikê*. When Protagoras spells out the prospectus for the *politikê technê* he claims to teach, it is articulated in terms of the management (*dioikein*) of the affairs of one's household and ability in acting and speaking where the affairs of the city are concerned (*Prot.* 318E–319A); and for Isocrates what marks out ability in *politikê* is management (*dioikêsis*) of the city as a whole (*Evagoras* 46; he is drawing a contrast with the ability to gratify the *dêmos*).

92. A similar story could be told about the *Laws*, which is wholly devoted to developing a framework for political and social order. Discussions of the educational system fundamental to sustaining it occupy most of Books 1 and 2 (focused on character development) as well as rounding off the entire work (the end of Book 12 deals with the academic studies appropriate for those who are charged with reviewing the legal code). See further Ch. 1, Section 5.

93. In this paragraph I am reproducing material first published in Schofield 1997: 221–2.

94. There is an interesting discussion of the significance of Plato's choice of an anonymous Visitor from Elea as main speaker in *Sophist* and *Statesman* by Blondell 2002: ch. 6. See also Gonzalez 2000, which answers the question put in its title—'The Eleatic stranger: his master's voice?'—more negatively than I shall be doing.

95. For the evidence, see Gifford 2001.

96. See Ch. 1, Sections 2 and 3.

97. See Strauss 1972: 43. The contrast is emphasized, and its implications explored, e.g. by Rosen 1995 and Kochin 1999.

98. See my discussion in Ch. 2, Section 3.3, and Ch. 7, Section 3.2, with Bobonich 1991 and Kamtekar 2004.

99. It is also briefly introduced at 276E, where the Visitor proposes that kingship is distinguished from tyranny because it is rule by consent, not compulsion. This distinction (found also e.g. in Xenophon: *Mem.* 4.6.12) is evidently superseded by the discussion at 292B–293D (so Klosko 1986:

191–2). Despite its evident merit, it is to be seen in context as an over-hasty and superficial attempt to correct the confessedly flawed account of kingship given in the opening section of the dialogue (261A–268D): over-hasty because it is proffered without the benefit of the profound reflections on philosophical method still to come (277A–287A), and before the mad logic of the doctor analogy of 292B–293D takes over. See further the excellent note on 276E in Rowe 1995a: 200.

100. But John Cooper observes (Cooper 1997a: 92–7) that later in his exposition, when explaining how the expert ruler will approach the task of government, the Eleatic Visitor envisages him presiding over a community in which (as in the *Laws*) the education of the citizens into virtue is seen as the major challenge, with coercion mentioned only in connection with the treatment of persons with an 'evil nature' (*Plt.* 308D–309D). The Visitor speaks of the need for a 'divine bond' in their souls, consisting in 'really true opinion about what is fine, just and good, held securely' (309C). So in practice it seems likely that he would ordinarily want to govern with the willing cooperation of the citizens, even if that is not how scientific government is defined.

101. See again Ch. 2, Section 3.3.

102. Cooper 1997a: 100 n. 37.

103. For more on why—according to the *Republic*—philosophers will agree to rule, see Ch. 7, Section 2.5.

104. I quote the formulation of Lane 2005: 336.

105. See Samaras 2002: ch. 8; quotations from pp. 144–6.

106. See Section 4 above.

107. McCabe 1997: 115–16; cf. e.g. Dorter 2001. Against the attempt to assimilate the statesman with the philosopher ruler, see e.g. Zuckert 2005, e.g. p. 8: 'According to the Stranger's definition, neither Socrates nor his philosopher-king is a statesman.'

108. Lane 2005: 337. She goes on to add (with reference to *Sophist* 216B–217A): 'This suggests the need for a careful interpretation of the way in which Socrates fills in the possible ways in which philosophers appear to non-philosophers' (ibid. 342).

109. The need for review had been indicated at the very start of the concrete legislative programme (beginning with the marriage laws of Book 6). Here Plato makes another application of the *Republic*'s painter analogy. Just as even the best painting will need repair work over time, so with the legislator's efforts (6.769D–E): 'His purpose is first to write laws with as much precision as he can. But then as time progresses and he puts his decrees to the test of practice, do you think any legislator so foolish as not to appreciate that his work inevitably has many omissions which must be corrected by some successor, so that the system and the ordering of the city he has founded may be always improving, not deteriorating at all?'

110. See e.g. Stalley 1983: ch. 4; Bobonich 2002: 119–23. Book 1 ends with the Athenian Visitor remarking (1.650B): 'So insight into the nature and disposition of people's souls will rank as one of the most useful aids to the expertise which is concerned with fostering a good character. And that,

I take it, we agree to be political knowledge or statesmanship.' Cleinias agrees.

111. Lane 1998a: 137; see also Lane 1995.
112. See e.g. the discussion of Part 3 of the *Theaetetus* in Burnyeat 1990.
113. For suggestions along similar lines relating to the difficulties in the *Statesman* discussed in (A) above, see Kamtekar 2004: 164; and relating to the treatment of kingship and law (discussed in Ch. 3, Section 5.1), Michelini 2000.
114. Here Plato's pen is drenched in irony and paradox (cf. Schofield 1997: 230–41). Roberto Polito has suggested in discussion that a clue to the point of the irony may be a bitter implicit contrast: between the Athenian Visitor's requirements of the tyrant and the city he rules, and what Plato found at Syracuse on his disastrous visits to the court of the young Dionysius II. Two such prerequisites are distance from a good harbour (through harbours gold and silver flood in—and all the vices they enable citizens to pay for), and restraint (despite a 'tyrannized soul') in the young tyrant: *Laws* 4.704A–705B; 709E–710A. Restrained was precisely what Dionysius wasn't; and the thing everyone knew about Syracuse was that it possessed a great harbour.
115. See the discussion in Section 6 (B) above.
116. This need not mean that when he wrote the *Laws*, Plato had abandoned the *Republic*'s vision of philosopher rulers as a vision. Here as elsewhere the *Laws* offers an approximation to an ideal which it characterizes as suitable only for 'gods and children of gods' (5.739B–E). For a fuller treatment of this material in the *Laws*, see further Laks 1990 and Schofield 1997: 230–41.

5

Utopia

1. Against Utopia

1.1 Late twentieth-century inquests

One thing everybody knows about the *Republic* is that it is the first great work of political utopianism ever written—although it was not for another 2,000 years that the word 'utopia' was invented (by Sir Thomas More, early in the sixteenth century). In some minds that description will at once ring warning bells. Wasn't the construction of utopias a blind alley for political thought and (still more) for the pursuit of happiness? And isn't it an activity—whether literary or political—we are now thankfully rid of? Not for nothing, it might be said, was the second half of the twentieth century punctuated by inquests on the entire enterprise: *After Utopia*,[1] *The End of Ideology*,[2] *Das Ende der Utopie*,[3] *The End of Utopia*,[4] and (ambiguously, but perhaps most notoriously of all) *The End of History*,[5] even if the note they were striking was seldom uncomplicatedly triumphalist. Utopianism sometimes looks like a nightmare that disfigured much of European historical experience over the last two centuries or so—and which is now over, to be replaced by a different and global repertoire of social and political trauma in our own time.[6] Here is one particularly succinct and comprehensive verdict:[7]

The dream of a rational and organized society was held not just by Stalinists but was part of a persistent faith within western societies from the Enlightenment onwards. As with Saint-Simon, the vision of a managed society in which efficiency prevailed is one which unites Victorian patriarchs and 20th century social democrats, welfarists, corporatists and technocrats. The charnel-house terminal point of this version of utopia is to be found in the slave labour and death camps of Auschwitz, Dachau, Treblinka, Bergen-Belsen and Ravensbruck—the whole roll call of horror that has indelibly stained and falsified European pretensions to civilization.

The authors then cite Zygmunt Bauman's analysis of the Holocaust as an actual expression of modern civilization 'in its industrialized, bureaucratized genocide'. The argument is that the development and execution of the idea of the Holocaust owed much to a prevailing conception of society as 'a collection of so many "problems" to be solved, as "nature" to be "controlled", "mastered" and "improved" or "remade", as a legitimate target for social engineering, and in general a garden to be designed and kept in the planned shape by force'.[8] Underlying that characteristically utopian conception is a presumption of knowledge: its proponents presumed a knowledge about the world and about what is best for other people that was no doubt always questionable and objectionable (every utopia arguably a dystopia), and with the final collapse of communism is now generally perceived as an illusion.[9]

1.2 Assessments of the *Republic*

The best known of twentieth-century accounts of the political vision of Plato's *Republic* situated it precisely within the context just described. Karl Popper's book *The Open Society and its Enemies*[10] was originally published at the end of the Second World War (in 1945), and is among other things a response to fascist and Marxist ideologies by a refugee from Nazi Austria: an attempt to expose what he regarded as their utterly wrong-headed intellectual foundations. Volume One of the work is devoted mostly to Plato, because Popper saw in the *Republic* the first wholesale rationalizing project for a closed authoritarian society in the Western tradition. He took the dialogue to be advocating the use of totalitarian methods, first to entrench a regressively archaizing class system, and then to protect it from the possibility of subsequent change. Popper was in no doubt that Plato intended a blueprint for action, and indeed for vesting power as a philosopher ruler in his own hands.[11]

Popper was trying among other things to break 'the spell of Plato', as he put it. Should we heave a sigh of relief that with the general demise of the utopian hope of imposing rational order on society, Popper's project is no longer necessary—and read the *Republic*, if we read it, for other reasons? Before we start to ponder that reaction, I want to present two other interpretations of Plato's vision which raise further problems for the idea that he might be worth reading *for* his utopianism. One of these denies—with conscious paradox—that Plato *was* a utopian thinker. This is the interpretation associated with Leo Strauss, like Popper a refugee from the Nazi regime. Strauss construed the *Republic* as an *anti*-utopian work.[12] His Plato makes it clear enough to the careful, initiated reader that the political scenario he paints—especially the women guards, the sexual communism, the eugenic breeding programme, the philosopher rulers of the central books—is a comic fantasy in Aristophanic vein. The fantasy is designed to lead us to the conclusion that any attempt to reconstruct the realm of the political on rationalist lines would generate a dystopia built on injustice, not justice, doomed anyway to impracticability because it ignores the natural basis of the relationship between the sexes and the exigencies of sexual desire. The moral? We are left to draw that for ourselves. But since the recipients of Socrates' teaching in the dialogue are young 'gentlemen'—Glaucon and Adeimantus—whose motivations and potentialities are the subject of discreet comment as it unfolds, we like them are presumably meant to infer that traditional aristocratic leadership is the best practical option in a necessarily imperfect world. Strauss's *Republic* is obviously in many ways the polar opposite of Popper's. For one thing, Strauss was intensely preoccupied with the problems that utopian *writing* unavoidably poses for the reader: something to which Popper seems to have been tone deaf. But they share some premises. Both see Plato as engaging in utopianism as a practical agenda—in Popper's eyes to endorse it, in Strauss's to represent it as fantastic, and so to subvert it. For both, utopianism is a rationalist nightmare. Both were obsessed with the form it assumed with communism.[13]

There is an affinity between these reactions to the utopianism of the *Republic* and the horrified fascination with Plato and the Platonist legacy that readers of Nietzsche recognize as a fundamental leitmotiv running through many of his writings.

Nietzsche's response to Plato is a third reaction I want to consider. In the preface to *Daybreak* (1881: an early instance) he asks (§3):

Why is it that from Plato onwards every philosophical architect in Europe has built in vain? That everything they themselves in all sober seriousness regarded as *aere perennius* is threatening to collapse or already lies in ruins?

By way of possible answer he mentions—only to reject it—the need for a *critique* of reason (the Kantian recipe), and then continues:

The correct answer would rather have been that all philosophers were building under the seduction of morality, even Kant—that they were apparently aiming at certainty, at 'truth', but in reality at '*majestic moral structures*' (*Critique of Pure Reason* II, p. 257).

The preface to *Beyond Good and Evil* (1886) compares dogmatic philosophy to astrology, the classic example of the projection of human hopes and fears into what is then asserted as the truth about the nature of the universe. From a vantage point of liberation and confidence Nietzsche strikes an attitude of sadness:

It seems that all great things first have to bestride the earth in monstrous and frightening masks in order to inscribe themselves in the hearts of humanity with eternal demands: dogmatic philosophy was such a mask; for example, the Vedanta doctrine in Asia and Platonism in Europe. Let us not be ungrateful to it, although it must certainly be conceded that the worst, most durable, and most dangerous of all errors so far was a dogmatist's error—namely, Plato's invention of the pure spirit and the good as such. But now that it is overcome, now that Europe is breathing freely again after this nightmare and at least can enjoy a healthier—sleep, we, *whose task is wakefulness itself*, are the heirs of all that strength which has been fostered by the fight against this error.

For Nietzsche Plato's entire philosophical project constitutes a radical refusal of reality, masquerading as an assertion of ultimate truth: utopianism in the worst sense of the word.

2. *A Question of Seriousness*

Commenting on Nietzsche's preference for Thucydides over Plato ('What is it I love in Thucydides? Why do I honour him more highly than Plato?' *Daybreak*, §168), Bernard Williams offered some reflections on the shape of the wishfulness discerned by Nietzsche in the whole architecture of Platonist philosophy (although sometimes Nietzsche doubted Plato's actual commitment to a doctrine like the immortality of the soul: *The Will to Power*, §428). Near the end of *Shame and Necessity* he wrote:[14]

The important question ... is whether or not a given writer or philosophy believes that, beyond some things that human beings have themselves shaped, there is anything at all that is intrinsically shaped to human interests, in particular to human beings' ethical interests. In the light of that question and the distinctions it invites, Plato, Aristotle, Kant, Hegel are all on the same side, all believing in one way or another that the universe or history or the structure of human reason can, when properly understood, yield a pattern that makes sense of human life and human aspirations. Sophocles and Thucydides, by contrast, are alike in leaving us with no such sense. Each of them represents human beings as dealing sensibly, foolishly, sometimes catastrophically, sometimes nobly, with a world that is only partially intelligible to human agency and in itself is not necessarily well adjusted to ethical aspirations. In this perspective the difference between a Sophoclean obscurity of fate and Thucydides' sense of rationality at risk to chance is not so significant.

These remarks prompt the main question I want to address in this chapter. It can be expressed in terms of a particular kind of choice between Thucydides and Plato.[15] Thucydidean realism about human nature and the sheer contingency of things discounts hope as 'almost invariably deluding' and 'overwhelmingly destructive' in its effects.[16] Is that the only truly rational approach to political understanding, whether on the part of interpreters or for political agents themselves? Or does the kind of utopianism Plato explores in the *Republic* offer a way of thinking seriously about how things might be different which avoids false optimism, and indeed false consciousness, regarding the prospects for fulfilling common human aspirations? What I have in mind is not any suggestion that the substantive utopian proposals of the *Republic*—such as the communistic social arrangements it spells out, or its recourse to philosopher rulers—are options for the twenty-first century. My concerns are about the *manner* in which Plato explores such possibilities. Does it exhibit a grip on what a Thucydides might recognize as reality?[17] Does it yield an approach to the ideal that contains anything we might now find compelling or penetrating (despite the dangers of metaphysical illusion)? In developing an assessment which has positive as well as negative components, I shall argue first that there is reason to believe that utopian thinking of one form or another is an inescapable human constant. Then I shall point to a number of ways in which the *Republic* takes pains to confront the realities of human nature and social existence in working out its powerfully articulated but highly contentious ideal of community. Finally, I shall consider the highly nuanced position Plato's Socrates adopts on the issue of the practicability of the programme, and in that context we shall find ourselves reflecting on Plato's preoccupation with the problem of utopian writing.

3. *A Future for Utopianism*

The inquests have been pronounced. Yet is utopian thinking necessarily located the other side of a historical divide making this dimension of the *Republic* alien to us, not just in content but in the very idea of it? Or—as I shall be arguing—is it simply taking new forms, as one might expect if there was reason to judge it to be an inescapable ingredient in the intellectual life of any vigorous political society of any sophistication? Let us start with a definition. I propose without originality that we define utopian thinking very broadly, as the imagining of a blueprint for a desired world which is nevertheless located in present-day concerns, with questions about practicability and legitimacy not necessarily excluded, but regarded as secondary.[18] And now the argument for holding that utopianism will always be with us. It might go like this: Human thought is always dealing with the possible as well as the actual. Where it engages with the practical—what should I do? what is the best thing for us to do?—there is often no option but to explore alternatives. The picturing of alternative possibilities is accordingly a fundamental human activity, and something we all of us engage in virtually all the time, whether in reaching small- or large-scale decisions for ourselves, family, friends and sometimes country, or in our professions and occupations as plumbers, doctors, cellphone salesmen, musicians, engineers or whatever. Utopian thinking could be regarded as a particularly ambitious and comprehensive exercise in the imagination of alternatives: the attempt to envisage how the whole structure of society—its spatial organization, its communications systems, its patterns of work and leisure, its educational arrangements, the role it recognizes for individual choice—might be differently and better constituted.[19]

Hope without a utopian dimension is liable to be too unambitious for our own good. This might be thought a particular drawback to faith in Western liberalism. As Raymond Geuss writes:[20]

Liberalism has for a long time seemed to lack much inspirational potential; it is good at dissolving traditional modes of life and their associated values, but less obviously good at replacing them with anything particularly distinctive or admirable. It fits all too comfortably with some of the more ignoble aspects of commercial society. What contribution could liberalism conceivably make to thinking about the general degradation of the planetary environment? Liberal ideals like individualism, toleration, or limitation of state power seem either short-sightedly confused or mere covers for hegemonic designs.

In principle utopian thinking could take any number of different forms. For example, it could involve radical rejection of whatever dominant assumptions might be supposed to underpin society as it is at present. Or (not necessarily alternatively) it could be articulated as a projection of existing developments and potentialities into a new dominant general pattern. And one might expect it to be expressed in a variety of literary or other forms of representation, from analysis to narrative, and from science fiction to the futuristic models of planners and architects. Once you start looking, you can in fact find utopian thinking everywhere. Begin with a website—try typing 'utopia' into a search engine.[21] For those who prefer older technologies, *The Faber Book of Utopias* starts with the anonymous Egyptian 'Tale of a Shipwrecked Sailor' from the early years of the Middle Kingdom (1940–1640 BC), but it ends with various pieces published in the last thirty years of the twentieth century AD.[22] These include scientific projection, Disneyland as dystopia (something of an obsession among academics), an extract from the last chapter of Julian Barnes's *A History of the World in $10\frac{1}{2}$ Chapters* (1989), and the account of the utopian country of Aleatoria (under the title 'The Lottery State') by the political theorist Barbara Goodwin, from her book *Justice by Lottery* (1992). Of the same era is Philip Allott's *Eunomia: New Order for a New World* (1990): 'an unashamedly *idealist* social philosophy', as he put it in the preface to the 2001 paperback edition, which works out a vision of an international social order that is already 'beginning to socialize itself in spite of itself'. Nor have analytic philosophers abandoned utopia as a category. Robert Nozick's *Anarchy, State, and Utopia* (1974) proposes a version of utopia as a framework in which people can realize their own communal visions of the good life—the positive possibility inherent in what he calls the 'minimal state': the state as the protective agency preventing violations of rights to life, liberty and property (and doing nothing more), which Nozick argued was its only morally justifiable form. Thomas Nagel's *Equality and Partiality* (1991) takes 'the problem of utopianism' (the title of an early chapter in the book) to constitute a standing hazard for *any* political theory: i.e. the danger of neglecting to ensure that the impersonal ideals the theory posits are consonant with the motivations people are likely to be able to develop in practice as agents with personal commitments.

The ideal of the global village is perhaps the most potent form of utopianism in evidence today.[23] Perhaps one reason why we do not instantly recognize it as such is that it often defines itself as a contemporary realism, filling the spaces left by the demise of attempts to implement the centralized and bureaucratized visions of a society organized for happiness mentioned at the beginning of the chapter. It is often identified with the idea of a liberalized, globalized free market, as articulated in the so-called 'Washington consensus': 'the dominant orthodoxy over the last twenty years in leading OECD countries, and in the international financial institutions'.[24] That was an *idea* long before it started to resemble a description of how at least parts of the modern world actually work, notably as proposed in the most general philosophical terms by Friedrich von Hayek in *The Constitution of Liberty* (1960). It is, of course, utopian thought of a very different kind from the modes it has displaced. That might make it harder to recognize *as* utopian. What it envisages is 'a deconcentration of capital, fragmented and flexible organisational forms, erosion of class as a meaningful identifier and a declining role for the State', effected by a visible, not invisible hand.[25] But it evokes the same fervour as earlier utopian agendas (Philip Allott calls it 'a fundamentalist religion').[26] It sometimes makes claims to historical inevitability reminiscent of Marxism, founded on the same presumption of knowledge.

201

And some of the vocabulary it has characteristically appropriated and helped to foster—'empowerment', 'enterprise', 'flexibility', 'lifelong learning', for example—testifies to the hope of a new form of human identity and fulfilment, just as other utopianisms had promised in their own terms.

Everything about globalization is contested, however. I am referring not just to the bitter opposition to the global market orchestrated by the anti-globalization movement.[27] Different visions of a globalized world are on offer.[28] Some point instead to the ideal of a globalized civil society, and argue that—as with the global market—this is an ideal already realized in a 'vast, sprawling non-governmental constellation of many institutionalized structures, associations and networks within which individual and group actors are interrelated and functionally interdependent', encompassing religion, sport, science, medicine, the media and the internet, and the activities of NGOs, to mention but a few salient instances, and enabling 'its participants—athletes, campaigners, musicians, religious believers, managers, aid-workers, teleworkers, medics, scientists, journalists, academics— . . . to regard this society as *theirs*'.[29] Others argue that the time is ripe for a political project: global social democracy. History is seen as preparing the way, as the deficiencies of neoliberalism and the anti-globalization response become ever more apparent in the face of the sorts of challenge posed by global terrorism and global environmental damage: 'The contemporary phase of globalization is transforming the foundations of world order, leading away from a world based exclusively on state politics to a new and more complex form of global politics and multilayered governance.'[30]

In short, utopian visions are in no less plentiful supply today than in the past. Some inevitably will be more attractive than others, in substance and method too. While utopianism on my argument constitutes a fundamental and constant strain within Western political thought, it would plainly be naive to expect anything other than a huge variety in the forms that speculation of this kind will have taken over the centuries. The position is rather like the one that obtains with religion. Religion is always and everywhere. But religion in ancient Greece is a very different phenomenon from religion in contemporary America; and in ancient Greece and modern America alike it assumes different forms and finds many different modes of expression. In particular, once we consider *literary* expression, we are immediately confronted with the problem of what a writer is *doing* with the material—how he or she plays with it, what specific questions are addressed, how the writer positions him- or herself relative to those who may be considered as rivals, what genre and medium are adopted, and so forth. It should therefore go without saying (to return to Plato and the *Republic*) that we cannot simply take it for granted that its enquiry into justice is anything like the same kind of exercise as—for example—the one John Rawls undertook in *A Theory of Justice* (1972), even though Rawls's treatise might well be described as utopian.[31] In considering whether the way Plato does utopia retains some interest or appeal despite its remoteness from us, I return first to the Nietzschean question of realism. Is Plato's utopianism a flight from reality, or a way of coming to terms with it?

4. Plato's Utopian Realism

4.1 The Golden Age and the swollen city

In Book 3 of the *Laws* Plato sketches his own picture of a Golden Age. What would conditions for humans be like after the flood (not Noah's Flood, but its Greek equivalent—Deucalion's Flood). He makes three crucial suppositions. First, they would live in small, isolated rural communities. Second, an abundance of flocks and herds would suffice for an ample diet of milk and meat, further supplemented by hunting; they would also be well supplied with clothing, bedding, housing and pottery. Third, all knowledge of metals and metal-working would have been lost—they would have no iron or bronze, no gold or silver. The consequence? No *stasis* (civil strife), no war, no arts of war—including under these litigation and all the other means humans have devised for inflicting harm and injury on each other. These would be virtuous people and friendly communities. In fact what Plato sees as developing among them is a great nobility and simplicity of character. They would be braver and at the same time more restrained and all round more full of justice than the present generation—even if the heights of goodness and the depths of vice would not have been within their reach (*Laws* 3.677E–679E).[32]

There is no such innocence in the good city of the *Republic*. It is set in a world Thucydides would have had no difficulty in recognizing: where the appetites—above all materialistic appetites—are rampant, and where in consequence war and *stasis* rage.[33] The political argument begun in Book 2 does start with the model of a reciprocal community of farmers and artisans (and eventually merchants, retailers and hired labourers) which has something of the same simplicity as the post-deluvial settlements described in the *Laws* (*Rep.* 2.369B–372D). This simplicity is something of an arbitrary hypothesis on Socrates' part: with foreign trade and a market already in operation, there seems to be no structural reason why members of such a community should be content with having only their basic needs met. As Rachel Barney asks: 'What is to prevent the appetites of such people from becoming immoderate?'[34] In any event, Socrates goes on immediately to complicate the model.

He imagines this 'first city' no longer content to have the necessities of life supplied, but saturated with luxuries of every conceivable sort: a swollen and inflamed city. Satisfying its appetites will require an imperialistic acquisition of more territory, and the next inevitable step will be war. Socrates in the *Phaedo* had located the root cause of war and *stasis* and fighting in the body and its appetites (*Phd.* 66C). The *Republic* too makes this the origin of war in particular (2.373D–374A; cf. 372E–373C), and of the evils permeating private and public life in cities more generally (2.373E; cf. 5.473D, 6.501E); hence the downfall of the ideal city itself (8.546D–547B). For waging war a new class has to be introduced: to give the city its military capacity (2.373E–374E).

There is not much mystery about Socrates' decision to develop this more complex model of a political community. As he implies, the kind of complexity he introduces will assist the project of discovering the origins of justice and injustice in cities (2.372E)—and consequently in the individual soul, too. What that thought presumably carries with it is a recognition that no theory of what human goodness consists in, or of what it is to be a properly functioning political community, will be worth much *unless* it takes due account of human appetite and the forces of evil it unleashes within societies of a size and complexity typical of the civilized world. Primitivism, in short, is not a serious option.[35]

However if a complex political community *is* to function properly—to be the good city Socrates will claim in the *Republic* he has constructed (4.427E)—it is plainly out of the question for it to remain swollen and inflamed. Reflecting on Plato's way of ensuring that it doesn't will take us to the core of his thinking about war and society and the role of a warrior class within it. His starting point seems to have been Sparta.[36] In the scenario Socrates paints in Book 2, what necessitates the introduction of a military class in the first place is an expansionist economy: something in the first instance predicated of the community he and Glaucon are imagining, but immediately assumed to be the condition of neighbouring cities too (2.373D). Yet the presence of a militia provides the opportunity for radical reshaping of the whole orientation of a society. If the warrior class can be trained to value virtue not wealth, and if it does not merely protect the city from external dangers, but controls the way society operates within, then it is possible to create a community 'purged' of luxury (to use Socrates' own expression, 3.399D–E). That inference is not spelled out in so many words. Presumably Plato did not think he needed to do so.

The obvious reason for the silence lies in the Spartan associations conjured up by Socrates' description of the warrior class. Although Spartan brutalization is negated by his stress on the fundamental importance of music and poetry (simplified and reformed, to be sure) for education in virtue, he does not leave everything to education. In order to remove the guards from the temptations of wealth acquisition, he resorts to institutional arrangements that are unequivocally Spartan in inspiration. Summer and winter alike (i.e. not just in the campaigning season) they are to live and eat together in a garrison (as in Sparta). They are to have no private land, virtually no private property, no money, and above all (as at Sparta) no use of gold and silver (cf. Xen. *Lac. Pol.* 7.6).[37] In short, they are to be soldiers, not businessmen (416A; Xenophon explains the Spartan attitude to money in the same terms: *Lac. Pol.* 7.1, 6). As in Sparta, so here it was simply to be expected that society as a whole would reflect in one way or another the priorities of the governing military class. Certainly Socrates is represented as assuming that his city will generate only modest economic resources. He assumes extremes neither of wealth nor poverty, and doesn't bother to question Adeimantus' obviously extravagant inference that the city itself has no money (4.421D–422A).[38]

4.2 Athens vs. Atlantis: a 'Thucydidean' narrative of war and greed

What prompts Adeimantus' expression of concern that the ideal city will have no money is a doubt about its ability in that event to fight a war—i.e. to equip the warriors who have been the chief subject of discussion for the last fifty pages of the dialogue for the job that defines their existence as an element within the city. How could it take on an adversary, especially if compelled to go to war with a great and wealthy city? Socrates responds in witty vein with an analogy that he develops with baroque extravagance. Think of a well-trained boxer taking on not one but two rich, fat non-boxers—or even more. He'd pick each of them off in turn, hitting them repeatedly in the sun and the stifling heat. In fact it would be like pitting a pack of hard lean dogs against fat tender sheep. However Adeimantus wonders whether, if the wealth of all other cities were concentrated in just one, the good city *would* then be endangered. In response, Socrates now questions the premise of the entire line of objection to which he has been responding so far. *No* other city *is* 'one'. All are really two cities: a city of the rich and a city of the poor. So none is greater than the good city—since none actually is a city (4.422A–423B).

This is scarcely the most strenuous stretch of argumentation in the *Republic*, nor one that obviously contributes to understanding justice and injustice, the main concerns of the dialogue.[39] It occupies a mere page of text. However its themes have extensive resonances in Plato. His preoccupation with the unity of the city is something that will engage us in Section 5 of this chapter. As for the ability of the good city to fight successful wars, that exemplifies what Stephen Halliwell describes as 'Plato's anxiety' to avoid the charge of utopian fantasy by imagining his community 'as existing in the actual, i.e. non-ideal, Greek world, and as maintaining a variety of relations with other Greek cities, as well as with barbarian peoples outside Greece'.[40] In the relevant passage in Book 5 (469B–471C), Plato makes Socrates an eloquent advocate of the Panhellenism that became a constant in the Greeks' self-image from the time of their successful repulsion of the Persian threat in 490 BC and then again in 480 and 479,[41] and took programmatic form in political rhetoric from time to time.[42] It was in the air again at the time Plato was writing the *Republic*, notably on account of the publication in 380 of the *Panegyricus* of Isocrates, who was to continue to advise the Greeks to settle their differences and unite once more against Persia throughout the rest of his writing career.

Plato gives Panhellenism a very distinctive and indeed radically original twist. The suggestion is not that Greeks should not fight Greeks: not for him bland optimism that there is any realistic possibility of that. But when they do fight, they should regard what they are engaged upon not as warfare but as *stasis*. That should impose an important constraint on behaviour, preventing them from devastating land and firing houses—since both sides know that after the conflict they will have to continue living in the place. Socrates is in effect made to focus on the *particularity* of the ideal city and its physical and cultural situation.[43] It's to be a Greek, not a barbarian city. The argument is that that has consequences (5.470E–471B). Its citizens will be attached to *Greece* as their *own* 'nurse and mother';[44] and they will share in the same religious practices as the other Greeks.[45] Therefore they will pursue their differences with other Greeks on the understanding that eventually they will be reconciled with them; 'moderating' them, not punishing them with enslavement or destruction. This line of thought raises many questions, not least about the very identity and structure of the ideal city. And it seems to function as ideology, rather than as anything that could be supported by philosophical theory, notably when Socrates claims that Greeks and barbarians are *natural* enemies. For our present purposes what matters is precisely Plato's willingness to dirty his hands with such issues in such a style.[46]

Plato's exploration of the topic of the ideal city at war is not confined to the *Republic*. He makes it the explicit focus of the entire intellectual enterprise originally proposed for the *Timaeus* and the unfinished sequel to the *Timaeus*, the *Critias*. In the event the *Timaeus* is devoted largely to expounding a theory of cosmology and of the constitution of the natural world, with a long final section on human beings and their place in the overall scheme of things. Formally speaking, however, the exposition of that theory figures only as a preface to an account of the good city's victory in war over a larger, wealthier adversary: of the conflict (as told by Solon to Critias' grandfather) between a rather Spartan prehistoric Athens and the non-Greek peoples of Atlantis (*Tim.* 27A–B; cf. 20D–27A).

Plato presents the narrative as developing a topic naturally suggested by the *Republic*, but not addressed there (although the boxer analogy does in fact constitute a first sketch). He begins the *Timaeus* by having Socrates recapitulate a conversation held the day before, when he presented arguments on the question of the best *politeia* (*Tim.* 17C–19A; cf. *Critias* 111C–D). As the recapitulation proceeds, it becomes evident that these arguments must have been a version of the argument of Books 2 to 5 of the *Republic*. Socrates rehearses the principle of specialization in skills and the division of the classes, the education of the guards, the provision for women guards, the abolition of the family, the eugenic programme and the social mechanisms needed to sustain it. He then goes on to something new. He wants to see the scheme they have been working out put into action, with the city they have described tested in warfare against other cities (*Tim.* 19C):

I'd love to hear an account of the contests our city engages in against other cities, and of how it distinguishes itself, both in the way it gets to the point of going to war, and in the way it conducts war. I want one that shows how it deals with each of the other cities in ways that reflect positively on its own education and training, in word and deed alike—in how it behaves towards them, and in how it negotiates with them.

Socrates disclaims any ability to provide this himself. Nor does he think poets or sophists are up to the task. It is a job for those who have gifts and experience in both philosophy and politics (*Tim.* 19C–20C).

The challenge is taken up by Critias: not the leader of the junta of thirty tyrants of 404–3 BC, but his grandfather, a significant Athenian politician active in the same era as Themistocles, and now a very old man.[47] He retells the story—claimed to be true, but transparently a fiction[48]—of Athens and Atlantis. And he makes it relevant by imagining the city and citizens Socrates has described mapped on to ancestral Athens (26D): 'The congruence will be complete, and our song will be in tune if we say that your imaginary citizens are the ones who really existed at that time.' The Athens he portrays is set in a more fertile and more extensive territory than the contemporary city (*Critias* 110D–111E). To all appearances it is a land power only, acknowledged leader of Greece, and indeed described as ruling the peoples of the Mediterranean in general: supreme in war, but notable above all for the handsome bodies and the variety and range of the virtues displayed by its citizens (*Tim.* 25B; *Critias* 108E, 112E). Its ruling military caste makes no use of gold or silver, and there is no sign that they harbour any materialistic ambitions. The huge and hugely wealthy island of Atlantis, by contrast, is an aggressive, bureaucratically organized imperialistic state made up of ten different cities. It relies on a navy as much as an army, and has already conquered many islands in the Atlantic, the Mediterranean as far north as Etruria in Italy, and north Africa as far as Egypt (*Critias* 114A–C). Despite their vast wealth, for a long while prior to these conquests the people of Atlantis were not corrupted by luxury, and indeed remained paragons of virtue. But in time human nature won out, and they were consumed with greed (*pleonexia*) regardless of justice, and by power. The ensuing conflict with Athens is represented as divine punishment for *hubris*. But the *Critias* breaks off at the point where Zeus prepares to pronounce the way in which this will be the fate of Atlantis (*Critias* 120D–121C). Eventually the island will sink beneath the waters of the Atlantic (*Tim.* 25C–D).

What Plato is giving us in Critias' narrative is a multidimensional historical allegory. Perhaps at a first reading one is put in mind of the heroic Athenian victories over the Persian empire in 490 (Marathon) and 480 (Salamis): precisely the period when Critias the politician was crossing swords with Themistocles. Certainly some of the rhetoric Critias employs conjures up that association, and incidentally expresses Panhellenist sentiments already voiced in the *Republic* (*Rep.* 5.469B–471C). He makes the Egyptian priest[49] who is alleged to be Solon's informant say (*Tim.* 25D–E):

Then it was, Solon, that the power of your city was made manifest to all mankind in its valour and strength. She was foremost of all in courage and the arts of war, and first as the leader of Hellas, then forced by the defection of the rest to stand alone, she faced the last extreme of danger, vanquished the invaders, and set up her trophy. The peoples not yet enslaved she preserved from slavery, and all the rest of us who dwell within the bounds set by Heracles she freed with ungrudging hand.

But Plato's prehistoric Athens sounds 'like a picture of *Sparta* lodged in an Attic locale', to borrow Christopher Gill's formulation (my italicization).[50] And there are numerous ways in which by contrast Atlantis obviously resembles the imperialistic

Athens of the fifth century—for example, in its extensive mining operations;[51] its navy, dockyards and system of harbours full of vessels and merchants from all over the world, making a commotion and hubbub night and day; its varied formulae for military contributions from the satellite cities (reminiscent of those exacted by Athens from the members of the Delian league); and not least the grandiose architecture of its acropolis, covered with temples, and crowned by a virtual facsimile of the Parthenon: the shrine of Poseidon, with its huge golden statue of the god (*Critias* 114D–119B *passim*).[52] The presence of the Syracusan Hermocrates as a discussant along with Socrates, Timaeus and Critias reinforces the point.[53] In the pages of Thucydides he emerges as the politician who did most to rally his people to unite with the other cities of Sicily to withstand the most strikingly ambitious demonstration of its power ever mounted by the Athenians: the disastrous naval expedition to Sicily despatched in 414 BC. To judge from the speeches Thucydides puts in his mouth (4.59–64, 6.33–4, 72, 76–80), Hermocrates had the percipience to take the threat seriously, but also to give his audience a cool but sanguine assessment—thoroughly justified in the event—of its chances of failure. What he is made to hear in the *Critias* from Critias will not be news to him. In the story of Atlantis a Hermocrates would be reminded only too vividly of the Periclean and post-Periclean Athens he knew so well.[54] Critias' pseudo-history is a vehicle for a critical commentary on the actual history of Periclean and post-Periclean Athens.

How convincing is Critias' narrative as an answer to Adeimantus' question about the military capacity of the ideal city? It does not matter that philosophy and philosopher rulers are emphatically edited out of the account of the city's *politeia* (the resumé of the *Republic* at *Tim.* 17C–19A omits them entirely, although there are enough hints that they are being omitted and enough allusions to philosophy to signal that this is not because Socrates has forgotten them).[55] In the *Republic* itself the whole of the treatment of war and the warrior class is completed before philosopher rulers are introduced (at 5.473C–E). Nor does it matter that the fit between the militia governing the prehistoric Athens of the *Critias* and the *Republic*'s warrior class is not exact.[56] The *Critias'* militia also live in isolation from the rest of the population, they have the same communal institutions, and among them too men and women train together. But they have their own families, and they build private dwellings to accommodate them (*Critias* 110C–D, 112B–C). So this Athens both is and is not the same as the good city of the *Republic*. It is presumably some sort of approximation to it, rather as the city constructed in the *Laws* is an approximation. However, for the purposes of Adeimantus' question there seems no reason why an approximation will not do well enough.

The general moral Plato means to communicate seems clear. What history suggests, he appears to be saying, is confirmation of the answer to Adeimantus that Socrates had already offered in the *Republic*. If a modestly equipped city subordinates the economy and economic motivations to virtue, as in the good city of the *Republic*, it will in the end triumph over the greed and ambition of an imperialistic power devoted to the accumulation and display of wealth. The philosophical construction of the good city does not evade what history counts as reality and realism.

Whether this represents some convergence of outlook between Plato and Thucydides is nonetheless far from clear. Thucydides was once regarded as both the great scientific historian, the paradigm of the accurate, impartial, objective reporter, and the great theorist of realism, understood in the sense of Realpolitik: the idea that international politics is inevitably conducted by states only on the basis of calculated pursuit of their own best interests. Judged against that kind of benchmark, Plato's fiction of the war between Athens and Atlantis—to say nothing of his political philosophy more generally—looks unThucydidean in every conceivable dimension. In more recent scholarship, however, a very different Thucydides has emerged: an ironist and a pessimist, for whom all political undertakings (and all interpretations of them) are liable to be subverted by chance, folly, hope and greed; a narrator whose truth is as much emotional and immediate as factual and reflective, selected and shaped with supreme care and rhetorical cunning.[57] In short, he begins to sound much more like Plato.

Yet Plato certainly felt himself to be at odds with Thucydides' apparent conviction that Athenian imperialism was a glorious project so long as it was safe in the hands of Pericles. Contemporary scholars—differing here from many of their distinguished predecessors—doubt that the *History does* communicate any such conviction.[58] In Plato's eyes it clearly did so,[59] to judge from the *Gorgias* and particularly the *Menexenus*, which are designed to get us to see Pericles in an altogether harsher light. For Plato, Pericles was merely a late episode in a story of self-indulgence and consequent degeneration that he himself told in one mode or another again and again, allegorically now in the *Critias*, and for a last time in Book 3 of the *Laws* (3.698A–701E).[60]

5. The Idea of Community

5.1 The principle of unity

So far in this chapter the aspect of Plato's ideal city that has been most prominent is its thoroughgoing Spartan regimentation: reflecting the emphases particularly of Books 2 and 3 of the *Republic*. The aspect that gets the pulses of Socrates' interlocutors racing is not that but something else: the prospect of a society sharing wives and children, that they get him to develop in Book 5 of the dialogue (5.449C–450D; cf. 4.423E–424A). The idea or ideal of community (*koinônia*) is in fact the key concept shaping the vision at the heart of its utopianism.[61]

The city, Aristotle observes in the very first sentence of his *Politics*, is a sort of association or community or (as we might say) 'sharing system' (*koinônia*)—in fact as he sees it the most important form of community, embracing all smaller units (the family, the village and so on) (*Pol.* 1.1, 1252a1–6). After the preliminaries of Book 1 he begins Book 2 with a statement of the enterprise he is undertaking in the work (*Pol.* 2.1, 1260b27–33):

Since our plan is to consider the political community which is the best of all for people who are able to live so far as possible as they would wish (*kat' euchên*), we must also examine other social and political systems, both those actually operative in the cities that are said to be well governed (*eunomeisthai*), and any others that may have been propounded by particular individuals and are thought to be good systems—so that we can see what is useful and on the right lines.

What this prospectus introduces is Aristotle's critical survey of the schemes put forward by individual thinkers—Plato in the *Republic* and *Laws*, Phaleas of Chalcedon, and Hippodamus—and then of the *politeia* at Sparta, in Crete, and at Carthage, with an appendix on celebrated lawgivers like Solon in Athens, and Zaleucus and Charondas in southern Italy.

Aristotle next explains what he takes to be the natural focus of the enquiry (*Pol.* 2.1, 1260b36–1261a4):

To begin with we must take as our starting-point the natural point of departure for this enquiry. It is necessarily the case that all citizens share everything, or they share nothing, or they share some things but not others. Sharing nothing is clearly impossible: the *politeia* is a sort of community or 'sharing system' (*koinônia*), and there must at least be a common or shared locality—a city that is one city must have one locality, and the one city is what the citizens share in. But is it better for a city that is to be well ordered to share in everything which can possibly be shared? Or is it better to share some things but not others?

And now he thinks it is time for an example (*Pol.* 2.1, 1261a4–9):

It would be possible for the citizens to share children and wives and property with each other, as in Plato's *Republic*. In that work Socrates says that the children and the wives and the property must be in common. Well then, which is the better system—the one we have now, or the one that conforms to the law set out in the *Republic*?

For Aristotle the fundamental preoccupation of political philosophy is the idea of political community. Its chief job is to consider the best form of political community ideally available. The first question that project requires the philosopher to tackle is: how *much* should the members of such a community—as a 'sharing system'—share with each other? The first example given to illustrate the question is the treatment of the subject in Plato's *Republic*.

In his focus on the idea of community, and in the question he goes on to ask about it, Aristotle articulates Plato's fundamental concerns in political philosophy as well as his own. It has often been thought that Aristotle is curiously selective in his treatment of the political ideas of the *Republic*: no mention in Book 2 of the *Politics* or elsewhere, for example, of the dialogue's main argument about justice, nor of the introduction of philosopher rulers. The opening chapter of Book 1 of the *Politics* actually continues with a critique of the initial thesis of *another* dialogue (the *Statesman*): the proposition that there is no intrinsic difference in the rule exercised by a king or a statesman or a householder. This has prompted the suspicion that Aristotle sees *that* dialogue as Plato's principal theoretical treatment of politics.[62] But the *Republic* itself makes it clear that when Aristotle takes the idea of community as his focus, Plato would have agreed that this *is* what political philosophy should make its principal subject. It is not distorting anything in the *Republic* to read it in that way. Plato's engagement with the idea of community is already apparent in the discussion of the basic model of a reciprocal economy in Book 2 of the dialogue. Specialization of functions is from the outset conceived as enabling a plurality of persons to act as 'sharers and helpers' with each other (2.369C): each farmer or artisan makes his product 'common to all', 'sharing it with others' (369E). This is the basis on which 'we established the city'—'the genuine city', as it is described a little later (372E)—'and made it a community (*koinônia*)' (371B). It is a genuine city precisely because it is a 'sharing system'.

Aristotle begins his consideration of the *Republic*'s account of the topic with a critique of its invocation of unity as a fundamental principle of community (*Pol.* 2.2–3). He is right about the key role played in Plato's thinking by the appeal to unity.[63] The crucial passage comes in Book 5. Socrates has finished explaining what it is for women and children to be 'in common' among the guards, and now moves on to consider whether this is a provision consistent with the rest of the political system he has described, and whether this is community or sharing at its best. He continues (5.462A–B):

'If we want to settle this, isn't it a good starting-point to ask ourselves what is the greatest good we can come up with for the organization of a city—the thing the lawgiver should be aiming at as he frames his laws—and what is the greatest evil? And then to ask: "Do the proposals we have just been through fit the footprint of the good, and fail to fit those of the evil?"'

'Yes, that's the best possible starting-point,' he said.

'Well, then, can we come up with a greater evil for a city than something that tears it apart and makes it many cities instead of one? Or any greater good than what binds it together and makes it one?'[64]

'No, we can't.'

At this point Socrates goes on to propose a hypothesis about the identity of the unifying factor he is speaking of. We should interpret him as effectively distinguishing between: (i) the general formula for the good; (ii) a specific recipe which constitutes (as it were) a way of realizing the formula—what Socrates calls 'the footprint of the good'; and (iii) the institutional arrangements which in their turn make it possible to put the recipe into effect.

The formula (i) is expressed in terms of what we may call the Unity Principle (UP):

UP   The greatest good for a city is what unifies it.

The recipe (ii) which specifies a way of achieving the unification identified by UP as the good is at once articulated (5.462B–C):

'Does community of pleasure and pain unite it, when so far as possible all the citizens are equally afflicted by joy or grief over the same gains and losses?'

'Absolutely so,' he said.

'Whereas privatization of these feelings is divisive? When the city and the people in the city have the same experiences, but some get distraught and others delighted?'

'Of course.'

'Is this because expressions like "mine" and "not mine" are not applied by people in the city on one and the same occasion? And the same with "somebody else's"?'

'It certainly is.'

'Does that mean the best regulated city is one where most people apply these expressions "mine" and "not mine" to the same thing in the same way?'

'Much the best.'

Socrates makes a comparison (anticipating St Paul) with the way things are with a single person. When someone's finger gets hurt, then because all the parts of the body form a community governed by the soul, the entire community is conscious of feeling the hurt, too—so that what we say is: *That person has a pain* in the finger' (5.462C–E). Finally, in (iii) Socrates goes on to argue that the detailed proposals for the organization of the city which he has been developing through Books 2 to 5 will indeed have effects that fit 'the footprint of the good' (as indicated by simultaneous communal use of possessive pronouns), and will therefore be the cause of its greatest good (5.462E–464B).

The force and attractiveness of UP is obvious. Unless a city is *one* city, it will not be a city at all. Its very identity as a city is a function of its unity. There could scarcely be anything more important or beneficial than whatever it is that generates such unity—at any rate in the sense that *without* such a unifying cause no other good is possible for a city, because there will then *be* no city to be the beneficiary of any other good. The Unity

Principle is something of fundamental importance for the whole argument of the *Republic*.[65] We should not be deceived by UP's deferral to Book 5 into missing its more general significance. As the analogy of city and soul would lead one to expect, UP has already been foreshadowed in the wording of the account of justice as psychic harmony at the end of Book 4 (443D–E), which is itself anticipated by the treatment of *sôphrosunê* (restraint) in city and individual alike earlier in the book (4.431E–432A). The individual, says Socrates, has to put his own house in order, and tune the three elements in the soul just like three fixed points in a musical scale—top, bottom, intermediate—'and if there turn out to be any other elements in between, he must *bind all these together* and become *a complete unity out of many*, restrained and in harmony with himself'. Earlier still in Book 4 (427E) Socrates obtained agreement that the city they have been describing is 'perfectly good' (assuming that the basis of its construction is right)—no doubt because the community as a whole enjoys as much happiness as any city can (4.420B–421C). It will not be *two* cities at war with each other, a city of the poor, and a city of the rich (4.423E–424A). The enunciation of UP in Book 5 also points forward to the metaphysics of Books 6 and 7. The most important thing the philosopher rulers of the good city have to come to understand is the Form of the Good (6.504C–505B). The Form of the Good is Plato's ultimate principle of *reality*. This makes it unsurprising that in what *it* says about the good, the Unity Principle similarly reflects an analysis of what it is to *be* a city, or that Plato's approach to the question of what is the best form of political community (like Aristotle's after him) is developed through consideration of the conditions that need to be satisfied if there is to be a city at all.

Platonic political philosophy may at this point look as far removed from the philosophical presuppositions of modern political liberalism as it would be possible to be. In his *Political Liberalism*, for example, John Rawls explicitly contrasts the sort of position he holds with the 'dominant tradition' which he finds in Plato and Aristotle, and in medieval Christian thinkers and utilitarian political philosophy alike.[66] In their commitment to the idea that there can be only one 'reasonable and rational good', these philosophers fall on one side of a deep divide separating them from advocates of pluralism. The liberal typically maintains that there are many *conflicting* comprehensive views of life, each with its own conception of the good, but all 'compatible with the full rationality of human persons, so far as that can be ascertained with the resources of a political conception of justice'.

Is the Unity Principle the place to look for evidence of the chasm between Plato and liberalism? There is more in common between UP and principles to which Rawls would subscribe than might be supposed. Despite his well-known doctrine of the priority of right over good,[67] Rawls insists that in truth the two are complementary, and that implicit in justice as fairness is an idea of the good of political society as such.[68] That good consists (just as in the *Republic*) in social unity. And social unity is for Rawls the condition of a well-ordered society where everyone accepts and knows everyone else, and accepts the same principles of justice; where it is recognized that the basic structure of society satisfies those principles; and where citizens actually practise justice so conceived for the most part. There could scarcely be a better description of the connections between political justice, unity and the good that are worked out by Socrates in the *Republic*. In articulating what the unity of the good city will depend upon, Book 4 makes political restraint a matter of unanimity (*homonoia*) between superior and inferior elements in society as to which should rule and which should be ruled (432A); and subsequently it becomes clear that their agreement reflects the principle of political justice requiring everyone to perform for the city the functions that are 'their own'—since that is what they are naturally best equipped to do (433A–434C; cf. 443C–444A). General acceptance of that principle is doubtless to be secured either as it is refracted in myth (through absorption of the Noble Lie in childhood), or ultimately through philosophical understanding (in the case of philosopher rulers).[69]

A civic republican position similar to Rawls's liberalism has been defended by Ronald Dworkin.[70] Once again the formal connections between justice and the good of social unity are highly reminiscent of those drawn in the *Republic*. Dworkin develops the Rawlsian position further, in arguing that political community has an ethical primacy over individual lives to the extent that a person counts his or her own life as diminished when there are failures of justice in formal political decisions (legislative, executive and administrative): 'an integrated citizen accepts that the value of his own life depends on the success of his community in treating everyone with equal concern'. He continues in Rawlsian vein: 'Suppose this sense is public and transparent: everyone understands that everyone else shares that attitude. Then the community will have an important source of stability and legitimacy even though its members disagree greatly about what justice is.' Dworkin concedes that 'all this is utopian'—and none the worse for that: 'We are now exploring utopia, an ideal of community we can define, defend, and perhaps even grope our way towards, in good moral and metaphysical conscience.' And then he makes a start on suggesting why we might find the ideal attractive by himself exploiting an explicit comparison with Plato's view of the relationship between justice and well-being in the *Republic*.[71]

There are, of course, other versions of liberalism which share no common ground with Platonic utopianism.[72] One powerful tradition is grounded in a more Hobbesian approach to political theory: what Bernard Williams called 'political realism'. The liberalism of the political realist 'takes the condition of life without terror as its first requirement and considers what other goods can be furthered in more favourable circumstances, it treats each proposal for the extension of the notions of fear and freedom in the light of what locally has been secured.' In fact: 'It regards the discovery of what rights people have as a political and historical one, not a philosophical one.'[73] From this perspective there is no surprise in discovering a degree of convergence between Rawls's or Dworkin's political liberalism and Platonic utopianism. Like Plato, they count as proponents of 'political moralism'—they 'make the moral prior to the political'.[74]

5.2 Collectivism without metaphysics

Ingredient (i) in Plato's theory of the political good—the formal Principle of Unity—might therefore commend itself even to modern liberal thought. Nor would it have been likely to strike Plato's contemporaries as a particularly novel or adventurous or contentious claim in itself.[75] Anxiety about *stasis* in Athens at the end of the Peloponnesian War seems to have been the catalyst which made of *homonoia*, unanimity or consensus, a key expression in the vocabulary of politics and political philosophy. It was employed initially and fundamentally to formulate a precondition of the internal stability of the city, vital if individual or factional interests are not to prevail.[76] In any historical

Greek *polis* of Plato's time, the relatively close-knit fabric of society, emphasized during frequent episodes of warfare against neighbouring communities, was such that Socrates' treatment of unity as the good of the city would doubtless have been widely regarded as a restatement of the obvious.

What is not compatible with liberalism is Socrates' recipe (ii) for achieving the unity that constitutes the good: uniformity of emotional response to experiences—or, more precisely, experience of anything good or bad (5.462D–E)—which affect the city or its inhabitants. To be sure, Dworkin's 'integrated' citizens all feel diminished by events that damage their community as a *political* community. But these constitute a strictly limited subset among the experiences by which citizens are affected. Failures in justice are the only experiences that count in this context. If a fellow citizen has a bereavement in the family, or loses a contest in the Olympic games, or suffers loss of a valuable cargo through shipwreck, that is nothing to me as a citizen, although if I am his friend or a relative it may affect me on that account. Dworkin compares the communal life of an orchestra. It is similarly limited: 'it is *only* a musical life'.[77] Hence:

The musicians treat their performances together as their orchestra personified, and they share in its triumphs and failures as their own. But they do not suppose that the orchestra has a sex life, in some way composed of the sexual activities of its members. ... Though the first violinist may be concerned about a colleague's sexual habits or deviance, this is concern for a friend that reflects altruism, not self-concern for any composite unit of agency which includes him. His moral integrity is not compromised by the drummer's adultery.

To think otherwise is to succumb to 'anthropomorphism'. Dworkin's indictment of any such metaphysical view of integration and community reads like a commentary on Plato's Pauline analogy with the body and its parts (5.462C–D). The presupposition is 'that a communal life is the life of an outsize person, that it has the same shape, encounters the same moral and ethical watersheds and dilemmas, and is subject to the same standards of success and failure, as the several lives of the citizens who make it up'.[78]

What motivates the thoroughgoing integration of individual with communal experience envisaged in Plato's recipe for unity? One answer might be that he was all along committed to what since Hegel has been called the organic theory of the state.

A famous passage at the beginning of Book 4 of the *Republic* (4.420B–421C) has often been thought to attribute a metaphysical primacy to the city over the individuals or classes that constitute it. If that interpretation is correct, it might prompt us to reconsider whether Book 5's Principle of Unity can after all be plausibly construed in the neutrally formal way just proposed in Section 5.1. I shall argue that it isn't correct, and so we needn't.

In Book 4 Plato's Socrates certainly talks of the city as something that can be happy or enjoy well-being, and that can exhibit virtues as such (analysis of these ideas is indeed central to his political argument). There have been attempts to give reductionist readings of what such talk commits him to. For example, Gregory Vlastos argued against Grote and Popper, in particular, that Socrates conceives the happiness of the whole city as nothing more than a shorthand for the happiness (so far as it can be achieved) of all the citizens.[79] But while this *is* the way Aristotle seems to understand the attainment of the good life by a political community,[80] Lesley Brown has shown that when Socrates discusses the question (4.420B–421C) he treats the city as an organic whole with its own needs and characteristics, above all a need for unity and harmony.[81] Asking whether elements within it are happy or as happy as they might be is not the right question, as Adeimantus has done with respect to the guards, any more than would be asking of a statue whether its eyes are as beautiful as they might be. What matters is that the individual parts are so painted that the statue as a whole is beautiful. So *mutatis mutandis* with the city and its happiness. Socrates is in effect commandeering Adeimantus' word 'happy' to insist that good order in the city is a more important value than the satisfactions and successes of individuals or groups which the expression usually conveys. 'Happy' predicated of the city conveys the notion of its social harmony, just as by the end of Book 4 it will become apparent that happiness for the individual is constituted by harmony in the soul.[82]

The happiness of the city is therefore not reducible to the happiness of individual citizens.[83] It does not follow that the city is an entity metaphysically prior to the citizens, any more than Dworkin's orchestra is ontologically more fundamental than the musicians who constitute it. Nor, as Socrates develops his argument in the rest of Book 4, does he treat it as though it were. What will make the city good—what its good order and therefore its happiness consists in—is above all its being the case that 'each person, whether child or woman, slave or free, craftsman, ruler, ruled, does their own job and doesn't meddle with what is other people's' (4.433D): in other words, social justice (as the *Republic* defines it) at work, precisely as is required by Rawls's definition of a well-ordered society. The harmony of the city simply consists in the properly regulated performance of those activities that are relevant to its functioning as a political community: that is, the economic, military and governmental roles necessary for its survival. Dworkin calls this the *practice* (as opposed to the metaphysical) view of the identity of an integrated community. As he says, this should not be taken to indicate that the concept of a community reduces to some claim about the behaviour of individuals as individuals:[84]

When an integrated community exists, the statements citizens make about it, about its success or failure, are not simply statistical summaries of their own successes or failures as individuals. An integrated community has interests and concerns of its own—its own life to lead. Integration and community are genuine phenomena, even on the practice view. But on that view they are created by and embedded in attitudes and practices, and do not precede them.

So, in Plato's treatment of the city as an organic whole at the beginning of Book 4, there is no anticipation of the collectivist recipe (ii) spelled out in Book 5 (462B–D) for achieving the unity that constitutes the good. It tends rather to confirm the analysis of the Principle of Unity (i) offered above in Section 5.1. The collectivist recipe is motivated by something else: not a metaphysical conception of the city, but reflection on a specifically social and political anxiety. 'Can we come up with a greater evil for a city than something that tears it apart and makes it many cities instead of one?', is the first question Socrates asks in this context (5.462A–B). It is important to notice the point in his argument at which he gives expression to this anxiety. The question is put very near the *end* of his account of the good city. That is to say, Socrates has already developed at length the theory of political justice as a function of the social harmony that prevails when each of the three classes he has specified (economic, military, governing) performs its own and only its own function. The worry he now raises is introduced as a question about his own theory, and in particular about the way it all hangs together (5.461E). We can rephrase Socrates' question to bring this out more explicitly: 'Have enough safeguards really been built into the theory to pre-empt what might most threaten the unity of the city: the dangers of social division?' The affirmative answer supplied by his collectivist recipe—uniformity in emotional response—shows what he took to be the origin of the threat: appetites, emotions or attitudes that create or express division between people. So the challenge he undertakes is that of showing that (iii) the institutional arrangements developed throughout the course of Books 2 to 5 are the right ones to preempt the development of any such appetites, emotions or attitudes, and more positively create the social conditions in which the terms of the collectivist recipe (ii) are satisfied.

5.3 Collectivist psychology

Plato's basic concept of political unity is not of itself collectivist, as became clear in our discussion of (i) the Principle of Unity. But he conceives the only effective way of achieving political unity to be the development of (ii) a collectivist social psychology, promoted by (iii) collectivist social and political institutions. The idea basic to this line of thought is a simple one. Our emotional aspirations and reactions are functions of our attachments to things and people. Our attachments in turn are shaped by the arrangements for ownership and use of property, and for marriage and the upbringing of children, that are in force in society. So, if ownership and use of property is mostly private, and if the approved social unit for marriage and child rearing is the nuclear family, attachments and emotions too will be 'privatized', with massive potential for social divisiveness. As Stephen Halliwell argues, Plato seems actually to have coined the abstract noun 'privatization' (*idiôsis*)—never to use it again—to characterize the condition of our emotions in such circumstances: 'when the city and the people in the city have the same experiences, but some get distraught and others delighted' (5.462B–C).[85] Communal institutions, by contrast, will foster communal attachments. Because women and children are 'in common', every guard will assume he or she is related to everyone else among the guards, and is bound to them by the duties of care and respect that family members have towards each other. Together with the abolition of private property earlier discussed, these ties will ensure (as Socrates works out in some detail) that the usual sources of division within a society will either not exist or become subject to social and psychological controls that rob them of their potential for evil.

An apparent difficulty now presents itself. What Plato wants to secure is the unity of the *city*. But what he has to say about communal emotional responses to experience relates only to one *element* in the city: the guards—the rulers and the military. And the collectivist social institutions he has introduced are likewise institutions governing the life of the guards, not of the farmers, craftsmen and the rest of the economic class. In his critique of the *Republic*, in Book 2 of the *Politics*, Aristotle is sometimes charged with confusing Plato's proposals for securing unity in the class of guards with his treatment of the unity of the city as such. Yet UP *is* a principle about the city itself, and what Socrates claims is that the guards' sharing of women and children and the use of property fits the 'footprint' of the *city*'s good.[86] Moreover, when in the *Laws* Plato recalls the *Republic*'s conception of the good *politeia*, he takes the communistic ideal to be one which should be realized so far as possible 'throughout the whole city' (*Laws* 5.739B–C).[87] So, if there is confusion, it looks as though it is Plato who is mostly responsible for it.[88] Nor is the confusion necessarily harmless. Is not discontent in the economic class a major potential threat to the unity and stability of the city? If what *enhances* the guards' sense of mutuality is having women, children and property in common, will not their sense of unity with the rest of the population inevitably be diminished?[89]

It is clear however that Plato wants to argue that the relations *between* the guards and the economic class itself exhibit the community of feeling needed for political unity. The ground has been prepared by the charter myth for the good city—the Noble Lie—retailed at the end of Book 3 (414B–415D). As Nicole Loraux puts it, the Noble Lie is 'a moment of ideology' designed to inculcate in *all* the citizens the conviction that *all* of them are members of the kind of family that the argument of Book 5 for communal sharing of women, children and property will predicate of the guards:

The recourse to myth comes first [i.e. before the account of the 'political construction' in Book 5], as a way of convincing the citizens of their common autochthonous origin, by virtue of which, all born from the earth, they are 'all brothers'.[90]

The myth is actually addressed in the first instance to the guards, and focuses more specifically on the recognition that *they* must in consequence think of the *other* citizens as their brothers (3.414E). Since Plato then goes on to make the second instalment of the myth legitimate the class structure—his fiction roots it in nature, or rather in gold, silver, iron and bronze natures—he evidently saw no irresoluble tension between the idea of the city as family and its tripartite division.[91] Indeed, in Book 4 he has Socrates make it clear that he regards specialization of functions as crucial to the unity of the city: 'by applying himself to his own one function each will become one person, not many, and that way the entire city will grow to be one, not many' (423D). When in Book 5 Socrates makes his attempt to show that the institutions of the good city *do* promote community of feeling, he begins not with the collective life of the guards, but with the terms in which guards and the *dêmos* talk about each other (463A–B). In the good city the producers will call the rulers not 'masters' (as in most regimes) nor even 'people who exercise rule' (as with the expression *archôn*, in a democracy like Athens), but 'saviours' (or 'preservers') and 'helpers'—as well as like themselves 'citizens'. They in their turn will call the producers not 'slaves' but 'wage providers' and 'sustainers': signifying recognition of the similarity of their own role to that of a hired labourer, a job they undertake for the benefit of others, not as anything good or noble, rewarded only by consequential avoidance of being ruled by someone worse than themselves (cf. 1.346E–347D). The common theme is recognition of mutual support and dependence between fellow citizens, and the keynote is mutual gratitude. There is no reference here to the Noble Lie, nor to any of the other mechanisms Plato may take to be operative in ensuring robust and voluntary commitment to the political settlement that is constituted by the *Republic*'s system of political justice (on this issue see further Chapter 6). But they are presumably presupposed by the apparent confidence with which Socrates is made to describe the mutual regard of rulers and workers.

Evidently it is any potentiality for dissension *within* the ruling class that Plato takes to present a much more real and serious threat to the unity of the city than unrest in the economic class. After all, they are the repositories of all military resources, all political authority, and the whole ethos of the city's culture.

Adam was quite correct to say of the discussion in Book 5 which immediately concerns us:

Plato's object throughout this episode is to keep the whole city 'one' by preventing *one* of its constituent factors, viz. the guardians, from becoming 'many'. If the guardians are united—so he holds—no danger to the city's unity need be apprehended from the others (465B).[92]

In seeing *stasis* as the disease to which an aristocracy (which is what the *Republic*'s guards are) is distinctively prone,[93] Plato follows a model: Herodotus, in the famous debate of the Persian nobles about the merits of monarchy, oligarchy (not distinguished from aristocracy) and democracy (*Histories* 3.80–2). The argument presented for aristocracy in the debate is that power is thereby placed in the hands of the best men, those best qualified for deliberation (3.81.3). The argument against is that in an aristocracy strong private animosities develop: which lead to feuding (*stasis*), which leads to murderous bloodletting, which leads to—monarchy (3.82.3). Plato's collectivist proposals in Book 5 of the *Republic* are designed to secure the advantage of aristocracy so defined while pre-empting its characteristic disadvantage.

One of the more interesting observations Aristotle makes in his discussion of Platonic communism is this comment (*Pol.* 2.5, 1263b37–40):

It is strange that the very philosopher who intends to introduce a system of education, and believes that by that means the city will be morally good, should think that he can reform it by these kinds of measures [i.e. the communistic arrangements], instead of by acquisition of good habits and by philosophy and by laws.

The criticism certainly exposes a complexity in Plato's thought. He stakes a great deal on education and on general acquisition of at least 'popular' virtue. At the same time he shows limited faith in human nature and its capacity for improvement—hence the resort to social engineering of various sorts, including eugenic manipulation. Perhaps it might be said—in mitigation of the contrast—that education and regulation are only different and complementary modes of socialization. But there is a crucial difference between them: one is a form of persuasion; the other of control. Plato is well aware of the duality of his approach. The citizens are to be brought into harmony with one another 'through both persuasion and compulsion' (7.519E). In the case of the *Republic*'s argument that collectivist institutions will promote a collectivist psychology, the underlying assumption is that *control* of emotion and desire is required, even for a natural elite whose upbringing is specifically designed to develop a balance between the fiercer and the gentler emotions, and whose imperviousness to temptation or fear is tried and tested (3.410B–414A). The private satisfactions and dissatisfactions associated with acquisition of property and with relationships within the nuclear family seem to be regarded as powerful enough to undermine the effects of *paideia* (education).

So, as precaution against greed the guards are confined to a barracks on the Spartan model, where they are supported by taxation of the economic class and denied any use of gold and silver or of money (3.415D–417B). Where management of the emotions is concerned, it is a similar story. Socrates makes much of the potential for controlling anger, violence and the fractiousness of litigation implicit in the alternative arrangements he advocates. It is almost as though—like Aristophanes in the *Assemblywomen*—he is simply thinking of the way in which ordinary unreformed Athenians would behave if you effected a radical and liberating change in their circumstances. For example (in fact, an example already found in Aristophanes), so far as violence by the young against the old is concerned, a different set of emotions and associated behaviours will be fostered: respect (all older people will be treated as parents) and fear (of punishment by the extended family of the victim).[94] Ambition in the military auxiliaries will be satisfied by honours finer than those awarded to Olympic victors—bestowed however not for individual achievement, but for saving the whole city (5.463B–466C).

Aristotle produced a whole battery of reasons for thinking that the *Republic*'s collectivist institutions would fail to deliver these supposed benefits. Most of them turn on the thought that under that system positive attachments to people and property are likely to be diluted, and hostile attitudes and behaviour become more prevalent. For example, if each citizen has a thousand sons, and these are not theirs individually, but *any* boy is undifferentiatedly the son of *any* citizen, then all will take undifferentiatedly little notice of their 'sons'. Similarly with property: property that is common to the greatest number of owners receives the least attention (*Pol.* 2.3, 1261b32–40). On the other hand, the dilution of true family ties will tend to weaken sanctions against antisocial and criminal behaviour towards true family members: such behaviour 'is bound to occur more frequently when people do not know their relations than when they do' (*Pol.* 2.4, 1262a30–1).[95] As for common ownership of property, 'if both in the enjoyment of the produce and in its production people prove unequal, complaints are bound to arise between those who enjoy or take much but work little, and those who take less but work more' (*Pol.* 2.5, 1263a11–15). Within their own terms of reference these points are not without force.[96] But, of course, they make some unargued assumptions about the limits to the transformation of human motivations that a radical reorganization of society and radical reform of education could achieve. That is no doubt what Plato might have said in reply, observing as he does that abolition of the nuclear family (and associated webs of kinship) and its control of property would cut off at the root much of the most intense dissension actually experienced by Greek cities (5.464D–E). He would not have been surprised by the phenomenon of millions throughout the world mourning (even as I write) the death of the first pope of the globalized era—as the loss of the father of their own catholic family.

5.4 Plato the feminist?

Where Plato exhibits rather more confidence in the potentialities of human nature is in the vigour and tenacity with which he has Socrates argue for women warriors and rulers as well as men—on the ground that there is no relevant difference in their nature between the two sexes. The first principles Socrates invokes in this connection include no reference to anything recognizable as women's rights or equal rights for all citizens,[97] nor to the need to consider women's well-being or needs and desires in determining the proper basis for a social and political system. In the eyes of some readers, this makes Book 5 of the *Republic* immediately irrelevant to any contemporary consideration of the social and political position of women,[98] although for others 'all the major issues of sexual equality are touched on in the arguments of the *Republic*'.[99] What Socrates does appeal to is the argument that communistic arrangements are at once the most beneficial for the city, and the ones that are best suited to human nature.

The main tactic he employs to make this point about human nature is use of the 'alienating' image—alienating us both from convention and from our deep-seated sense of ourselves—of guard dogs and hunting dogs.[100] If you keep dogs, then you expect male and female dogs alike to keep guard, go hunting, and in fact do—and be trained to do—everything 'in common', even if (as Glaucon observes) males are stronger, and females weaker. Bearing and raising puppies does not exempt the bitches from any of that (5.461D–E). Again, your best hunting dogs and birds will be thoroughbreds, and so far as possible you mate them with others in their prime to maintain quality stock; similarly with your horses and other animals (5.459A–B). These practices simply reflect the nature of the animals in question. Why should not similar practices be appropriate to *human* nature?

Socrates anticipates resistance. 'Isn't a woman's nature completely different from a man's? And by the principle of specialization of functions, isn't some work essentially woman's work (work to which women but not men are naturally suited), with other work naturally suitable for a man?' Socrates gives this line of argument fairly short shrift. Only a woman, of course, can bear children, following insemination by a man. But it is the social and political sphere that is under discussion. Here the evidence suggests that 'none of the activities connected with running a city belongs to a woman because she is a woman, nor to a man because he is a man' (5.455D). Socrates appeals to men's capacities at weaving, cooking and baking. Praxagora in Aristophanes' *Assemblywomen* (210–40) had drawn attention to the versatility and competence of women in managing the household.

Assemblywomen, produced in Athens somewhere around 392–90 BC, in truth anticipates much in the main nexus of ideas that Socrates puts forward in this part of the dialogue.[101] The women of Athens disguise themselves as men, pack the Assembly, vote to transfer power to themselves, and elect the heroine Praxagora as general (the office Pericles had so often held). The plan for thoroughgoing reform of Athenian society that she puts forward (*Assemblywomen* 583–710) contains the following major elements: common ownership and use of all property, resulting in a common and equal lifestyle (590–607); sharing of women in common, with anyone allowed to produce children with anyone they want (611–15), although with rules to ensure that the old and ugly don't miss out (615–34); children to regard all older men as their fathers, with consequent reduction in violence (635–43); no lawsuits—the misdemeanours that occasioned them no longer being committed (655–72); the whole city constituting a single household, with all eating and drinking together (673–710). The conversation in which Praxagora explains all this to her husband Blepyrus and a neighbour of his is saturated with gross sexual ribaldry. Otherwise there is little in the programme that is not replicated lock, stock and barrel in Plato.

Scholars have argued with each other as to whether Aristophanes knew an early version of the *Republic*, or whether both he and Plato drew on some common unknown theoretical tract (despite Aristotle's assertion of the uniqueness of Plato's proposals: *Pol.* 2.12, 1274b9–10).[102] Aristophanes' systematic use of communistic vocabulary does suggest that such ideas must have been circulating at the time. As for the *Republic*, for all Socrates' references to jokes, ridicule, playfulness and so forth, there is no self-consciously signposted echo of Aristophanes' play in the text of Book 5, even though it is highly probable that the *Assemblywomen* lies behind it. Readers have often felt that Plato was having some fun with *them* here. I think that fun consists precisely in arguing out in all seriousness and from first principles a social and political programme which (as the author and his first readers knew very well) had quite recently been most memorably acted out as a sexual extravaganza on the Attic stage.[103] Much of what Socrates has to say regarding the mockery attracted by proposals such as these is in fact an exercise in pointing out its merely conventional basis: people once thought, for example, that the Cretan and Spartan practice of exercising naked was ridiculous, until they came to appreciate that you could engage in that kind of activity better naked than clothed (5.452A–E).

Socrates expresses the conclusion that his argument reaches in the following terms (455D–E):

Natural abilities are evenly distributed between the sexes, and a woman is naturally equipped to participate in all activities, and a man the same—though in all of them woman is weaker than man.

The qualification about the relative weakness of the woman (already prepared for, of course, by the bitch analogy) is modified by Glaucon's remark that 'plenty of *individual* women are better at all sorts of things than individual men' (5.455D). But it is reflected in most of Plato's references to women in other dialogues, and elsewhere in the *Republic*, too. Women are frequently portrayed as cowardly and emotional and undisciplined (e.g. 3.395E, 4.431B–C, 5.469D, 10.605C–E). By the time he wrote the *Timaeus*, at any rate, Plato was taking this to be a sign of a *natural* tendency, as is evident from his assumption that men will be reincarnated as women in their next life if they have failed in this (*Tim.* 42B–E; cf. 90E–91A). And the *Laws* is explicit that 'female nature is inferior in goodness to that of males' (*Laws* 6.781B).[104] Nonetheless in the eschatology of the myth of Er in Book 10 of the *Republic*, all souls—those of men and women alike—have the power and responsibility to *choose* the life they will next lead (including whether it is to be a human life, and if so what sex they will be), predisposing though their natures and previous experiences may be (*Rep.* 10.617D–620D).[105] And the fact remains that in Book 5 the Platonic Socrates is clear that there are women as naturally suited to every occupation—including ruling and fighting for the city—as men. That is precisely what we should expect on other grounds. It was Socratic teaching that there is the same kind of virtue for a man and a woman.[106]

Broadly speaking, contemporary readers have responded in two very different ways to what they find in Plato on this theme. One is summed up in the slogan 'the maleness of reason'.[107] On this view, Book 5 of the *Republic* identifies qualities of reason and vigour in male terms, according them supreme social and political value; construes them however as universals of human nature; and attributes them to women, therefore, only insofar as it assimilates woman to man[108]—and scarcely surprisingly finds that the assimilation is in general less than complete. Sometimes interpretations on these lines have no quarrel in principle with the idea of an ungendered philosophical reason, but argue that from Plato on attempts to articulate it, particularly in the sphere of ethics, have historically ended up heavily gendered. That history invites us to 'invent a cultural tradition' to which the prevailing image of woman as excluded from reason and culture 'would no longer correspond'.[109] Other interpretations along the same lines take a more essentialist view of the failure of his attempt to appeal to nature. As Luce Irigaray puts it: 'The natural is at least two: male and female. All the speculation about overcoming the natural in the universal forgets that nature is not *one*.'[110] If there is no such thing as *human* nature, it would be possible to diagnose Plato's theory of a pure rational and immortal soul as an articulation only of patriarchal male nature, in contrast with the symbolic figure of a Penelope, expressing in her quite different form of astuteness (*mêtis*)—as she weaves and unweaves her web of deceit—the embodied mind of an impenetrable and distinctively female subjectivity.[111]

This style of response has the advantage, if it is an advantage, of finding a sort of consistency running through virtually everything Plato says about women. An alternative reaction differs in two main dimensions.[112] First, a sharp distinction is made between how humans are by nature (summed up in the claim that for the Plato of the *Republic* the soul is 'fundamentally sexless'),[113] and how he conceives the way people are in existing circumstances, where dismissive sociocultural stereotypes inform many of his references to women. Second, statements asserting or implying the *natural* inferiority of women to men in *Timaeus* and *Laws* are taken as evidence of a shift away from the position of the *Republic*—despite what is said about the comparative weakness of women in Book 5 of the dialogue—whether because of encroaching philosophical and political conservatism, or because of changing thoughts on the nature of the soul. So far as the *Republic* is concerned, the ideal of equal participation by women and men alike in the key roles on which government of a society depends, on the grounds of what all are naturally equipped to contribute to it, remains 'a triumph of imaginative impartiality'[114] over an inherited prejudice from which Plato could not otherwise break free.

Angela Hobbs suggests that his position in the dialogue 'may be deliberately ambivalent, designed to accommodate the fact that his immediate audience is almost certainly male'. Plato 'genuinely wishes to convince them of the Socratic theory that the virtues are gender neutral'; on the other hand, he wants to portray philosophy and the activities of the guards in 'robustly active terms' likely to convince young males that this is a life for 'real men'.[115] The ambivalence may not be just a matter of Plato's rhetorical registers. It is hard to avoid the impression of a philosopher struggling to have a serious argument with himself: trying to reconcile two rather different sets of ideas about men, women and human nature, both of which he found powerfully attractive, in the service of a vision of the benefits for the political community that would flow from taking 'sharing among friends' really seriously. The *Laws* confirms the impression. At the most general level, it continues to insist that sharing women and children and property is the paradigm to which we should aspire when working out our conception of *politeia*. It implies that that remains the way to achieve the ideal of unity—a condition where all rejoice and grieve at the same time (*Laws* 5.739B–E). But the *Laws* embarks on a different project from that undertaken in the *Republic*. There is no attempt here to work out that ideal literally in practice. We have to be content with approximations. So the Athenian Visitor withdraws as impracticable—given the 'birth, upbringing, and education here assumed'—the abolition of private land ownership and housing proposed for the guards in Book 3 of the *Republic*, and similarly the mating arrangements involving the abolition of the family in the 'second wave' passage of Book 5, although (for example) he insists that those who have land apportioned to them should still *regard* it as common to the city itself (*Laws* 5.739E–740B; presumably treating property as available for common *use*, as Aristotle advocated: *Pol.* 2.5, 1263a21–40).

On the other hand, the *Republic*'s more strenuously argued thesis that women should receive the same training and education for the same occupations as men is reiterated in the *Laws* with more force and passion than ever. One outburst on the advantage for the happiness of the city in revising and reforming all its practices to make them common to both women and men is prompted by reflection on the neglect in Crete and Sparta of arrangements for governing the life of women, and particularly of any provision of common meals for them (*Laws* 6.780D–781D).[116] Another—occasioned by consideration of detailed specifications for the educational programme—deserves quotation. I adapt Trevor Saunders' spirited rendering of the Visitor's explanation of why the programme will apply to females as well as males, without any reservations about having women, too, learning horse-riding or the use of weapons (*Laws* 7.805A–D):

Visitor: I maintain that since this state of affairs *can* exist [i.e. one where women like the Sauromatians in the Black Sea region engage in pursuits the Greeks regard as a male preserve, riding horses and using the bow and other weapons: 804E–805A], the way things are now in our corner of the world—where men and women do *not* have a common purpose, and do *not* throw all their energies into the same activities—is absolutely stupid. Almost every city, under present conditions, is only half a city, and develops only half its potentialities, whereas with the same cost and effort it could double its achievement. Yet what a staggering blunder for a legislator to make!

Cleinias: I dare say. But a lot of these proposals, Visitor, are incompatible with the familiar social and political systems. However, you were quite right when you said that we should give the argument its head, and only make up our minds when it had run its course. You've made me reproach myself for having spoken. So carry on, and say what finds favour with you.

Visitor: The point I'd like to make, Cleinias, is the same one as I made just a moment ago. There might have been something to be said against our proposal, if it had not been proved by the facts to be workable. But as things are, an opponent of this piece of legislation must try other tactics. We are not going to withdraw our recommendation that so far as possible, the female gender should share in education and everything else with the male.

Plato's vision is one thing. The strength of his determination to work out its implications in the detail of his recommendations of (for example) the system for holding political office is much more questionable. They leave much to do with the position of women in the society in obscurity, and scholars differ in their assessment of whether anything radically different from the norms of subordination prevailing in contemporary Athens is envisaged.[117]

In *Republic* and *Laws* alike Plato envisages more resistance to the collectivist idea of abolishing the household and the nuclear family than to the participation of women as well as men in political and military activity. There is an interesting relationship here with Thomas Nagel's discussion of the change in attitudes towards what he identifies as the three main sources of socio-economic inequality that would be needed to overcome resistance to an egalitarian system.[118] The members of his triad are: discrimination (for which the remedy is removal of obstacles to equality of opportunity); hereditary advantage, principally associated with the family (which can be softened by public support for childcare, education, social benefit systems, forms of positive discrimination and so on); and variation in natural ability (where attempts might be made to sever the connection between superior talent and superior economic reward). Nagel suggests that as the sources of inequality move from those purely external to the individual (discrimination) to those with a strong internal component (variation in ability), so resistance will inevitably and reasonably increase to moves to counter them in the direction of greater equality. In the *Republic*'s provisions for the guards, radical attacks are made on the first two members of the triad: discrimination (women to be guards as well as men, and to share the same training) and the role of the family (it is to be abolished).[119] But Socrates made it clear that he anticipated a more formidable 'wave' of resistance to his second proposal than to his first: just as Nagel's theory would lead one to expect. The *Laws* exhibits a similar kind of gradation in its treatment of issues of community and equality. It allows the family back in, but it still seeks to regulate the economic system in such a way as to minimize the differentials in wealth usually associated with the family, for instance by providing that all landholdings are equal in size and inalienable, as well as by debarring those who are to count as citizens from commercial activity, with no gold or silver permitted in the city at all. But the *Laws* retains the *Republic*'s rejection of discrimination between women and men—at least in its most general theoretical statements—with undiminished fervour.

6. *Epilogue: The Question of Fantasy*

No doubt some utopian writers in some periods have formulated what they conceived as plans for action, even if their critics judged them to be what Karl Marx referred to contemptuously as 'recipes ... for the cookshops of the future', or, to put it in Hegel's more prosaic formulation, 'instructions on how the world ought to be'.[120] But sometimes (and sometimes simultaneously) an opposite assumption is made about utopianism—that if it is appropriate to describe a set of ideas as utopian, that carries with it the implication that they are impossible to realize in practice: that 'ought' doesn't here imply 'can'. The assumption may or may not be conjoined with the further thought that the utopian author *intended* only to compose a fantasy. What interpretative options are suggested by the text of the *Republic*? Once we pose the question, it quickly becomes apparent that its author was himself much exercised by the possibility that the communistic ideas introduced initially in Book 5 might appear fantastical, like an Aristophanic comedy.

In fact Socrates imagines himself having to withstand three 'waves' of disbelief and ridicule. He makes it clear that what he fears will prompt the criticism is the perception that his views are just wishful thinking, or more precisely mere 'prayers' (5.450D, 456C, 7.540D). As Myles Burnyeat shows in his article 'Utopia and Fantasy', the overarching argument of Books 5 to 7 is systematically organized so as to demonstrate at each stage that what is proposed is both beneficial and feasible to implement.[121] Take the first idea put forward: that women should be guards of the city as well as men, sharing with them a single way of life, and engaging in the same shared pursuits, including warfare and government. Here Socrates first establishes—on the grounds we have considered—that women are as naturally suited for these functions as men, and then that it is desirable accordingly for them like the men to be educated to undertake them (5.450C–D, 456C, 457B–C).

He confesses at the outset that he expects his second idea—that wives and children are to be shared in common—to meet with much greater resistance, not as to whether it would be beneficial, but as to feasibility (5.457C–D; but Glaucon assures him he can expect plenty of disagreement on both counts: 457E). In fact Socrates begins his treatment with an elaborate apology for deferring the issue of possibility until he has shown that a highly regulated sexual communism and a communal system for rearing children would be 'of the greatest possible benefit to the city and the guards' (5.457E–458B).[122] And that is what he proceeds to do over the next few pages, before engaging in further discussion about the guards' actual practice of war (that then drifts on to a broader consideration of the *ethics* of warfare). Any very specific questions about the feasibility of sexual communism seem to have dropped from view. Eventually Glaucon is provoked (5.471C–E) into demanding an answer to the different and more general question of whether and how a *politeia* incorporating the arrangements so far described could *come into existence*.

This is the question which prompts Socrates' introduction of the notion of philosopher rulers. They *could* make it happen. They would have both the wisdom and the power requisite for instituting such a *politeia* (5.473C–E). That paradoxical notion itself then becomes the topic of the third and final stage of the argument, in which Socrates faces the largest and most formid-able 'wave' of criticism, and discharges a responsibility to show that rule by philosophers would be beneficial, and is not something which *could* not happen (6.499B–D, 502B–C; cf. 7.540D). It represents a change, he says, that is 'not small nor easy, but possible' (5.473C).

Here the principal difficulty is not that it would be impossible to find anyone suitable. True, by the time he wrote the *Laws* Plato had decided that anyone with the knowledge and understanding required for good government who became absolute ruler of a city would succumb to corrupting self-interest, unless they had something of divinity in their nature (9.875A–E).[123] In the *Republic*, at the end of quite strenuous argument on the subject, Socrates sums up as follows (6.502A–B):

'Will anyone challenge our contention that it is possible for the offspring of kings and rulers to be born with philosophical natures?'

'Not a soul,' he said.

'And if they are born with philosophical natures, can anyone claim that there is absolutely no way they can avoid being corrupted? That it is difficult for them to be saved from corruption, even we admit. That in the whole of time not one out of all of them will ever be saved from it—is there anyone who will make that contention?'

'How could they?'

'But surely one like that would be enough to bring about all the things that people aren't convinced about, provided that he has a city which listens to him?'

'Yes, that would be enough,' he said.

The twist is in the tail: how to secure a population willing to accept the guidance of a philosopher ruler? Plato seems to be confronted here with a conundrum analogous to the one Rousseau faces in 'taking men as they are and laws as they might be' (preface to *Le Contrat Social* 1). How is a people ever going to come to know and trust political arrangements that reconcile order and freedom (as Rousseau envisages), unless they have already had an experience of them that establishes the requisite knowledge and trust?

Rousseau invokes the figure of the Founder (*Le Contrat Social* 2.7). History shows that lawgivers like Moses and Lycurgus have commanded an authority which inspires confidence in their legislation—and gets the show on the road. All Plato has to say at this juncture, however, is the following (6.502B–C):

'After all, if a ruler establishes the laws and the way of life we have gone through, it is presumably not impossible that the citizens will be willing to implement them.'

'Not in the least impossible.'

'Or is it astonishing that arrangements which seem a good idea to us should seem a good idea to other people as well?'

'Well, *I* don't think so,' he said.

This makes it sound as though Socrates is refusing to address Rousseau's version of the problem. He appears not to be attempting to explain *how* people would develop the knowledge or belief, together with the trust needed, to get the institutions and way of life of the good city started, but is settling for the claim *that* it's *not impossible* that they should implement the system. Given that the passage is part of the concluding discussion of the desirability and possibility of rule by philosophers, we must take it that that is indeed all Plato thinks needs to be established—as is confirmed by the terms in which Socrates finally sums up the whole argument about 'legislation' pursued by him from the beginning of Book 5 (6.502C): 'Our arrangements are the best, if only they could be put into effect, and while it is difficult for them to be put into effect, it is not impossible.'

Yet Plato's approach is closer to Rousseau's than the discussion so far suggests. When Socrates says that popular implementation of the provisions for which he has been arguing is not an impossibility, he does not mean—minimally—that in a contingent world anything not inconsistent with human nature could happen.[124] In the immediate context he appeals to a more substantial possibility: that people would find the same sorts of consideration 'a good idea' as have he and his interlocutors. And over the previous couple of pages (from 499D) he has taken the line that 'the many'—if left to themselves, and not influenced by the image of philosophy projected by 'gate-crashers' (500B; Plato's rival Isocrates evidently thought he was the target of this remark: see *Antidosis* 260)—could be *persuaded* by one means or other to drop their hostility to philosophy and to the political solution to human misery that rule by philosophers represents. Adeimantus expresses reservations (501E). His scepticism seems well founded. Socrates has presented virtually nothing by way of argument for the view about the efficacy of persuasion that he is advancing here. It flies in the face of most of what is said, on much stronger grounds in theory and experience alike, about popular attitudes to Socrates and to philosophy, both elsewhere and in other parts of the *Republic* itself.[125]

'The many' of 499Dff. and 'the citizens' of 502B are presumably not the same body of people. 'The many' seem to be 'men as they are', who might at least be shamed into going along with Socrates' view of philosophy and philosophers (502A). 'The citizens' who think the way of life for which he has 'legislated' is a good idea must be 'men as they might be' under the *politeia* the philosopher ruler will establish. Elsewhere in the dialogue Plato shows himself keenly aware of the difficulty of converting the one into the other. As we shall explore further in Chapter 7, the Noble Lie—the charter myth of the good city which teaches that all citizens are earth-born brothers—is a story all of them, and the guards especially, must be persuaded to believe if they are to care about the welfare of the city as they should. But Glaucon says he thinks there is no device by which the original citizens could be persuaded of it, though possibly their children and subsequent generations might be (3.414B–415C). At the end of Book 7 Socrates seems to be trying to deal with what we might call the conversion problem in another way. Philosopher rulers should banish everyone over ten years old into the country, so that children can be weaned from their parents' lifestyle and moulded on a new system (7.540E–541A). The problem with this scenario is not (as is sometimes objected) that it is too extreme and too violent to implement for Plato to mean it seriously. At Athens under the junta led by Critias in 404–03 BC, all but 3,000 sympathizers were forcibly expelled from the city. As G. R. F. Ferrari comments, we need to 'bear in mind the ease with which cities in the Greek world could be rebuilt, relocated, or started from scratch', even if there was 'no historic parallel for removing a whole class of parents to the countryside without their children'.[126] The difficulty is rather that the exercise presupposes that the philosopher ruler has recruited an adult militia moulded by his ideals already.

No wonder, then, that Socrates acknowledges that the most significant challenge he has to meet is the 'wave' of criticisms likely to greet his thesis about philosopher rulers. Yet the most important things Plato has to say about the possibility of realizing utopia come in a passage of dialogue just before Socrates introduces the idea of philosopher rulers (5.472B–473B). In response to Glaucon's increasingly insistent demands for an answer to the question of possibility, Socrates reminds him of the point of the whole discussion. In launching an enquiry into what justice is, and what the perfectly just man would be like if he existed, they have been trying to delineate a model or paradigm: *not* to show that the model could exist, but to get agreement that somebody who came as close as possible to it would get as close as possible to perfect happiness. Similarly with the good city (472D–E):

'Can't we claim to have been constructing a model of a good city in speech?'

'We certainly can.'

'In which case, do you think we are doing any less of a good job in speaking with that end in view if we are unable to demonstrate that it is possible for a city to have the arrangements we were describing?'

'Of course not,' he said.

Here, too, Socrates will suggest (473A–B), an approximation will suffice.

On its own this one passage, crucially positioned as it is in Plato's argument, is sufficient to rebut both the Popperian and the Straussian readings of the *Republic*. For Popper and Strauss alike, the application or applicability of its political ideal to human society is the key issue for interpretation. Popper takes the dialogue as a manifesto for action. Strauss supposes that because (as he sees the matter) its political vision *can't* be implemented, Plato must have deliberately designed it that way, and cannot therefore have meant it seriously—he can be serious only about its impossibility. But the stretch of dialogue between Socrates and Glaucon just summarized and quoted makes it crystal clear that *the issue of possibility or impossibility is not in the end what we should be concentrating on.* So what *should* be our focus? In a word: community—the idea of community (*koinônia*); the idea—articulated in all the specific proposals of Book 5—that sharing is what makes a city a real or a good city.

As with justice, so with the good city: the principal thing the *Republic* seeks to offer is *philosophical understanding*. In the nature of things, Socrates goes on to say (473A), speech (i.e. philosophical dialogue) gets more of a grip on truth than action does—*truth* is evidently what he is interested in.[127] His approach to questions about justice and community is all of a piece with his treatment of the mathematical sciences later on in the dialogue. A modern reader will not be surprised to find him arguing that arithmetic and geometry are concerned with intelligible, not sensible, objects. The shock comes when Socrates takes a similar line on astronomy: the study of the heavens is to be pursued only as a way into *true* astronomy, which deals with a purely intelligible realm of perfect geometrical forms in perfect motions: 'true patterns of movement achieved by real speed and real slowness in true number, with all of the figures they form true ones'—a domain accessible to reason alone (7.529D).[128]

But why, either side of the fundamentally important piece of text about truth at 473A–B, does Socrates press various questions of possibility, not just desirability, so relentlessly? That is explained by the misgivings he expresses that his ideas might be dismissed as no more than fantasy. Plato has to negotiate his way between a Scylla and a Charybdis. To show that his communistic proposals represent a serious contribution to the understanding of social and political life, he needs to demonstrate that they are more or less practicable. But at the same time he has to indicate that the main point of the philosophical conversation represented in the *Republic* is not to provide assurance that their implementation can be engineered—because practicability is only a fallible sign of truth, not what it consists in, even in the sphere of ethics and politics. In short, he shapes up to the same sort of problem as confronts virtually any philosopher who writes on (say) equality or justice or democracy. These are ideals which we want to have purchase on our social and political lives. At the same time we want to acknowledge their validity as ideals, even granted that it is immensely difficult to offer an adequate account of what an equal or just or democratic society would actually be like, or of how it could actually be realized.

Notes

1. Shklar 1957.
2. Bell 1960.
3. Marcuse 1967.
4. Jacoby 1999.
5. Fukuyama 1992. As Melissa Lane has commented to me, while Fukuyama's book reflects on the demise of totalitarian ideologies, it argues that liberal democracy *is* the form of society satisfying man's 'deepest and most fundamental longings' (p. xi) which in broadly Hegelian style is the final

outcome—for us 'who live in the old age of mankind' (p. 334)—of the historical process. In other words, his 'end' is a *telos* as well as a termination. Yet he concedes (ibid.) that 'those who remain dissatisfied will always have the potential to restart history'. Whether that will happen is something we cannot know (p. 339).

6. Eloquently summarized in Allott 2001: xxii–xxvi.

7. Grey and Garsten 2002: 15.

8. Bauman 1989: 18. The general line of argument was pioneered in Arendt 1951; a powerful restatement in Traverso 2003.

9. So Grey and Garsten 2002: 9. I am much indebted to this article both for its general approach to utopianism and for its references to other literature.

10. Popper 1961 [1945]. *The Open Society* generated a huge amount of controversy, not least over its treatment of Plato: see e.g. the lengthy rebuttal of Levinson 1953, and the papers collected in Bambrough 1967. A lucid and balanced assessment of Popper's account of Plato, warmly acknowledged by Popper himself (p. x), is Robinson 1951. A good recent discussion: Samaras 2002: ch. 5.

11. Popper's philosophical pedigree and mindset were scarcely Nietzschean, but on this last point he and Nietzsche spoke with one voice: see *Daybreak* §496. Almost the only reference to Nietzsche in *The Open Society* (p. 284 n. 60) relates to a quotation from Plato's *Theages* (in *The Will to Power* (§958)) concerned with the same general issue. (Neither Nietzsche nor Popper concern themselves with the authenticity of the *Theages*, now universally agreed to be post-Platonic.)

12. A major statement is Strauss 1964: ch. 2; other treatments by Strauss of 'Platonic political philosophy' may be found e.g. in two posthumously edited collections of his essays: Strauss 1983; 1989. A treatment of the *Republic* on Straussian lines is offered by his most famous pupil, Allan Bloom, in the 'interpretive essay' included in Bloom 1968. A good guide to Strauss's Plato is supplied by Zuckert 1996: chs 4–6. A fierce critique: Burnyeat 1985.

13. See further Lane 1999.

14. Williams 1993: 163–4. Another dimension of Thucydidean realism he finds suggested by Nietzsche's remarks in *Daybreak* is the impartial way in which 'the psychology he deploys in his explanations is not at the service of his ethical beliefs' (by contrast with Plato's psychological theorizing) (ibid., p. 161). On Nietzsche's Plato, see further Zuckert 1996: ch. 1 and Geuss 2005; and for more on questions about Thucydides' 'realism', Section 4.2 below.

15. Affinities (despite differences) between Thucydides' political history and Plato's political philosophy are explored from a vantage point different from mine or Williams's, in Strauss 1964: 139–44, 236–41.

16. So Geuss 2005: 224.

17. However, in thinking about the *Gorgias* and the *Menexenus* in Ch. 2, we have already seen Plato questioning the 'truth' the *History* (or indeed history) succeeds in conveying about Pericles and Athens, even if his analysis of rhetoric is heavily indebted to Thucydides. Examination of the *Critias* (Section 4.2 below) will reinforce the point. It goes without saying

that fundamental to Platonic metaphysics and epistemology is the denial that true reality can be located in the physical world at all, subject as it is to change and time.

18. So Grey and Garsten 2002: 10. Other definitions are of course current. The idea of utopia as a tool of social criticism is also crucial, as expressed for example in the following account (borrowed by Clay and Purvis 1999: 2, from Gibson 1961): 'A utopia should describe in a variety of aspects and with some consistency an imaginary state or society which is regarded as better, in some respects at least, than the one in which the author lives.... Most utopias are presented not as models of unrealistic perfection but as alternatives to the familiar, as norms by which to judge existing societies.' M. Whitford translates Luce Irigaray as saying (in Irigaray 1992: 26): 'I am militating politically for the impossible, which doesn't mean I am a utopian. Rather what I want does not yet exist, as the only possibility of a future.' Whitford aptly comments that 'Irigaray both affirms and denies the utopian impulse' (Whitford 1994: 382).

19. So, for example, John Keane writes that his argument will 'presuppose that periodic fascination with big ideas is a necessary condition of imagining a social order' (Keane 2003: xi).

20. Geuss 2002: 320–1.

21. At the time of writing there is a gateway to a range of information at <http://users.erols.com/jonwill/utopialist.htm> (but of course URLs are subject to Heraclitean flux). The first page you can open is a list of 'definitions'—from Oscar Wilde, for example: 'A map of the world that does not include Utopia is not worth even glancing at, for it leaves out the one country at which Humanity is always landing. And when Humanity lands there, it looks out, and seeing a better country, sets sail. Progress is the realisation of Utopias.' Or try the Society of Utopian Studies' site at <http://www.utoronto.ca/utopia> for news of its journal, annual conference, etc.

22. Carey 1999. The introduction to this book brings home very forcibly the extent to which so many of the key utopian preoccupations of the *Republic* and the *Laws* recur in subsequent utopian writing.

23. Its ancient antecedents lie not in Plato but in Stoicism: see e.g. Schofield 1991; Nussbaum 1996, 1997; Brown 2006.

24. So Held 2004: 55.

25. I quote the formulation in Grey and Garsten 2002: 17.

26. Allott 2001: xi.

27. In this connection, see the reflections on the 2005 G8 summit in Nairn 2005.

28. As one might expect if Perry Anderson (commenting on the ideas of Frederick Jameson) is right that utopianism flourishes most intensively in periods when people correctly sense that their world is on the brink of radical change: Anderson 2004. He notes the dystopian flavour of much contemporary expectation of developments in science, notably as regards the prospects for genetic engineering, and wonders whether Huxley's *Brave New World* is more the text for our time than Orwell's *1984*.

29. Keane 2003: 11, 7.

30. Held 2004: 162. See also e.g. Unger 1998.
31. See Geuss 2003.
32. For further discussion of this *Laws* 3 passage, see Dillon 1992: 30–3; Cole 1967: ch. 7 (on its sources); Boys-Stones 2001: 13–17 (particularly on its probable development by Aristotle's pupil Dicaearchus of Messene).
33. On this theme in Thucydides, see (for example) Balot 2001: ch. 5.
34. Barney 2001: 220.
35. On this point, see Vidal-Naquet 1986a: 297–8.
36. See above, Ch. 1, Section 5.
37. On the prohibition on gold and silver at Sparta, the curious iron 'pancakes' used instead, the pressures to which the prohibition gradually succumbed, and much else, see Figueira 2002.
38. Compare Aristotle's quip (*Pol.* 2.9, 1271b13–15) that at Sparta the legislator achieved the opposite of what would have been advantageous: he made the city moneyless (as Adeimantus thinks is the prospect for Socrates' city), but the individuals in it lovers of money (this charge, commonly made against Sparta, is implicit in Socrates' treatment of timarchy (*Rep.* 8.548A–B)).
39. But the unity of the good city will turn out to be a function of its justice, and the disunity of other societies a sign of their injustice—and these conditions mirror the state of the just and the unjust soul.
40. See Halliwell 1993: 21.
41. An early and particularly memorable instance is supplied by the reply of the Athenians to the Macedonians after the naval engagement at Salamis but before the land battle at Plataea, where in refusing to contemplate a separate deal with the Persians, they cite 'Greekness': common blood ties, common language, common religion and common ways (Herodotus 8.144.2).
42. A good introduction to Panhellenism remains Finley 1975b. There is an interesting detailed study of its treatment in Thucydides in Price 2001: ch. 3.
43. This is an idea we shall be pursuing further in Ch. 7, Section 2.5, in connection with the myth of the Noble Lie.
44. The phrase echoes a key expression in the Noble Lie (3.414E).
45. This is presumably ensured by making Apollo at Delphi—the Panhellenic cult centre—the authority for the ideal city in all matters religious (4.427B–C).
46. For an excellent discussion of the passage and the issues it raises, see Halliwell 1993: 23–5, 191–2.
47. Scholars do not agree on which Critias is meant. For arguments in favour of the view adopted here, see Lampert and Planeaux 1998–9: 95–100; Nails 2002: 106–8.
48. See Clay 1999.
49. The Egyptian dimension—not unique in Plato's later dialogues: see e.g. *Phaedrus.* 274C–275B; *Philebus* 18B–D; *Laws* 7.798E–799B—is worth a discussion all to itself. Some at least of its significance probably consists in response to Isocrates' critique of the *Republic* in his sophistic exercise entitled *Busiris.* Here (*Busiris* 15–27) Isocrates had insinuated that the social and political system of the *Republic* constituted a repressive

regime maintained by a discipline and fear more akin to Egyptian religious superstition than to the Greek ideal of liberal education cultivated by the Athenians. In the story told to Solon we may see Plato's witty response. So far from its being true that the ideas of the *Republic* are borrowings from Egypt, alien to Athens, an Egyptian priest vouchsafes that the *politeia* of the *Republic did* once have an ancient historical incarnation resembling the *politeia* of contemporary Egypt—but in a prehistoric Athens, where it developed first and quite separately. He seems to think that ancient Athens like his own Egypt has a priestly caste (*Tim.* 24A), but in Solon's version we hear only of guards (*Critias* 110C–D). For treatment of the whole issue—including the date (contested) of the *Busiris*—see the discussion in Eucken 1983: ch. 5.

50. Gill 1977: 295.
51. Not silver, as at Laurion in Attica, but *oreichalkos*, 'mountain copper', yellow copper ore, which is valued by the people of Atlantis second only to gold, and used to create glittering surfaces, for example, in the wall surrounding their acropolis. I take it that Plato here implies another criticism of Periclean Athens: there is really nothing to choose between the precious metal silver, by which it set such store, and the base metal the Atlantidans use instead.
52. See the classic study of Vidal-Naquet 1986b.
53. See Lampert and Planeaux: 1998–9: 100–7. They might have noted that Thucydides' testimony to his general perspicacity and his experience and outstanding courage in war (6.72) chimes nicely with Socrates' requirements of wisdom and political experience in discussants, to ensure they are capable of coping properly with Adeimantus' question (*Tim.* 19E), and presumably marks him out as one of the many witnesses to Hermarchus' qualifications mentioned by Socrates (*Tim.* 20A).
54. For an account of what Hermocrates was up against—and stressing the way 'their community's civic ideology conditioned the Athenian citizens from youth on to accept war as inevitable and even desirable'—see Raaflaub 2000.
55. See the discussion in Schofield 1997: 213–15. Some aspects of my arguments on this point are disputed in Rowe 2004.
56. On the different ways in which primitive Athens and Magnesia in the *Laws* approximate to the condition of the *Republic*'s good city, see Laks 1990: 216–17.
57. See e.g. Stahl 1966; Connor 1984; Ober 2000.
58. The older view received a classic formulation, e.g. in de Romilly 1963. The contemporary view: e.g. Stahl 1966; Connor 1984. More references to opinion on either side are usefully collected in Orwin 1994: 15 n. 1.
59. Most other Athenian writers and thinkers of the fourth century BC appear to have thought the same, and indeed to have appropriated for themselves the same view of Pericles: references in Yunis 1996: 143 n. 13.
60. Why is the *Critias* unfinished? We do not know, and speculation has not been very profitable. The dialogue breaks off at the point where Zeus has summoned the other gods to hear how Atlantis is to be punished for its hubris. A narrative of its war with Athens and an account of its eventual

physical submersion would presumably have followed. Perhaps by simultaneously introducing and withdrawing a Homeric council of the gods Plato wanted to signal that what was now ending was a myth, or more precisely an unhistorical history. He had after all already written enough of the *Critias* to make the point he seems to have wanted to make.

61. There is an authoritative commentary on Book 5 of the *Republic*—the core text for Plato's treatment of *koinônia*—in Halliwell 1993, which like any good edition gives crisp, balanced and often penetrating consideration to many of the issues Plato's discussion raises, as well as supplying all manner of pertinent information.

62. See *Plt.* 258E–259C, with discussion in Cooper 1997a: 73–80. The suspicion: see Annas 1999: 90–2.

63. In this chapter I confine discussion of Plato's approach to political unity largely to the *Republic*. But it is a theme that can be pursued through a whole sequence of dialogues, from *Menexenus* to *Laws*. The development of Plato's preoccupation with unity is the principal theme of Pradeau 2002.

64. Compare Socrates in the *Phaedo*: 'They [i.e. materialists] do not think at all that in truth it is the good and what is binding that binds and holds together' (99C), and what the Athenian Visitor says in the *Laws*: 'The true art of politics must make not what is private but what is common its concern—the common interest binds cities together, whereas private interest tears them apart' (9.875A).

65. See further Burnyeat 2000 (especially pp. 74–81).

66. Rawls 1993: 134–5.

67. See Rawls 1972: 446–52.

68. See Rawls 1993: 201–2.

69. It had become a commonplace by Plato's time that 'unanimity' (*homonoia*) was the solution to a city's social and political discontents, as reflected e.g. at *Rep.* 1.351D; Xen. *Mem.* 4.4.16. See further de Romilly 1972.

70. See Dworkin 1989: 501–2.

71. Plato's substantive principle of political justice is of course irreconcilable with Rawls's or Dworkin's or any other liberal principle. The liberal assumes an equality of free status in the population that constitutes the membership of the society, and articulates justice accordingly in terms of their rights to liberties and their entitlement to social and economic benefits and opportunities. Plato makes a different assumption: the basic functions that have to be performed if society is to be efficient, secure and stable require that differential status be assigned to different categories of citizen, and justice has to be conceived accordingly in terms of proper discharge of societal functions. Similarly, the circumstances in which he envisages that the principle of political justice will achieve general acceptance (see further on this in Ch. 6, Section 5) are utterly different from those which Rawls or any political liberal would regard as appropriate. But both in Rawls's formal specification of a well-ordered society and in Dworkin's delineation of the ideal of a community, reference to any *particular* set of principles of justice is avoided. Both formulations are in fact neutral as between a liberal and a Platonic conception of justice—to take the two examples of immediate concern to us.

72. On varieties of liberalism, see Geuss 2001: ch. 2; 2002.
73. Williams 2005: 61.
74. Williams 2005: 3.
75. 'Classical Greece itself *is* Platonic when it comes to this most commonly shared belief on the nature of the political': Loraux 2002: 94. Loraux's *The Divided City* is a wide-ranging meditation on the way division figures—in Heraclitean fashion—in the Greek imagination as what (contrary to Plato's argument in the *Republic*) simultaneously sunders *and unites* the profoundly agonistic political life of the *polis*. See also her article Loraux 1991.
76. See de Romilly 1972.
77. Dworkin 1989: 495.
78. Dworkin 1989: 492.
79. See Vlastos 1995: II.80–4. The same position is taken in Taylor 1986: 17: 'the whole structure of his [Plato's] theory requires that the *polis* is an organization devised with the paramount aim of promoting individual *eudaimonia*'.
80. See Miller 1995: ch. 6.
81. See Brown 1998.
82. On this dimension of the city-soul analogy see Taylor 1986: 18–22.
83. So far from making promotion of individual happiness the 'paramount aim' of the *polis* (Taylor 1986: 17), Socrates concludes his discussion of the happiness of the city with the remark that with the whole city flourishing in accordance with the principle of each 'doing his own' and being well governed on that basis, things must just be allowed to take their course so far as sharing in happiness for each of the classes within it is concerned (4.421C). Of course, the basic rationale for having a community in the first place is for people to secure mutual benefits (2.369B–C; cf. 7.519E–520A). But achievement of benefits will not make them happy: for that they will need to develop virtue or some approximation to it—presumably a prospect that *will* be realized if the city does truly flourish as it should, and in particular if education for rulers and the military and the mechanisms Plato envisages as inducing restraint in the rest of the population are effective.
84. Dworkin 1989: 494.
85. See Halliwell 1993: 172, where among other illuminating comments is the suggestion that the expression embraces 'all the ways in which individuals can conceive themselves as independent agents, with interests and needs ("pleasures"/"pains") of their own: it would arise, in other words, wherever something might be spoken of as "personal", "private", or "individual" '. Halliwell goes on: 'This means that Plato's argument is aimed not merely at selfishness (cf. *Laws* 5.731D–732B), but at the psychological basis of individuality.' It is certainly noteworthy that when Plato reformulates this idea of a collectivist psychology in the *Laws*, he talks of 'contriving it that so far as possible even things that are naturally private may have become at least in a sort of way common/communal—with (for example) eyes, ears, hands being thought to see and hear and do things in common' (5.739C–D).

86. As Peter Garnsey has stressed to me, Plato's communism is a matter of what might broadly be called common *use*, not of the communal *ownership* of persons or things (although it is true that Aristotle thought common ownership of property was envisaged: see pp. 226–7 above).

87. Aristotle does seem to treat the formulation of the collectivist ideal in Book 5 of the *Republic* and its restatement in Book 5 of the *Laws* as interchangeable. For example, his account of the aim of the *Republic*'s proposals as giving the city 'as much unity as possible' (*Pol.* 2.3, 1261b16–17) relies on a formulation in the *Laws* version (5.739D) rather than on any explicit statement in the *Republic* itself.

88. See Stalley 1991: 183–6; cf. also Laks 1990: 219–21.

89. See Halliwell 1993: 174, 181 (notes on 463B1, 466B1).

90. Loraux 2002: 198.

91. The solution might consist in recognizing the grades or modes of brotherhood to which Plato might be thought to be logically committed. One could say that guards (gold or silver in nature) have one grade or mode of brotherhood with other guards, another with farmers, artisans and people involved in commerce (iron or bronze).

92. Adam 1902: I.305 (note on 462B9). The rest of the city won't be divided either against the guards or against one another, says Socrates, echoing in the word for 'division' (*dichostatein*) Solon's great meditation on *stasis*, in the poem that survives as his Fragment 4 (so Halliwell 1993: 179).

93. Of course, the *Republic* sees *stasis* between rich and poor as the condition endemic and prevalent in existing societies generally (4.422E–423A). It takes care to eliminate the possibility of this kind of division from the good city, principally by denying the ruling class possessions or the use of gold and silver at all: see further Ch. 6.

94. The points about litigation (464D–E) and respect for the elderly (465A–B) are anticipated in Aristophanes' *Assemblywomen* (655–72, 635–43 respectively); entitlement of any older person to give orders and punishments to anyone younger (465A) in the Laconizing literature (Xen. *Lac.Pol.* 2.10). As elsewhere in Book 5, Plato challenges the reader to ask why what Aristophanes represents as comic fantasy should not actually come true in the circumstances he envisages.

95. But Plato might have observed that in myth, at least, brotherhood undiluted is all too often paradigmatic of mutual hatred: see Loraux 2002: ch. 8.

96. Aristotle does not comment on the difficulties inherent in the *Republic*'s proposals for eugenic breeding, which Plato himself seems to have thought the most problematic of his collectivist ideas (see below, n. 117). For a full discussion of these difficulties and related issues for questions of kinship, see Halliwell 1993: 16–21.

97. Contrary to the interpretation of Vlastos 1989. He defended his use of the vocabulary of rights in this context in a postscript to Vlastos 1978, published in the reprinted version at Vlastos 1995: II.123–5. For remarks relevant to the propriety of this kind of modernizing interpretation of the categories of Greek political thought, see Schofield 1995–6.

98. So e.g. Annas 1976.

99. Bluestone 1987: 165.

100. For the notion of an alienating description, see Burnyeat 1992: 183–4 (pp. 306–7 of the reprinted version in Fine 1999).
101. But many other elements in Plato's cultural inheritance, all relating in one way or another to the role and status of women in society, also doubtless helped to constitute the context in which the ideas of Book 5 of the *Republic* were developed. For a brief survey, see Halliwell 1993: 9–12; at greater length: Dawson 1992: ch. 1.
102. A useful summary of the evidence and the arguments in Halliwell 1993: Appendix (pp. 224–5), which is overly sceptical about the likelihood that Plato would have recalled the play. As he says, it is hard to improve on the thorough and judicious discussion in Adam 1902: I.345–55 (Appendix 1 to Book 5), which is less hesitant on this point.
103. Contrary to the influential interpretation of Strauss 1964: 61–2, expanded in Bloom 1968: 379–89, which treats the echo of Aristophanes as indicating that the *Republic*'s own proposals are nothing but comic fantasy, whose impracticability is designed to wean us from utopianism (a similar view in Saxonhouse 1976, 1985: 45–52). For criticism of the Straussian reading, see Bluestone 1987: 41–50, 154–62; Burnyeat 1992; Kochin 2002: 81–2.
104. Fuller collections of similar passages are conveniently available in Wender 1973: 80–2; Irigaray 1985: 152–9.
105. Homer's Epeios chooses in his next life the 'nature of a woman skilled in crafts' (10.621C). This scarcely reflects failure in his previous life—he wins a boxing match at the funeral games for Patroclus (*Il.* 23.664–99), and under Athena's inspiration is principal architect of the Trojan horse (*Od.* 8.492–3)—but presumably indicates the power of his devotion to the goddess.
106. Vlastos 1995: II.140 rightly stresses the importance of Socrates' stance for Plato's approach to the issue. The key text is *Meno* 72D–73C (where Socrates does not endorse Meno's belief that virtue for a man functions within the public sphere, but within the domestic for a woman); cf. e.g. Xen. *Symp.* 2.9; Arist. *Pol.* 1.13, 1260a20–2; D.L. 6.12 [Antisthenes], 7.175 [Cleanthes].
107. See e.g. Lloyd 1993.
108. An observation at least as old as Rousseau, who at the beginning of Book 5 of *Emile* says: 'Having got rid of the family there is no place for women in his system of government, so he is forced to turn them into men.' The suggestion that it is abolition of the family that drives the proposal of women guards has been repeated in the modern literature (e.g. Okin 1977), but plainly runs against the grain of the text.
109. Lovibond 1994: 99.
110. Irigaray 1996: 35.
111. With Cavarero 1995: ch. 1. At one point Cavarero goes so far as to apologize to her female readers for imposing on them 'the labour of my analytical reading of philosophical texts': ibid. 123 n. 3.
112. For a classic statement, see Vlastos 1989.
113. So Smith 1983: 472; endorsed by Levin 1996.
114. Vlastos 1995: II.143.
115. Hobbs 2000: 246–7.

116. But this is precisely the context in which the Visitor is made to assert that 'female nature is inferior in goodness to that of males' (781B).

117. Subordination is argued, e.g. in Annas 1976; Okin 1979: 60–70; Levin 2000: 81–9. Participation in most aspects of political and civic life is argued in Cohen 1987; Brisson 2005: 98–106; and (with much caution) in Saunders 1995. A judicious summary treatment of the issues is offered in Bobonich 2002: 385–9.

118. See Nagel 1991: ch. 10.

119. There is no attempt to surmount Nagel's third obstacle: differences in ability are of course what is made to shape the whole structure of the *Republic*'s sociopolitical system.

120. I owe these quotations—the first from the 'postface' to the second edition of *Das Kapital*, the second from *Philosophy of Right*—to Waldron 1995: 160.

121. Burnyeat 1992.

122. Socrates' evasiveness about the feasibility of the mating and breeding arrangements he describes as appropriate for guards becomes more intelligible in the light of the detail of his discussion (5.458C–461E). If men and women do everything together, including their physical training, then it is inevitable that sexual encounters will occur: an erotic, not a geometric necessity, as Glaucon puts it. So effecting a successful breeding programme will require formidable social control (as well as esoteric knowledge), involving large-scale deception. It is scarcely surprising if Plato was not prepared to have Socrates vouch at all explicitly or specifically for the workability of such arrangements; and it is interesting that mistaken calculations about appropriate matings are subsequently identified as the symbolic cause of contamination of the stock, with ultimately disastrous consequences for the good city (8.545D–547A). See further Halliwell 1993: 16–21.

123. It is not clear whether the author of the *Republic* would have agreed—since it is unclear whether the dialogue's philosopher rulers hold absolute power in the sense envisaged in *Laws* 875A–E. For some further discussion, see Schofield 1997: 230–41.

124. On what Plato means by 'possibility' with regard to realizing the ideal city (and the rule of philosophers that is the precondition of that), see Laks 1990: 213–17.

125. As H. Yunis says, 'the reader's first response may well be astonishment' (Yunis 1996: 16). W. K. C. Guthrie comments (Guthrie 1975: 502 n.1): 'This good-hearted but misinformed crowd [i.e. the many of 499Dff.] sounds very different from 'the great beast' of 492B–493D, the real cause of trouble, whose whims the Sophists merely follow. No doubt Plato's attitude to the *dēmos* was in fact ambivalent.'

126. Ferrari and Griffith 2000: xvii, 251.

127. My argument here converges with Jeremy Waldron's view of what in general the great political theorists of the Western canon were about (as set out in Waldron 1995).

128. On this topic, see further Burnyeat 2000.

6

Money and the Soul

---

1. The Ethics and Politics of Money

In 1932 John Maynard Keynes wrote as follows:[1]

When the accumulation of wealth is no longer of high social importance, there will be great changes in the code of morals. We shall be able to rid ourselves of many of the pseudo-moral principles that have hag-ridden us for two hundred years, by which we have exalted some of the most distasteful human qualities into the position of the highest virtues. We shall be able to afford to dare to assess the money-motive at its true value. The love of money as a possession—as distinguished from the love of money as a means to the enjoyments and realities of life—will be recognized for what it is ... one of those ... semi-pathological propensities which one hands over with a shudder to the specialists in mental disease.

This is a protest not just against 'the money-motive', but against the Enlightenment, its values and its analysis of social good. Keynes is evidently looking back to the eighteenth century, and to the revolution in moral thought given classic expression in the writings of David Hume and Adam Smith. The pioneering work was Bernard Mandeville's satirical verse tract *The Fable of the Bees* (the 1714 title of a work first published in 1705). The poem championed the shocking idea that the egoistic acquisitiveness of individuals, pursued by disreputable means as well as fair ones, was no threat to the public good. On the contrary, it was actually what sustained society:

> Thus Vice nurs'd Ingenuity,
> Which join'd with Time and Industry
> Had carry'd Life's Conveniences
> It's real Pleasures, Comforts, Ease,
> To such a Height, the very Poor
> Liv'd better than the Rich Before,
> And Nothing could be added more.

It was left to Hume and Smith to state and elaborate the moral: such 'vice' is no vice at all. In his essay 'Of Commerce' of 1741-2, Hume contrasted the civility, peace and progress generated by trade, and by the pursuit of the refined pleasures of luxury, with the militaristic conception of what made for the public good associated with Spartan ideals. He is famous for the scorn he poured on the 'monkish virtue' of celibacy, mortification and self-denial. Pride in oneself and the achievements of one's own industry was for him both fundamental for the existence and prosperity of civilized society, and a pre-eminent example of a quality of mind 'useful or agreeable to the person himself or to others'—Hume's own definition of a virtue. A little later in the century, Adam Smith incorporated similar ideas in his account of the way a market economy works, above all in his magnum opus *An Inquiry into the Nature and Causes of the Wealth of Nations* (1776), with its formulation of the notion of the Invisible Hand ensuring that while each 'intends only his own gain', despite himself he 'frequently promotes that of the society more effectually than when he really intends to promote it'.[2]

The classic expression of the traditional view of acquisitiveness overturned by these thinkers of the British Enlightenment is to be found in the *Republic*. Keynes might almost have been offering a summary of the view of the love of money taken in Plato's dialogue. But Plato echoed a long Greek tradition of political reflection, from Hesiod and Solon through many fifth- and fourth-century writers, in seeing greed as a prime force for destructiveness in human affairs, whether in fuelling *stasis* within a city, or in powering and then destroying imperialistic ambition,[3] and in focusing particularly on the power of money.[4] The tradition is reflected in Attic tragedy and comedy alike. The venality of both politicians and the *dêmos* they flatter is a favourite theme in Aristophanes. We may forget that in Sophocles' *Antigone*, a drama exploring as it does such fundamental polarities as male and female, civic and family obligation, Olympian and chthonic religion, another counter in the dialectic between Creon and most of the other main characters is money and its power.[5] At one point (*Antigone* 295–301) Creon has this to say:

No currency ever grew up among humankind so evil as money (*arguros*). This lays waste even cities, this expels men from their homes. This instructs and perverts good minds among mortals, tilting them towards shameful acts. It has shown people how to be villainous, and how to know impiety in their every deed.

One instance of this phenomenon that Plato might have found particularly disturbing might be found in the conduct of the junta of the thirty tyrants (404–3 BC). Contemporary Athenian critics who diverged in their own political sympathies as widely as Xenophon and Lysias agreed in complaining that much of their behaviour was motivated by nothing more ambitious than plain greed.[6] Xenophon in his *Hellenica* (his continuation of Thucydides' *History*) has Critias come clean about this (*Hell.* 2.3.16):

It is impossible for those who want to have more (*pleonektein*) to avoid getting rid of those people who are most likely to form an opposition. And you are naïve if you think that, just because we are thirty and not one, we have to keep any the less close a watch on this rule of ours, just as if it were a tyranny.

Here Critias is made to use the sort of language that Plato's Thrasymachus uses to articulate his immoralism, and that Thucydides associates with Athenian imperialism (not least in the echo of Pericles' famous acknowledgement that it constitutes a form of tyranny: 2.63.2—but Critias appropriates the vocabulary and the sentiment to justify *internal* oppression).[7]

Where Plato pushed the analysis of the desire 'to have more' far beyond any of his predecessors was in his exploration of its roots in the human psyche. His theory of the soul constitutes the key to the ethical and political theory worked out in the *Republic*. Analysis of the soul is not pursued simply to throw light on society—whether the good society or degenerate forms—by analogy. It already assumes and then enriches a conception of human beings as political animals whose motivations have an inevitably social dimension. The psychoanalyst Adam Phillips suggests that in our own time political theory and psychological understanding have become divorced from one another:[8]

Designs for a good life, of which the whole notion of sanity must form a part, have been left to political theorists; and descriptions of the bad life, of a life lived in thrall to one of the many modern pathologies, have been left to neurologists, psychiatrists and psychologists, the masters of modern mental health.

The *Republic*, by contrast, takes both these projects to require a complex form of reflection that is simultaneously both political and psychological. Having pondered utopia, we need to consider next the threat to utopia posed by materialistic desire.

2. The Analogy of City and Soul

I shall approach the topic by considering one of the difficulties Bernard Williams thought he saw in the *Republic*'s analogy of the city and the soul. Williams diagnosed a failure of match between the dialogue's description of the city's economic class and its account of appetite (*epithumêtikon*) as the corresponding element in our psychological make-up.[9] He drew a contrast particularly with the spirited element (*thumoeides*). How do we get a purchase on the identity of the psychological motivation to which Plato applies the word 'spirited'? By thinking of a character-type: a type concerned (as John Cooper has suggested)[10] with self-image and self-esteem, as expressed in competitive behaviour and displays of pride—and dominated by *anger* among all the emotions (we only understand anger if we see its focus on threats to self-image). But we best understand that competitiveness in its turn from the form of life—military, aristocratic, Homeric—in which it is played out, and which defines the *Republic*'s class of guards; or rather its warrior auxiliaries, once their seniors have been allocated the responsibility of ruling as their function (3.412B–C, 414B). The way Plato's Socrates identifies appetite, Williams suggested, is quite different. It has an independent psychological and physiological foundation, which Socrates explains when he represents appetite as a motivation which conflicts with reason, like an archer pushing on the bowstring with one hand and pulling the bow itself with the other. For example, something within a thirsty person pushes and says: 'Drink'; but something too may pull and say: 'Don't drink'. Socrates says that the advice not to drink will invariably be due to some reasoning, whereas the injunction to drink arises from 'feelings and physical disorders'. More formally: 'The part with which we feel sexual desire, hunger, thirst and the turmoil of the other appetites can be called the irrational and appetitive element, the companion of certain repletions and pleasures' (4.439D). Whether or not this description *sufficiently* captures what Socrates will mean by appetite, it doesn't on the face of it seem likely that there is any associated character-type or way of life which we can or need to refer to for further illumination. He tells us comparatively little about the city's economic class, but in Williams's view any idea that in general the lives of (for example) cobblers are dominated by the sorts of appetites just listed seems highly implausible.

Williams's treatment of the issue depended heavily (although not very explicitly) on a single passage: the analysis of psychological conflict towards the end of Book 4. A broader look at the evidence indicates that for Plato the motivations of appetite have just as strong a social and cultural dimension as do those he associates with the spirited element in the soul. A good place to start from is a sequence in Book 9, where Socrates reviews the theory of soul developed in Book 4 and used extensively in Books 8 and 9.[11] Here is his summary treatment (*Rep.* 9.580D–581A):

'The first part [i.e. of the soul], we say, is the one with which a person learns, the second one with which he gets angry. To the third, on account of its diversity, we found it impossible to give its own unique name, so we gave it the name of its largest and strongest element. We called it appetitive—because of the intensity of its appetites for food, drink, sex, and everything that goes with these—and money-loving, because money is the principal means of satisfying these kinds of appetites.'

'And we were right,' he said.

'So if we were to say that the thing it took pleasure in and had a love for was financial gain, would that be the best way of concentrating our argument under one heading? Would we that way make it clear to ourselves what we mean when we talk about this part of the soul? And if we called it money-loving and gain-loving, would we be right?'

'Well, *I* certainly think we would,' he said.

In recapitulating the account of appetite, Socrates certainly starts with a reference to the conflict passage in Book 4 on which Williams relied (4.436A–B). But he goes on at once to associate appetite with the love of money. And he then suggests that for the purposes of the argument—that is, the main ethical argument of the *Republic* about what kind of life brings a person happiness—the most helpful way of understanding this third part of the soul is as the element within us devoted to the love of money and financial gain. It goes without saying that money is paradigmatically a social and cultural phenomenon, only intelligible in terms of social and cultural structures. What Socrates implies is that when we imagine a lifestyle devoted to satisfaction of the appetites, we should think not just of a person fixated on pleasures of food, drink and sex, but also—and indeed typically and primarily—of someone obsessed with money. That obsession is generated by realization that money is the master key giving access to all the pleasures of the flesh. But the obsession takes on a life of its own. Acquiring and possessing money comes to seem the greatest pleasure of them all.

When Socrates associates appetite with love of money, he makes it just one kind of human motivation among others. He will go on at once (9.581A–B) to identify love of victory and honour as a function of spirit (the *thumoeides*) and love of learning and wisdom as a function of reason (the *logistikon*). In this part of the *Republic* talk of parts of the soul is focused primarily on the different forms taken by human aspiration and the behaviour it motivates. Much contemporary discussion of Plato's division of the soul in the dialogue has concentrated attention on something very different. Interpreters have been preoccupied with the arguments from psychological conflict in Book 4 for the presence in the soul of distinct elements with which we perform different mental activities: reason, get angry, feel physical desires—the different elements referred to here in Book 9 at 580D–E. This preoccupation has generated a large literature devoted to the ontological status of the elements Plato distinguishes and the logical coherence and adequacy of the resulting model of the mind.[12]

For example, Plato has been suspected of making the mind disintegrate into *homunculi* (or mini-minds) with their own beliefs and goals, and of leaving in consequence no room for 'I'—despite indications that such an outcome is far from what he intends. It is the oligarchic *person* who 'enthrones the appetitive and money-loving element, and makes it the great king within *himself*' (or, as he otherwise puts it, within his own soul), 'sitting the rational and spirited elements on the ground on either side beneath it and reducing them to slavery' (8.553C–D). What Plato presupposes here is a conception of the person or self as *deciding*—in this instance—to identify with the motivations of appetite rather than with those of reason (as a philosopher does) or of spirit (like the timocratic man). In fact, I think he *always* presupposes a 'he' or 'she' whose identification with the promptings of one or other element in the soul—sometimes successively, as e.g. in the description of righteous indignation at 4.440C–D—is what determines behaviour and, in the end, character. Thus the just person, by contrast with the timocratic or oligarchic, 'rules *himself*' (or herself), and by binding the parts of his or her soul together becomes 'one from many' (4.443D–E). Indeed the *soul*'s choice of one life rather than another is to be the major theme of the Myth of Er (10.617D–621D).[13]

These issues about the model of the mind elaborated at the end of Book 4 have an importance and fascination of their own. We shall be returning at various points—although mostly in the notes rather than the main text—to aspects of them. Yet what also needs to be registered is the presence already in Book 4 of the preoccupations of Book 9. In fact these set the context for the whole enterprise of soul division. Before Socrates launches his main argument about the soul (4.436A–441C), it is apparent that what will most interest him about the elements he distinguishes (unsurprisingly, given the analogy he wants to make with the city) is not conflict but something else: the different forms of aspiration and the consequent behaviour he associates with them—love of learning (not just any and every form of reasoning), love of honour, love of money. This trichotomy pre-dates soul division in Plato's writing. It is already presented as familiar in the *Phaedo* (*Phd.* 68B–C; cf. 82C), where love of honour and love of money are treated as things you would expect of a 'body-lover', not a philosopher. When at *Rep.* 9.581A Socrates remarks that 'we called it [appetite] money-loving and gain-loving', he is referring back to the passage in Book 4 which immediately precedes the soul division (4.435E–436A). Here the thesis that we must each have within us the same elements and characteristics as are found in the city is argued by appeal to national traits. In the case of the spirited element, Thracians, Scythians and in general northerners are instanced; the love of learning is particularly characteristic of the Greeks; and 'love of money is something you could say is especially associated with the Phoenicians and the Egyptians' (4.436A). The claim is that the only reason for ascribing such traits to these nations is that the human beings populating them are like that. The further assumption Socrates

seems to make is that (for example) the love of money so characteristic of the Phoenicians and the Egyptians is nonetheless
something that we are all aware of in our own souls, whether it
is dominant there or not.[14]

The money-loving element in the soul corresponds to the
money-making function within society. It is worth noting, however, that what I have been calling the 'economic' class was
not characterized in terms of money-making when Socrates
first started describing his good city. He began by positing an
extremely small community indeed, designed to meet at any
rate basic needs: a farmer, a builder, a weaver and a shoemaker
would perhaps suffice (2.369B–370C). Arguments for expanding
it were immediately developed; and the expansion is progressively focused on buying and selling, money, and the operation
of the market. But the primary functions of production continue
to dominate the way the *politeia* is presented. In the myth of
the Noble Lie, for example, Socrates refers to 'craftsmen or farmers' (3.415C); and when he contemplates the possibility that the
guards might acquire their own land and houses, and money in
their pockets, he says only that they will then become house-
holders and farmers instead of guards (4.417A).[15] We can actually
pinpoint the place where he switches to a different nomenclature.
After making a point about the impact on society if carpenters
and shoemakers were to exchange roles, Socrates starts his next
question by mentioning 'someone who is a craftsman or some
other sort of businessman [*chrêmatistês*, "money-maker"] by
nature' (4.434A). From then on his way of identifying the third
class is to talk of the business or money-making class (4.434C,
441A), anticipating the specification of 'gain-loving' as one of the
three species of human being in Book 9 (9.581C).

Partly this is a matter of convenience. Plato needs a single
term to catch the economic class as a whole, at any rate once he
starts to develop the city–soul analogy. More importantly, it is
one of the ways in which he gradually articulates more and more
of the presuppositions of his whole understanding of society.
Money and greed do not make their first entry in the *Republic*
midway through Book 4. Much of Book 1—which anticipates
so many key themes of the rest of the work—is devoted to
discussion of these topics, in a dramatic context calculated to
remind the reader of the horrors of civil conflict.[16] Reflection on
the principle of specialization introduced in Book 2 at once shows

that the conception of a minimal city of farmers and craftsman is unstable: an expanding economy, with money and a market, is inevitable once you have a society structured to achieve efficient exchange (the picture Socrates paints of rustic simplicity is no more than a pleasant conceit on his part).[17] The corrupting effects of money and private property, and above all of gold and silver, are what motivate Socrates' insistence that the guards are to have nothing to do with them (3.415D–4.421C). So in calling the economic class 'money-making' he is only making explicit something taken for granted all along. In any developed society, those whose work sustains the economy will be motivated by the desire for gain. In the good city, to be sure, farmers and artisans will exercise those roles because they have the natural talents and the training for them: that is what suits them to membership of the third class. Moreover, the political settlement to which they are deemed to have subscribed prescribes this as the contribution they are to make to society. But what drives them all to get up in the morning is the desire to make money. [18]

3. The Psychology of Money

To get clearer about the dominant position of money in the structure of appetite, it will be helpful to look at a few more passages. First, here is one from the beginning of the account of psychic harmony that ends Book 4. After reminding Glaucon of the way the rational and spirited elements in the soul are made concordant by the education recommended in Books 2 and 3, Socrates says this (4.442A):

When these two elements are brought up on a diet of this kind, when they truly receive the teaching and education appropriate to them, then the two of them will exercise rule over the appetitive element, which in any individual is the largest part of the soul, and *by nature quite insatiable where money is concerned.*

Money is not a natural phenomenon. It doesn't grow on trees. Once it starts to structure the very fabric of society, however, in a soul dominated by appetite it will become the natural focus of naturally unlimited human desire, and we won't understand appetite unless we appreciate its dominant role in appetite. In describing it as *naturally* insatiable, Plato's Socrates presumably means that left to itself—unless regulated some-how by reason—then it is distinctive among the appetites in its insatiability.[19] The same kind of idea recurs in the *Laws*. The Athenian Visitor is discussing in general terms the causes that turn people into murderers (9.870A):

The chief cause is appetite, which controls a soul that is made savage by cravings. Murder is something committed particularly because of the form of lust most people experience most often and most intensely. Human nature and bad education make them succumb to a power which breeds in them a million passions for money and for its insatiable and limitless acquisition.

Plato here comes close to the Freudian diagnosis of the love of money as a form of insanity, which Keynes was enunciating in the quotation that opened this chapter.[20]

Another particularly indicative passage comes early on in Book 8 of the *Republic*, where Socrates starts to describe the spiral of decline into progressively more depraved lifestyles, once the love of money gets a hold in the good city, in utopia. Here is what he says about the lifestyle typical under timarchy, i.e. the sort of social and political system found in Crete or at Sparta, which he envisages as replacing the ideal city once the proper basis of the class system is undermined (8.548A–B):

'Desirers of money', I said, 'is what these sorts of people will be, like people living in oligarchies, with a fierce but secret reverence for gold and silver. They will have treasuries and strongrooms of their own where they can store their wealth in secret. And they will ring the city with places that are quite simply private nests, where they can spend a fortune on women or anyone else they fancy.'

'Very true,' he said.

'They will also be mean about money, as you might expect of people who reverence it and do not acquire it by open means. But their appetites will make them love spending other people's, and plucking the fruits of pleasure in secret, running away from the law like children from their father, since their education will have operated not by persuasion but on the basis of compulsion.'

In any individual, citizens of utopia included, most springs of motivation are located in appetite. But an ethically based code of behaviour, if properly internalized, will effectively inhibit them. If it is *not* properly internalized, but experienced as external enforcement, and if the institution of private property has been introduced, then money will become a focus of desire and secret acquisition by the guards of what *was* the good city in two potentially conflicting ways. Here we need to observe a crucial distinction: (a) first, money will be desired by the elite as the *means* to secret satisfaction of more basic appetites, on a scale hugely more lavish than they themselves would have thought of attempting in the good city; (b) second, precisely because it is the key which unlocks so much else, it will be desired *for itself* ('reverenced' or 'honoured')—hence their wish to refrain from spending their own money at all so far as possible. The distinction between (a) a focus on money as means and (b) a pursuit of it as goal will be a resource for interpretation that I shall be exploiting throughout the rest of this section.

Questions relating to the distinction start at once to crowd in. Here are three. (A) Is it the love of money in mode (b) that is *naturally insatiable* or in mode (a)? (B) In either mode, is the love of money a *necessary* desire—required for our survival or well-being—or an unnecessary one (for the distinction see 8.558D–559C)? (C) Isn't the love of money in mode (a) *inherently in conflict* with love of it in mode (b)?

(A) We might think that when Socrates says that the appetitive element in the soul is *naturally insatiable* where money is concerned (4.442A), he must be thinking of money as a focus of desire in mode (a).[21] Somebody dominated by the appetitive element in the soul as such will love money not for its own sake, but just because it enables the satisfaction of appetites—and the more of it you have, the more you can satisfy more and more appetites.[22] The love of money is for him or her not one appetite among others (as in mode (b)), but a controlling second-order appetite: 'an appetite for appetite', in Adam Phillips's phrase.[23] But there are also things to be said for the view that mode (b) is what is in question. Here are two arguments for this verdict. First, on the account just articulated, it is not primarily the love of money that is insatiable, but appetite itself—money is just a way of giving effect to its insatiability. Second, Plato is here replaying in his own register an old theme in Greek moral reflection. At the beginning of the sixth century Solon had written (Fr.13.71–6 West):

No limit to wealth has been set that has become apparent to men:[24] those of us who now have the wealthiest lifestyle just redouble our efforts to get more. What degree of it would satisfy everyone? Making gains is to be sure something the immortals have bestowed on mortals, and from them comes derangement—different people get it at different times when Zeus sends it as punishment.

As this passage goes on, it gets to sound more and more like love of money in mode (b). Much closer in time to the writing of the *Republic* was the production of Aristophanes' last surviving play, *Wealth* (388 BC). The relevant passage is nicely summarized by Richard Seaford:[25]

The unlimit of money takes brilliant form in Aristophanes' *Wealth*. Not only does Wealth have power over everybody and everything, it is also distinct in that of everything else (sex, bread, music, honour, courage, soup, and so on) there is satiety, whereas if somebody gets thirteen talents he desires the more strongly to get sixteen, and if he achieves this, then he wants forty and says life is not worth living until he gets them.

This is clearly someone money mad: obsessed with a craving for money in mode (b). It seems safest to conclude that for Plato insatiable desire for money could be a matter of love of it in mode (a) or mode (b) or both.

(B) The love of money does not fit very easily, or at any rate straightforwardly, into the typology of necessary and unnecessary desires. On the one hand, if the desire for money is naturally insatiable for the sorts of reasons intimated by Solon and Aristophanes, it looks like a paradigmatically unnecessary desire. On the other hand, it is significant that Socrates offers 'moneymaking' as a general characterization of the necessary desires, in contrast to 'spendthrift' for the unnecessary (8.558D). The need for a money-based economy is explicitly asserted in Socrates' account of the 'true' and 'healthy' city (2.371A–372E); and in the fully developed 'good' city, even though the guards are to have nothing to do with money, the economic class must deal in it if the guards' basic desires for food, drink and clothing—like those of the rest of the population—are to be satisfied.

Aristotle had presumably been puzzling over this very problem in the *Republic* when he very characteristically proposed two different types of acquisition (*chrêmatistikê*). One is something the manager of a household must engage in to ensure the supply of things 'either necessary for life or useful to the political or the household community' (*Pol.* 1.8, 1256b28–30). This is explicitly denied to be the unlimited form of wealth accumulation that Solon was castigating. The other is the unnecessary activity which usually gets called acquisition: a form of expertise in business transactions generally assumed to be tied to a money economy. This is what 'gives rise to the opinion that there is no limit to wealth and property' (*Pol.* 1.9, 1256b41–1257a1; he endorses the opinion: ibid. 1257b23–35).[26] Aristotle goes on to say that people intent on physical pleasure turn all other forms of expertise—e.g. military or medical—into acquisition in this sense, 'as though to make money were the one aim, and everything else must contribute to that aim' (ibid. 1258a13–14). The premise of this reasoning is the claim that hedonism consists in excess (ibid. 1258a6–7). If that is what is in the driving seat, Aristotle must here be associating limitless desire with the love of money in mode (a).

So far as concerns the proper acquisition of the necessities of life required by the city or household, however, Aristotle seems to want to dissociate that from the love of money altogether. The position taken in the *Republic* is less idealized. Although Plato could have been more explicit than he is on the subject, those who constitute the economic class in the good city are apparently to focus on being businessmen who make money from their various crafts and occupations, practised in the first instance (no doubt) in order to meet the needs and promote the well-being of the guards and the rest of the population. How Plato might have envisaged such a state of affairs being achieved is an issue we shall take up in the final section of this chapter.

(C) There clearly is a conflict inherent in the differing attractions of desire for money in mode (a) and in mode (b). Plato dramatizes it in the account first of how the son of someone of timarchic character becomes an 'oligarchic' person (8.553A–554B), and then of how in turn the son of someone with just such an oligarchic character develops into the 'democratic' person (8.558C–561A). Socrates imagines a timarchic man whose characteristic pursuit of honour in public life has finally met with impeachment at the hands of his enemies, and crucially the loss of all his possessions following death, exile or disenfranchisement. The ambition his son had similarly begun to nurture seeps away in consequence. Feeling himself demeaned by his poverty, he turns to making money, banning his rational element from any calculation or enquiry except about how to turn a little money into a lot, and allowing his spirited element to admire only wealth and the wealthy. He toils away, counts every penny, and in satisfying 'only the most pressing and necessary of his desires, refuses to spend money on anything else, and keeps all his other desires in subjection, since he regards them as idle' (8.554A). In short, he becomes the archetypal miser. Love of money in mode (b) is dominant, just as in an oligarchic social and political system money is the prevailing value because its possession is what defines membership of the elite (8.550D–551B), the governing principle of oligarchic ideology (its hypothesis, as Aristotle would have put it: *Pol.* 6.1, 1317a35–2, 1317b1). Mode (a)—love of money as means—will, of course, represent a temptation, at any rate where there is opportunity to spend other people's money. Fear of arousing the 'spending' or 'spendthrift' desires is generally likely to make it a temptation successfully resisted. However, just because it constitutes a standing temptation, the oligarchic person is someone divided against himself: 'he is two individuals, not one, though for the most part his better desires have the upper hand over his worse desires' (8.554D–E).

With the democratic person, the situation is reversed. Socrates now imagines what might happen if the miser he has described had a son. The young man would initially acquire his father's habits, forcing himself to master those appetites that are spend-thrift and not focused on money-making: the 'unnecessary' desires whose satisfaction is not required for our survival or well-being, unlike (for example) the desire for bread and cooked food. But then he might well fall into wild company, offering him the 'democratic' prospect of 'pleasures of every kind, hue and variety' (8.559D). He is vulnerable to their appeal—he has had no proper education, so his reason does not control the appetitive element in his soul, but is at its beck and call. A struggle between the oligarchic and democratic tendencies within his dominant appetitive element may ensue, but it is all too likely that eventually he will live his life 'spending as much money, effort and time on unnecessary as on necessary desires' (8.561A). The love of money in mode (b) has lost its grip on him. Now he wants it only to spend it: mode (a).

In the passages we have just been surveying, Plato is clearly not working with a conception of appetite that confines it to unthinking physical urges. The very idea of the unnecessary or spendthrift pleasures implies desire not confined to the drive to satisfy the needs of the body. An extreme instance is the case of the 'democratic' person in Book 8, who gratifies all his passing appetites indiscriminately, and so may spend a lot of time in political activity, and even sometimes doing what he takes to be philosophy (8.561C–E).[27] These and similar appetites are clearly permeated by thought.[28] As Christopher Gill has brought out, Plato takes it that the shapes taken by all our motivations, appetite included, are dependent on the beliefs we have come to acquire, above all from our response to the kind of education and upbringing we have had. When Socrates illustrates what he means by unnecessary appetites, by taking the case of desire for food over and above what will contribute to well-being, he says that it 'can be eliminated, in most people, by discipline and education from early childhood' (8.559B). But 'most people' is not everyone. Thus the emergence of the kind of person who is tyrannized by lawless desire 'occurs through the replacement of beliefs (*doxai*) implanted in childhood about what is fine and disgraceful by beliefs which were formerly suppressed and which manifested themselves only in dreams'.[29]

The *Republic* never offers a formal account of what makes all these desires appetites. But in the initial specification of the *epithumêtikon* in the argument from psychological conflict in Book 4 it is described as 'the companion of certain repletions and pleasures' (4.439D); and a little later reason and spirit, if properly developed and educated, are said to guard against its 'filling itself with the so-called pleasures of the body' (4.442A). It is consistent with this focus that in his sketch of the democratic person, where a much more catholic scope for appetite is assumed, Socrates makes much of the way all *pleasures* are put on an equal footing (8.561A–C). So perhaps what he thinks is characteristic of all appetites as such is that they are directed to the pursuit of pleasure in the first instance,[30] as Aristotle seems to have taken to be a philosophical commonplace.[31] So long as desire is focused on pleasure, as in the case of someone who does a bit of philosophy because it's enjoyable (rather than because he wants to learn the truth about something), it will count as a function of the *epithumêtikon*.

4. *Greed, Power and Injustice*

There is little evidence in the *Republic* to judge whether in the ordinary way of things people whose lives are motivated principally by love of money are assumed to love it primarily in mode (a) or mode (b). The dialogue is written to illuminate the extraordinary: extremes of justice and injustice located far beyond the horizons of the ordinary materialist as represented by Cephalus in the opening pages of Book 1.[32] The narrative of degeneration developed in Books 8 and 9 is designed above all to bring us to an understanding of what a paradigm of injustice would be like. From this perspective there is crucial significance in the transition from the person of oligarchic character (who values money primarily in mode (b)) to the person of democratic disposition (whose interest in money is simply that it will enable him or her to satisfy any and every appetite he or she happens to want to indulge: love of money in mode (a)). Democracy—as Plato will write in the *Laws*, plainly recapitulating the thought of Book 8 of the *Republic*[33] —'has a soul longing for pleasures and appetites, and wanting to have them filling it up' (4.714A).[34] It is then only the shortest of steps from indiscriminate democratic cultivation of the appetites to the behaviour of the person with the soul of a tyrant: the epitome of injustice. All restraint in indulging the appetites is now abandoned, especially where and perhaps because its abandonment violates fundamental moral, religious and legal sanctions.

That, not the love of money, is what dominates Socrates' account of the tyrannical person. But none of Plato's first readers would need much prompting to see greed as a hallmark of the tyrant. It was a commonplace of Greek moral reflection. Sophocles' Oedipus tells Creon not to try to wrest tyranny from him without friends and mass support: it is something captured by mass support and money (*Oedipus Tyrannus* 540–2). And to quote Richard Seaford again, this time on the encounter between Creon, now tyrant himself, and the blind seer Teiresias in *Antigone*: 'Teiresias, when accused by Creon of venality, responds, "No, it is tyrants who love disgraceful gain", and Teiresias is never wrong'.[35] In fact, Socrates devotes his first two pages on the lifestyle of the tyrannical person to a detailed account in mode (a) of the increasingly lawless, impious and violent methods of securing the money that will be needed to sustain it (9.573D–575C; the financial appropriations made by the person who actually becomes a tyrant have already been described: 8.568D–569C).

This is the point at which the *Republic* establishes contact with the debate about power staged in the *Gorgias*. It might perhaps be supposed that the main argument of the *Republic* does not really engage with questions about power, although grasping control and knowing how to exercise it is of course the central issue in the ship of state analogy (6.488C–D). Any such preconception would be quite mistaken. Certainly the dialogue shows little interest in the military and political capabilities of cities in the international arena that so fascinated Thucydides, nor in what we might conceptualize as the power of the state over its citizens or subjects.[36] But the personal access to political power enjoyed by those who hold office under the various regimes characterized in Books 8 and 9 is a constant preoccupation, albeit hardly thematized. And in his accounts of the individual characters corresponding to political systems, Plato gives increasing prominence to the power to satisfy an individual's aspirations—to achieve 'whatever someone wants'—as what people look for in their lives.[37]

A preoccupation with power so understood figures prominently in the argument with Thrasymachus in Book 1, and in Glaucon's restatement of Thrasymachus' position at the beginning of Book 2. Glaucon's story of the magic ring, which confers invisibility on the freerider who possesses it, and his argument about how it would be used, in fact reworks the line of thought put in Polus' mouth in the *Gorgias*. Glaucon, too, argues that someone with the opportunity to do whatever he wanted would take *pleonexia*, 'greed', 'having/getting more' (of anything, not just money or possessions), as his good, and would constitute a paradigm of injustice (2.359B–360D; cf. *Gorgias* 466B–468E).[38] The only difference is that he speaks of *exousia*, 'opportunity', 'licence', 'freedom', where Polus had spoken in terms of *dunamis*, 'power', 'capacity'.

It is true that Plato is in no rush to show what is wrong with this way of thinking. This is only because of the deliberately measured and indirect route he has Socrates take in engaging with the fundamental question that Glaucon and Adeimantus

have posed about the profitability of justice (2.357A–367E). A
first line of response is indicated at exactly the point in the
Republic one would expect: at the end of Book 4, in Glaucon's
own concluding reflections there on justice and injustice within
the soul (4.445A–B):

'When the body's natural constitution is ruined, life seems not worth
living, even with every variety of food and drink, and all manner of
wealth and political power (*archê*). Is someone's life going to be worth
living when the natural constitution of the very thing which enables
us to live is upset and ruined, *even assuming he can do anything
he wants*—anything apart from what will release him from evil and
injustice, and win him justice and goodness (given that the two of them
[i.e. justice and injustice] have been shown to be the sorts of conditions
we have explained)?'

'Even assuming he can do anything he wants': that assumption
is eventually withdrawn by Socrates—in the *Republic* as in the
Gorgias—in his final treatment of the topic in the dialogue, five
books further on. He imagines someone with a tyrannical soul
who actually exercises tyrannical power in a city. Is it true that
(in the words of Sophocles' *Antigone*) 'not least among all the
many blessings of tyranny is this: it can do and say whatever
it wants' (Soph. *Ant.* 506–7)? Or (as with the popular sayings
the Athenian Visitor in the *Laws* produces) that high on the
list of good things in life is 'being a tyrant and doing whatever
you desire' (2.661A–B)? No, says Socrates: 'The tyrannical nature
never gets a taste of freedom or true friendship' (9.576A), living as
it does in continual suspicion and fear. And he argues that such
a person is at every point enslaved by the insatiability of his own
appetites: 'the soul which is being tyrann*ized* will be *the last
one to do what it wants*' (577D–E). Life becomes imprisonment
(579B–C):

'He has the nature we have described, full of many and varied fears and
lusts. And greedy though his soul is, he is the only one living in the
city who cannot go abroad anywhere, or go and see any of the places
other free men so desire to see. He spends most of his life submerged
from view at home, like a woman. He envies the other citizens, if one
of them does go abroad and sees some fine sight.'

Socrates' final verdict begins as follows (579D–E):

'The truth is, whatever some people may think, that the real tyrant
is really a slave—abjectly ingratiating and servile, and someone who

sucks up to thoroughly depraved people. If you know how to look at the soul as a whole, it is apparent that he does not *satisfy* his appetites in the least, but lives in acute need of nearly everything, and in true poverty.'

'Plato's tyrant', says Julia Annas, 'would not last a week.' His portrait of the tyrant, she goes on, might suit 'a Caligula, someone effortlessly presented with absolute power who finds that with the removal of all normal inhibitions reality and fantasy merge until sanity is lost'. But successful dictators in the real world (Lenin and Stalin are instanced) have actually been 'tireless bureaucrats with conventional opinions and unimaginative private lives'.[39] This line of objection misses its target. Plato's Socrates does not claim that all actual tyrants *are* like the person he describes. It is made quite clear that he is considering *only* the Caligula scenario: where absolute power is achieved by someone whose mind is already tyrannical (9.578C). And, as Dorothea Frede comments, there is no reason to think Plato would have rated the chances of such a person's tenure on power very high—any higher than Caligula's in his short reign.[40] Plato chooses to imagine the scenario where someone really does have *absolute* power because that is the one that interests both him and his interlocutors: Polus and Callicles in the *Gorgias*, Thrasymachus, Glaucon and Adeimantus in the *Republic*. Annas appears to concede the strength of his critique of power as they conceive it: the demonstration that the ability and opportunity to do whatever one wants is actually a nightmarish prospect—a recipe for misery.[41] In Frede's words again, Plato's tyrant, 'driven to near-madness by his erotic desires, is a paper-tiger in the literal sense of the word: he is a tiger who exists on paper only, as a demonstration that utmost injustice is not feasible'.[42]

The identification of the paradigmatically unjust life as a species of tyranny provides a clue to the resolution of a cluster of puzzles which have much troubled the commentators. The *Republic*'s central proposal—that justice for the individual is psychic harmony—is perceived by many readers as a fundamental flaw in the execution of the dialogue's basic project.[43] In the first place, the main argument presented for the proposal towards the end of Book 4 is invalid. It appeals to the principle that where two things x and y are both called 'F', the basis on which 'F' is predicated of x must be the same as or analogous to the grounds for predicating '*F*' of *y*. So, if the city is called 'just' because each class does its own job and no other's, the reason why an individual is called 'just' will similarly be because each element in the soul performs its own function and no other (434D–435C). The principle supporting this inference is false as a general principle. It assumes that words are univocal. But—as Aristotle was fond of pointing out—univocal they very often are not. It is not plausible, for example, that if individuals are to be called 'healthy' because of their robust constitution, this will be the reason why we do or should predicate 'healthy' of cities. A healthy city is rather one which provides a physical and social environment tending to promote health in individuals.

Second, Book 4 does not make much effort to show that justice as psychic harmony is characteristically associated with just behaviour, i.e. fair or moral treatment of *other* individuals. It *asserts* that someone whose soul is in this condition will not be party to embezzlement, theft, betrayal or oath-breaking, nor adultery, disrespect towards parents or neglect of the gods (442D–443A). But it does not try to prove the point; and just action is actually explicitly redefined, not in such a way as to attempt to capture the idea of honest or dutiful behaviour towards others, but as 'what preserves this inner harmony and helps to bring it about' (443E). So Plato's Socrates faces the charge of having made justice something which is of intrinsic benefit to the just individual only by turning it into a characteristic unrecognizable as justice.

The *Republic*'s view of justice and injustice emerges from Book 9's treatment of the tyrannical soul in an altogether more convincing light.[44] To begin with, the association of injustice with the lawless appetites being indulged by someone with absolute power is something common opinion, as represented by Glaucon and Adeimantus, already accepts. It is built into Glaucon's picture of the freerider Gyges as the perfectly unjust man. So Socrates can treat as uncontroversial the proposition that unjust behaviour, in its most rampant form, is the product of lawless appetites. Now, all he needs to sustain his own position on injustice and to undermine Glaucon's thesis—directly the claim that injustice is intrinsically preferable to justice, but indirectly therefore the social contract account of justice—is to take three further steps. These are the suppositions that, first, rampantly unjust conduct is rampant because lawless appetites are insatiable; second, insatiable appetites are necessarily anarchic; third, since psychic anarchy is the cause of rampant injustice, it is best interpreted *as* the core of injustice itself: which will be a supremely wretched condition because of the insatiability of the desires that constitute it. If we now ask what sort of person would be *least* likely to engage in the behaviour characteristic of the perfectly unjust man, there seems much plausibility in *Republic*'s proposal that it is someone whose soul is in a condition of psychic harmony as far removed as can be conceived from the psychic anarchy which is to be equated with injustice.[45]

5. Taming the Beast Within

In *any* individual, Socrates has claimed in Book 4, the appetitive element is 'the largest part of the soul, and by nature quite insatiable where money is concerned' (4.442A).[46] This makes it potentially dangerous, both to the soul and to society at large. The danger is that by satisfying desires for food and drink and sex, it extends its range and becomes strong, and no longer performs its own function: above all the necessary job of driving people to keep themselves alive, and of acquiring the resources to support life.[47] Instead it may attempt to enslave and govern reason and spirit, and end up 'turning upside down everyone's entire life' (4.442B). The way to guard against this happening is also indicated. Reason and spirit need to be properly developed, learning their own jobs (governing the soul, or in the case of spirit supporting reason in that activity), and being educated, whether through intellectual pursuits (reason) or by exposure to the civilizing power of music and poetry (spirit). In Book 6, when rational rulers have been turned into philosophers, Socrates conceives that their passion for truth will have atrophied any enthusiasm for acquiring and spending money (6.485D–E). Here he talks of the need to keep a watch on appetite, precisely to guard against its taking control of the soul.

How that is to be done is an issue both for psychology and for politics; or, rather, for the fusion of the two that is Plato's characteristic mode of analysis in the *Republic* and the *Laws*. The basic psychological mechanism he envisages is presented in a colourful passage at the end of Book 9. Here Socrates offers us one of his most memorable images in a dialogue full of memorable images.

We are to think of ourselves as one of those hybrid creatures who populate some of the stranger regions of Greek myth: the Chimaera, for example (a combination of lion, fire-breathing goat emerging from its back, and a snake for a tail). The largest component (representing appetite) is a monster with a ring of animal heads of different species—some gentle, some fierce—which it can alter and grow from itself at will. Next largest (corresponding to the spirited element) is a lion. The smallest (our rational self) is a human being. Someone who thinks (as Thrasymachus does) that injustice is what is in our self-interest is really saying that it pays to feast and strengthen the monster and the lion within us, but starve and weaken the human being, so that our humanity is dragged about wherever one of the bestial elements takes it. If we want the human being inside us to have control over us as humans, on the other hand, then we must identify with the human element within us, acting and speaking in such a way that the man within 'looks after the many-headed monster like a farmer, feeding and nursing the gentle growths, but not allowing the fierce ones to sprout' (9.589B). All depends on reason: reason refusing to allow fiercer appetites to develop; reason giving active encouragement to gentler ones. The horticultural simile is significant. Here appetites are not even treated metaphorically as alternative centres of consciousness, but as requiring the sort of treatment appropriate for hair or toenails.[48]

The key to the ability to exercise this control over appetite—as the Book 4 passage makes crystal clear—is education. And time and again it is the unavailability of education and upbringing of the right kind that gets stressed in Socrates' account in Books 8 and 9 of the way in which degenerate societies and individual character-types degenerate still further. In a timarchic system, for example, the older generation will have less consideration for music and poetry than they should, and they will also begin to neglect physical training (8.546D). As for the timarchic person, although he has a passion for physical training and hunting, he 'has missed out on the finest of all guardians' (8.549B): reason, blended with education in music and poetry—the only thing that remains with someone throughout life as the protector of virtue once a person has it in them. Similarly the oligarchic person 'never applied himself to his education' (8.554B), and the democratic type is brought up in the same uneducated and cheeseparing manner (8.559D). The deficient upbringing

Socrates' timarchic and oligarchic characters *do* get is described in detail. One thing above all that marks out the good city, by contrast, is the time, care and energy invested in an appropriate education for rulers and the military (4.423D–E).

Here we face a political problem. Such an education will indeed develop in the rulers reason's natural capacity both for government and for rule over the other parts of their own souls, and in the military a tempering of spirit which makes it responsive and obedient to the voice of reason in the soul, and turns them into protagonists obeying and supporting the rulers' decisions. Appetite, however, is what rules the souls of money-lovers (9.581C), and presumably therefore individuals belonging to the economic class in the good city. What will be the impact of education on it and them? The *Republic* maintains an almost total silence on how the economic class is to be educated. Plato's overwhelming preoccupation is with the elite. His hopes rest with them. At one point Socrates makes a passing reference to education in a particular craft (leather-cutting: 5.456D), with the implication that that is what for craftsmen compares with the education in music and poetry enjoyed by the guards described in Books 2 and 3. And not just enjoyed by the guards—specifically designed for individuals whose lives are to be governed principally by reason and spirit, and much of it articulated in terms only apposite to an aristocratic elite. It seems fairly clear that Plato does not envisage it as applying to those who are to be farmers, craftsmen and people in business,[49] except in indirect and secondary ways.[50]

Yet, although the education that is represented as all-important for controlling the appetites is not to be made available to the economic class, Plato is quite explicit not merely that the appetites of the 'ordinary majority' have to *be* controlled (4.431C–D), but that they must themselves recognize and accept constraints on their behaviour.[51] Restraint (*sôphrosunê*) as a property of the city depends on agreement on the part of *all* classes—the economic included—that the class responsible for wise deliberation about its affairs should rule (4.431D–E). And restraint is exhibited in the mass of the people by obedience to the rulers (4.431C–D),[52] and by the control they themselves exercise over their physical pleasures: something apparently regarded as a truth of general applicability, not just in the ideal city (3.389D–E). What Plato must be supposing is that this outcome will be achieved in

Kallipolis by cultural means: by a combination above all of ideology and law—which can be assumed to be reflected in the kind of upbringing and moral education children of farmers and craftsmen and business people will receive.[53] Agreement on their part that the guards should rule must be primarily due to their absorption of the civic ideology encapsulated in the Noble Lie. The Noble Lie will implant the *beliefs* people hold about the structure of society and their naturally ordained role within it, and thereby motivate them to make sure that their business activity is such as to make an appropriate contribution to the city. I shall be discussing the Lie at length in the next chapter. Obedience to the rulers, by contrast, will be primarily a matter of obeying the law. In the rest of this chapter I shall discuss the way Plato seems to envisage the achievement of this outcome.

We may begin with a question about how the process of acculturation is *psychologically* possible for members of the economic class. If what rules their souls is appetite, and if it is unlikely that their upbringing (whatever exactly it may consist in) is deliberately designed to foster any but limited respect for reason,[54] *how* do they internalize the kind of restraint that on Plato's premises only government by reason (assisted by spirit) can produce? Help with this question is sometimes sought in Socrates' continuing exploration of the implications of his version of the Chimaera image (9.590C–D):

'Why do you think menial work or using your hands to produce things brings discredit and criticism? Isn't the reason just this? It happens when the best element in a person is naturally weak, and so he is unable to control the creatures within him, but instead becomes their servant. All he can do is learn how to appease them.'

'Apparently.'

'So if we want someone like this to be under the same kind of rule as the best person, we say he must be the slave of that best person, don't we, since the best person has what is divine ruling within him? And when we say he needs to be ruled, it's not that we mean any harm to the slave, which was Thrasymachus's view of being ruled. It's simply that it's better for everyone to be ruled by what is divine and wise. Ideally he will have his own divine and wise element within himself, but failing that it will be imposed on him from outside, so that as far as possible we may all be equal, and all friends, since we are all under the guidance of the same commander.'

'Yes, that is what we say. And rightly.'

These heavily paternalistic remarks have been read as a fairly straightforward statement of the thesis (anticipating Aristotle's justification of 'natural' slavery)[55] that in the ideal city the economic class will be governed not by their own reason, but by the wisdom of the philosopher rulers.[56] However Socrates is not talking here about Kallipolis. He is producing a number of considerations—considerations drawn from ordinary experience that might appeal to the ordinary person—for thinking that our true advantage lies not with the greed and self-aggrandizement championed by Thrasymachus, but in having the human being within us in control of the lion and the monster instead. There is no reason to think that the farmers and craftsmen and businessmen of the good city will be very like the menial or manual worker characterized here. Socrates never suggests that those in the economic class are generally speaking weak in reason (even if it is not what rules their souls), still less that they cannot control their appetites. Certainly they do not have the status of slaves.[57]

Nonetheless the way Socrates continues the conversation does take us some distance with the issue that concerns us. He supports the general moral that he draws from his treatment of the example of menial and manual workers with further evidence from common experience (590E): 'That is clearly the aim both of the law, which is the ally of all the inhabitants of the city, and of our own governance of our children.' He then comments on the way children aren't given freedom until we have established a regime within them, as in a city. Nothing more is said about law. But here in embryo is the theory of law in the *Laws*. Law is treated as a form of wisdom—even (as in the *Laws*) as divine wisdom—controlling the behaviour of citizens through its prescriptions.

At this point in the *Republic* Socrates does not try to specify the psychological mechanism by which that effect is achieved. But if we put it as a question about the operation of law in the ideal city as it bears down on the souls of individuals in the economic class, two alternatives—not necessarily exclusive—suggest themselves. One is the deterrent impact of what law issues by way of threats for non-compliance—something fully elaborated in the *Laws*. In Book 8 (554C–D) Socrates envisages the oligarchic person as 'using something decent within himself' to suppress evil desires by 'compulsion and fear'. Perhaps something similar will take place in the souls of the businessmen of the ideal city. And perhaps the 'something decent' might derive from assimilation of legal prescription. The other possibility is that law has the effect of habituating the *way* the appetites control their souls. Although it is appetite that has most influence on their behaviour, and although appetite if left to itself is naturally insatiable, nonetheless any temptation to let its demands breach the limits of the law, and the belief that doing so is the way to get pleasure, will wither away if people get used to confining it within the law. Back in Book 4 much is made of the way an ethos 'seeps imperceptibly into people's characters and habits' (4.424D; cf. 3.401C–D). The satisfaction of *limited* desires—'simple and moderate', as Socrates puts it in Book 4 (4.431C)—will then be experienced as sufficient, and indeed as *true* pleasure (cf. 9.586E).

These possibilities indicate at any rate the sort of explanation Plato needs of how the economic class can come to internalize the restraint of appetite which reason would dictate, even though the reason in their own souls is never going to be in the driving seat, and therefore never able to command the resources needed to direct their behaviour by rational persuasion.[58] Such restraint can clearly be at best an approximation to the *sôphrosunê* of the individual as defined in Book 4: the state of 'friendship and concord' that arises when the ruling part of the soul and the elements that are ruled 'share the belief that the rational part should rule and that they should not wage civil strife against it' (4.442C–D).[59] Nonetheless it will be individual restraint of a kind, since persons in this condition of mind will certainly be 'rulers *themselves* over the pleasures of drink, sex, and food', as Book 3 describes the sort of *sôphrosunê* appropriate to the general population (3.389D–E). Plato would presumably count it a form of what he later calls 'demotic' or popular virtue (6.500D).

The problem of how to restrain the appetites of the economic class remains with us. Capitalism does not share Plato's principled aversion to the naturally insatiable desire for money. But capitalism has only ever been tolerable when tempered by something else, whether by the institutions of the state and of civil society, or by social democracy asserting itself in some shape or form. Finding more effective ways of exercising some control over it remains an urgent need.

Notes

1. Keynes 1932: 369 (Keynes is projecting a future of plenty and leisure). I owe knowledge of this passage to Phillips 2005: 187.
2. For the material in this paragraph I have drawn primarily on Porter 2000.
3. See the full study of Balot 2001, and particularly his analysis of Thucydides in ch. 5. By contrast Kallet 2001 argues that, unlike earlier authors, Thucydides detaches acquisition of money and resources as such from the moral sphere and therefore from automatic association with greed. She sees him as applauding its use under Pericles as the engine of power. For her it is only under his successors that on Thucydides' account greed and profit become the dominant motivations, blurring public and private interest, with corrosion of power the result—as exemplified above all in the Sicilian expedition.
4. See Seaford 2004: ch. 8.
5. See Seaford 2004: 158–60, who quotes the passage I cite.
6. See Balot 2001: 219–24, from whom I borrow the Xenophon quotation; also Section 1 of Ch. 3, p.105 above.
7. How far we can believe Xenophon or Lysias is another matter. Both may be suspected of preferring the simplicities of moralizing rhetoric to the complexities of muddy reality, and Xenophon (who had sided with the thirty) had every reason to want to distance himself from Critias: see Notomi 2000: 240–2. In his writings Critias was a firm advocate of restraint and measure: see e.g. Wilson 2003: 181–206. Following the arguments of Bultrighini 1999, Wilson also questions too easy an acceptance of the fourth-century 'scapegoating' of Critias which resulted in his comprehensive *damnatio memoriae* (ibid. p. 200 n. 12).
8. Phillips 2005: 220.
9. See Williams 1973.
10. See Cooper 1984: 12–17; cf. also Hobbs 2000: 30–7.
11. Cf. Reeve 1988: 43–50.
12. A good starting point for entering this territory is Annas 1981: ch. 5; see also Irwin 1995: ch. 13. A treatment that presses the disintegration reading lucidly and relentlessly is Bobonich 2002: chs. 3 and 4 (on which see the penetrating review of Kahn 2004). Price 1995: ch. 2 offers a subtle and more open-ended exploration, pursuing a variety of different interpretative possibilities. Other treatments to which I am particularly indebted are Lorenz 2004; and R. Stalley, 'Persuasion and the tripartite soul', unpublished MS. Both reject the view that Plato's tripartition of the soul commits him to denying the unity of the person, particularly the version of the view espoused by Bobonich.
13. For the argument developed in this paragraph, see further Gerson 2003: 109–17.
14. See Lorenz 2004: 84–5.
15. But in this same context Socrates insists that the guards are to have housing suitable for soldiers, not businessmen (*chrêmatistikai*: 4.415E).
16. See in particular Algra 1996; Gifford 2001.

17. See further Schofield 1993.
18. In Book 1 Socrates had of course already argued against Thrasymachus that the skill someone requires to make money is distinct from the skill a doctor or pilot or whoever needs to cure patients or to steer a boat, even if they make money by practising their profession (341C–342E; cf. 346A–E). And the same point is made about shepherding (345B–E). One would suppose that in general members of the economic class acquire to some degree or other skill in the money-making for which they have a natural desire. But, if so, it would seem to follow that anyone who does must practise *two* crafts, not restricting themselves to one alone, even though Socrates is so insistent on that for all classes in the city. The qualification to the 'one person, one job' rule envisaged at 4.434A does not cater for the tension between craft skill and money-making Socrates flags up a little earlier at 4.421C–422A, where he is insistent that concentration on wealth accumulation—and the idleness and luxury (not to mention the political unrest) it generates—could detract from the quality of a person's practice of their basic role. Ibn Rushd (Averroes to the medieval West) was so struck by the problem that he concluded—I take it wrongly—that Plato must have have denied property and the use of gold and silver to craftsmen as well as guards (see Rosenthal 1956: 147–8). I am grateful to Antony Hatzistavrou and Christopher Rowe for raising the issue with me, and to Peter Garnsey for drawing attention to Ibn Rushd's treatment of it.
19. Its distinctiveness in this regard is well brought out by Aristophanes at *Wealth* 187–97: a passage summarized below.
20. See further Phillips 2005: Pt Two, ch. IV: 'Money Mad'.
21. There seems no reason to think that love of gain as such is intrinsically insatiable, any more than is the desire to eat or play chess.
22. One might be put in mind of Epicurus on the pleasures of the flesh (*KD* 20): 'The flesh takes the limits of pleasure as unlimited, and unlimited time brings it [sc. unlimited pleasure] about.'
23. Phillips 2005: 194.
24. A line quoted by Aristotle in his discussion of acquisition (*Pol.* 1.8, 1256b32–4).
25. Seaford 2004: 168 (the key lines are at *Wealth* 187–97). He goes on (ibid. pp. 168–9) to mention a fascinating passage of Xenophon's *Ways and Means* (4.6–7) where silver-mining is cited as the one industry in which excess supply is never produced: 'nobody ever possessed so much silver as to want no more, and if he has a massive amount, he takes as much pleasure in burying as in using it'.
26. For a discussion of Aristotle's analysis, see Meikle 1995. Aristotle offers an unconvincing basic explanation as to *why* money-making is a matter of unlimited appetite. The reason is a preoccupation with living rather than living well. Because the desire for living is unlimited in persons in this condition, their desire for the things which produce it is equally unlimited (*Pol.* 1.9, 1257b40–1258a2). But just for living one *doesn't* need unlimited wealth, as Aristotle himself had pointed out. More interesting is his construction of money-making as a perverted way of pursuing the *good* life (ibid. 1258a2–14: discussed below).

27. These instances are discussed in Cooper 1984: 9–12. I agree with him in interpreting these *as* all of them functions of the *epithumêtikon*: I take it part of Plato's object is to show what happens to appetite once no preference is given to satisfaction of necessary over unnecessary appetites. For an alternative interpretation, see Scott 2000: 22–6. Cooper presents a broader view of appetite than Williams, but at no point refers to the *Republic* passages associating appetite with the love of money.

28. The love of money must involve at least the thought that money is the means to satisfaction of desire, even if working out *how* to build up the financial resources to do so is a job for reason (and indeed the purpose for which in the case of the oligarchic person it has been enslaved: 8.553D): see Price 1995: 60–1. Lorenz 2004: 110–12, despite interesting remarks on how love of money is culturally inculcated, takes an implausible line on this issue.

29. Gill 1996: 245–60; quotation from p. 253, where Gill is paraphrasing 9.574D–E.

30. Philosophy and the pursuit of honour bring their own characteristic pleasures (9.581C–E; contrasted with those of appetite in a lengthy comparison: 581E–588A), but the pleasure is not a primary object of concern for philosophy or ambition.

31. So e.g. at *EN* 3.2, 1111b17; 7.6, 1149a34–b1; *EE* 2.7, 1223a34; 2.8, 1224a37.

32. On Cephalus see Gifford 2001: 52–69.

33. Book 4 of the *Laws* is saturated in reminiscences of the *Republic*: see Schofield 1997: 230–41; 2003.

34. Compare once again Adam Phillips's characterization of the love of money as 'an appetite for appetite' (Phillips 2005: 194); and notice the projection of the condition of the democratic person on to the democratic city (cf. Ferrari 2003: ch. 3).

35. Seaford 2003: 105.

36. On the 'statelessness' of the ancient Greek *polis*, see Cartledge 2000: 17–20.

37. In the *Hippias Minor* (366C) Socrates offers this unargued and uncontested specification of what it is to have power: someone has the power to do something if he 'does what he wants when he wants'.

38. As Giles Pearson points out to me, for a Thrasymachus or a Glaucon, greed (*pleonexia*) takes for its object not just money and material possessions, but *anything* a person could want to have: e.g. sex with anyone you desire, killing or rescuing from prison anyone you like (2.360C; see also e.g. 9.579B–C, on the tyrannical person, quoted above, p. 267). Aristotle similarly treats as 'greedy' (*pleonektai*) self-lovers who gratify their appetites by assigning to themselves 'the greater share' (*pleion*) of wealth, honours and bodily pleasures (*EN* 9.8, 1168b15–21). Myles Burnyeat observes (Burnyeat 2005–6: 20–1): 'Thrasymachus assumed, and Glaucon did not deny, that what lies deepest in human nature is *pleonexia*. This term covers *both* the desire for more and more *and* the desire for more than others have. It is both greed and competitiveness, all rolled into one. The doctrine of the divided soul separates these two aspects: greed is a vice of appetite, assertiveness a vice of spirit.' Nonetheless in a tyrannical person appetite dominates to such an extent that the motivations of assertive spiritedness will be enlisted wholly

in its service—and will inevitably require appropriating the property of others.

39. Annas 1981: 304.

40. D. Frede 1996: 265–6. In a letter written on 2 May 49 Cicero, appealing to Plato's view of tyrants, predicted that Caesar's reign would not last six months (*ad Att.* 10.8.6–8).

41. As described by Annas, a dictator sounds in some ways more like the *Republic*'s oligarchic person, *mutatis mutandis* (8.554A–E), although politically speaking Stalin's modus operandi in particular fits the profile of the tyrannical leader who has emerged as champion of the people, particularly as regards disposal of any possible opposition and the slavery he ends up imposing on his city (8.565D–569D). Plato does not deny that such a tyrant can be successful in ordinary political terms. But his drab soul, akin to the miser's in its obsession with control, will not command the admiration of a Thrasymachus or a Callicles.

42. D. Frede 1996: 266. For penetrating reflections on absolute power and absolute freedom, and on their delusion and weakness, see Eagleton 2005: ch. 3 *passim* (also pp. 11, 24). He aptly quotes Shakespeare's *Troilus and Cressida* (I.iii) (at p. 72):

> Then everything includes itself in power,
> Power into will, will into appetite,
> An appetite, an universal wolf,
> So doubly seconded with will and power,
> Must make perforce an universal prey,
> And last eat up himself.

43. So influentially Sachs 1963; other views: e.g. Vlastos 1971; Annas 1978; Dahl 1991; Smith 1997.

44. The interpretation proposed here follows that of Kraut 1992b: 311–37.

45. The final three paragraphs of this section are lightly adapted from Schofield 2000a: 229–30.

46. It is largest because there are many different forms of appetite (9.580E, 588C). One verb will serve to characterize what reason and spirit do ('learn' or 'reason out', 'get angry'). For appetite an open-ended list is needed, starting with 'hunger', 'thirst', 'lust'.

47. Plato spells out a distinction between necessary and non-necessary desires at 8.558D–559C: necessary are those we can't 'fend off' (notably sexual desire, doubtless) or which if satisfied benefit us (hunger and thirst—and the desire to make enough money to supply our real needs). Hence presumably the use of the term 'money-making', in contrast to 'spendthrift' non-necessary appetites, as a general characterization of the necessary ones—one more sign of the importance of acquisitive desire in Plato's conception of appetite.

48. This is a passage which needs to be borne in mind when reflecting on Socrates' remark in Book 8 about the oligarchic person's use of compulsion and fear to keep down evil desires he harbours, instead of 'making them gentle by reasoning' (8.554C–D). The remark is produced by Bobonich as one among several proof texts for recognition on Plato's part of appetite's being not merely an independent seat of consciousness, but capable of engaging in

'rational interaction' by virtue of its responsiveness to persuasion (Bobonich 2002: 242–4). But rational interaction is impossible either with a monster or with the growths a farmer has to deal with. I conclude that Plato—always the dramatist of the theatre of the soul—has *no* non-metaphorical way of articulating his theory of mind. If we were to donate him with one, I would prefer a version which makes the talk of reasoning with appetites at 554C–D a shorthand for the *self* reasoning with *itself* about why it would be better not to indulge evil desires—and so *mutatis mutandis* in similar contexts.

49. See Reeve 1988: 186–9. Reeve's positive suggestion is that training in a craft will in fact supply such moral education as is needed by 'future producers': it 'releases an appetitive psyche from the rule of unnecessary appetites . . . and causes it to abandon the pleasures of food, drink, and sex for the more pleasant pleasure of making money' (ibid. p. 190). I can see no evidence in the text that training in a craft has any of these effects.

50. Nobody at all—young or old—is to hear stories that make the gods responsible for evil (2.380B–C); mothers are not to terrify their children with tales of nocturnal visitations by deities who assume other shapes and forms (2.381E); nor must anyone represent a god like Apollo as telling prophetic lies (2.383B–C). See Burnyeat 1999: 261: 'norms for art in the ideal city will reshape the whole culture'. Thus variety and elaboration in music are off the agenda for shepherds, not just guards (3.399D). The placing of this prescription is significant. Almost the next remark Socrates makes is his exclamation (3.399D–E): 'Ye dogs! Without noticing it, we've been very thoroughly purging the city we said not long ago was a place of luxury.' The comment about shepherds makes the point—with all possible understatement—that purging the *city* means more simplicity in the economic class as well as in the lifestyle of the guards.

51. For thoughtful remarks on this point, see Kahn 2004: 350–3.

52. After contrasting (without initial reference to the ideal city) the range and variety of desires and pleasures and pains in the general population (anywhere, presumably) with the simple and moderate desires of the rational minority who have the best natural endowment and the best education, Socrates extrapolates to utopia: 'Well, do you see the same sort of phenomenon in our city? And are the desires of the morally inferior majority *controlled* here by the desires and wisdom of the morally superior minority?' Following assent from Glaucon, he concludes: 'So if any city can be called the master of its pleasures and desires, and indeed of *itself*, this one can?'

53. Some sense of the way law will be used to promote the values of the ideal city among the whole citizen body may be gauged from the rule forbidding craftsmen to 'represent whether in pictures or in buildings or in any manufactured object anything indicative of bad character, anything undisciplined, mean, or graceless' (3.403B).

54. Not least because children will be brought up and educated by members of their own appetite-dominated class.

55. *Pol.* 1.3–7; see further Schofield 1990; Garnsey 1996: ch. 8.

56. For example, Reeve 1988: 48; Irwin 1995: 351.

57. Contrary to what appears to be the assumption in Reeve 1988: 285 n. 3.

58. This seems to me an adequate answer to a question pressed insistently in different variants by Bernard Williams in Williams 1973. In one form the puzzle consisted in asking how we are to picture the acquiescence of persons potentially violent in their appetites and passions when the *logistikon* (in the form of other persons) rules, as it does in the ideal city. I am suggesting that social control imposed by the exercise of reason through e.g. law is what shapes and moderates the habitual pattern of appetite—naturally insatiable, to be sure—in the economic class.

59. I incline to the view that speaking of appetites as concordant, or as holding shared beliefs, can only be a metaphorical way of expressing the point that there is no conflict between a person's appetites and a true understanding on their part of what is good. The issue is controverted (see e.g. Bobonich 2002: ch. 3; Price 1995: ch. 2; Kahn 2004: 353–4): so much of the psychology of the *Republic* is dramatized that it is often difficult—as Kahn brings out nicely (ibid. p. 356)—to gauge just what theoretical significance the dramatization might carry. Fortunately we do not need to pursue the issue further for present purposes.

7

Ideology

---

1. Ideology and Religion

The nightmare of society tearing itself apart in mutual hatred and the pursuit of self-interest is a spectre omnipresent in Plato's thinking about politics:[1] a nightmare for our own times. Plato's recipe in the *Republic* and the *Laws* alike for dispelling it has various components: tightly controlled institutional structures; a common education—at least for the ruling classes—designed to develop or control (as needed) every element in the human psyche for the promotion of virtue; government conducted with wisdom and an overriding concern for the public interest. Another ingredient is the subject of this final chapter: ideology. Not Plato's word, of course (a late eighteenth-century French coinage). And a word with a range of meanings, although its use as a critical tool by Marx, Marxists and other theorists of false consciousness is perhaps the most celebrated.[2] Taken as a purely descriptive term, however, it does express something Plato evidently thought it essential to build into his account of how a harmonious society might be made to work. What I have in mind is ideology as a highly articulated system of widely and deeply held beliefs and cultural values that is strongly influential on behaviour.[3]

Does a *utopia* need ideology? Perhaps it might not if—for example—the citizen body were composed exclusively of Stoic sages. What Stoicism conceives as the impulse to perfect rationality inherent in human nature would in that case be sufficient to make all their behaviour wholly appropriate to their social and political situation. But Plato's utopianism is premised on a more Thucydidean view of human nature and its social impulses. Even in a utopian society most people will never succeed in fully assimilating the rational basis on which a good human life needs to be lived. And nobody is ordinarily capable of achieving rationality without a strong cultural formation in an ordered institutional framework. Nor will the ideal city survive unless its values and rationale are absorbed through inculcation of an ideology that is shared by all its citizens. In short, utopia for Plato faces the same kinds of problem as do actual societies. He takes it that the resources needed to deal with them will be more effective versions of the resources that actual societies deploy for the purpose much more fitfully.

These assumptions are common to both *Republic* and *Laws*. And both dialogues turn to religion when it comes to prescribing an ideology for utopia. In the *Republic* the brief passage in Book 3 introducing and recounting the myth of the Noble Lie is the key text. Although it offers us only a glimpse of the way an ideology for Plato's city might look, in this chapter it gets the lion's share of discussion, because of the many issues in moral and political philosophy it opens up—not least the relationship between politics and philosophy that we began to consider way back in Chapter 1. The *Laws'* use of religion, by contrast, pervades the dialogue from beginning to end. If the Noble Lie is indeed a fiction best inculcated in childhood, the moral and religious rhetoric of the *Laws* is intended as truth—of a sort—for adults.

The very idea of lying or of using religion for political ends immediately prompts suspicion of the need to invoke a less neutral concept of ideology in diagnosing what Plato is about. Lying and using in whose interest? Isn't this ideology mediating a distorted representation of reality designed to deceive and thereby control those who can be got to believe it? To the first question Plato would reply: in the interests of those lied to, or in whom religion is to be inculcated. In other words, he would enter the defence of paternalism. With the second question he would reject the charge of distortion. What the *Laws'* religious rhetoric and the *Republic's* Noble Lie communicate is truth. Admittedly, they do so in ways which fall short of full philosophically argued disclosure. But that need not mean that what they communicate is not truth—as Plato sees it—in any sense. Questions about truth and rationality are tricky in both dialogues: but perhaps more complex in the *Laws* than in the *Republic*, to which we shall now turn.

2. *The Noble Lie*

2.1 The Phoenician myth

The Noble Lie of the *Republic* (3.414B–415D) is presented to the reader as a myth (415A). It is really two myths, or a myth in two parts: a 'Phoenician' theme (414C), on which Socrates then plays a no less important Hesiodic variation (cf. 8.546E). The Phoenician element is Plato's rewriting of the story of how Cadmus sowed a field with dragon's teeth, and how from the earth there then sprang up a race of armed men: the 'earthborn' or 'Spartoi' (the sown ones). These Cadmus set fighting among each other by throwing a stone into their midst. But five survived, and these helped him build Cadmea, the citadel of what was to become Thebes in Boeotia, whose aristocracy claimed them as ancestors.[4]

The story is a thoroughly Greek tale, a foundation myth presumably used to explain and legitimate the status of the established Theban landed elite. Cadmus, however, was by birth Phoenician: an immigrant to Greece from the city of Tyre. This is what allows Plato to indicate the model for his own myth by the designation 'Phoenician'. The *point* of calling it Phoenician is presumably something different: to suggest that there is something not entirely Greek about the story—that is (I take it) something not readily compatible with civilization. The suggestion is then reinforced by Socrates' confession that although—according to the poets—there have been many places where the indigenous peoples have sprung from the earth in this kind of way (the Athenians themselves had their own local version of just such a myth of origins),[5] it is not the sort of thing that has happened in their own time—and he does not know if it *could* happen. In other words, the story is archaic as well as barbaric.

Glaucon accuses Socrates of being reluctant to tell the myth, and Socrates doesn't demur (414C). Nor in fact when it comes to it *does* he tell a story. What he offers is not a narrative, but the briefest of summaries of the gist of what he would try to persuade the citizens of Kallipolis to believe (414D–E):

I have to try and persuade first of all the rulers themselves and the soldiers, and then the rest of the city, that the entire upbringing and education we gave them, their whole experience of it happening to them, was after all merely a dream, something they imagined, and that in reality they spent that time being formed and raised deep within the earth—themselves, their weapons and the rest of the equipment which was made for them. When the process of making them was complete, the earth their mother released them, and now it is their duty to be responsible for defending the country in which they live against any attack—just as they would defend their mother or nurse—and to regard the rest of the citizens as their brothers, born from the earth. (Trans. T. Griffith)

Socrates makes not the slightest attempt to supply any circumstantial detail which might enable the reader to imagine what the process of formation within the earth might be like or what would be involved in 'releasing' those formed within it: pre-eminently, it seems, as in the original myth of Cadmus, warriors (with the rulers the principal targets of the persuasion), but the other citizens too. The whole thing is strictly unimaginable and for that reason unnarratable;[6] or, rather, imaginable only at the cost of being quite incredible. So Socrates attempts to cut his losses by placing the concluding emphasis on the moral imperative that the myth is meant to convey to the rulers and the soldiers on whom they rely. They are to deliberate on behalf of their country and defend it *as mother and nurse*, and to think of other citizens *as brothers and as earthborn.* 'As really being', or 'as if they were'? Within the framework of the story the earth, i.e. their native soil, figures as mother (not 'mother, as it were'). But since it would be hard to know what *literally* believing that might be like, the alternatives dissolve into one.

There are few myths in Plato whose rationale is so transparent. Socrates introduces the Noble Lie with the proposal that at this point in the exercise they need as a 'device' one of 'the falsehoods which are to be used as need dictates' (414B–C). This is a reference to the sorts of lies which may legitimately be told to friends or enemies if that is the best way to benefit the city (2.382C, 3.389B–C). Elsewhere in the *Republic* they are called 'drugs' (5.459C–D; cf. 3.389B), reminding modern readers of Marx's famous dictum identifying religion with the opium of the people. What is this particular drug designed to effect? If the section of text quoted above does not already make that clear, Socrates' statement at the end of the entire Noble Lie passage spells the point out. The idea is to get the citizens 'to care more (*kêdesthai*) for the city and for each other' (415D). Plato has introduced this theme two or three pages earlier in Book 3 (412C–E). When Socrates finally brings to completion his account of the education those who have the potential to become guards of the ideal city are to receive, he gets swift agreement that the best of those they have educated are the ones who would actually qualify as guards (with a distinction between those exercising rule and those providing military support for them now explicitly marked, or beginning to be marked: 412C, 414B). 'Best' is defined in terms of suitability for guarding, and that in turn in terms of the combination of wisdom, capacity and care for the city. Socrates elaborates on care (*kêdesthai*). If they are to be good at their job and care as they should, guards will need to *love* the city, which they will do only if they identify its interests with their own, and assimilate the conviction that they must put all their efforts into securing what they judge to be best for the city.

How, then, to induce the conviction and engender love for the city? Neither here in Book 3 nor anywhere else in the *Republic* is Socrates made to propose that these are things people can be argued into by rational considerations, or (to put it another way) from the perspective of Book 7's dialectic. At various points reasons are given as to why contributing to the good of the community is in a person's own best interest: e.g. in the Book 1 argument on why good people will consent to exercise rule (1.346E–347D); or in Book 2's account of how communities are formed (2.369B–C); or (but less explicitly and indeed much more controversially) in the famous passage in Book 7 on why philosophers will agree to return to the Cave and take their share in government (7.519D–520E). But locating one's own best interest in the good of the city is one thing. *Loving* the city and living out a *conviction* that promoting what one takes to be its best interests is what deserves one's greatest efforts is something else. It is something Plato evidently took to require not reason or argument, but the production of a generally accepted ideology: accepted not just by the citizens at large, but by the rulers and military, too, and indeed *principally* by them (3.414C, 414D). He does not explain that or why this should be so. He simply has Socrates assert the usefulness of medicinal lies in certain circumstances (2.382C, 3.398B), and announces the need for one without argument on the specific occasions when he takes it to be needed (3.414B, 5.459C–D). He has in mind what is required to sustain the ideal city constructed in this particular dialogue. However, the notion that only ideology can sustain devotion to a political community is one of quite general application—and presumably does a good deal to explain the pervasive role of religion in the social and political theory of the *Laws*.

The thought that the Noble Lie, and specifically its Cadmeian element, consists in telling people something literally false about their origins, does not appear to be anything Plato finds disconcerting in itself. He has no Kantian or absolutist aversion to lying so far as the human sphere is concerned (however, falsehood is incompatible with divinity: 2.380D–383C).[7] Quite how we should understand the main connotation of 'noble' (*gennaion*) in the expression 'noble lie' is unclear. Perhaps it is only ironic, or a term of literary appraisal: an impressively massive lie, a right royal lie.[8] But it is easy enough to see why Plato might think it noble. Devotion to one's city was a widely accepted and frequently hymned Greek ideal, familiar from Homer (particularly in the figure of Hector in the *Iliad*) to the Athenian funeral oration. So a myth designed to promote such devotion to what Socrates will describe as the *good* city (e.g. 4.427E) might well be regarded as something noble.

Whether Plato really thought it likely to be persuasive—i.e. to do its job in fostering conviction and devotion—is another matter. The issue of persuasion is one he makes Socrates highlight both in introducing the Noble Lie and in reflecting on it once told. That cities were once founded by earthborn warriors (or the like) is something of which the poets have succeeded in persuading people. But this is not the way cities get founded nowadays. To persuade people otherwise would require 'a lot of persuading' (414C). Socrates doesn't know what effrontery (*tolma*) or words (*logoi*) to use (414D).[9] At the end of the whole passage he asks Glaucon: 'Can you think of any device (*mêkhanê*) by which they [i.e. the citizens] could be persuaded of this story (*mûthos*)?' 'No way', says Glaucon, 'so far as they themselves are concerned.' Given that believing the story would require them to suppose that they had been born and brought up quite differently from the way they know they were actually brought up, Glaucon's reaction is not surprising. But he thinks that their sons and descendants and people in later generations generally might be persuadable (415D). Socrates replies that even that would be enough to motivate them to care more for the city and each other.

I take it he has the Cadmeian element in the myth particularly in mind (that was what prompted expression of the original concern over persuasion, and caring for the city and each other is *its* explicit and distinctive message). The idea is presumably that if you think your children and descendants will be persuaded of it, you accept that they will consequently become devoted to the welfare of the city above all—and because they are *your* sons and descendants, and its welfare something your family is committed to, you will want yourself to share in that devotion. Plato very likely shared the qualified optimism he ascribes to Glaucon and Socrates. Myths of *distant* origins, where nobody really knows what happened, are among the falsehoods he has Socrates explicitly acknowledge as 'useful' in Book 2 of the *Republic* (2.382D). And in a sort of commentary on our passage in the *Laws*, he makes the Athenian Visitor cite the myth of Cadmus as one of thousands of stories of which people can easily be persuaded, lacking in credibility though it is. That myth is in fact presented as an important example for the legislator to ponder: an example of how—with the greatest good of the city in mind—he can persuade the souls of the young of whatever he tries to persuade them. He needs to find any and every device (*mêkhanê*, again) he can to get the people of his community to give expression to this simple goal in songs and stories and other forms of speech throughout their lives (2.663E–664A). As we might put it, the aim is to get them to make that goal true for them, by using whatever falsehoods will do the trick. Here, as in the *Republic* (2.378E–379A), Plato evidently sees this as a project requiring the legislator to call upon the services of the poets, or at any rate the resources of poetry.

2.2 The myth of the metals: fraternité, inégalité, la parole de Dieu

'Hear the rest of the myth,' says Socrates to Glaucon (415A). The rest of the myth is a rewriting of the Hesiodic 'myth of ages': a synchronic version of the narrative in *Works and Days* of successive eras of human existence, or rather of degeneration from a Golden Age through silver to bronze and—after a glorious period when heroes bestrode the earth—iron (*Works and Days* 106–201).[10] Unlike his Cadmeian myth, Plato's myth of metals is actually told. Socrates begins in the second person plural, imagining (as he says) that he is telling it to the citizens (415A–B). Once he starts complicating the relationship between gold, silver, bronze and iron strains in the citizen stock, verbs in the second person are no longer employed. But that can't be taken to show that the original audience drops out of sight or mind. It is presumably just that once the focus is on how different 'metallic' groups are allocated their roles in society, use of the comprehensive 'you' is no longer appropriate.

A properly ordered *politeia*, according to the *Republic*, is one in which different functions necessary to sustain the life of the city are undertaken only by those who possess the natural capacity to perform them well, and who are assigned on that basis to mutually exclusive classes within the society. In the myth of the metals Socrates assumes that the citizens to whom it is to be addressed occupy and understand the different roles specified by this model of a *politeia*. Ruling, providing military support, farming and the practice of crafts are the ones mentioned in Book 3 (3.415A–C). Built as it is on this assumption, what does the myth seek to achieve? First, theological justification for the way the capacities of individuals—and therefore the roles they perform and the places within the system that they occupy—are determined and hierarchically ordered. Second, and evidently the main preoccupation, a theological imperative designed to prevent that system being undermined by nepotism, or at any rate by the false assumption that natural capacity is always or necessarily inherited (415B; cf. 4.423C–D):

The first and most important instruction god gives the rulers is that the thing they should be the best guards of, the thing they should keep the most careful eye on, is what gets mixed in with the souls of the offspring.

Third, divine prophecy of the dire consequences of ignoring the imperative.

The whole line of argument is adroitly predicated on the brotherhood of all citizens—that is, on the idea promoted at the conclusion of the immediately preceding Cadmeian myth. Brotherhood is apparently not conceived as compromised by the differences in natural capacity associated with the different metals. And it is *because* of the kinship between all citizens that parents of one 'race' will not always produce offspring of the same race. Sometimes silver will be born from gold, gold from silver, and so for all the other possible combinations. Compliance with the imperative to ensure that in that case the child must be relocated to the class for which it is naturally suited will presumably be encouraged by the ideology of universal brotherhood.

Plato seems to envisage (here as in the further use he makes of the myth in explaining degeneration from the ideal *politeia*: 8.547A–B) that every individual is either gold or silver or bronze or iron. There is no question of someone having (say) a preponderance of bronze but a tincture of gold. The language Socrates uses might perhaps mislead one into thinking otherwise. He talks of 'admixture' of metals (*paramemeiktai*), and of the production by gold or silver parents of a child who is *hupokhalkos* or *huposidêros*—perhaps 'veined with bronze' or 'veined with iron' (3.415B; but one then has to pretend that bronze is a bit like an ore). It is not excluded linguistically that this might imply that the child is for all that predominantly silver or gold. But such an interpretation is not *secured* by the linguistic possibility. Moreover there is a strong argument on theoretical grounds for rejecting it. When Socrates considers the case of someone who is the *hupokhrusos* or *huparguros* offspring of a farmer or a craftsman ('veined with gold/silver'), he takes it that the divine injunction will require promotion of the child to the class of guards or to the military, just as the reverse situation will require expulsion from it (415C).[11] Yet, if in metallic composition such a person were still *predominantly* bronze or iron, promotion would be inappropriate—and indeed would threaten a range of destabilizing consequences. We must accordingly suppose that by 'admixture' Socrates means admixture of a given metal with the other non-metallic components of human nature. And calling someone (for example) *huparguros*, 'veined with silver', will indicate that silver and silver alone is the metal of that person's soul.

If the first part of the Noble Lie is a foundation myth, one might call this second part a myth of succession and survival. The *Republic*'s eugenic programme will not be introduced until Book 5, and as we have seen it will form no part of Kallipolis' ideology. But a concern with the need to preserve the purity of the stock of the guards and the auxiliaries is already apparent, and indeed highlighted by the very use of the vocabulary of metals and its associations. In the passage preceding the Noble Lie, Socrates had spoken of the need to put potential guards to the test (*basanizein*) and ensure that they are uncontaminated (*akêratos*)—both of these being expressions used elsewhere in Greek literature for testing gold (3.413E–414A). When the passage is recapitulated in Book 6, Socrates now talks quite explicitly of testing them 'like gold in the fire' (6.503A). Of course, the overriding object is to ensure that nothing endangers proper performance of the functions of guards. Yet the myth of metals stresses the supreme *value* which gold confers on the guards (3.415A).

There is nothing remotely egalitarian or democratic about the myth of metals. In making sure that it wasn't, Plato must have been perfectly well aware that he was taking a stance that might be regarded as idiosyncratic (at best) or (potentially more uncomfortable) anti-Athenian. Idiosyncratic: because the myth of metals is presented as an elaboration of the Cadmeian myth of autochthony. And the default expectation of any myth of autochthony was doubtless that it would legitimate *equally* the claims to high status of any families who could plausibly represent themselves as descendants of the original earthborn founders of the *polis*. (Certainly there is evidence of a fiercely egalitarian ethos among early Greek aristocracies.)[12] Anti-Athenian: in that Athenians saw no incompatibility between their democracy and their own traditional claims to be autochthonous. This is registered nowhere more clearly than in Plato's own *Menexenus*, his pastiche of the rhetoric of the funeral oration—a political art form portrayed by Nicole Loraux as the definitive self-celebration of the Athenian democracy, and never more memorably than in the famous speech over the war dead delivered by Pericles, which is echoed by Socrates at some crucial points.[13] 'We and our dependants,' says Socrates (*Menex.* 238E–239A), 'all born brothers of a single mother, make the justified claim that we are not one another's slaves or masters. Instead our natural equality of birth compels us to seek by lawful means equality under the law, yielding to each other in nothing except reputation for virtue and wisdom.'

The *Republic* itself elsewhere echoes the renunciation of a power structure analogous to the master–slave relationship (5.463A–B). But the myth of metals is plainly irreconcilable with any suggestion of natural *equality* of birth and with endorsement of the hallmark democratic slogan 'equality under the law', conveying as it did something like our 'equal rights'. That said, the myth of the metals passage does not read as though it is written to make a pointedly anti-Athenian point. It helps to constitute a natural culmination to the long initial treatment of the role and education of the guards which began forty pages earlier in Book 2. The guards, their functions and their lifestyle, are much more Spartan in inspiration than Athenian, of course, even if Socrates' stress on music and the soul, rather than gymnastics and the body, introduces a civilizing 'Athenian' element into the picture.[14] By the time he reaches the Noble Lie, the reader is not expecting to be reminded of Athenian institutions, even by indirection or implicit negation.

The Noble Lie therefore affirms fraternity without equality. And liberty? The other key component of the conceptual fabric of the Noble Lie is not liberty but god: divine declaration, injunction and prophecy. The ideology of the *Republic*'s ideal city is explicitly authoritarian and theistic. This should come as no surprise, given Book 2's prominent and critical emphasis on the need for poetry to communicate and reflect a true conception of god, if guards are to be educated correctly, and a healthy society is to be created (2.377E–383C). The theism of the *Republic* in fact anticipates the much more elaborate and highly developed theistic discourse of the *Laws*: a dialogue which notoriously makes its intentions plain from the outset, beginning as it does with the very word 'god' (1.624A). Religion is to be pervasive in the life of the form of ideal society imagined in the dialogue—starting with the words addressed by the legislators to the first citizens of Magnesia (as it is called) on their arrival. It consists of a speech laying out the whole theological framework of human life and its ethical parameters, sustained over two and a half pages of monologue, and opening with the Orphic dictum: 'God, as the old saying has it, holds beginning and end and middle of all the things that are' (4.715E–718C).[15] Just so in the Noble Lie: the beginning and the middle and the end of the city are presented in a divine perspective. Plato's rationale for writing god into the popular ideology of *Republic* and *Laws* alike is not hard to understand. He wants to appeal to a source of authority that is unchallengeable, which will underpin the traditions of the society, and whose pronouncements can be immediately persuasive to the population at large. God fits the bill.

2.3 The politics of lying

'We want one single, grand lie', Socrates says when he introduces the Noble Lie (3.414B–C), 'which will be believed by everybody—including the rulers, ideally, but failing that the rest of the city.' Grand lie? Noble lie?[16] This is not the only point on which there might be argument about the translation. Some prefer to 'lie' the more neutral 'falsehood' (which need not imply deliberate deception), others 'fiction' (perhaps trying to prescind from questions of truth and falsehood altogether). Cornford had 'bold flight of invention'.[17] I think 'lie' is exactly right (but the argument for that will emerge later, in Section 2.4). The *Republic*'s explicit reliance on such a mechanism to secure assent and commitment to the political arrangements it proposes still has the capacity to shock and offend. It makes the Noble Lie a natural focus for many of the major questions the dialogue provokes.

First, and most obviously, the use of the Noble Lie is what more than anything may prompt the charge that the *Republic*'s preoccupation with political unity is a recipe for 'the collectivist, the tribal, the totalitarian theory of morality', to quote Popper's formulation—inasmuch as it licenses wholesale deception of individual citizens as the means to secure the good of 'the state' (as Popper conceptualized Plato's city).[18] Such deception is quite incompatible with the assumption of modern liberal political philosophy since Locke that the only valid way of legitimating the political order is by appeal to reason: to *rational* considerations which have the power to motivate acceptance of a political authority by those who are to be subject to it. It is similarly and connectedly in conflict with the fundamental moral requirement, often associated above all with Kantian ethics, that people be treated as ends, not means. The Noble Lie seems an affront to human dignity, and something that undermines the human capacity for self-determination in particular.

Our own time is seeing both an explosion in knowledge and the media by which it is communicated, and unprecedented levels of concern about standards of probity in public life, and about lying and the manipulation and suppression of information in particular. Not that it would be reasonable to expect these ugly processes to stop. As John Dunn wrote back in 1979 (commenting on realization that moral and practical insight is not the preserve of any elite):[19]

If this realization dictates a hugely more democratic conception of political rights and capabilities than Plato favoured, it neither dictates nor indeed permits that ruthlessly evasive and disingenuous egalitarianism which pervades the ideologies of the modern world, capitalist and socialist alike, and pretends that the problems of power have been solved or would be solved if the power of human beings was rendered equal. And since the structural inequality of power in the societies of the modern world, however drastically reorganized these might be, is so intractably vast and since such power cannot be rendered safe, insulated from the capacity to harm, it is clear enough that one of the most widely deplored characteristics of the Platonic Republic, the noble lie, has at least as guaranteed a place in any possible structures for our world as it had in that of Plato.

Plato is in fact nowhere more our contemporary than in making similar preoccupations—knowledge, virtue, truth, deception—central to his own vision of what matters in politics.

Nor is that just a contemporary perspective. In having Socrates sanction lying as a basic ingredient in political discourse, Plato must have known he was breaching the norms of the democratic political ideology of his own time and place. It is true that Odysseus the trickster is held up as a figure commanding admiration from the readers of the *Odyssey*. That was a reflection of the archaic worldview symbolized by Hesiod when he made Zeus first marry Metis ('Resource') and then, when she is pregnant with Athena, turn her own powers against her, 'deceiving her wits by trickery with wily words' and swallowing her whole (*Theogony* 886-91). *Mêtis* involves 'flair, wisdom, forethought, subtlety of mind, deception, resourcefulness, vigilance, opportunism ... and experience'. It has to do with 'the future seen from the point of view of its uncertainties', and is at a premium in 'transient, shifting, disconcerting and ambiguous' situations. As Marcel Detienne and Jean-Pierre Vernant have shown, *mêtis* encapsulates a cluster of attributes and values that remained prized (although not characteristically by the philosophers) throughout Greek literature and thought down to Oppian's *Treatise on Fishing* in the second century AD and beyond.[20]

Odysseus was not always presented as he had been in the *Odyssey*. More pertinent for our purposes is Sophocles' *Philoctetes* of 409 BC, a profound meditation—played out in the theatre before the Athenian *dêmos*—on the moral corrosiveness and dubious political advantage of Odysseus' attempt to get the youthful Neoptolemos to hoodwink Philoctetes into what was to be an enforced return to the Greek camp at Troy. The Athenians generally thought of lying and deceit as the way not they but the Spartans conducted political life, as is testified above all by Pericles' antitheses on the subject in the funeral speech attributed to him by Thucydides (2.39.1). A democratic political culture, by contrast, required a general commitment on the part of speakers in the Assembly to tell the truth. As Demosthenes put it on one occasion (*On the False Embassy* 184):

There is no greater injustice anyone could commit against you than to speak falsehoods. For where the political system depends on speeches, how can political life be conducted securely if these are not true?

Hence the Athenians' intense resentment against speakers they suspected of manipulating them: the demagogues who figure so prominently in Aristophanic comedy and Thucydidean history. Hence too Diodotus' reflections during the debate on Mytilene of 427 BC (again as reconstructed by Thucydides) about the spiralling debasement of democracy and democratic rhetoric produced by widespread contravention of the norm of veracity (3.43.2–4):

It has become the rule also to treat good advice honestly given as being no less under suspicion than bad, so that a person who has something good to say must tell lies in order to be believed, just as someone who gives terrible advice must win over the people by deception. Because of these suspicions, ours is the only city that nobody can possibly benefit openly, without thoroughgoing deception, since if anyone does good openly to the city, his reward will be the suspicion that he had something secretly to gain from it.

What Diodotus sees as the ultimate degradation of political culture—an outcome where 'a person who has something good to say must tell lies in order to be believed'—is apparently embraced by the Platonic Socrates as no more troubling than the white lies someone tells a child when getting it to take some medicine.[21]

'One *single*, grand lie' might suggest a possible line of defence on Plato's behalf. Did he perhaps think that relations between citizens in general and between rulers and ruled in particular should exhibit openness and candour—but that there had to be just one exception: the myth that spelled out the basis on which that relationship was founded? No, that is not what Plato thought. The Noble Lie might with luck be the one thing needed to induce in the citizens an overriding concern for the good of the city. But lying and falsehood are seen as pervasive necessities in the politics and culture of the good city, and in this regard there is an asymmetry between rulers and ruled. One particularly chilling remark on the subject occurs in Socrates' discussion in Book 5 of the mechanisms that will be needed to sustain belief in the eugenic system for controlling breeding. 'It will be a necessity', he says (459C), 'for the rulers to use many drugs.' He then explains what he has in mind (459C–D): 'It looks as though the rulers are going to have to use a great deal of falsehood and deception for the benefit of those they are ruling.' So in this instance the ruled (here not the economic class, but the young soldiers who are to support the rulers) will be told that the mating arrangements are simply the outcome of a lottery. The ruled, by contrast, should have nothing to do with lying. For an ordinary citizen to lie to the rulers is worse than for a patient or someone in training to lie to his doctor or trainer about his physical condition, or for a sailor not to tell the navigator the truth about the state of the ship and those sailing it. If a ruler catches any of the artisans lying like this, 'he will punish him for introducing a practice which is as subversive and destructive in a city as it is in a ship' (3.389 B–D).[22]

Socrates' insistence on the need for lying to sustain the political order is all of a piece with his general treatment of culture and society more broadly. The Cave analogy of Book 7—the most striking and memorable image in the entire dialogue—represents uneducated humanity as imprisoned by illusions, feeding uncritically on third-hand images of reality (7.514A–515C, 516C–D, 517D–E). When Socrates subsequently argues that philosophers must be compelled to return to the Cave to exercise their function as rulers, the implication is presumably that most of those they are to govern, although citizens of an ideal city, have very little ability to resist deception or to respond to anything better than images of truth (cf. 520B–C). That implication is not contradicted by the radical programme of censorship of the poets that he works through in Books 2 and 3, in the context of his treatment of the upbringing of the guards.

Of course, there is an important sense in which the reason why Homer and Hesiod are attacked, and great tracts of their poetry ruled unfit for consumption, is that they tell falsehoods. Sometimes Socrates seems to mean by this that gods or heroes are represented as doing things which they did *not* do: for example, it simply isn't the case (according to Socrates) that Cronos took revenge on his father Ouranos by castrating him (2.377E–378A), or that Achilles dragged Hector round the tomb of Patroclus and slaughtered prisoners taken alive on his funeral pyre (3.391B). But the reason why Socrates disputes what we might call the factual truth of these accounts is that they are at odds with the conceptions of god and of moral virtue which should inform the education of the guards.

His real objection is that such stories are 'not admirable' (2.377D–E) and are 'impious' (3.391B). In fact in the passage in which he first introduces the notion of lies as useful drugs, he concedes that with stories like those told by Homer and Hesiod, we don't *know* where the truth lies so far as events long ago are concerned. In these circumstances the right thing is to 'make falsehood as much like the truth as possible' (2.382B–C): i.e. to tell a story which encapsulates *moral* truth even if—inevitably—it is fanciful if conceived as fact. Education *has* to begin with stories like this—'broadly speaking false, though there is some truth in them' (2.377A). In other words, the culture is and must be saturated with myths that are literally false, and deceptive if believed to be factually true. But the deception is legitimate if like the Noble Lie and the stories Socrates *wants* the young to hear, they are morally admirable fictions that drug people into sound convictions and lead them to virtue (2.377B–C, 378E–379A). What is wrong with Homer and Hesiod is not in the end that they lied, but that there was nothing morally admirable in most of the lies they told (2.377E).[23]

2.4 The morality of lying

So far we have been looking at ways in which the Noble Lie, and the whole conception of a well-ordered society it represents, conflict with the outlook of ancient Athenian ideology and modern liberal ethical and political thought alike—even if ideological mechanisms of this sort may be a political necessity. It could also be argued that some deep-seated tensions in the project of the *Republic* itself rise to the surface at this point. The Platonic Socrates is quite explicit that his proposals for a role for the philosopher in government will be perceived as generally paradoxical (5.473C–E), and nothing 'fine' or 'good' so far as the philosophers for their part are concerned (7.540B; cf. 1.347C–D, 7.520D, 521A). The need to employ lies and deceit to maintain the social and political fabric is presumably itself one of the reasons why Plato has him attribute that view to them. Popper thought such lying and deceit by philosopher rulers actually incompatible with the *Republic*'s own definition of genuine philosophers as those who love truth and the contemplation of truth.[24] Getting to grips with this issue will take a little time.

In a key passage of Book 2 Socrates finds it helpful in his discussion of the question whether the gods lie or dissemble to distinguish between lies in the soul and lies in speech—between the true or real lie and a spoken imitation or image of it, something that is 'not quite an unadulterated lie' (2.382B–C). He goes on at once to observe that the true lie is hated not only by gods but by humans, whereas lying in speech has uses (for humans, not gods) that don't merit hatred (2.382C–E). What does he mean by the 'lie in the soul'? Nothing very exalted, he assures us. 'All I am saying is that to lie, and to be deceived, and to be ignorant about reality in one's soul, to hold and possess the lie there, is the last thing anyone would want.' And this—the true lie—is then defined as 'the ignorance in the soul of the person who has been deceived' (2.382B).

Socrates' distinction is a simple one. It turns on the implicit thought that lying is such a profoundly disturbing thing that we ought to try to identify what it is that is so disturbing about it, and let that control our use of the expression 'lie'. What is disturbing about lying is not in the end saying something false out loud in words to someone else, nor deliberately trying to mislead them, but *saying something false in your own mind to yourself*, particularly something false about 'the most important things' (2.382A). So we should adjust our use of the language of truth and falsehood accordingly. Saying something false to another with intent to deceive is certainly a lie (the 'lie in words'), but the outcome lying in speech tries to achieve—belief in a falsehood—is what the real evil of lying consists in: the true lie (the 'lie in the soul'), therefore. It's still appropriate (Socrates seems to think) to speak then of a *lie*, not just the internal enunciation of a falsehood, because that falsehood expresses the state of mind of someone who is *deceived* into believing what they say to themselves. To put it differently, deception is an ambiguous notion. It can mean being deceived by oneself or by another (real deception), or it can mean trying to deceive someone else —which, if the deceiver is not himself or herself deceived, is 'not unadulterated' deception, but a mere image of the real thing (the fact that you are saying something false makes it sound as though you are deceived, even though you aren't).

The Stoics seem to have built on this distinction in developing their own absolutist solution to the problem of reconciling philosophical love of truth and the expediency of lying for political and other prudential reasons. According to them, the wise person—i.e. the person who is perfectly rational—will sometimes say things that are false (*deliberately* say such things, as the standard examples they recycled make clear). But there will be no intent to deceive, even if the speaker knows very well that the outcome will be deception. And the wise will say what is false 'without assent'. So their words will not count as lying, 'because they do not have their judgment assenting to what is false'. This is as much as to say that the wise are not in the grip of what the *Republic* describes as the true lie, the lie in the soul. The difference is that the Stoics stick to common usage in reserving the word 'lie' exclusively for speech-acts. Of course, the upshot is an innovative conception of lying in speech: someone counts as lying only if they are *themselves* deceived in some way (although presumably not the same way as the person to whom their falsehood is uttered is deceived)—above all, no doubt, regarding what is good and bad. The root cause of such deception of soul would be a morally bad disposition, as emerges in the Stoics' treatment of examples of falsehoods that may legitimately be told. Something false told by a doctor to his patient or a general to his troops is not a lie provided their intention is not bad. Just so, the Stoics' wise person says false things from a morally good disposition. The implication of their radical conception of lying is the counter-intuitive proposition that the Platonic Socrates' useful medicinal lies are not lies at all.[25]

Just because the lie in words (to revert now to Socrates' own categories) is a lie only in words, not in the speaker's soul also, and therefore 'not quite an unadulterated lie', it obviously does not follow that there is any blanket justification for telling such lies. To say that they are 'not quite unadulterated' suggests a shade of grey a lot closer to black than white. And it is not hard to think of reasons why Socrates might want to encourage general aversion to them: not least because a successful lie in words will be responsible for deception—a 'true lie'—in the *hearer*'s soul (although like the Stoics he might have wished to insist that principally and ultimately it is everyone's *own* responsibility whether they give their assent to a falsehood). Exceptions would always need a special defence, such as the argument that the telling of the right kind of myths to children induces not deception but *truth* in their souls in regard to 'the most important things' (2.382A).

Nonetheless we should not be surprised that the *Republic* allows for such exceptions. It was Augustine, not Plato, who was the first notable champion of what we might call the absolutist position on the morality of lying: holding that all lying is wrong, and forbidden by God as sinful. Indeed Augustine represents a watershed between antiquity and modernity in the history of the moral philosophy of lying. The massive influence of his view on the matter was such that much subsequent discussion has felt obliged at least to grapple with the absolutist position, even though few have embraced it like Kant without qualification.[26] The questionability of the absolutist stance is brilliantly exhibited in the chapter entitled 'Sincerity: Lying and Other Styles of Deceit' in Bernard Williams's last book, *Truth and Truthfulness*.[27] But in treatments of lying by Greek and Roman authors before Augustine there is not much to suggest that it even occurred to people that absolutism was a serious option. It is the Stoics who stand out as exceptions to the general rule—but exceptions only of the highly qualified kind we have just glanced at. The *Republic*, however, unquestionably envisages justifications for lying.

In the passage at the end of Book 2 that we have been considering, Socrates lists a few types of occasion on which lying may be 'useful, so as not to be deserving of hatred' (2.382C). Stories about events long ago—the myths he subjects to censorship—constitute one category of useful lie. The other cases he mentions form a pair: lying to enemies and lying to one's so-called friends, if in derangement they are attempting to do something bad. These two sorts of useful lie are no less important for him. Their articulation as such is probably not due to Plato. I suspect that the category of the useful lie is one he took over from Socrates himself. In Xenophon's *Memorabilia*, for example, Socrates engages in rather more extended and pointed discussion of the topic of whether it is just to lie to one's friends as well as one's enemies, with permissible examples including

lying to a depressed and indeed suicidal friend, lying to children
to induce them to take medicine when they need it, and lying by
a general to encourage his downhearted troops (*Mem.* 4.2.14–18;
the last of these examples is mentioned as a commonplace in a
speech to the Athenian Assembly by Andocides delivered in 391
BC: 3.34). This anticipates Socrates' initial characterization of
useful lies in general as 'taking the form of a drug (*pharmakon*)',
the point being that just as only doctors—the experts—should
administer drugs, so in the public sphere it is appropriate for the
rulers alone to lie, for the benefit of the city, whether as regards
enemies or citizens (3.389B–C).

The example of the deranged or depressed friend who needs
to be lied to for his or her own good takes us right back to the
beginning of the *Republic*. In the initial conversation between
Cephalus and Socrates, the idea begins to emerge that justice
might be a matter of telling the truth and repaying one's obligations. Socrates raises the case of the deranged friend by way of
objection. Suppose such a person had when of sound mind lent
you weapons and now asks for their return, then it *wouldn't* be
the act of someone behaving justly to comply with the request,
or to tell the whole truth. So 'this isn't the definition of justice,
speaking the truth and giving back what one takes' (1.331A–D).
The issue of truth-telling and indeed of its ambiguity is thereby
marked out as something we may expect to figure on the agenda
of the dialogue as a whole. Socrates' position—that there will
always be cases where truth-telling *wouldn't* be just—is later
reinforced by epistemological and metaphysical considerations
advanced at the end of Book 5. There he argues quite generally that *any* particular exemplification of beauty or justice,
or largeness or heaviness, and so on, may turn out to be an
exemplification also of precisely the opposite: ugliness, injustice,
smallness, lightness. So it would be a mistake to suggest that
they could constitute part of the essence of beauty or justice and
so on, and qualify as objects of knowledge rather than opinion
(5.479A–480A). An absolutist position on truth-telling proves
therefore to be incompatible with Platonism. In Platonism the
realm of the absolute is held to be the Forms, not the world of
human experience and activity.

In his account at the beginning of the next book of the dispositions which must become second nature to the philosopher
as one devoted to knowledge, Socrates early on lists 'aversion to

falsehood' (6.485C), which he explains as 'not willingly accepting falsehood in any form—hating it, but loving truth'. In the conversational exchange which then ensues, it is argued that this requirement simply follows from the philosopher's love of wisdom. Someone who genuinely loves learning things 'must make every possible effort, right from earliest childhood, to reach out for truth of every kind' (6.485D). James Adam in his great commentary on the Greek text of the *Republic* thought 'truth' here meant 'metaphysical truth'—what someone whose soul harboured a lie about 'the most important things' would be ignorant of.[28] I'm not sure Plato meant to be so restrictive. 'All truth' or 'truth of every kind' sounds as though it might include truth in speech as well as truth in the soul.[29] Adam was right, however, in the main thing he wanted to deny. Plato cannot be tacitly withdrawing the claim that in their capacity as rulers philosophers will necessarily resort to deception in order to maintain the social and political fabric of the city.

What does follow (on the more inclusive view of what 'truth of every kind' encompasses) is that even as they tell politically expedient lies, philosopher rulers will hate doing it. There really is a tension at this point between their aspirations as philosophers and the constraints under which they must operate as rulers. A little later Socrates asks (6.486A): 'Do you think, then, that the mind which can take a large view, and contemplate the whole of time and the whole of reality, is likely to regard human life as of any importance?' Everything to do with ruling—as preoccupied exclusively with the affairs of humans—must for a philosopher be irksome triviality, and that presumably includes the need to tell lies.

The still influential political philosopher Hannah Arendt wrote in 1967 as follows:[30]

I hope no one will tell me any more that Plato was the inventor of the 'noble lie'. This belief rested on a misreading of a crucial passage (414C) in the *Republic*, where Plato speaks of one of his myths—a 'Phoenician tale'—as a *pseudos*. Since the same Greek word signifies 'fiction', 'error', and 'lie' according to context—if Plato wants to distinguish between error and lie, the Greek language forces him to speak of 'involuntary' and 'voluntary' *pseudos*—the text can be rendered with Cornford as 'bold flight of invention' or be read with Eric Voegelin ... as satirical in intention; under no circumstances can it be understood as a recommendation of lying as we understand it.

It will by now be evident that Arendt was simply wrong about the interpretation of *pseudos*. The Noble Lie is specifically introduced as one of the 'falsehoods that get created as needed which we were talking about a little while back' (3.414B). Socrates is referring to the useful medicinal lies first exemplified in Book 1 by the case of the deranged friend's dagger, and then categorized near the end of Book 2. The Noble Lie, like the entire discussion of acceptable and unacceptable narratives in Books 2 and 3, is conceptualized in terms of the polarity of lying and truth-telling, and resonates as such with discussions of political expediency in many other Athenian texts of the late fifth and fourth centuries, as well as with Plato's own metaphysical preoccupation with truth. Carl Page rightly comments on 'how deeply woven into the fabric of the entire conversation' is his treatment of lying.[31] Nietzsche was a surer guide than Arendt when he congratulated Plato on 'a real lie, a genuine, resolute, "honest" lie' (*Genealogy of Morals* 3.19).

2.5 Ideology and the philosopher

The Noble Lie is the *Republic*'s principal device for instilling in the guards the conviction that they should invest their best energies into promoting what they judge to be the city's best interests, and for inspiring consequent devotion to its well-being. The first generation of guards will not actually believe the Lie, but—by a mechanism we have discussed—it will nonetheless encourage in them that conviction and devotion. Later generations will absorb and accept it in childhood.[32]

The introduction of the Lie at the end of Book 3 long precedes the revelation towards the end of Book 5 that these guards must be philosophers if the ideal city is to come into being and remain in being. Will the philosophers' understanding of reality, and above all of the Good, give them an *alternative* and more deeply rooted source of conviction and devotion—conceivably displacing that implanted by the telling of the Noble Lie? Since Plato never has Socrates explicitly address this question, any answer must be to a degree speculative. A full examination of the possibilities would require a review of the whole issue of the relationship between philosophy and politics in the *Republic*. I shall offer a brief indication of some grounds for answering our question in the negative: philosophy supplies *no* alternative source of motivation.

My argument begins with the section of Book 6 in which Socrates turns to consider what preparation philosophers will need for undertaking the task of government (at 6.502D). Here is the key passage (502E–503B):

'Our account of women and children has been completed, but the selection of rulers is something we need to tackle more or less from square one. What we said, if you remember, was that they must prove their patriotism by being tested in the fire of pleasure and pain. It must be clear that they will not surrender their convictions through hardship, fear or any other twist of fortune. Those who fail the test must be disqualified, while those who emerge pure, like gold tested in the fire, should be appointed rulers, and given rewards and prizes both in their lifetimes and after their deaths. That was the kind of thing we were saying, while the argument put on her veil and slipped by us, afraid of stirring up the trouble we now find ourselves in.'

'You're absolutely right,' he said. 'I do remember us saying that.'

'Yes, we were reluctant to say the things we have now been bold enough to say. Anyway, let's now stand by our new-found boldness, and say that if we want guards in the most precise sense of the word, we need philosophers.'

'Very well. Let's go on record as saying that.' (Trans. T. Griffith)[33]

Socrates does not mention the Noble Lie here, but he does resume the gist of the section preceding it in Book 3, where tests are prescribed for *verifying* a guard's patriotism: ensuring that conviction and devotion can withstand a full range of dangers and temptations (3.412D–414A). It is not suggested here that these tests will not after all adequately guarantee what they are designed to guarantee (cf. 6.503E, 7.535A–C). Nor is it suggested that the influences Books 2 and 3 regarded as essential for training the guards (including the Noble Lie) are in themselves inappropriate or ineffective. In particular, there is no hint of a doubt as to whether someone who had successfully absorbed those influences would actually be patriotic (*philopolis*).

To be sure, the present passage suggests that something crucial was missing from the process for selecting guards: something deliberately suppressed back in the argument of Book 3. That something was precisely the need for guards to be *philosophers*: the requirement which will now prompt the treatment of a *philosophical* education that occupies the rest of Books 6 and 7.

Now there is no difficulty in grasping what it is that the guards will be provided with by philosophy and philosophical education. It is the knowledge and understanding they will need for the job of ruling. These are the exclusive focus of the Sun, Line and Cave, and Socrates' subsequent explications of these (6.504D–7.534E). Not patriotism. In fact it is precisely the experience of doing and living philosophy that may cause philosophers to waver in their patriotism. Doing and living philosophy may well appear more attractive than doing their patriotic duty. Hence the blend of compulsion and persuasion that will in that event be needed to get them to return to the Cave (7.519B–520A). But the persuasion on offer—reminding philosophers of the justice of reciprocating their education by the city (520A–E)—could only be effective with someone who recognizes that he or she is before all else a *citizen* of the good city. And that recognition presupposes the underlying devotion to it inspired initially by the Noble Lie.

In the Noble Lie's Cadmeian myth citizenship is articulated in terms of filial obligation.[34] The force of that metaphor is what underpins the overriding commitment to the good of the city required of its rulers, supported by its military. There is no non-metaphorical piece of political theory developed elsewhere in Books 2 to 4 into which it can be translated (contrast the story of the metals). And crucial to it is an existential dimension untranslat*able* into theory. In effect it says to the rulers: '*This*—the city—is *your* mother, *you* must deliberate on her behalf and defend her.' We have to wait until Book 5 for a non-mythical articulation of the relationship between city and citizens which could transform the metaphor into something more literal (though still an imaginative projection). There, the radical eugenic breeding provisions that Socrates proposes require a reconceptualizing of the family. All the young are to think of *anyone* else who was evidently conceived during the same mating festival as brothers or sisters, and parents are to treat *all* such children as their sons and daughters (5.461D–E). In fact every time one guard meets another, he or she will *assume* it is a brother or sister or mother or father, or the child or parent of one (5.463C). In such a city, more than in any other, the binding unity which Socrates calls the 'footprint' of the good will be apparent. Everyone will use 'I' and 'my' simultaneously. All will rejoice and grieve over exactly the same events (all saying with reference to the same thing 'I'm really upset by that', etc.). They will behave like the parts of one body, which are all affected by pain or pleasure in any one of them (e.g. the finger), so that we say 'the *person* feels pain *in* the finger' (5.462A–D, 463E–464B).[35]

What this passage in Book 5 brings home is something of essential importance for an understanding of the Noble Lie. Plato evidently sees no way of developing the motivation to care for the city *independent* of the creation of what one might call a holistic political ideology. The metaphor of filial obligation or recompense is his favourite way of articulating such an ideology. Something like it recurs in the famous discussion in Book 7 of the return of philosophers from contemplation of eternal truth to the cave of human existence. At the end of the Cave analogy, Socrates says that 'the best natures' must not be allowed to avoid descending from their philosophical studies back into the Cave—to fulfil their duty to take their turn as rulers over the other citizens. Glaucon objects (7.519D): 'What? Are we going to do them an injustice, and make them live a worse life when a better is possible for them?' On the second point Socrates issues a reminder that their concern as legislators is the good of the whole city, not of any particular class within it. His reply on the first point does not (as some commentators would have preferred) invoke the metaphysics of the Forms, but turns on considerations of reciprocal obligation. Significantly he moves into direct speech to address his argument direct to the philosophers. He appeals to the understanding *they* need to have of *their* existential situation.

Other cities, Socrates has remarked, do nothing to nurture the political potential of their philosophers. 'But we have produced *you* as leaders and kings', he begins, 'and have educated you accordingly, so that you can share in both the philosophical and the political life.'[36] When his quite sustained speech to them is complete, he asks Glaucon: 'Then do you fancy those we have nurtured will disobey us after hearing this, and refuse to take their turn in sharing in the exertions of the city?' 'Impossible', says Glaucon, now convinced: 'It is a just instruction, and they are just.' It is striking how he couches his verdict in terms of justice. The verdict is prepared for not by reflection on justice as it comes to be conceived in the main argument of the *Republic*, but on justice as Simonides thought of it—paying back what you owe to somebody (1.331D–E).[37] Not that the dialogue in the end sees any necessary incompatibility between these two conceptions of justice. The first thing we are told about the characteristic behaviour of the just person as defined at the end of Book 4 is that he is someone who repays his debts (442E–443A). Such a person counts behaviour in the political as in other spheres 'just' when it preserves and promotes psychic harmony (443C–E: presumably a necessary, not a sufficient condition).[38]

There is a notable anticipation in the earlier *Crito* of the pattern of argument I am detecting in these passages of the *Republic*. In that dialogue the issue for Socrates' friend Crito is why the philosopher will not effect an escape from the prison to which he is confined, awaiting execution of the sentence of death passed on him by the Athenian court. The main body of the explanation Socrates offers him is contained in an extended piece of political rhetoric put in the mouths of the personified laws of Athens, and addressed in the second person direct to Socrates himself and to his existential situation (compare the *Republic* contexts that we have been considering). The laws appeal for the most part to Simonidean justice, and in the first instance to paternalistic considerations with which we are now familiar. The laws and the city produced Socrates—it was under their auspices that his parents married and brought him to birth. They too are similarly responsible for his upbringing or nurturing and his education. So, if the laws and the city now decide that Socrates must perish, the reciprocity of obligation dictates not that he should do what he can to destroy the laws and the city (which is what ignoring their jurisdiction would amount to), but that he should obey the decision out of filial respect (*Crito* 50D–51C).[39]

The issues at stake in all three of these texts—the *Crito* passage, the treatment of the return to the Cave in Book 7 of the *Republic*, and the Noble Lie—are closely comparable: how to *persuade* the individual to do something required by the good of the city. In each case the considerations put forward in favour are drawn not from the deeper resources of Socratic or Platonic philosophy, but from more popular discourse. In the *Crito* and the return to the Cave passage, the argument is presented as a piece of political rhetoric addressed in the second person to the philosopher, while in the Noble Lie Socrates has recourse in myth to another popular form—and again in its second part adopts a more urgent mode of expression by addressing the citizens in the second person. The second person is for the Platonic Socrates peculiarly appropriate to communication between members of a family about their obligations and commitments. 'I was always concerned with you,' he tells the Athenians at his trial (*Apol.* 31B), 'approaching each one of you like a father or an elder brother to persuade you to care for virtue.' When there is a need to move people to make particular commitments to a particular community, the arguments Plato produces for elevating the good of the city above that of the individual have nothing metaphysical about them.

One might worry (scholars have worried a great deal) that there *ought* to be, at any rate in the case of the *Republic*'s philosophers, who have after all been deeply immersed in study of the Form of the Good and all it entails.[40] But let us suppose that they had indeed been persuaded in childhood of the myths of the Noble Lie. And let us further suppose that they have never lost either the conviction thereby instilled in them that above all they must care for the city as a matter of reciprocal obligation, or (yet more importantly) the motivation to do so that the conviction supports. What will have changed for them now that they have achieved philosophical understanding? First, they will no longer believe the myths as myths. They will have the sort of grasp of the rationale for the good city that is articulated in the philosophical argument of the *Republic* (cf. 6.497C–D). Second, they will have become only too aware that in the pursuit of knowledge of eternal truth they have discovered something incomparably more important than the city, and something also far more desirable as a good. They will consequently need to be *compelled* to take their turn at ruling. But patriotic conviction—'hard to wash out', and tested in every kind of trial—will remain writ deep in their souls: something Socrates stresses once again after he has introduced the topic of an education fit for philosopher rulers, even as he allows that the discussion back in Book 3 glided past and veiled the difficulty which would be presented by that perspective (6.503A).[41]

On this supposition it should follow that, however clear and universal the philosophical vision they enjoy outside the Cave, and however small human life appears from that perspective, or again however preoccupied they might be with the health and happiness of their own souls, nonetheless the philosophers' conviction of their political duty and the sense of their own identity that goes with it are so deeply entrenched that its unphilosophical and pre-dialectical dictates will in the end trump all other considerations.[42] The problem of adjusting perspective on re-entry to the Cave is alluded to, and may mean that they need *reminding* of it—hence the argument about reciprocation that Socrates imagines himself and the other interlocutors putting to them. But any lapse in recollection of what they have all along been committed to could be no more than temporary. And a reminder of their obligation, together with a statement of the contribution they are uniquely capable of making thanks to their philosophical grasp of truth, is all that will be necessary for them to recover themselves. In short, what Plato makes Socrates say, philosophically undemanding as it may be, turns out to be the appropriate thing to say, precisely because of the depth of the conviction and motivation it appeals to.

The city—any political community—is (to use the vocabulary of the contemporary political theorist Michael Walzer) an involuntary association. Most of us 'are born citizens (unless we are very unlucky) and are rarely invited to agree our citizenship'. The world of involuntary association does not function on the basis of purely rational values chosen by agents operating in conditions of ideal freedom. To picture things otherwise is 'an example of bad utopianism'. Most of the time, however, it 'gives us reasons for operating within that space rather than moving wholly outside it. These reasons include loyalty to particular people, the sense of being at home with those people, and the longing for generational continuity. Men and women who choose to operate within a given association are not necessarily victims of false consciousness.'[43] Plato's philosophers return to the Cave because they acknowledge their membership of their own involuntary association, and the power of the reasons for returning that—not philosophy—exerts upon them.

3. *Law and Religion*

3.1 Legislating for theocracy

'There never was a legislator', says Machiavelli (*Discorsi* 1.11), 'who in introducing extraordinary laws to a people did not have recourse to God, for otherwise they would not have been accepted, since many benefits of which a prudent man is aware are not so evident to reason that he can convince others of them.' And he goes on to name names: 'Hence wise men, in order to escape this difficulty, have recourse to God. So Lycurgus did; so did Solon, and so have many others who have had the same thing in view.'[44] Plato's Athenian Visitor is one of those others, and indeed in modern assessments is a more convincingly documented example—although, as we shall see, the religion of the *Laws* is to have a rational underpinning, and rational persuasion will be part and parcel of the dialogue's legislative enterprise. Here is the prayer (*Laws* 4.712B) with which the Visitor launches his discussion of the main project of the *Laws* in Book 4, following the preliminary discussions of the first three books:

Let us therefore call upon God as we undertake the founding of the city. May he hear our prayer, and having heard it come graciously and in kindly concern for us to join in establishing the ordering of the city and its laws.

The project is itself in some strong senses a religious project, and that is reflected and given symbolic expression in the Visitor's invocation—in the Greek, 'God' is in fact the first word of the prayer, as indeed it is the very first word of the whole dialogue (1.624A). It is made clear enough a little later in Book 1 that the project will also be a *critical* undertaking. The god-given status of Cretan law—supposedly imparted to Minos by Zeus himself (624A–B)—is quickly problematized, at least by implication. Cleinias, the Cretan participant in the conversation, thinks their laws are predicated on the assumption that war is a city's overarching aim (1.630D). But the argument has already shown that, if so, those laws rest on a misconception.[45] Cleinias is tempted to infer: 'So much the worse for our lawgiver.' The Visitor prefers to insist that Cleinias' premise must be mistaken: Lycurgus and Minos must have been wanting to promote the whole of virtue, not only courage (1.630D–631B). This is surely just politeness.[46] What is more important is the explicit association he goes on to make between virtue and the divine. The four cardinal virtues are 'divine goods', presumably because restraint and justice and courage all reflect wisdom (*phronêsis*)—and so all 'look to reason as their guide' (1.631B–D). The divine status of reason itself is spelled out subsequently, in Book 4, but for the present we can note the transformation which the very notion of god has in effect already undergone—the Visitor's god must be the rational god of the philosophers.[47]

Soon after the beginning of Book 4, the Visitor articulates an underlying assumption (4.709B): 'that the all-directing agent in human affairs is God, and together with God chance and opportunity'—although he goes on at once to say: 'A less uncompromising way of putting it is to acknowledge that there must be a third factor, expertise (technê), to follow up the other two.' Here again we may be reminded of Machiavelli, in the same chapter of the *Discorsi*, on Romulus' successor Numa Pompilius:

All things considered, therefore, I conclude that the religion introduced by Numa was among the primary causes of Rome's success, for this entailed good institutions; good institutions led to good fortune; and from good fortune arose the happy results of undertakings.

The Athenian Visitor's view is that within the framework of divine providence, there is scope for the skilled legislator to make the best of the opportunities chance may throw up. Religious observance inculcating a sense of divine power and divine justice turns out to be a priority for the legislator's agenda. His very first act (4.715E–718A) will be delivery of an address attempting to instil reverence for the gods in the immigrants who are to become the citizens of Magnesia—the new Cretan city whose foundation is being imagined. Solemn religious rhetoric conveying ethical imperatives buttressed by theology is what in the *Laws* takes the place of the *Republic*'s Noble Lie, in its function as a foundation myth for the founding generation of rulers of the good city.

What is the political framework within which the rhetoric is to function? The short answer is: theocracy. It is true that Plato never uses that word, and indeed that he perhaps makes the Visitor convey distaste for the idea that the best *politeia* should be called *any* sort of '-ocracy': no doubt because *kratos* suggests the domination (*despoteia*) of naked *power* (4.713A). But if it *were* to be given a name of that sort, the city the interlocutors are imagining that they are founding should be called after the 'god who exercises true domination (*despozontos*) over those who have reason' (ibid.)'. That god turns out to be Cronos, according to Greek theology displaced as supreme deity by Zeus, but treated here as reason itself. The main argument for this claim about divinity and rationality runs from 713A–715D. From a retelling of the myth of the Golden Age of Cronos, the Athenian derives what he represents as the truth that 'wherever cities have a mortal, not a god, for ruler, there is no respite for them from miseries and hardships' (713E). The right *politeia* will therefore be one in which reason—the immortal element in us—is what we obey.[48] And an ordering of the city in accordance with reason can be named 'law'.[49] Then the Athenian discusses and dismisses an alternative view of things: the idea that justice is the advantage of whichever faction in the city is strongest. He ends with a linguistic innovation. When law is at the mercy of the ruler, ruin for the city is not far off; 'rulers' ought to be, and be called, 'servants of the law'[50]—and then we shall see salvation and (to return to the point of departure) the blessings gods bestow on cities.

So the account of the rationally ordered law-based *politeia* of the *Laws* as—in the sense defined—a theocracy is what provides the background for the oration the Visitor envisages being delivered to the first citizens of Magnesia on their arrival. As in many passages of the dialogue, Plato seems to have multiple audiences in view.[51] At the beginning and end of the oration, it is certainly the new colonists who are the target of persuasion. Thus the speech starts with a contrast between the just and god-fearing person who will secure happiness, and (described much more eloquently and at much greater length) the unjust, who in his abandonment by god will before long bring total ruin to himself, his family and his city.[52] After some intricate discussion designed to stress the basis of piety in sound moral character, the speech turns to its main and final business: a hierarchically structured exhortation to perform religious duties. Here there are two curiosities. Much the greater part of this concluding section is taken up with the need to give *parents* due respect in life and in death alike: this is the message about proper piety that the new colonists will have ringing in their ears as they disperse (4.717B–718A). The emphasis is all of a piece with the gerontocratically flavoured paternalism permeating the whole of the *Laws*. Treatment of the honours to be paid to gods (Olympian, civic, underworld), *daimones* (divine guardian spirits) and heroes is much more cursory (717A–B),[53] and seems to be preoccupied with an esoterically expressed Pythagorean ranking of Olympian over underworld gods. At this juncture Plato seems to be talking more to his intimates in the Academy (who will already have been alerted by the Orphic theological quotation which launches the speech: 715E–716A) than to the colonists.

What animates the conception of religion in the laws is not reverence for the gods of Homer and Hesiod, but something else: 'for the author of the *Laws*, it is the stars that are the real gods'.[54] That does not mean that Plato envisages the abolition of traditional cults for other deities. Early in Book 5 he writes a striking passage on Apollo's oracles at Delphi and similar oracles elsewhere, in which the Athenian Visitor is made to declare that none of their injunctions nor any other long-established religious practices ought to be subjected to even the slightest alteration by the legislator (5.738B–D; cf. 6.759A–760A).[55] The *Laws* accordingly recognizes (for example) Zeus the Protector of the City (11.921C; cf. 5.745B, 8.842E), Zeus god of strangers (5.730A, 8.843A, 12.953E), Zeus god of tribesmen (8.843A). Again, it makes provision for the proper observance of funeral rites that will respect the divinity of the gods both of the underworld and of this world (12.958C–960C). Further examples would be easy to list.[56]

But the dialogue is not undiscriminating in matters of religion. Religious practice is in fact strictly controlled. The Visitor prohibits the introduction of unauthorized private cults, principally on the grounds that they often involve witchcraft of various kinds (including necromancy: 10.909D–910E; cf. 11.933A–E). He associates such practices with atheism, which is notoriously to be punished in extreme cases with death, or (worse) with solitary confinement and (as with the Polyneices of Sophocles' *Antigone*) deprivation of rights to burial in the city's territory (10.907D–910E). And he requires the institution of not less than 365 festivals, so that every day of the year there will be sacrificing to a god or *daimôn* on behalf of the city, the citizens and their possessions. There are to be monthly feasts to the twelve gods who give their names to the twelve tribes into which the city body is distributed (8.828A–D).[57] The objective? 'To ensure first that we enjoy the favour of the gods, and promote their cult; and second that we should become familiar and well acquainted with each other, and promote every kind of social contact (6.771D).' An earlier passage adds that there is no greater good for the city than such mutual knowledge—transparency promotes sincerity (5.738D–E).

In prescribing monthly sacrifices the Visitor refers to the need to conform to 'the revolution of the universe' (6.771B). He does not identify the astral deities who are presumably to be the true recipients of this worship. But a belief in the divinity of the heavenly bodies is evidently what the astronomical reference implies. Plato gives this old belief a new underpinning, first with an insistence on a proper education in an up-to-date astronomy (8.820E–822C) and then with a theological explanation of the motions of the heavenly bodies (10.897B–899B). But there is another no less significant innovation. As E. R. Dodds commented:[58]

The great novelty in Plato's project for religious reform was the emphasis he laid, not merely on the divinity of sun, moon, and stars (for that was nothing new),[59] but on their cult. In the Laws, not only are the stars described as "the gods in heaven", the sun and moon as "great gods", but Plato insists that prayer and sacrifice shall be made to them by all; and the focal point of his new State Church is to be a joint cult of Apollo and the sun-god Helios, to which the High Priest will be attached and the highest political officers will be solemnly dedicated.[60]

This ceremony is one that requires the whole city to gather together for the purpose (12.945E).

What is remarkable about the Laws is not that it makes religion so central to its argument. The centrality of religion to the life and well-being of a city is something most of Plato's contemporaries would have accepted without demur. The religious historian Christina Sourvinou-Inwood writes:[61]

The Greek polis articulated religion and was itself articulated by it; religion became the polis' central ideology, structuring, and giving meaning to, all the elements that made up the identity of the polis, its past, its physical landscape, the relationship between its constituent parts. Ritual reinforces group solidarity, and this process is of fundamental importance in establishing and perpetuating civic and cultural, as well as religious, identities. ... The perception that religion was the centre of the polis also explains, and is revealed in, a variety of stories and practices. It is also related to the perception that it is the relationship of the polis with its gods that ultimately guarantees its existence.

Plato however thinks through this conception of religion quite explicitly as an integrated and overarching ideology, not just in a few pivotal passages, but at many different levels: including many of the explanations supplied for specific pieces of legislation, as well as in prescriptions for cult and in the theology worked out towards the end of the dialogue in Book 10. The Laws thus constitutes a systematic exploration of the way religion should perform its ideological role unparalleled until Augustine's *City of God*. There is nothing to match it in Aristotle's treatment of an ideal *politieia* in Books 7 and 8 of the *Politics*, for example, despite their many other echoes of the *Laws*.

3.2 Moral rhetoric

The Athenian Visitor offers some commentary on the address he has given to the Magnesian colonists, and particularly about its bearing on the theory and practice of legislation (4.718C–D). Reflection on it will assist us to analyse the characteristic features of the *Laws'* main mode of religious discourse:

Athenian: I should like the citizens to be as open to persuasion towards goodness as is possible to achieve; and clearly this is the outcome the legislator will try to promote throughout his legislation.
Cleinias: Of course.
Athenian: It occurs to me that the sort of approach I've just articulated, provided it is not addressed to an utterly savage soul, will help to make people more amenable and better disposed to listen to what the lawgiver recommends. So even if the address has no great effect, but only makes the listener a trifle easier to handle, and so that much easier to teach, the legislator should be well pleased. People who are eager to achieve moral excellence as much and fast as they can are pretty thin on the ground. Most only go to prove the wisdom of Hesiod's remark that 'easy is the road to vice' and that it's no sweat to travel it, since it's very short, but (he says)

> In the approach to goodness the immortal gods
> Have set the sweat of toil. The path
> Is long and steep, and rough at first.
> But when the crest is won, hard though it be
> Easy then the road is to endure.

This is a very different paternalism from that implicit in the telling of the *Republic*'s Noble Lie.

The contrast might be expressed as one between an Athenian and a Socratic form of paternalism. The distinction may be approached by asking how Plato might have gone about the business of working out the means by which the population of the ideal *politeia* of the *Republic* might be got to accept an ideology motivating care for the city. If I am right that the whole intellectual project of the *Republic* is a *Socratic* project[62]—an attempt to think through how Socrates might have conceived of an ideal political system—then at this point, too, Plato may have tried to draw on Socratic resources, and found himself turning to the category of useful or medicinal lies (I have argued in Section 2 of this chapter that Socrates himself may well have had resort to this idea): hence the Noble Lie, and in that sense a Socratic form of paternalism. In the *Laws*, on the other hand, there should be no surprise if the Athenian Visitor who leads the conversation looks to a very different resource in considering how the population can be brought to accept and internalize the values which underpin the good city he is imagining. Section 2.3 of this chapter drew attention to Athenian pride in the openness and honesty of their public discourse, and their apprehensions of the threat to democracy posed by lying speakers. The resort to public persuasion that the Visitor advocates here should be seen as precisely the kind of approach an *Athenian statesman* of Solonian stamp (we still possess some of the poems Solon addressed to his fellow citizens on social and political disorder and its remedy) could be expected to adopt. The resulting rhetoric differs from the Noble Lie in a number of significant ways accordingly. Above all, as Dodds argues, religion in the *Laws* is not 'simply a pious lie, a fiction maintained for its social usefulness'.[63] He suggested an alternative interpretation: 'Rather it reflects or symbolizes religious truth at the level of *eikasia* [imagination] at which it can be assimilated by the people. Plato's universe was a graded one: as he believed in degrees of truth and reality, so he believed in degrees of religious insight.'

In the first place, citizens are to be addressed as the adults they are, capable of understanding general propositions in ethics, and not treated as if they were children for whom 'stories' would be the appropriate mechanisms for communicating the truths they need to grasp. This becomes yet more apparent when at the end of Book 4 the Athenian undertakes to cover for their benefit the topics so far omitted in the oration with which the new settlers are to be greeted (723D–724B). The first nine pages of Book 5 (5.726A–734E) offer a highly abstract account (delivered—like the whole of the book—as a monologue) of the right valuation to be set on the soul and the body and on property; then of proper social dealings with friends, relatives, foreigners and other citizens; next the excellences of character that should be developed, beginning with trustworthiness, stressing virtues that are socially oriented, and condemning self-love as the most pernicious of vices; and turning finally from questions like these, which one way or another involve consideration of the higher and potentially more 'divine' aspects of human nature, to the problem of how to deal with the merely human phenomenon of pleasure and pain. In fact the passage constitutes an impressive lesson in *souci de soi*—a primer of proper self-respect. The Visitor prefaces all of this with an injunction (5.726A): 'Everyone who was listening to the address just now about the gods and our dearly beloved ancestors should now pay attention.' In the first instance that presumably means the assembled original settlers, as the prime target audience for that address. But as we have seen several other audiences were also being spoken to. And no doubt you and I—the readers—are included.

Second, and relatedly, whereas the Noble Lie is aimed primarily at the carefully educated elite that Plato imagines as rulers and defenders of the *Republic*'s good city, the citizens who are to benefit from the exercises in moral rhetoric of *Laws* 4.715E–718A and 5.726A–734E are conceived as ordinary people, with an ordinary capacity for moral improvement not yet fostered by distinctively Platonic education—like many of the readers the author of the dialogue is doubtless envisaging.[64] They are neither very uncivilized (no one with an utterly savage soul) nor in general eager for moral excellence. These assumptions are sustained throughout the dialogue (9.853C–D):

Unlike the ancient legislators, we are not framing laws for heroes and sons of gods. The lawgivers of that age, according to the story told nowadays, were descended from gods and legislated for people of similar stock. But we are human beings, legislating in the world today for the children of human beings, and we shall give no offence by our fear that one of our citizens will turn out to be, so to speak, a 'tough egg', whose character will be so 'hard-boiled' as to resist softening; powerful as our laws are, they may not be able to tame such people, just as heat has no effect on tough beans.

A bit later in Book 5, in fact as a preface to the first substantive topic the Visitor proposes (selection of office-holders, deferred to Book 6), there is discussion of the general problem of ensuring that the population contains no bad elements. The Visitor contemplates introducing drastic measures for purging these. But partly because he does not want to assume that his legislator has dictatorial powers, and partly because his project is a theoretical one, he advocates the prophylactic strategy of thorough advance screening, to prevent the vicious from becoming citizens in the first place (5.735A–736C). As for the moral rhetoric to which the potentially virtuous potential backsliders are to be exposed on arrival, he recognizes that he may have to settle for an outcome that leaves many of them just 'more amenable'—'a trifle easier to handle, and so that much easier to teach' (4.718D).[65] This formulation has been taken as suggesting that 'the purpose of persuasion is to win over the emotions of those addressed'.[66] It is true that the opening passage of the speech to the immigrants, for example, is designed among other things to instil fear of the penalty for living an unjust life: abandonment by God, total ruin for oneself, one's household and one's city (4.716A–B). But thereafter, while the rhetoric will have its desired effect only with someone who aspires to self-respect and wants to avoid self-damage, the appeal is generally to the understanding—although (given the nature of the audience) not to an intellectual appetite for philosophical dialectic. The Visitor's expression 'easier to *teach*' therefore deserves to be allowed its full weight.

Third, with the shift in focus from the ruling classes of a rigidly stratified society (as in the *Republic*) to a much more homogeneous community comes simplification of the content of the rhetoric. The legislator of the *Laws* can concentrate all his talk on moral goodness: for example, on 'enlarging cities' through the social influence of virtue (5.731A). The Noble Lie, by contrast, was necessarily oriented to more explicitly political concerns. It had to justify and communicate the imperative of keeping ruling, military and business classes uncontaminated, yet at the same time to insist on the brotherhood of all the citizens. The *Laws* consigns business activity to *non*-citizens, and in making the citizens a more homogeneous body with a considerable degree of equality (e.g. in property holdings, in communal eating arrangements and in educational experience) it thereby generates conditions in which friendship might be expected to flourish. In other words, it attempts to solve by a combination of moral education and social engineering a political problem for which the *Republic* had suggested something else was also essential: acquisition of a specifically political conviction of the need to care for the city.

I have been speaking of moral education. The Visitor himself presents the treatment of soul, body and property he is about to launch into at the start of Book 5 as a contribution to education (4.724B). Moreover, both the original address to the settlers (4.715E–718A) and its continuation (5.726A–734E) are presented as together constituting the 'prelude' to the entire legislative programme (5.734E; cf. 4.723D–724A).[67] And when reflecting in general terms on preludes, the Visitor remarks that the legislator who prefaces his laws with preludes is not legislating—i.e. not *merely* making law—but 'is educating the citizens' (9.857E). This evaluation, together with the style and content of the speeches to the settlers that we have been considering, strongly suggests that Plato conceives the rhetoric of a prelude as designed primarily to appeal to reason, and indeed to encourage development of a rational approach to life—for example, in the way one thinks of soul, body and property.[68] It is only reinforced by the illustration the Athenian provides of the difference between law as bare prescription and law in the 'double' version incorporating a prelude, when introducing the topic of preludes (4.721A–E):

Athenian: Now then, to start with, let's have the simple form. It might run more or less like this:

A man must marry between the ages of thirty and thirty-five. If he does not, he must be punished by fines and disgrace—

And the fines and disgrace will then be specified. So much for the simple version of the marriage law. This will be the double version:

A man must marry between the ages of thirty and thirty-five, reflecting that there is a sense in which nature has not only somehow endowed the human race with a degree of immortality, but also planted in us all a longing to achieve it, which we express in every way we can. One expression of that is the desire for fame and the wish not to lie nameless in the grave. Thus mankind is by nature a companion of eternity, and is linked to it, and will be linked to it, forever. Mankind is immortal because it always leaves later generations behind to preserve its unity and identity for all time: it gets its share of immortality by procreation. It is never a holy thing voluntarily to deny oneself this prize, and he who neglects to take a wife and have children does precisely that. So if a man obeys the law he will be allowed to go his way without penalty, but if a man disobeys, and reaches the age of thirty-five without having married, he must pay a yearly fine (of a sum to be specified; that ought to stop him thinking that life as a bachelor is all cakes and ale), and be deprived too of all the honours which the younger people in the city pay to their elders on appropriate occasions.

In amplifying the core prescription, this sample prelude offers a rational explanation of its propriety in terms of a theory of human nature, and—because of the affinity to divine nature exhibited in the account—of a consequential religious imperative making marriage something mandatory.

The exemplary prelude on marriage has incurred criticism. R. F. Stalley comments:[69]

There undoubtedly is an argument here, but it is an embarrassingly bad one. ... It seeks to attach the rather vague yearnings for immortality which most people are supposed to have to a very specific law about the age of marriage, without any attempt to justify the claim that all men by nature desire immortality, or to demonstrate that we ought to act on this desire, or to show that this requires marriage between the age of thirty and thirty-five. The fact that Plato himself failed to act on the law only intensifies one's suspicions.

These remarks fail to take account of the main datum Plato obviously seeks to explain: the fundamental truth about humans that—as with many other species—sexual reproduction is their means of perpetuating themselves indefinitely. What the marriage prelude assumes is the idea that this is our way of approximating to immortality or to eternal being, and is what as such explains sexual desire (as well as the other sorts of desire Plato mentions). That idea is one both Plato and Aristotle spell out elsewhere.[70] As a piece of explanation it imports some substantial metaphysics, but neither the metaphysics nor the explanation is lacking in rational appeal, even if neither will be likely to win many converts in a post-Darwinian intellectual era.

It is interesting that Plato opts for a *metaphysical* premise with theological resonances. It would have been possible to argue the need for a law requiring marriage on grounds of political utility. Indeed, the selection of the right time for a man to marry as between thirty and thirty-five is so specific that the legislator and his audience must anyway be supposed to have a fairly complex and particular set of social and political considerations in mind. Here it is important to appreciate—against what Stalley claims—that the prelude does *not* treat the requirement of marriage at that age as *following* from the metaphysical explanation of the desires it alludes to: in that sense no *argument* is here presented for the requirement. That only goes to confirm that the persuasive rhetoric of the prelude is designed to do something else: to get people to see themselves and their lives in a framework larger than politics—in fact in the light of the theological ethics that is articulated in the speeches to the newly arrived citizens of Magnesia.

The *Laws'* paternalism typically functions through sermons rather than myths, at least so far as the adult population is concerned. It is still paternalism. Regulations are to be written 'in the styles of a loving and prudent father and mother', not 'posted on walls as instructions and threats the way that a tyrant or despot would do' (9.859A). What is *not* envisaged is the tabling of the legal code which shapes the life of the city and its citizens for open debate. There is no provision for them to vote on whether to accept or reject any of its articles, still less to develop a political culture in which choosing between such alternatives would be a meaningful exercise.[71] The legislator knows best; and the preambles with which his laws are prefaced or 'doubled' educate the citizens by providing a reasoned account of what is good for them and for the city, and above all by explaining the way the 'divine' goods constituted by the virtues of character are fostered by his legislation. He 'gives advice on what is noble and good and just, teaching people about what it consists in and how it should be reflected in our conduct if we are to be happy' (9.858D). The ingredients of which advice in the preludes is made up are broadly the same as we have identified in the rhetoric of the addresses to the original settlers and in the sample prelude on marriage. It is true that in the law on homicide there are a number of increasingly elaborate references to the respect due to the 'ancient myth' that the spirit of the murdered man turns his anguish and fury in vengeance on his murderer (9.865D–E, 870D–E, 872D–873A). But myths are the exception, not the rule, and are apparently envisaged (as at 870A–E) only as supplementary to the generalities more usual in preludes.

3.3 Philosophical foundations

With Book 9 (on criminal law) the *Laws* moves into a different register. It presents the reader with a more challenging set of reflections on law and the business of legislation. Fairly early on in the book, the Athenian raises the issue of inconsistencies in moral vocabulary and belief, as a preface to discussion of a major problem for the whole project (9.860E–861C): ordinary language accepts a distinction between voluntary and involuntary acts of injustice, but he holds that nobody is unjust willingly (a version of the famous Socratic paradox, although Socrates' name is never mentioned). There follows a dense and difficult discussion with Cleinias of the difference between harm and injustice, and of the various ways a distinction between voluntary and involuntary might be conceived and applied (roughly speaking, the Athenian wants to restrict its use in the legislative context to harmful acts).[72] This is followed in turn by consideration of the different psychological causes of wrongdoing, and the senses in which it is due to ignorance, functioning as a prelude to laws on theft, and including perhaps 'the most radical penological manifesto ever written' (861C–864C).[73] Another example: a few pages later, in introducing his legislation on grievous bodily harm, the Visitor prefaces it with some observations on law as an expedient, second-best to the knowledge of an expert ruler with the best interests of the city at heart. These remarks strike a note not obviously in harmony with the idea of law as the expression of divine reason celebrated in the Cronos myth of Book 4, and rather closer to its treatment in the *Statesman* (295A) as something valid only for 'the majority of cases' (9.875D). They serve to launch a general discussion (875D–876E) on the desirability if possible, when someone has been convicted of a criminal offence, of letting juries assess penalties to suit the individual case. The punishments the Visitor then goes on to propose for different types of case are accordingly presented merely as 'models' for those giving judgment to imitate.

The following Book 10 is almost entirely given over to a long and elaborate proof (which serves as the prelude to the law on impiety) that providential gods exist.[74] Not merely is this a quite different kind of prelude from any of its predecessors, but it assumes a different audience and constitutes a different genre of religious discourse. First, the audience. The Visitor suggests that blasphemous talk or behaviour will typically be perpetrated by people with no scruples whatsoever. What makes them unscrupulous is either that they are out-and-out atheists, or that they think the gods have either no interest in human affairs or (if they have) can be bought off (10.885B–E). Young people in particular are represented as vulnerable to relativist or reductionist views about the gods and about moral values (888B, 890A). *They* constitute the primary audience that needs to be persuaded of the truth. The Visitor is quite explicit that he is principally thinking of the situation at Athens (886A–B), but Cleinias takes him to be describing something that potentially threatens public and private life in cities at large. So the theological arguments of Book 10 have a relevance not confined to Athens or indeed to Magnesia. And they require of the interlocutors Cleinias and Megillus an altogether more strenuous and sophisticated intellectual engagement than they have had to display so far. The Visitor invokes an analogy with travellers attempting to ford a river in flood (892D–893A):

Imagine the three of us had to cross a river in spate, and I were the younger and had plenty of experience of currents. Suppose I said, 'I ought to try first on my own account, and leave you two in safety while I see if the river is fordable for you two older men as well, or if not, just how bad it is. If it turns out to be fordable, I'll then call you across and put my experience at your disposal in helping you to cross; but if in the event it cannot be crossed by old men like yourselves, then the only risk has been mine.' Wouldn't that strike you as fair enough? The situation is the same now: the argument ahead runs too deep, and men as weak as you will probably get out of your depth. I want to prevent you novices in answering from being dazed and dizzied by a stream of questions, which would put you in an undignified and humiliating position you'd find most unpleasant.

But Cleinias at any rate is portrayed as equal to the challenge, once the argument gets under way, and is even credited with a modest number of independent responses and suggestions.

Right at the outset the argument is marked as a prelude (885B). In fact Cleinias has not heard much about atheism and its dire moral effects before he is insisting that such an argument 'would be the best and finest prelude we could have to *all* our laws' (887C), even if it is protracted (890D–891A) and might be thought to 'step outside legislation' (891D–E). Once written down it can be examined and gone over again and again, he comments, by people who find learning difficult (890E–891A).

Presumably Plato is not meaning to indicate that the theological argument of Book 10 would after all have been the best initial introduction to the dialogue's legislative project for the audience envisaged back in Books 4 and 5. The point is doubtless rather that once the theistic underpinnings of the project are *challenged*, a philosophical argument proving the existence of gods and the nature of their control over human affairs would *then* provide it with the ideal preface (it is only in the later books of the dialogue that Plato is ready to move into a more reflective mode capable of accommodating such challenges). The proof is beautifully integrated with the focus of the earlier prefaces on a proper understanding of the soul and its primacy over the body. Its core ingredient is the argument that the first source of all movement and change must be soul, which therefore has to be what governs the universe (893C–896E). And the rational order of the universe is such that we may infer the divinity of the soul that is its cause (896E–899D). The Visitor then assumes that such a being must be omniscient, omnipotent and supremely good, from which it must follow that the gods exercise a providence over all things, human affairs included (900C–905B). Humans for their part need to remember that the universe exists 'not for your benefit—it is you that exist for its sake', as a part exists to contribute to the whole (903B–D).

Here is a form of religious discourse which—unlike the sermons that constitute the other preludes—really does *argue* for its first principles. But a question remains concerning what status we should suppose we are to accord to the theology of Book 10 of the *Laws*. Is it 'Plato's theology'—i.e. the theory about the divine that we can suppose to represent Plato's own best guess on the subject? Or is it rather what one might call his civic or political theology—i.e. that theological system, no doubt seen by him as that true theological system, which gives the kind of foundation for the religious political theory of the dialogue that will justify its pervasively religious cast as well as the moral order it asserts? The second option is the more cautious interpretation—assessing the *Laws*' theology as it does relative to its function in the dialogue, and to what might be called *philosophical limitation*.[75] In the formulation of R. Hackforth:[76]

Plato is not concerned to give us the whole of his metaphysics, or even of his philosophy of religion; in the *Laws* his object is to lay down the necessary minimum of philosophical doctrine required for a sound basis of religion and morality; and from that point of view it was not necessary to go into the difficult question of the relation of *nous* [intellect] to the universe, or (what is the same thing) the relation of *nous* to *psuchê* [soul], the principle of movement in the universe. Indeed it would have been unreasonable to expect Cleinias and Megillus, or the citizen body to whom the 'preambles' to the laws are addressed, to follow him if he had. As Timaeus says (*Tim.* 28C): 'To find the maker and father of this universe is hard enough, and even if I succeeded, to declare him to everyone is impossible.' Why should that be 'impossible' in the *Timaeus* if it can be done by straightforward scientific argument in the *Laws*?

Someone inclined to take this second 'civic theology' option might want to leave open the possibility that in other contexts Plato would have located the truest form of divinity elsewhere than in soul. One such possibility might be intellect conceived as a more ultimate cause (the *Philebus'* position, and indeed implicit in the *Laws'* own treatment of law as divine because it is the voice of reason). Another might be something metaphysically fundamental such as—in the *Republic's* scheme of things—the Form of the Good.

4. *Conclusion*

Plato's decision to construct the political discourse of the *Laws* within a religious framework is not hard to fathom. I take it that he wanted three things above all of the rhetoric he was to develop in dialogue, in the most sustained and complex exercise in ideology he ever attempted. First, the rhetoric should reflect and embody a sense of a transcendent moral framework for political and social existence. Second, it should be capable of being persuasive—and above all generally intelligible—to the population at large, not to just an intellectual elite, provided they are prepared by their education and acculturation to listen to reason. Third, and consequently, it should be effective in promoting a respect for law and attachment to virtue. As Sections 3.1 and 2 have indicated, it was religious discourse, reformed and redirected as necessary, which could best meet these three requirements.

There is nothing much here which political liberals of any persuasion will find congenial. Yet liberalism has arguably failed to provide from its own resources a convincing explanation of what it is that makes a society cohesive.[77] In most places at most times—perhaps pre-Buddhist China is the major exception—it is religion that has played a key ideological role in cementing societies together. Conceivably the relative social calm enjoyed by materialistic Western democracies in the post-Christian era of the last half of the twentieth century was the aberration. Certainly religion has once again become a major ingredient in the life of some nation states—and in their global interactions—in a way that would have seemed inconceivable forty or fifty years ago. So Plato's concern that the religion shaping the life of a society should be rational religion may be something that social and political theorists need to take seriously again.

Notes

1. As noted in Ch. 5 (p. 245 n. 63), this perception supplies the organizing theme for Pradeau 2002.
2. See e.g. Geuss 1981; Thompson 1984.
3. There are many formulations of ideology as descriptive term currently on offer. This one combines elements from Geuss 1981: 10 and Figueira 2002: 147.
4. The basic sources for the myth of the Spartoi are Apollodorus, *Library* 3.4.1; and Hyginus, *Fabulae* 178–9: both compilations of perhaps the second century AD. Pausanias (of the same period) also knows the story: *Description of Greece* 8.11.8, 9.5.3, 9.10.1. But it is of much earlier origin, as can be inferred not only from Plato's use of it but e.g. from Pherecydes Fr.22 [Jacoby]; Aeschylus, *Seven against Thebes* 474; Euripides, *Phoenician Women* 931–46.
5. See Loraux 1993: ch. 1.
6. Although the Hellenistic poet Apollonius Rhodius would only have been spurred on by the challenge: as in the baroque Homeric similes with which he attempts to capture Jason's ploughing of a field of earthborn sown warriors at the end of the third book of the *Argonautica* (3.1354–1407). Ovid's treatment of Cadmus' sown men is tame by comparison: *Metamorphoses* 3.95–114.
7. See further Section 2.4 below.
8. John Ferrari has a good note on the question: 'The lie is grand or noble (*gennaios*) by virtue of its civic purpose, but the Greek word can also be used colloquially, giving the meaning 'a true-blue lie', i.e. a massive, no-doubt-about-it lie (compare the term 'grand larceny').' See Ferrari and Griffith 2000: 107 n. 63. Ironic uses in Plato of the word *gennaios* are documented in Jowett and Campbell 1894: III.46 (on 348C).

9. On the sophisticated embarrassment Plato communicates through Socrates' comments on the story, see further Section 5 of Schofield 2007, forthcoming.

10. This was not the only occasion on which Plato drew on Hesiod's myth of ages and combined it with something Cadmeian. Along with other mythical resources, it is put to quite different use in his dialogue *Statesman*: see *Plt.* 270C–272E, where the account of the Golden Age incorporates the idea that humans then were 'earthborn'. For a stimulating interpretation of Hesiod's original, despite the exaggeration of its denial that the decline of the human race is what he is illustrating, see Most 1997.

11. The myth makes no pretence that being of bronze or iron race is just as good in its way as being golden or silver. There is an elite club within the ideal city: promotion (*anaxousi*) and expulsion (*ôsousin*) are therefore the appropriate vocabulary, although Plato makes Socrates talk of an appropriate 'honour' (*timê, timêsantes*) accorded by both of the processes.

12. See e.g. Morris 1996; Raaflaub 1996.

13. See Loraux 1986. For more on the *Menexenus*, see Ch. 2, Section 2.3, above.

14. See Ch. 1, Section 5 above.

15. See further Section 3.1 below.

16. See p. 287 (with n. 8) above.

17. Cornford 1941: 106.

18. Popper 1961: 107.

19. Dunn 1993: 116. Williams 2005: ch. 13 argues that political principles and social forces favouring democratic freedom of expression as a bulwark against the tyranny of power do not necessarily nor obviously promote a system well adjusted to discovering and transmitting truth or to fostering truthfulness (on the part either of rulers or ruled). Plato would have agreed: see Ch. 2, Section 2.

20. Detienne and Vernant 1978. Quotations from pp. 3–4, 107.

21. For an excellent treatment of the material surveyed in this paragraph (and of a great range of similar evidence), see Hesk 2000.

22. In the prelude introducing legislation to govern sale and exchange of goods the *Laws* construes adulteration of coinage as a form of lying and deceit, and treats someone who does it as in effect guilty of swearing a false oath. It pronounces that anyone who commits this sort of crime will be 'most hateful to the gods' (cf. *Rep.* 2.382A) as well as liable to a flogging (*Laws* 11.916D–918A).

23. For fuller treatment of the topic covered in this paragraph, see e.g. Ferrari 1989: 108–19; cf. also Burnyeat 1999.

24. Popper 1961: 138.

25. The relevant texts are: Plutarch, *On Stoic Contradictions* 1055F–1056A, 1057A–B; Sextus Empiricus, *Adversus Mathematicos* 7.42–5; Stobaeus, *Eclogae* 2.111.10–17; Quintilian, *Institutio* 12.1.38. For discussion, see Bobzien 1998: 271–4.

26. See Bok 1978: ch. 3. Although in the end absolutist, Augustine's treatment of the topic (primarily in *De Mendacio* [late 390s AD] and *Contra Mendacium* [422 AD]) is highly nuanced and extremely subtle: for an analysis, see Kirwan 1989: 196–204.

27. Williams 2002: ch. 5.

28. Adam 1902: II.4.

29. Does 7.535D–E suggest otherwise? According to Socrates a 'crippled' soul hates telling or hearing a deliberate lie, and gets terribly cross about it, but puts up with the 'unwilling lie', wallowing in ignorance and experiencing no distress when its ignorance is revealed for what it is. This is someone who has an inverted and perverted sense of the relative importance of the lie in words and the lie in the soul. It would be wrong to infer that lies in words are *not* to be viewed with distaste. But they are small beer compared with 'true' lies.

30. Arendt 1968: 298 n. 5.

31. Page 1991: 2.

32. Here I am summarizing material presented more fully in Section 2.1 above.

33. But I replace Griffith's 'guardian' with 'guard': see Ch. 1, p. 49, n. 67.

34. For an emphatic statement of this point, see Hahm 1969.

35. For further discussion of this passage, see Ch. 5, Section 5.1, above.

36. Whether their counterparts elsewhere would be regarded by Socrates as having any political obligations reciprocating for their education and upbringing is a moot point. If one supposed it legitimate to extend the argument made by the laws of Athens in the *Crito* to other cities generally, an affirmative answer might be inferred. But the *Republic* takes the view that in most actual or conceivable *politeiai* education and upbringing are so deficient that keeping one's hands free from impiety and injustice may often be the most one can reasonably expect of a philosopher (cf. 6.496A–E, 9.592A–B).

37. For this reading of Socrates' argument as an appeal to justice as reciprocity, see e.g. Gill 1996: 287–307; Nightingale 2004: 131–7.

38. Here I glide past issues much debated in recent scholarship. See e.g. Annas 1978; Dahl 1991; Smith 1997.

39. This argumentation in the *Crito* has been much discussed. For a powerful recent treatment, see Harte 1999.

40. For an excellent recent review of the debate about the issue, see Brown 2000; cf. also Sedley 2007a, forthcoming.

41. Adam has a good note on this point: see Adam 1902: II.46.

42. For the concept of the pre-dialectical (in contrast to the post-reflective) in the ethics of the *Republic*, see Gill 1996: chs 4.4 and 4.5 (e.g. at pp. 267–8).

43. For these quotations, see Walzer 2004a: 1, 8, 12.

44. The stakes, he argued (ibid.), are high: 'As the observance of divine worship is the cause of greatness in republics, so the neglect of it is the cause of their ruin. Because where the fear of God is wanting, it comes about either that the kingdom is ruined, or that it is kept going by the fear of a prince, which makes up for the lack of religion.' But that provides only a temporary stay of execution: 'princes are short-lived'.

45. See further Ch. 1, Section 5, pp. 41–2.

46. Cf. Strauss 1975: 6.

47. See, for example, the theological fragments of the Presocratic philosopher poet Xenophanes: Kirk, Raven and Schofield 1983: 168–72.

48. The chief object of statesmanship and legislation is throughout the dialogue identified as producing *virtue* in the citizens (see e.g. 12.963A). But the

Laws makes virtue itself a matter of the control of passions and appetites by reason—so that while this is achieved most immediately through courage and restraint, courage and restraint depend above all on the wise judgement that is assured by reason (see e.g. 1.631B–D; cf. also 5.726A).

49. Plato suggests an etymological derivation of *nomos* (law) from *nous* (reason). The god with whose name *nous* is associated is presumably Cronos—at any rate if Plato has in mind the etymology of Cronos in the *Cratylus*: *koros noū*, 'undefiled purity of reason' (*Crat.* 396B). Strauss suggests that Plato here 'conceals completely the fact that the rule of law is the rule of laws laid down by human beings' (Strauss 1975: 58). But the *Laws* never pretends that law is anything other than the work of human legislators. It is simply that at this point the godlike quality of the rationality that needs to inform human legislation is what it wants to emphasize.

50. An interestingly different recommendation from the *Republic*'s proposal that they be called 'saviours' and 'helpers' (5.463A–B): although salvation is still the goal.

51. See Schofield 2003.

52. Even here, however, Plato cannot resist painting what is pretty clearly yet another portrait of the young Alcibiades and his downfall—evidently for a knowing Athenian audience. In the immediate sequel (716B–D) the Visitor seems to break off for a brief conversation with Cleinias which plays with Protagoras' famous 'man the measure' thesis, and with Plato's own favourite theme of assimilation to god—here cast in terms of the love of like for like: 'In our view it is God who is preeminently the "measure of all things", much more so than any "man", as they claim. So someone who is to become a person loved by a god of such a nature must so far as possible make his own nature like God's. So on this reasoning those of us whose characters are marked by restraint will be loved by God, because they are like him, whereas the person who is not restrained is unlike him and at odds with him—and the unjust person, too; and the same reasoning applies to all the other virtues and vices.' When the Visitor resumes the speech proper (at 716D), it is now as though he is—for a while, at least—telling Cleinias how it will go, rather than actually delivering it.

53. E. R. Dodds found 'little or no religious warmth in any of Plato's references' to the gods of traditional religion: Dodds 1945: 22.

54. Reverdin 1945: 52.

55. The authority for the ideal city of Apollo at Delphi in all matters of religion was already pronounced as 'the greatest, noblest, and first of all laws' in the *Republic* (4.427B–C).

56. See e.g. Morrow 1960: 434–70.

57. Further complications—entailing more monthly gatherings for sacrificial purposes—are spelled out not altogether lucidly at 6.771A–772A (see Thompson 1965).

58. Dodds 1951: 220–1; cf. Dodds 1945: 24–5.

59. But Plato gave it a more strenuous astronomical and theological basis, in the cosmology of the *Timaeus* and the theology of Book 10 of the *Laws*.

60. See especially 8.820E–822C, 12.945E–947E. As Morrow says (1960: 447–8): 'The identification of Apollo with the brightest of the astral gods provides a

natural bridge between the common man's ideas and those of the intellectuals.'

61. Sourvinou-Inwood 1990: 304–6.
62. See Ch. 1, Section 2.
63. See Dodds 1951: 234 n. 89; cf. Dodds 1945: 23–4. At the same time one suspects that Plato will have found it rather easier to put extended talk of this kind in the Athenian's mouth than in Socrates'. It is not that Socrates was irreligious; but his piety—above all his belief in the voice of his own inner *daimonion*—was unconventional, making him an unobvious choice as advocate of religion as the basis of social order (cf. Burnyeat 1997). Interestingly, religion has a much less pervasive and prominent role in the political thought of the *Republic*.
64. This dimension of the *Laws* is thoroughly explored by Bobonich 2002.
65. Rather as with the Noble Lie, so with the legislative programme of the *Laws* it is recognized that, to begin with, the original settlers won't accept the laws of Magnesia at all readily (though this is not a point about belief but about behaviour). That is much more likely to happen with those who imbibe them in infancy in the next generation, and grow up used to them and participating in institutions governed by them (6.752B–C).
66. Stalley 1994: 170.
67. For an account and analysis of the theory of a 'prelude', see Ch. 2, Section 3.3.
68. See above Ch. 2, Section 3.3. The case for taking preludes as exercises in rational persuasion is argued at length by Bobonich 1991; also his Bobonich 2002: 97–119.
69. Stalley 1994: 171–2.
70. See Plato, *Symposium* 207C–208B; Aristotle, *Generation of Animals* 2.1; *On the Soul* 2.4. The *Symposium* treats physical reproduction as the lowest form taken by the pursuit of immortality, far transcended by the production of spiritual 'offspring' achieved by the virtuous lover in his educational influence on his beloved (208E–209E) and above all by the philosopher in his encounter with the Form of Beauty (211D–212B). The *Laws* settles for the lowest common denominator where the desire for immortality is concerned.
71. See above, Ch. 2, Section 3.3, p. 98 n. 104.
72. But the Visitor seems prepared after all to call voluntary harm committed from an unjust disposition a voluntary act of injustice (862D). Conceivably Plato took the view that provided it is understood that what is voluntary is the act of harm, not strictly speaking the injustice, the familiar talk of involuntary injustice can stand. No wonder, however, that he makes Cleinias request further clarification on the distinctions under discussion; though any light cast by the Visitor's further response looks to be at best oblique.
73. For a helpful brief treatment of this material, see Saunders 1991 (quotation from p. 144), with selective references to other discussions in the scholarly literature.
74. For discussion, see e.g. Stalley 1983: ch. 15 (with brief bibliography at p. 196). More recently: Carone 1994; Mason 1998. A valuable older work is Solmsen 1942: chs 8 and 9.

75. I develop this idea in Schofield 2003, from which material is incorporated and adapted in this and the next paragraph.
76. Hackforth 1936: 6. A similar view is taken in Vlastos 1939: 77–83. Cf. also Dodds 1951: 220–1; Menn 1995: chs 3 and 6.
77. See Geuss 2002.

Conclusion

In some quarters the end of utopia is still being celebrated or (as in this example from Evans 2005) regretted:

Ever since Plato, western thinkers have dreamed of ideal societies, utopias that could perhaps never be fully realized, but which at least gave us something to aspire to—noble, beautiful visions of what society might one day be like. Thomas More, Tommaso Campanella, Francis Bacon and Karl Marx all painted pictures in which there is a strong sense of community, in which work is fulfilling and leisure is used wisely and creatively. Now, at the dawn of the 21st century, this long tradition of idealism has all but vanished. We have no vision—just the paltry consolations of consumerism.

Not the sort of voice one immediately associates with the *Guardian* newspaper, contemporary standard-bearer of social democratic liberalism. The columnist who penned these words at once conceded that 'Marx's dream became, for millions, a nightmare'. But the atomistic and materialistic form of living which prevails in Western societies is in its turn symptomatic of an outlook marked by 'realism without imagination'. 'If this really was the end of history'—here the author alludes to Fukuyama's teleology—'it would be an awful anti-climax.'

This book has argued that there is still life in utopianism, and that its earliest surviving philosophical version—Plato's *Republic*—remains a powerful paradigm of utopian writing, not least for the subtleties of its reflections on the very project of utopian writing. The *Republic*'s idea of community rooted in principles of justice continues to find echoes in political philosophy. At the same time, Plato acknowledges and tries to cope with the inevitability of war more frankly than many subsequent utopian writers, from the Stoics onwards; and the refractory complexity of human nature has not often been analysed with more penetration. Much of his political theorizing recognizably inhabits the same world as the realist Thucydides', even if his conception of reality is ultimately very different.

No less important in Plato—as in later writers—is utopia's critical function. He has a field day with his devastating and still damaging critique of the shortcomings of democracy, and particularly the difficulty it has in acknowledging the authority of knowledge. Yet he is no less prepared to probe or suggest the limitations of the idea of expertise in political management as a recipe for good government. His analysis of human acquisitiveness—and particularly the love of money—as pathological, once it comes to exercising a controlling grip on society, puts another disturbing question which retains its relevance. Finally, Plato's conviction of the need even in utopia for the cohesive power of an ideology grounded in religion demands to be taken a lot more seriously in the early twenty-first century than it was in the relative calm of the secular post-war decades.

Plato has a vision of what a better society might be like. By now readers will know whether and how far they find that vision—and the complexities of the way it is explored—in the least appealing. But I hope 'exploration' has come to seem the right word to describe the philosophizing that Plato conducts within the intellectual framework it constitutes, and in establishing that framework in the first place.

Bibliography

Aalders, G. J. D. (1972). 'Political thought and political programs in the Platonic *Epistles*', in *Pseudepigrapha* I, *Entretiens sur l'Antiquité classique* 18. Vandoeuvres-Geneva: Fondation Hardt, 145–87.

Acton, J. E. E. D. (1956). 'The history of freedom in antiquity', in G. Himmelfarb (ed.), *Essays on Freedom and Power by Lord Acton*. London: Thames and Hudson, Ch. 2.

Adam, J. (1902). *The Republic of Plato*. Cambridge: Cambridge University Press.

Algra, K. A. (1996). 'Observations on Plato's Thrasymachus: the case for *pleonexia*', in K. A. Algra, P. W. van der Horst and D. T. Runia (eds), *Polyhistor: Studies in the History and Historiography of Ancient Philosophy*. Leiden: Brill, 41–59.

Allott, P. J. (2001). *Eunomia: New Order for a New World* (2nd edn). Oxford: Oxford University Press.

Anderson, P. (2004). 'Rivers of Time', *New Left Review*, 26: 67–77.

—— (2005). *Spectrum*. London and New York: Verso.

Annas, J. (1976). 'Plato's *Republic* and feminism', *Philosophy*, 51: 307–21; reprinted in G. Fine (ed.), *Plato 2: Ethics, Politics, Religion, and the Soul*. Oxford: Oxford University Press (1999), 265–79.

—— (1978). 'Plato and common justice', *Classical Quarterly*, 28: 437–51.

—— (1981). *An Introduction to Plato's Republic*. Oxford: Clarendon Press.

—— (1999). *Platonic Ethics, Old and New*. Ithaca and London: Cornell University Press.

—— and Rowe, C. J. (eds) (2002). *New Perspectives on Plato, Modern and Ancient*. Washington, DC: Center for Hellenic Studies, Trustees for Harvard University.

—— and Waterfield, R. (eds) (1995). *Plato: Statesman*. Cambridge: Cambridge University Press.

Arendt, H. (1951). *The Origins of Totalitarianism*. New York: Harcourt Brace.

—— (1968). 'Truth and politics', in H. Arendt, *Between Past and Future: Eight Exercises in Political Thought*. New York: Viking Press, Ch. 7.

Bakhtin, M. M. (1981). *The Dialogic Imagination*. Austin: University of Texas Press.

Balot, R. K. (2001). *Greed and Injustice in Classical Athens.* Princeton and Oxford: Princeton University Press.

Bambrough, R. (ed.) (1967). *Plato, Popper and Politics: Some Contributions to a Modern Controversy*. Cambridge and New York: Heffer.

Barker, A. (1995). 'Problems in the *Charmides*', *Prudentia*, 27/2, 18–33.

Barker, E. (trans., rev. R. F. Stalley) (1995). *Aristotle: The Politics*. Oxford: Oxford University Press.

Barnes, J. (1989). *A History of the World in $10\frac{1}{2}$ Chapters*. London: Cape.

Barney, R. (2001). 'Platonism, moral nostalgia, and the "city of pigs"', *Proceedings of the Boston Area Colloquium in Ancient Philosophy*, 17: 207–27.

Bauman, Z. (1989). *Modernity and the Holocaust*. Cambridge: Polity.

Bell, D. (1960). *The End of Ideology: On the Exhaustion of Political Ideas in the Fifties*. Glencoe, Ill.: Free Press.

Benhabib, S. (1986). *Critique, Norm, and Utopia: A Study of the Foundations of Critical Theory*. New York: Columbia University Press.

Blanning, T. C. W. (2002). *The Culture of Power and the Power of Culture: Old Regime Europe 1660–1789*. Oxford: Oxford University Press.

Blondell, R. (2002). *The Play of Character in Plato's Dialogues*. Cambridge: Cambridge University Press.

—— (2005). 'From fleece to fabric: weaving culture in Plato's *Statesman*', *Oxford Studies in Ancient Philosophy*, 28: 23–75.

Bloom, A. (trans.) (1968). *The Republic of Plato*. London and New York: Basic Books.

Bluestone, N. H. (1987). *Women and the Ideal Society: Plato's Republic and Modern Myths of Gender*. Oxford/Hamburg/New York: Berg.

Bobonich, C. (1991). 'Persuasion, compulsion, and freedom in Plato's *Laws*', *Classical Quarterly*, 41: 365–87.

—— (1995). 'The virtues of ordinary people in Plato's *Statesman*', in C. J. Rowe (ed.), *Reading the Statesman*. Sankt Augustin: Academia Verlag, 313–29.

—— (2002). *Plato's Utopia Recast: His Later Ethics and Politics*. Oxford: Clarendon Press.

Bobzien, S. (1998). *Determinism and Freedom in Stoic Philosophy*. Oxford: Clarendon Press.

Bohman, J., and Rehg, W. (eds) (1997). *Deliberative Democracy: Essays on Reason and Politics.* Cambridge, Mass., and London: MIT Press.

Bok, S. (1978). *Lying: Moral Choice in Public and Private Life.* New York: Pantheon Books.

Boys-Stones, G. (2001). *Post-Hellenistic Philosophy: A Study of its Development from the Stoics to Origen.* Oxford: Oxford University Press.

Bradford, A. S. (1994). 'The duplicitous Spartan', in A. Powell and S. Hodkinson (eds), *The Shadow of Sparta.* London and New York: Classical Press of Wales, 59–85.

Brandwood, L. (1969). 'Plato's seventh letter', *Revue de l'Organisation Internationale pour l'Etude des Langues anciennes par Ordinateur*, 4: 1–25.

Brisson, L. (trans. and ed.) (1987). *Platon: Lettres*: Paris: Flammarion.

——— (2005). 'Ethics and politics in Plato's *Laws*', *Oxford Studies in Ancient Philosophy*, 28: 93–121.

Brock, R., and Hodkinson, S. (2000). 'Introduction: alternatives to the democratic polis', in R. Brock and S. Hodkinson (eds), *Alternatives to Athens: Varieties of Political Organization and Community in Ancient Greece.* Oxford: Oxford University Press, 1–31.

Brown, E. (2000). 'Justice and compulsion for Plato's philosopher-rulers', *Ancient Philosophy*, 20: 1–17.

——— (2006). *Stoic Cosmopolitanism.* Cambridge: Cambridge University Press.

Brown, L. (1998). 'How totalitarian is Plato's *Republic*?', in E. N. Ostenfeld (ed.), *Essays on Plato's Republic.* Aaarhus: Aarhus University Press, 13–27.

Brunt, P. A. (1993). 'The model city of Plato's *Laws*', in his *Studies in Greek History and Thought.* Oxford: Clarendon Press, Ch. 9.

Bultrighini, U. (1999). *'Maledetta democrazia': studi di Critia.* Alessandria: Edizioni dell'Orso.

Burnyeat, M. F. (1985). 'Sphinx without a secret', *New York Review of Books* (30 May 1985): 30–6.

——— (1990). *The Theaetetus of Plato*, with a translation by M. J. Levett, revised by M. F. Burnyeat. Indianapolis/Cambridge: Hackett.

——— (1992). 'Utopia and fantasy: the practicability of Plato's ideally just city', in J. Hopkins and A. Savile (eds), *Psychoanalysis, Mind and Art.* Oxford: Blackwell, 175–87; reprinted in G. Fine (ed.),

Plato 2: Ethics, Politics, Religion, and the Soul. Oxford: Oxford University Press (1999), 297–308.

——— (1997). 'The impiety of Socrates', *Ancient Philosophy*, 17: 1–12.

——— (1998). 'The past in the present: Plato as educator of nineteenth-century Britain', in A. O. Rorty (ed.), *Philosophers on Education: New Historical Perspectives*. London and New York: Routledge, 353–73.

——— (1999). 'Culture and society in Plato's *Republic*', *The Tanner Lectures on Human Values*, 20: 215–324.

——— (2000). 'Plato on why mathematics is good for the soul', in T. J. Smiley (ed.), *Mathematics and Necessity: Essays in the History of Philosophy*. Oxford: British Academy, 1–81.

——— (2001). 'Plato', *Proceedings of the British Academy*, 111: 1–22.

——— (2005–6). 'The truth of tripartition', *Proceedings of the Aristotelian Society*, 106: 1–23.

Cairns, D. L. (1993). *Aidôs: The Psychology and Ethics of Honour and Shame in Ancient Greek Literature.* Oxford: Clarendon Press.

Cambiano, G. (1988). 'I filosofi e la costrizione a governare nella *Reppublica* platonica', in G. Casertano (ed.), *I Filosofi e il Potere nella Società e nella Cultura Antiche.* Naples: Guida Editori, 43–58.

Canfora, L. (1988). 'Crizia prima dei Trenta', in G. Casertano (ed.), *I Filosofi e il Potere nella Società e nella Cultura Antiche.* Naples: Guida Editori, 29–41.

Carey, C. (1994). 'Legal space in classical Athens', *Greece and Rome*, 41: 172–86.

Carey, J. (ed.) (1999). *The Faber Book of Utopias.* London: Faber and Faber.

Carone, G. R. (1994). 'Teleology and evil in *Laws* 10', *Review of Metaphysics*, 48: 275–98.

Carter, L. B. (1986). *The Quiet Athenian.* Oxford: Clarendon Press.

Cartledge, P. A. (2000). 'Greek political thought: the historical context', in C. J. Rowe and M. Schofield (eds), *The Cambridge History of Greek and Roman Political Thought.* Cambridge: Cambridge University Press, Ch. 1.

Cavarero, A. (1995). *In Spite of Plato: A Feminist Rewriting of Ancient Philosophy.* Cambridge: Polity; English translation of *Nonostante Platone.* Rome: Editori Riuniti (1990).

Clay, D. (1999). 'Plato's Atlantis: the anatomy of a fiction', *Proceedings of the Boston Area Colloquium in Ancient Philosophy*, 15: 1–21.

Clay, D. (2000). *Platonic Questions: Dialogues with the Silent Philosopher*. University Park, PA: Pennsylvania State University Press.

—— and Purvis, A. (1999). *Four Island Utopias*. Newburyport, MA: Focus Publishing/R. Pullins Co.

Cohen, D. (1987). 'The legal status and political role of women in Plato's *Laws*', *Revue internationale des droits de l'antiquité*, 34: 27–40.

—— (1993). 'Law, autonomy, and political community in Plato's *Laws*', *Classical Philology*, 88: 301–17.

—— (1995). *Law, Violence and Community in Classical Athens*. Cambridge: Cambridge University Press.

Cole, T. (1967). *Democritus and the Sources of Greek Anthropology*. Cleveland: American Philological Association.

Connor, W. R. (1984). *Thucydides*. Princeton: Princeton University Press.

Cooper, J. M. (1984). 'Plato's theory of human motivation', *History of Philosophy Quarterly*, 1: 3–21; reprinted in his *Reason and Emotion*. Princeton: Princeton University Press (1999), 118–37, and in G. Fine (ed.), *Plato 2: Ethics, Politics, Religion, and the Soul*. Oxford: Oxford University Press (1999), 186–206.

—— (1997a). 'Plato's *Statesman* and politics', *Proceedings of the Boston Area Colloquium in Ancient Philosophy*, 13: 71–103; reprinted in his *Reason and Emotion*. Princeton: Princeton University Press (1999), 165–91.

—— (ed.) (1997b). *Plato: Complete Works*. Indianapolis/Cambridge: Hackett.

—— (1999). 'Socrates and Plato in Plato's *Gorgias*', in his *Reason and Emotion*. Princeton: Princeton University Press (1999), 29–75.

Cornford, F. M. (trans.) (1941). *The Republic of Plato*. Oxford: Oxford University Press.

Csapo, E. (2004). 'The politics of the new music', in P. Murray and P. Wilson (eds), *Music and the Muses: The Culture of Mousike in the Classical Athenian City*. Oxford: Oxford University Press, 207–48.

Dahl, N. O. (1991). 'Plato's defence of justice', *Philosophy and Phenomenological Research*, 51: 809–34; reprinted in G. Fine (ed.), *Plato 2: Ethics, Politics, Religion, and the Soul*. Oxford: Oxford University Press (1999), 207–34.

Dawson, D. (1992). *Cities of the Gods: Communist Utopias in Greek Thought*. New York and Oxford: Oxford University Press.

Deane, P. (1973). 'Stylometrics do not exclude the seventh letter', *Mind*, 82: 113–17.

Delcomminette, S. (2000). *L'Inventivité dialectique dans le Politique de Platon*. Paris: Éditions Ousia.

Detienne, M., and Vernant, J.-P. (1978). *Cunning Intelligence in Greek Culture and Society*. London: The Harvester Press; English translation of *La ruses d'intelligence: la Metis des grecs*. Paris: Flammarion et Cie (1974).

Diès, A. (1935). *Platon, Oeuvres complètes*, Vol. IX.1. Paris: Société d'Édition 'Les Belles Lettres'.

Dillon, J. M. (1992). 'Plato and the Golden Age', *Hermathena*, 153: 21–36; reprinted in his *The Great Tradition: Further Studies in the Development of Platonism and Early Christianity*. Aldershot: Ashgate (1997).

Dodds, E. R. (1945). 'Plato and the irrational', *Journal of Hellenic Studies*, 65: 16–25.

___ (1951). *The Greeks and the Irrational*. Berkeley and Los Angeles: University of California Press.

___ (1959). *Plato: Gorgias*. Oxford: Clarendon Press.

Dorter, K. (2001). 'Philosopher-rulers: how contemplation becomes action', *Ancient Philosophy*, 21: 335–56.

Doyle, J. (forthcoming, 2007). 'Desire, power and the good in Plato's *Gorgias*', in S. Tenenbaum (ed.), *New directions in Philosophy: Moral Psychology*. Amsterdam: Rhodope.

Dunn, J. (ed.) (1992). *Democracy: The Unfinished Journey, 508 BC to AD 1993*. Oxford: Oxford University Press.

___ (1993). *Western Political Theory in the Face of the Future* (2nd edn). Cambridge: Cambridge University Press.

___ (2005). *Setting the People Free: The Story of Democracy*. London: Atlantic Books.

Dusanic, S. (1995). 'The true statesman of the *Statesman* and the young tyrant of the *Laws*', in C. J. Rowe (ed.), *Reading the Statesman*. Sankt Augustin: Academia Verlag, 337–46.

Dworkin, R. (1977). *Taking Rights Seriously*. London: Duckworth.

___ (1989). 'Liberal community', *California Law Review*, 77: 479–504; reprinted in S. Avineri and A. de-Shalit (eds), *Communitarianism and Individualism*. Oxford: Oxford University Press, 205–23.

Eagleton, T. (2005). *Holy Terror*. Oxford: Oxford University Press.

Elster, J. (1997). 'The market and the forum', in J. Bohman and W. Rehg (eds), *Deliberative Democracy: Essays on Reason and Politics*. Cambridge, Mass., and London: MIT Press, Ch. 1.

___ (ed.) (1998). *Deliberative Democracy*. Cambridge: Cambridge University Press.

Euben, J. P. (1994). 'Democracy and political theory', in J. P. Euben, J. R. Wallach and J. Ober (eds), *Athenian Political Thought and the Reconstruction of American Democracy*. Ithaca, NY: Cornell University Press, 198–226.

—— (1996). 'Reading democracy: "Socratic" dialogues and the political education of democratic citizens', in J. Ober and C. Hedrick (eds), *Dêmokratia*. Princeton: Princeton University Press, 327–59.

Eucken, C. (1983). *Isokrates: Seine position in der Auseinandersetzung mit den zeitgenössischen Philosophen*. Berlin and New York: de Gruyter.

Evans, D. (2005). 'The loss of utopia', *The Guardian* (27 October 2005): 32.

Farrar, C. (1988). *The Origins of Democratic Thinking: The Invention of Politics in Classical Athens*. Cambridge: Cambridge University Press.

Ferrari, G. R. F. (1989). 'Plato on poetry', in G. A. Kennedy (ed.), *The Cambridge History of Literary Criticism*, Vol.1. Cambridge: Cambridge University Press, Ch. 3.

—— (1992). 'Platonic love', in R. Kraut (ed.), *The Cambridge Companion to Plato*. Cambridge: Cambridge University Press, Ch. 8.

—— (2003). *City and Soul in Plato's Republic*. Sankt Augustin: Academia Verlag.

—— (ed.) and Griffith, T. (trans.) (2000). *Plato: The Republic*. Cambridge: Cambridge University Press.

Figueira, T. J. (2002). 'Iron money and the ideology of consumption in Laconia', in A. Powell and S. Hodkinson (eds), *Sparta: Beyond the Mirage*. London: Classical Press of Wales, 137–70.

Finley, M. I. (1975a). 'The ancestral constitution', in his *The Use and Abuse of History*. London: Chatto and Windus, Ch. 2; first issued as a separate pamphlet: *The Ancestral Constitution*. Cambridge: Cambridge University Press (1971).

—— (1975b). 'The ancient Greeks and their nation', in his *The Use and Abuse of History*. London: Chatto and Windus, Ch. 7.

Frede, D. (1996). 'Plato, Popper, and historicism', *Proceedings of the Boston Area Colloquium in Ancient Philosophy*, 12: 247–76.

Frede, M. (1992). 'Plato's arguments and the dialogue form', *Oxford Studies in Ancient Philosophy*, suppl. vol. (1992) 201–19.

—— (1996). 'Introduction', in M. Frede and G. Striker (eds), *Rationality in Greek Thought*. Oxford: Clarendon Press, 1–28.

Freeman, S. (1990). 'Reason and agreement in social contract views', *Philosophy and Public Affairs*, 9: 122–57.

Fukuyama, F. (1992). *The End of History and the Last Man*. New York and London: Hamish Hamilton.

Garnsey, P. D. A. (1996). *Ideas of Slavery from Aristotle to Augustine*. Cambridge: Cambridge University Press.

Gerson, L. P. (2003). *Knowing Persons: A Study in Plato*. Oxford: Oxford University Press.

Geuss, R. (1981). *The Idea of a Critical Theory: Habermas and the Frankfurt School*. Cambridge: Cambridge University Press.

——— (1999). 'Nietzsche on morality', in his *Morality, Culture, and History: Essays on German Philosophy*. Cambridge: Cambridge University Press, Ch. 7.

——— (2001). *History and Illusion in Politics*. Cambridge: Cambridge University Press.

——— (2002). 'Liberalism and its discontents', *Political Theory*, 30: 320–38; reprinted in R. Geuss, *Outside Ethics*. Princeton: Princeton University Press (2005), Ch. 1.

——— (2003). 'Neither history nor praxis', *European Review*, 11: 281–92; reprinted in R. Geuss, *Outside Ethics*. Princeton: Princeton University Press (2005), Ch. 2.

——— (2005). 'Thucydides, Nietzsche, and Williams', in R. Geuss, *Outside Ethics*. Princeton: Princeton University Press (2005), Ch. 13.

Gibson, R. W. (1961). *St Thomas More: A Preliminary Bibliography*. New Haven: Yale University Press.

Gifford, M. (2001). 'Dramatic dialectic in *Republic* Book 1', *Oxford Studies in Ancient Philosophy*, 20: 35–106.

Gill, C. (1977). 'The genre of the Atlantis story', *Classical Philology*, 72: 287–304.

——— (1995). 'Rethinking constitutionalism in *Statesman* 291–303', in C. J. Rowe (ed.), *Reading the Statesman*. Sankt Augustin: Academia Verlag, 292–305.

——— (1996). *Personality in Greek Epic, Tragedy, and Philosophy*. Oxford: Clarendon Press.

——— (2000). 'Protreptic and dialectic in Plato's *Euthydemus*', in T. M. Robinson and L. Brisson (eds), *Plato: Euthydemus, Lysis, Charmides*. Sankt Augustin: Academia Verlag, 133–43.

Giorgini, G. (1993). *La citta e il tiranno*. Milan: Giuffrè.

Gomme, A. W. (1962). 'The old oligarch', in his *More Essays on Greek History and Literature*. Oxford: Blackwell, 38–69; reprinted from *Harvard Studies in Classical Philology*, suppl. vol. 1 (1940): 211–45.

Gonzalez, F. J. (2000). 'The Eleatic stranger: his master's voice?', in G. A. Press (ed.), *Who Speaks for Plato? Studies in Platonic Anonymity*. Lanham, MD: Rowman and Littlefield, 161–81.

Goodwin, B. (1992). *Justice by Lottery*. London and New York: Harvester Wheatsheaf.

Gray, V. (2000). 'Xenophon and Isocrates', in C. J. Rowe and M. Schofield (eds), *The Cambridge History of Greek and Roman Political Thought*. Cambridge: Cambridge University Press, Ch. 7.

Grey, C. and Garsten, C. (2002). 'Organized and disorganized utopias: an essay on presumption', in M. Parker (ed.), *Utopia and Organization*. Oxford: Blackwell Publishing/The Sociological Review, 9–23.

Griswold, C. L. (1999). 'Platonic liberalism: self-perfection as a foundation of political theory', in J. M. Van Ophuijsen (ed.), *Plato and Platonism*. Washington, DC: The Catholic University of America Press, 102–34.

Grote, G. (1865). *Plato and the Other Companions of Socrates*. London: John Murray.

Gulley, N. (1972). 'The authenticity of the Platonic *Epistles*', in *Pseudepigrapha* I, *Entretiens sur l'Antiquité classique* 18. Vando-euvres-Geneva: Fondation Hardt, 103–43.

Guthrie, W. K. C. (1969). *A History of Greek Philosophy*, Vol. 3, Part I: *The World of the Sophists*. Cambridge: Cambridge University Press.

—— (1975). *A History of Greek Philosophy*, Vol. 4: *Plato, the Man and His Dialogues: Earlier Period*. Cambridge: Cambridge University Press.

Habermas, J. (1995). 'On the internal relation between the rule of law and democracy', *European Journal of Philosophy*, 3: 12–20.

—— (1996). 'Three normative models of democracy', in S. Benhabib (ed.), *Democracy and Difference: Contesting the Boundaries of the Political*. Princeton: Princeton University Press, 21–30.

Hackforth, R. (1936). 'Plato's theism', *Classical Quarterly*, 30: 4–9.

Hahm, D. E. (1969). 'Plato's "Noble Lie" and political brotherhood', *Classica et Mediaevalia*, 30: 211–27.

—— (1995). 'Polybius's applied political theory', in A. Laks and M. Schofield (eds), *Justice and Generosity: Studies in Hellenistic Social and Political Philosophy*. Cambridge: Cambridge University Press, Ch. 1.

Halliwell, S. (1993). *Plato: Republic 5*. Warminster: Aris and Phillips.

Hansen, M. H. (1990). 'Solonian democracy in fourth-century Athens', in W. R. Connor, M. H. Hansen, K. A. Raaflaub and

B. S. Strauss, *Aspects of Athenian Democracy*. Copenhagen: Museum Tusculanum Press, University of Copenhagen, 71–99.

Hansen, M. H. (1991). *The Athenian Democracy in the Age of Demosthenes*. Oxford and Cambridge, MA: Blackwell.

—— (1995). *The Trial of Sokrates—from the Athenian Point of View*, Historisk-filosofiske Meddelelser 71, The Royal Danish Academy of Sciences and Letters. Copenhagen: Munksgaard; reprinted in M. Sakellariou (ed.), *Démocratie athenienne et culture*. Athens: Académie d'Athènes 1996, 137–70.

—— (1996). 'The ancient Athenian and the modern liberal view of liberty as a democratic ideal', in J. Ober and C. Hedrik (eds), *Dêmokratia*. Princeton: Princeton University Press, 91–104.

Harrison, R. (1993). *Democracy*. London: Routledge.

—— (2003). *Hobbes, Locke, and Confusion's Masterpiece: An Examination of Seventeeth-Century Political Philosophy*. Cambridge: Cambridge University Press.

Harte, V. (1999). 'Conflicting values in Plato's *Crito*', *Archiv für Geschichte der Philosophie*, 81: 117–47.

Harvey, F. D. (1965). 'Two kinds of equality', *Classica et Mediaevalia*, 26: 101–46.

von Hayek, F. A. (1960). *The Constitution of Liberty*. London: Routledge & Kegan Paul.

Held, D. (2004). *Global Covenant: The Social Democratic Alternative to the Washington Consensus*. Cambridge: Polity.

Henderson, J. (2003). 'Demos, demagogue, tyrant in Attic old comedy', in K. A. Morgan (ed.), *Popular Tyranny*. Austin: University of Texas Press, 155–79.

Hesk, J. (2000). *Deception and Democracy in Classical Athens*. Cambridge: Cambridge University Press.

Hobbs, A. (2000). *Plato and the Hero: Courage, Manliness and the Impersonal Good*. Cambridge: Cambridge University Press.

Hodkinson, S. (1994). '"Blind Ploutos"?: contemporary images of the role of wealth in classical Sparta', in A. Powell and S. Hodkinson (eds), *The Shadow of Sparta*. London and New York: Classical Press of Wales, 183–222.

—— (2000). *Property and Wealth in Classical Sparta*. London: Duckworth.

—— (2005). 'The imaginary Spartan *politeia*', in M. H. Hansen (ed.), *The Imaginary Polis*, Historisk-filosofiske Meddelelser 91, The Royal Danish Academy of Sciences and Letters. Copenhagen: Munksgaard, 222–81.

Holmes, S. (1989). 'John Stuart Mill: fallibilism, expertise, and the politics–science analogy', in M. Dascal and O. Gruengard (eds), *Knowledge and Politics: Case Studies in the Relationship between Epistemology and Political Philosophy*. Boulder, San Francisco and London: Westview Press, 125–43.

Huffman, C. A. (2005). *Archytas of Tarentum: Pythagorean, Philosopher and Mathematician King*. Cambridge: Cambridge University Press.

Irigaray, L. (1985). *Speculum of the Other Woman*. Ithaca, NY: Cornell University Press; English translation of *Speculum de l'autre femme*. Paris: Minuit (1974).

____ (1996). *I Love to You*. New York and London: Routledge; English translation of *J'aime a toi*. Paris: B. Grasset (1992).

Irwin, T. H. (1995). *Plato's Ethics*. New York and Oxford: Oxford University Press.

Jacoby, R. (1999). *The End of Utopia*. New York: Basic Books.

Jowett, B. (trans.) (1875). *The Dialogues of Plato* (2nd edn). Oxford: Clarendon Press.

____ and Campbell, L. (eds) (1894). *The Republic of Plato: The Greek Text*. Oxford: Clarendon Press.

Kahn, C. H. (1963). 'Plato's funeral oration: the motive of the *Menexenus*', *Classical Philology*, 58: 220–34.

____ (1981). 'Did Plato write Socratic dialogues?', *Classical Quarterly*, 31: 305–20.

____ (1992). 'Vlastos's Socrates', *Phronesis*, 37: 233–58.

____ (1996). *Plato and the Socratic Dialogue: the Philosophical Use of a Literary Form*. Cambridge: Cambridge University Press.

____ (2002). 'On Platonic chronology', in J. Annas and C. J. Rowe (eds), *New Perspectives on Plato, Modern and Ancient*. Washington, DC: Center for Hellenic Studies, Trustees for Harvard University, 93–127.

____ (2004). 'From *Republic* to *Laws*: a discussion of Christopher Bobonich, *Plato's Utopia Recast*', *Oxford Studies in Ancient Philosophy*, 26: 337–62.

Kallet, L. (2001). *Money and the Corrosion of Power in Thucydides*. Berkeley/Los Angeles/London: University of California Press.

Kamtekar, R. (2004). 'What's the good of agreeing? *Homonoia* in Platonic politics', *Oxford Studies in Ancient Philosophy*, 26: 131–70.

Kateb, G. (1998). 'Socratic integrity', in I. Shapiro and R. Adams (eds), *Integrity and Conscience, Nomos* 40: 77–112.

Keane, J. (2003). *Global Civil Society?* Cambridge: Cambridge University Press.

Ker, J. (2000). 'Solon's *theôria* and the end of city', *Classical Antiquity*, 19: 304–29.

Kerferd, G. B. (1981). *The Sophistic Movement*. Cambridge: Cambridge University Press.

Keynes, J. M. (1932). *Essays in Persuasion*. London: Macmillan.

Kirk, G. S., Raven, J. E., and Schofield, M. (1983). *The Presocratic Philosophers* (2nd edn). Cambridge. Cambridge University Press.

Kirwan, C. A. (1989). *Augustine*. London: Routledge.

Klosko, G. (1986). *The Development of Plato's Political Theory*. New York and London: Methuen.

Kochin, M. S. (1999). 'Plato's Eleatic and Athenian sciences of politics', *The Review of Politics*, 61: 58–84.

—— (2002). *Gender and Rhetoric in Plato's Political Thought*. Cambridge: Cambridge University Press.

Koyré, A. (1945). *Discovering Plato*. New York: Columbia University Press.

Kraut, R. (1984). *Socrates and the State*. Princeton: Princeton University Press.

—— (1992a). 'Introduction to the study of Plato', in R. Kraut (ed.), *The Cambridge Companion to Plato*. Cambridge: Cambridge University Press, 1–50.

—— (1992b). 'The defense of justice in Plato's *Republic*', in R. Kraut (ed.), *The Cambridge Companion to Plato*. Cambridge: Cambridge University Press, 311–37.

Laks, A. (1990). 'Legislation and demiurgy: on the relationship between Plato's *Republic* and *Laws*', *Classical Antiquity*, 9: 209–29.

—— (2000). 'The *Laws*', in C. J. Rowe and M. Schofield (eds), *The Cambridge History of Greek and Roman Political Thought*. Cambridge: Cambridge University Press, Ch. 12.

Lampert L., and Planeaux, C. (1998–9). 'Who's who in Plato's *Timaeus*', *Review of Metaphysics*, 52: 87–125.

Lane, M. S. (1995). 'A new angle on utopia: the political theory of the *Statesman*', in C. J. Rowe (ed.), *Reading the Statesman*. Sankt Augustin: Academia Verlag, 276–91.

—— (1998a). *Method and Politics in Plato's Statesman*. Cambridge: Cambridge University Press.

—— (1998b). 'Argument and agreement in Plato's *Crito*', *History of Political Thought*, 19: 313–30.

—— (1999). 'Plato, Popper, Strauss, and utopianism: open secrets?', *History of Philosophy Quarterly*, 16: 119–42.

—— (2002). *Plato's Progeny*. London: Duckworth.

Lane, M.S. (2005). ' "Emplois pour philosophes": l'art politique et l'Étranger dans le *Politique* à la lumière de Socrate et du philosophe dans le *Théétète*', *Les Études philosophiques*, 60: 325–45.

Lanza, D. (1977). *Il tiranno e il suo pubblico*. Turin: Einaudi.

Lear, J. (1992). 'Inside and outside the *Republic*', *Phronesis*, 37: 184–215.

Ledger, G. R. (1989). *Re-counting Plato*. Oxford: Clarendon Press.

Levin, S. B. (1996). 'Women's nature and role in the ideal *polis*: *Republic* V revisited', in J. K. Ward (ed.), *Feminism and Ancient Philosophy*. New York and London: Routledge, 13–30.

—— (2000). 'Plato on women's nature: reflections on the *Laws*', *Ancient Philosophy*, 20: 81–97.

Levinson, R. B. (1953). *In Defense of Plato*. Cambridge, Mass.: Harvard University Press.

Lloyd, G. (1993) *The Man of Reason: 'Male' and 'Female' in Western Philosophy* (2nd edn). London: Routledge.

Loraux, N. (1986). *The Invention of Athens: The Funeral Oration in the Classical City*. Princeton: Princeton University Press; English translation of *L'Invention d'Athenes*. Paris: Mouton (1981).

—— (1991). 'Reflections of the Greek city on unity and division', in A. Molho, K. A. Raaflaub and J. Emlen (eds), *City States in Classical Antiquity and Medieval Italy*. Stuttgart: F. Steiner, 33–51.

—— (1993). *The Children of Athena: Athenian Ideas about Citizenship and the Division between the Sexes*. Princeton: Princeton University Press; English translation of *Les enfants d'Athéna*. Paris: Editions La Découverte (1984).

—— (2002). *The Divided City: On Memory and Forgetting in Ancient Athens*. New York: Zone Books; English translation of *La Cité divisée*. Paris: Editions Payot et Rivages (1997).

Lorenz, H. (2004). 'Desire and reason in Plato's *Republic*', *Oxford Studies in Ancient Philosophy*, 27: 83–116.

Lovibond, S. (1994). 'An ancient theory of gender: Plato and the Pythagorean table', in L. J. Archer, S. Fischler and M. Wyke (eds), *Women in Ancient Societies: An Illusion of the Night*. Basingstoke: Macmillan, 88–101.

McCabe, M. M. (1997). 'Chaos and control: reading Plato's *Politicus*', *Phronesis*, 42: 94–117.

—— (2002a). 'Indifference readings: Plato and the Stoa on Socratic ethics', in T. P. Wiseman (ed.), *Classics in Progress: Essays on Ancient Greece and Rome*. Oxford: British Academy, 363–98.

____ (2002b). 'Developing the good itself by itself: critical strategies in Plato's *Euthydemus*', *Journal of the International Plato Society*, 2 (available online at <http://www.nd.edu/~plato/plato2 issue/mccabe.htm>).

____ (2005). 'Out of the labyrinth: Plato's attack on consequentialism', in C. Gill (ed.), *Virtue, Norms, and Objectivity: Issues in Ancient and Modern Ethics*. Oxford: Clarendon Press, 189–214.

Macintyre, A. (1981). *After Virtue. A Study in Moral Theory*. London: Duckworth.

McKim, R. (1985). 'Socratic self-knowledge and "knowledge of knowledge" in Plato's *Charmides*', *Transactions of the American Philological Association*, 115: 59–77.

Marchant, E. C. and Bowersock, G. W. (eds) (1968). *Xenophon: Scripta Minora*. Cambridge, Mass., and London: Harvard University Press.

Marcuse, H. (1967). *Das Ende der Utopia*. Berlin [publisher not known]. Reprinted in his *Psychoanalyse und Politik*. Frankfurt: Europäische Verlagsanstalt; and Vienna: Europa Verlag (1968), 69–78.

Mason, A. (1998). 'Plato on the self-moving soul', *Philosophical Inquiry*, 20: 18–28.

Meikle, S. (1995). *Aristotle's Economic Thought*. Oxford: Clarendon Press.

Menn, S. (1995). *Plato on God as Nous*. Carbondale and Edwardsville: Southern Illinois Press.

____ (2005). 'On Plato's *Politeia*', *Proceedings of the Boston Area Colloquium in Ancient Philosophy*, 20.

Méridier, L. (1931). *Platon: Ouevres Complètes, V.1: Ion, Ménexène, Euthydème*. Paris: Société d'Édition 'Les Belles Lettres'.

Michelini, A. N. (2000). 'The search for the king: reflexive irony in Plato's *Politicus*', *Classical Antiquity*, 19: 180–204.

____ (2003). 'Plato's Socratic mask', in A. N. Michelini (ed.), *Plato as Author: The Rhetoric of Philosophy*. Leiden and Boston: Brill, 45–65.

Mill, J. S. (1978) *Collected Works of John Stuart Mill*, Vol. XI: *Essays on Philosophy and the Classics*, J. M. Robson (ed.) and F. E. Sparshott (introduction). Toronto: University of Toronto Press.

Miller, Jr., F. D. (1995). *Nature, Justice, and Rights in Aristotle's Politics*. Oxford: Clarendon Press.

Miller, M. H. (1980). *The Philosopher in Plato's Statesman*. The Hague and Boston: Nijhoff.

Mishima, T. (1995). 'Courage and moderation in the *Statesman*', in C. J. Rowe (ed.), *Reading the Statesman*. Sankt Augustin: Academia Verlag, 306–12.

Mitchell, B. G., and Lucas, J. R. (2003). *An Engagement with Plato's Republic*. Aldershot: Ashgate.

Monoson, S. S. (1994). 'Frank speech, democracy, and philosophy: Plato's debt to a democratic strategy of civic discourse', in J. P. Euben, J. R. Wallach and J. Ober (eds), *Athenian Political Thought and the Reconstruction of American Democracy*. Ithaca, NY: Cornell University Press, 172–97.

—— (2000). *Plato's Democratic Entanglements*. Princeton: Princeton University Press.

Moravcsik, J. M. E. (1983). 'Plato and Pericles on freedom and politics', in F. J. Pelletier and J. King-Farlow (eds), *New Essays on Plato. Canadian Journal of Philosophy*, Supp. Vol. 9: 1–17.

Morgan, K. A. (ed.) (2003). *Popular Tyranny*. Austin: University of Texas Press.

Morris, I. (1996). 'The strong principle of equality and the archaic origins of Greek democracy', in J. Ober and C. Hedrik (eds), *Dêmokratia*. Princeton: Princeton University Press, 19–48.

Morrow, G. R. (1960). *Plato's Cretan City: A Historical Interpretation of the Laws*. Princeton: Princeton University Press; reprinted 1993, with a foreword by C. H. Kahn.

—— (1962). *Plato's Epistles*. Indianapolis: Bobbs-Merrill.

Most, G. W. (1993). 'A cock for Asclepius', *Classical Quarterly*, 43: 96–111.

—— (1997). 'Hesiod's myth of the five (or three or four) races', *Proceedings of the Cambridge Philological Society*, 43: 104–27.

Nagel, T. (1991). *Equality and Partiality*. New York and Oxford: Oxford University Press.

Nails, D. (2002). *The People of Plato: A Prosopography of Plato and Other Socratics*. Indianapolis and Cambridge: Hackett.

Nairn, T. (2005). 'Democratic warming', *London Review of Books*, 27/15 (4 August 2005): 19–20.

Nehamas, A. (1998). *The Art of Living*. Berkeley/Los Angeles/London: University of California Press.

Newman, W. L. (1887–1902). *The Politics of Aristotle*. Oxford: Clarendon Press.

Nightingale, A. W. (1995). *Genres in Dialogue: Plato and the Construct of Philosophy*. Cambridge: Cambridge University Press.

—— (1999). 'Historiography and cosmology in Plato's *Laws*', *Ancient Philosophy*, 19: 299–326.

—— (2004). *Spectacles of Truth in Classical Greek Philosophy.* Cambridge: Cambridge University Press.

North, H. (1966). *Sophrosyne: Self-Knowledge and Self-Restraint in Greek Literature.* Ithaca, NY: Cornell University Press.

Norton, A. (2004). *Leo Strauss and the Politics of American Empire.* New Haven: Yale University Press.

Notomi, N. (2000). 'Critias and the origin of Plato's political philosophy', in T. M. Robinson and L. Brisson (eds), *Plato: Euthydemus, Lysis, Charmides.* Sankt Augustin: Academia Verlag, 237–50.

Nozick, R. (1974). *Anarchy, State, and Utopia.* Oxford: Blackwell.

Nussbaum, M. C. (1996). 'Patriotism and cosmopolitanism', in J. Cohen (ed.), *For Love of Country.* Boston: Beacon Press, 2–17.

—— (1997). 'Kant and Stoic cosmopolitanism', in J. Bohman and M. Lutz-Bachmann (eds), *Perpetual Peace: Essays on Kant's Cosmopolitan Ideal.* Cambridge, Mass., and London: MIT Press, 25–58.

O'Brien, M. J. (1967). *The Socratic Paradoxes and the Greek Mind.* Chapel Hill: University of North Carolina Press.

Ober, J. (1989). *Mass and Elite in Democratic Athens: Rhetoric, Ideology, and the Power of the People.* Princeton: Princeton University Press.

—— (1998). *Political Dissent in Democratic Athens: Intellectual Critics of Popular Rule.* Princeton: Princeton University Press.

—— (2000). 'Thucydides theoretikos/Thucydides histor: realist theory and the challenge of history', in D. R. McCann and B. S. Strauss (eds), *War and Democracy: A Comparative Study of the Korean War and the Peloponnesian War.* Armonk, NY, and London: M. E. Sharpe, 273–306.

—— (2003). 'Tyrant killing as therapeutic *stasis*: a political debate in images and texts', in K. A. Morgan (ed.), *Popular Tyranny.* Austin: University of Texas Press, 215–50.

Okin, S. M. (1977). 'Philosopher queens and private wives: Plato on women and the family', *Philosophy and Public Affairs*, 6: 345–69.

—— (1979). *Women in Western Political Thought.* Princeton: Princeton University Press.

Orwin, C. (1994). *The Humanity of Thucydides.* Princeton: Princeton University Press.

Osborne, R. G. (2003). 'Changing the discourse', in K. A. Morgan (ed.), *Popular Tyranny.* Austin: University of Texas Press, 251–70.

—— (ed.) (2004). *The Old Oligarch: Pseudo-Xenophon's Constitution of the Athenians Plato* (2nd edn). London: London Association of Classical Teachers.

Ostwald, M. (1969). *Nomos and the Beginnings of the Athenian Democracy*. Oxford: Clarendon Press.

Page, C. (1991). 'The truth about lies in Plato's *Republic*', *Ancient Philosophy*, 11: 1–33.

Palmer, J. A. (1999). *Plato's Reception of Parmenides*. Oxford: Clarendon Press.

Pelling, C. B. R. (2003). 'Speech and action: Herodotus' debate on the constitutions', *Proceedings of the Cambridge Philological Society*, 48: 123–58.

Penner, T. (1991). 'Desire and power in Socrates: the argument of *Gorgias* 466A–468E that orators and tyrants have no power in the city', *Apeiron*, 24: 147–202.

Perlman, P. (2005). 'Imagining Crete', in M. H. Hansen (ed.), *The Imaginary Polis*. Historisk-filosofiske Meddelelser 91, *The Royal Danish Academy of Sciences and Letters*. Copenhagen: Munksgaard, 282–334.

Phillips, A. (2005). *Going Sane*. London: Hamish Hamilton.

Popper, K. R. (1961). *The Open Society and its Enemies*, Vol.1: *The Spell of Plato* (4th edn). London: Routledge & Kegan Paul; first published in 1945.

Porter, R. (2000). *Enlightenment: Britain and the Creation of the Modern World*. London: Allen Lane.

Powell, A. (1994). 'Plato and Sparta: modes of rule and of non-rational persuasion in the *Laws*', in A. Powell and S. Hodkinson (eds), *The Shadow of Sparta*. London and New York: Classical Press of Wales, 273–321.

Pradeau, J.-F. (2002). *Plato and the City*. Exeter: Exeter University Press; English translation of a revised and extended version of *Platon et la Cité*. Paris: Presses Universitaires de France (1997).

Price, A. W. (1995). *Mental Conflict*. London and New York: Routledge.

Price, J. J. (2001). *Thucydides and Internal War*. Cambridge: Cambridge University Press.

Prior, W. J. (2002). 'Protagoras' great speech and Plato's defense of Athenian democracy', in V. Caston and D. W. Graham (eds), *Presocratic Philosophy: Essays in Honor of Alexander Mourelatos*. Aldershot: Ashgate, 313–27.

Raaflaub, K. A. (1983). 'Democracy, oligarchy, and the concept of the "free citizen"', *Political Theory*, 11: 517–44.

——(1990). 'Contemporary perceptions of democracy in fifth-century Athens', in W. R. Connor, M. H. Hansen, K. A. Raaflaub and

B. S. Strauss, *Aspects of Athenian Democracy*. Copenhagen: Museum Tusculanum Press, University of Copenhagen, 33–70.

—— (1996). 'Equalities and inequalities in Athenian democracy', in J. Ober and C. Hedrik (eds), *Dêmokratia*. Princeton: Princeton University Press, 139–74.

—— (2000). 'Father of all, destroyer of all: war in late fifth-century Athenian discourse and ideology', in D. R. McCann and B. S. Strauss (eds), *War and Democracy: A Comparative Study of the Korean War and the Peloponnesian War*. Armonk, NY, and London: M. E. Sharpe, 307–56.

—— (2003). 'Stick and glue: the function of tyranny in fifth-century Athens', in K. A. Morgan (ed.), *Popular Tyranny*. Austin: University of Texas Press, 59–93.

Raven, J. (1992). *Judging New Wealth: Popular Publishing and Responses to Commerce in England, 1750–1800*. Oxford: Clarendon Press.

Rawls, J. (1972). *A Theory of Justice*. Oxford: Clarendon Press.

—— (1993). *Political Liberalism*. New York: Columbia University Press.

Reeve, C. D. C. (1988). *Philosopher-Kings*. Princeton: Princeton University Press.

—— (1989). *Socrates in the Apology*. Indianapolis and Cambridge, Mass.: Hackett.

Reverdin, O. (1945). *La Religion de la cité platonicienne*. Paris: E. de Bocard.

Reydams-Schils, G. (2005). *The Roman Stoics: Self, Responsibility, and Affection*. Chicago and London: University of Chicago Press.

Rhodes, P. J. (1981). *A Commentary on the Aristotelian Athenaion Politeia*. Oxford: Clarendon Press; expanded edition (1993).

—— (2006). 'The reforms and laws of Solon: an optimistic view', in J. H. Blok and A. P. M. H. Lardinois (eds), *Solon the Athenian: New Historical and Philological Approaches*. Leiden: Brill.

Roberts, J. T. (1994). *Athens on Trial: The Antidemocratic Tradition in Western Thought*. Princeton: Princeton University Press.

Robinson, E. W. (ed.) (2004). *Ancient Greek Democracy: Readings and Sources*. Oxford: Blackwell.

Robinson, R. (1951). 'Dr Popper's defence of democracy', *Philosophical Review*, 60: 487–507; reprinted in his *Essays in Greek Philosophy*. Oxford: Clarendon Press (1969), Ch. 4.

de Romilly, J. (1963). *Thucydides and Athenian Imperialism*. Oxford: Blackwell; English translation of *Thucydide et l'impérialisme athénien*. Paris: Les Belles Lettres (1947).

de Romilly, J. (1972). 'Vocabulaire et propagande, ou les premiers emplois du mot *homonoia'*, in *Mélanges de Linguistique et de Philologie Grecques offerts à Pierre Chantraine*. Paris: Klincksieck, 199–209.

Roochnik, D. (2003). *Beautiful City: The Dialectical Character of Plato's 'Republic'*. Ithaca, NY: Cornell University Press.

Rosen, S. (1995). *Plato's Statesman: The Web of Politics*. New Haven and London: Yale University Press.

Rosenthal, E. I. J. (1956). *Averroes' Commentary on Plato's Republic*. Cambridge: Cambridge University Press.

Rowe, C. J. (ed. and trans.) (1995a). *Plato: Statesman*. Warminster: Aris and Phillips.

—— (ed.) (1995b). *Reading the Statesman*. Sankt Augustin: Academia Verlag.

—— (1996). 'The *Politicus*: structure and form', in C. Gill and M. M. McCabe (eds), *Form and Argument in Late Plato*. Oxford: Clarendon Press, 153–78.

—— (1998). 'Democracy and Sokratic-Platonic philosophy', in D. D. Boedeker and K. A. Raaflaub (eds), *Democracy, Empire, and the Arts in Fifth-Century Athens*. Cambridge, Mass., and London: Harvard University Press, 241–53.

—— (2000). 'The *Politicus* and other dialogues', in C. J. Rowe and M. Schofield (eds), *The Cambridge History of Greek and Roman Political Thought*. Cambridge: Cambridge University Press, Ch. 11.

—— (2001). 'Killing Socrates: Plato's later thoughts on democracy', *Journal of Hellenic Studies*, 121: 63–76.

—— (2004). 'The case of the missing philosophers in Plato's *Timaeus-Critias*', *Würzburger Jahrbücher für die Altertumswissenschaft*, 28b: 57–70.

—— (forthcoming, 2007). 'Plato and the Persian wars', in E. Bridges, E. Hall and P. J. Rhodes (eds), *Cultural Responses to the Persian Wars*. Oxford: Oxford University Press.

—— and Schofield, M. (eds) (2000). *The Cambridge History of Greek and Roman Political Thought*. Cambridge: Cambridge University Press.

Sachs, D. (1963). 'A fallacy in Plato's *Republic*', *Philosophical Review*, 72: 141–58.

Samaras, T. (2002). *Plato on Democracy*. New York: Peter Lang.

Saunders, T. J. (1970). *Plato: The Laws*. Harmondsworth: Penguin Books.

—— (1991). *Plato's Penal Code*. Oxford: Clarendon Press.

Saunders, T. J. (1995). 'Plato on women in the *Laws*', in A. Powell (ed.), *The Greek World*. London and New York: Routledge, 591–609.

Saxonhouse, A. (1976). 'The philosopher and the female in the political thought of Plato', *Political Theory*, 4: 195–212.

___(1985). *Women in the History of Political Thought*. New York: Praeger.

Scheid, J., and Svenbro, J. (1996). *The Craft of Zeus: Myths of Weaving and Fabric*. Cambridge, Mass., and London: Harvard University Press.

Schmid, W. T. (1998). *Plato's Charmides and the Socratic Ideal of Rationality*. Albany, NY: State University of New York Press.

Schofield, M. (1986). '*Euboulia* in the *Iliad*', *Classical Quarterly*, 36: 6–31; reprinted in M. Schofield, *Saving the City*. London and New York: Routledge (1999), Ch. 1.

___(1990). 'Ideology and philosophy in Aristotle's theory of slavery', in G. Patzig (ed.), *Aristotles' 'Politik'*. Göttingen: Vandenhoeck and Ruprecht, 1–27; reprinted with revisions and additions in M. Schofield, *Saving the City* (1999), Ch. 7.

___(1991). *The Stoic Idea of the City*. Cambridge: Cambridge University Press; expanded edition, Chicago: University of Chicago Press (1999).

___(1992). 'Socrates versus Protagoras', in B. S. Gowers and M. C. Stokes (eds), *Socratic Questions*. London and New York: Routledge, 122–36.

___(1993). 'Plato on the economy', in M. H. Hansen (ed.), *The Ancient Greek City-State*. Historisk-filosofiske Meddelelser 67, The Royal Danish Academy of Sciences and Letters. Copenhagen: Munksgaard, 183–96; reprinted in M. Schofield, *Saving the City* (1999), Ch. 4.

___(1995). 'Cicero's definition of *res publica*', in J. G. F. Powell (ed.), *Cicero the Philosopher*. Oxford: Clarendon Press. 63–83; reprinted in M. Schofield, *Saving the City* (1999), Ch. 11.

___(1995–6). 'Sharing in the constitution', *Review of Metaphysics*, 49: 831–58; reprinted in M. Schofield, *Saving the City* (1999), Ch. 8.

___(1997). 'The disappearance of the philosopher king', *Proceedings of the Boston Area Colloquium in Ancient Philosophy*, 13: 213–41; reprinted in M. Schofield, *Saving the City* (1999), Ch. 2.

___(1998). 'Plato', in *Routledge Encyclopedia of Philosophy*. London and New York: Routledge, 7.399–421.

Schofield, M. (1999a). *Saving the City: Philosopher-Kings and Other Classical Paradigms*. London: Routledge.

———(1999b). 'Zeno of Citium's anti-utopianism', in M. Vegetti and M. Abbate (eds), *La Repubblica di Platone nella Tradizione Antica*. Naples: Bibliopolis, 49–78; reprinted in M. Schofield, *Saving the City* (1999), Ch. 3.

——— (2000a). 'Approaching the *Republic*', in C. J. Rowe and M. Schofield (eds), *The Cambridge History of Greek and Roman Political Thought*. Cambridge: Cambridge University Press, Ch. 10.

——— (2000b). 'Plato and practical politics', in C. J. Rowe and M. Schofield (eds), *The Cambridge History of Greek and Roman Political Thought*. Cambridge: Cambridge University Press, Ch. 13.

——— (2003). 'Religion and philosophy in the *Laws*', in S. Scolnicov and L. Brisson (eds), *Plato's Laws: From Theory into Practice*. Sankt Augustin: Academia Verlag, 1–13.

——— (forthcoming, 2007). 'The Noble Lie', in G. Ferrari (ed.), *The Cambridge Companion to Plato*. Cambridge: Cambridge University Press.

Scott, D. (2000). 'Plato's critique of the democratic character', *Phronesis*, 45: 19–37.

Seaford, R. (2003). 'Tragic tyranny', in K. A. Morgan (ed.), *Popular Tyranny*. Austin: University of Texas Press, 95–115.

——— (2004). *Money and the Early Greek Mind*. Cambridge: Cambridge University Press.

Sedley, D. N. (2003). *Plato's Cratylus*. Cambridge: Cambridge University Press.

——— (2004). *The Midwife of Platonism: Text and Subtext in Plato's Theaetetus*. Oxford: Clarendon Press.

——— (forthcoming, 2007a). 'Philosophy, the Forms, and the art of ruling', in G. Ferrari (ed.), *The Cambridge Companion to Plato*. Cambridge: Cambridge University Press.

——— (forthcoming, 2007b). 'Myth, politics and punishment in Plato's *Gorgias*', in C. Partenie (ed.), *Plato's Myths*. Cambridge: Cambridge University Press.

Segvic, H. (2000). 'No one errs willingly: the meaning of Socratic intellectualism', *Oxford Studies in Ancient Philosophy*, 19: 1–45.

Shipley, G. (2005). 'Little boxes on the hillside: Greek town planning, Hippodamos, and polis ideology', in M. H. Hansen (ed.), *The Imaginary Polis*. Historisk-filosofiske Meddelelser 91, *The*

Royal Danish Academy of Sciences and Letters. Copenhagen: Munksgaard, 335–403.

Shklar, J. (1957). *After Utopia*. Princeton: Princeton University Press.

Sinclair, T. A. (1951). *A History of Greek Political Thought*. London: Routledge & Kegan Paul.

Skemp, J. B. (ed. and trans.) (1952). *Plato: The Statesman*. London: Routledge & Kegan Paul.

Skinner, Q. R. D. (1989). 'The state', in T. Ball, J. Farr and R. L. Hanson (eds), *Political Innovation and Conceptual Change*. Cambridge: Cambridge University Press, 90–131.

Smith, N. D. (1983). 'Plato and Aristotle on the nature of women', *Journal of the History of Philosophy*, 21: 467–78.

——— (1997). 'How the prisoners in Plato's Cave are "like us"', *Proceedings of the Boston Area Colloquium in Ancient Philosophy*, 13: 187–204.

Solmsen, F. (1942). *Plato's Theology*. Ithaca, NY: Cornell University Press.

Sourvinou-Inwood, C. (1990). 'What is *polis* religion?', in O. Murray and S. Price (eds), *The Greek City: From Homer to Alexander*. Oxford: Clarendon Press, 295–322.

Sprague, R. K. (1976). *Plato's Philosopher-King: A Study of the Theoretical Background*. Columbia: University of South Carolina Press.

Stahl, H.-P. (1966). *Thukydides: Die Stellung des Menschen im geschichtlichen Prozess*. Munich: Beck.

Stalley, R. F. (1983). *An Introduction to Plato's Laws*. Oxford: Blackwell.

——— (1991). 'Aristotle's criticism of Plato's *Republic*', in D. Keyt and F. D. Miller, Jr. (eds), *A Companion to Aristotle's Politics*. Oxford and Cambridge, Mass.: Blackwell, 182–99.

——— (1994). 'Persuasion in Plato's *Laws*', *History of Political Thought*, 15: 157–77.

——— (1997–8). 'Plato's doctrine of freedom', *Proceedings of the Aristotelian Society*, 98: 145–58.

Strauss, L. (1964). *The City and Man*. Chicago and London: University of Chicago Press.

——— (1972). 'Plato', in L. Strauss and J. Cropsey (eds), *History of Political Philosophy* (2nd edn). Chicago: Rand McNally, 7–63.

——— (1975). *The Argument and the Action of Plato's Laws*. Chicago and London: University of Chicago Press.

Strauss, L. (1983). *Studies in Platonic Political Philosophy*. Chicago and London: University of Chicago Press.

—— (1989). *The Rebirth of Classical Rationalism*. Chicago and London: University of Chicago Press.

Striker, G. (1994). 'Plato's Socrates and the Stoics', in P. A. Vander Waerdt (ed.), *The Socratic Movement*. Ithaca, NY, and London: Cornell University Press, 241–51.

Taylor, C. C. W. (1986). 'Plato's totalitarianism', *Polis*, 5/2: 4–29; reprinted in G. Fine (ed.), *Plato 2: Ethics, Politics, Religion, and the Soul*. Oxford: Oxford University Press, 280–96.

—— (2000). 'Democritus', in C. J. Rowe and M. Schofield (eds), *The Cambridge History of Greek and Roman Political Thought*. Cambridge: Cambridge University Press, Ch. 5.

Thesleff, H. (1982). *Studies in Platonic Chronology*. Helsinki: Societas Scientiarum Fennica.

Thompson, J. B. (1984). *Studies in the Theory of Ideology*. Cambridge: Polity.

Thompson, W. E. (1965). 'The demes in Plato's *Laws*', *Eranos*, 63: 134–6.

de Tocqueville, A. (2000). *Democracy in America*, trans. H. Mansfield and D. Winthrop. Chicago: Chicago University Press.

Todd, S. C. and Millett, P. C. (1990). 'Law, society and Athens', in P. A. Cartledge, P. C. Millett and S. C. Todd (eds), *Nomos: Essays in Athenian Law, Politics and Society*. Cambridge: Cambridge University Press, 1–18.

Trapp, M. B. (2000). 'Plato in Dio', in S. Swain (ed.), *Dio Chrysostom: Politics, Letters, and Philosophy*. Oxford: Oxford University Press, Ch. 9.

Traverso, E. (2003). *The Origins of Nazi Violence*. New York: The New Press.

Turner, F. M. (1981). *The Greek Heritage in Victorian Britain*. New Haven and London: Yale University Press.

Unger, R. M. (1998). *Democracy Realized: The Progressive Alternative*. London: Verso.

Vegetti, M. (trans. and comm.) (1998–). *Platone: La Reppublica*. Naples: Bibliopolis.

Versenyi, L. (1971). 'Plato and his liberal opponents', *Philosophy*, 46: 222–37.

Vidal-Naquet, P. (1986a). 'A study in ambiguity: artisans in the Platonic city', in his *The Black Hunter: Forms of Thought and Forms of Society in the Greek World*. Baltimore and London:

Johns Hopkins University Press, 224–45; English translation of *Le Chasseur noir*. Paris: F. Maspero (1981).

—— (1986b). 'Athens and Atlantis: structure and meaning of a Platonic myth', in his *The Black Hunter*, 263–84.

—— (1986c). 'Plato's myth of the statesman, the ambiguities of the golden age and of history', in his *The Black Hunter*, 285–301.

—— (1995). *Politics Ancient and Modern*. Cambridge: Polity; English translation of *La démocratie grecque vue d'ailleurs: essais d'historiographie ancienne et moderne*. Paris: Flammarion (1990).

Vlastos, G. (1939). 'The disorderly motion in the *Timaeus*', *Classical Quarterly*, 33: 71–83.

—— (1964). '*Isonomia politikê*', in J. Mau and E. G. Schmidt (eds), *Isonomia: Studien zur Gleicheitsvorstellung im griechischen Denken*. Berlin: Akademie Verlag, 1–35; reprinted in G. Vlastos, *Platonic Studies*. Princeton: Princeton University Press (1973), Ch. 8.

—— (1971). 'Justice and happiness in the *Republic*', in G. Vlastos (ed.), *Plato: A Collection of Critical Essays*, Vol. 2: *Ethics, Politics, and Philosophy of Art and Religion*. Garden City, NJ: Doubleday Anchor, 66–95; reprinted in G. Vlastos, *Platonic Studies*. Princeton: Princeton University Press (1973), Ch. 5.

—— (1977). 'The theory of social justice in the *polis* in Plato's *Republic*', in H. North (ed.), *Interpretations of Plato: A Swarthmore Symposium*. Leiden: Brill, 1–40; reprinted in G. Vlastos, *Studies in Greek Philosophy*, ed. D. W. Graham. Princeton: Princeton University Press (1995), II.69–103.

—— (1978). 'The rights of persons in Plato's conception of the foundations of justice', in H. T. Englehardt and D. Callahan (eds), *Morals, Science and Society*. Hastings-on-Hudson, NY: The Hastings Center, 172–201; reprinted in G. Vlastos, *Studies in Greek Philosophy*, II.104–25.

—— (1989). 'Was Plato a feminist?', *Times Literary Supplement* (17 March 1989): 276, 288–9; reprinted in G. Vlastos, *Studies in Greek Philosophy*, II.133–43.

—— (1991). *Socrates: Ironist and Moral Philosopher*. Cambridge: Cambridge University Press.

—— (1994). *Socratic Studies*. Cambridge: Cambridge University Press.

—— (1995). *Studies in Greek Philosophy*, ed. D. W. Graham. Princeton: Princeton University Press.

Waldron, J. (1995). 'What Plato would allow', in I. Shapiro and J. Wagner (eds), *Theory and Practice, Nomos*, 37: 138–78.

Wallace, R. W. (2004). 'Damon of Oa: a music theorist ostracized?', in P. Murray and P. Wilson (eds), *Music and the Muses: The Culture of Mousike in the Classical Athenian City*. Oxford: Oxford University Press, 249–67.

Walzer, M. (1987). *Interpretation and Social Criticism*. Cambridge, Mass., and London: Harvard University Press.

—— (1988). *The Company of Critics*. New York: Basic Books.

—— (2004a). 'Involuntary association', in M. Walzer, *Politics and Passion: Towards a More Egalitarian Liberalism*. New Haven and London: Yale University Press 2004, Ch. 1; an earlier version in A. Gutmann (ed.), *Freedom of Association*. Princeton: Princeton University Press (1998), 64–74.

—— (2004b). 'Deliberation, and what else...', in M. Walzer, *Politics and Passion*, Ch. 5; an earlier version in S. Macedo (ed.), *Deliberative Politics*. New York and Oxford: Oxford University Press (1999), 58–69.

Wardy, R. (1996). *The Birth of Rhetoric*. London and New York: Routledge.

Weiss, R. (1998). *Socrates Dissatisfied: An Analysis of Plato's Crito*. New York and Oxford: Oxford University Press.

Wender, D. (1973). 'Plato: misogynist, paedophile, and feminist', *Arethusa*, 6: 75–90.

White, N. P. (1992). 'Plato's metaphysical epistemology', in R. Kraut (ed.), *The Cambridge Companion to Plato*. Cambridge: Cambridge University Press, Ch. 9.

Whitford, M. (1994). 'Irigaray, utopia, and the death drive', in C. Burke, N. Schor and M. Whitford (eds), *Engaging with Irigaray: Feminist Philosophy and Modern European Thought*. New York and Chichester: Columbia University Press, 379–400.

Wilderbing, J. (2004). 'Prisoners and puppeteers in the Cave', *Oxford Studies in Ancient Philosophy*, 27: 117–39.

Williams, B. (1973). 'The analogy of city and soul in Plato's *Republic*', in E. N. Lee, A. P. D. Mourelatos and R. M. Rorty (eds), *Exegesis and Argument*. Aassen: Van Gorcum, 196–206; reprinted in G. Fine (ed.), *Plato 2: Ethics, Politics, Religion, and the Soul*. Oxford: Oxford University Press (1999), 255–64.

—— (1993). *Shame and Necessity*. Berkeley/Los Angeles/Oxford: University of California Press.

—— (2002). *Truth and Truthfulness*. Princeton: Princeton University Press.

_____ (2005). *In the Beginning was the Deed: Realism and Moralism in Political Argument*, ed. G. Hawthorn. Princeton: Princeton University Press.

Wilson, N. G. (1983). *Scholars of Byzantium*. London: Duckworth.

Wilson, P. (2003). 'The sound of cultural conflict: Kritias and the culture of *mousikê* in Athens', in C. Dougherty and L. Kurke (eds), *The Cultures within Ancient Greek Culture*. Cambridge: Cambridge University Press, 181–206.

_____ (2004). 'Athenian strings', in P. Murray and P. Wilson (eds), *Music and the Muses: The Culture of Mousike in the Classical Athenian City*. Oxford: Oxford University Press, 269–306.

Wolin, S. (1996). 'Fugitive democracy', in S. Benhabib (ed.), *Democracy and Difference: Contesting the Boundaries of the Political*. Princeton: Princeton University Press, Ch. 2.

Yunis, H. (1996). *Taming Democracy*. Ithaca, NY: Cornell University Press.

Zetzel, J. E. G. (ed. and trans.) (1999). *Cicero: On the Commonwealth and On the Laws*. Cambridge: Cambridge University Press.

Zuckert, C. (1996). *Postmodern Platos*. Chicago and London: University of Chicago Press.

_____ (2005). 'The Stranger's political science v. Socrates' political art', *Journal of the International Plato Society*, 5 (available online at <http://www.nd.edu/~plato/plato5issue/contents5.htm>).

Index of Passages

References in **bold** type indicate passages translated into English.

General Index

The index endeavours to capture all proper names of persons (ancient or modern) in the main text; in endnotes only references to persons whose views or activities are recorded or discussed in a degree of detail are listed.